Letts

GCSE
Success

Combined Science

Higher Tier

Revision Guide

Tom Adams
Dan Evans
Dan Foulder

Contents

Biology

Cell Biology

Transport Systems and Photosynthesis

Health, Disease and the Development of Medicines

Coordination and Control

Inheritance, Variation and Evolution

Ecosystems

Chemistry

Atomic Structure and the Periodic Table

Structure, Bonding and the Properties of Matter

Quantitative Chemistry

Cells are the basis of life. All processes of life take place within them. There are many different kinds of specialised cell but they all have several common features. The two main categories of cells are **prokaryotic** (prokaryotes) and **eukaryotic** (eukaryotes).

Structure of cells

Prokaryotes

Prokaryotes are simple cells such as bacteria and archaebacteria. Archaebacteria are ancient bacteria with different types of cell wall and genetic codes to other bacteria. They include microorganisms that can use methane or sulfur as a means of nutrition (methanogens and thermoacidophiles).

Prokaryotic cells:
> are smaller than eukaryotic cells
> have cytoplasm, a cell membrane and a cell wall
> have genetic material in the form of a DNA loop, together with rings of DNA called plasmids
> do not have a nucleus.

The chart below shows the relative sizes of prokaryotic and eukaryotic cells, together with the magnification range of different viewing devices.

A bacterium

Plasmid DNA: a small, commonly circular, section of DNA that can replicate independently of chromosomal DNA

Ribosomes: sites of protein manufacture

Chromosomal DNA: the DNA of bacteria is not found within a nucleus and is usually found as one circular chromosome

Cytoplasm

Cell wall: provides structural support to the bacteria (is not made of cellulose)

Flagella: tail-like structures that rotate to help some bacteria move

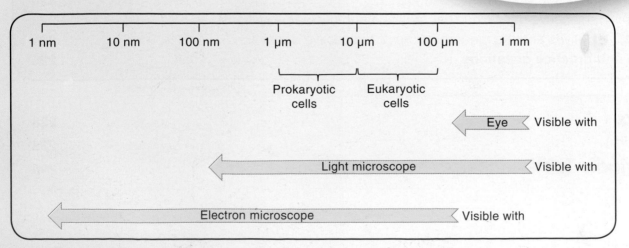

| 1 nm | 10 nm | 100 nm | 1 µm | 10 µm | 100 µm | 1 mm |

Prokaryotic cells

Eukaryotic cells

Eye — Visible with

Light microscope — Visible with

Electron microscope — Visible with

Eukaryotes

Eukaryotic cells:

➤ are more complex than prokaryotic cells (they have a cell membrane, cytoplasm and genetic material enclosed in a nucleus)

➤ are found in animals, plants, fungi (e.g. toadstools, yeasts, moulds) and protists (e.g. amoeba)

➤ contain membrane-bound structures called **organelles**, where specific functions are carried out.

Here are the main organelles in plant and animal cells.

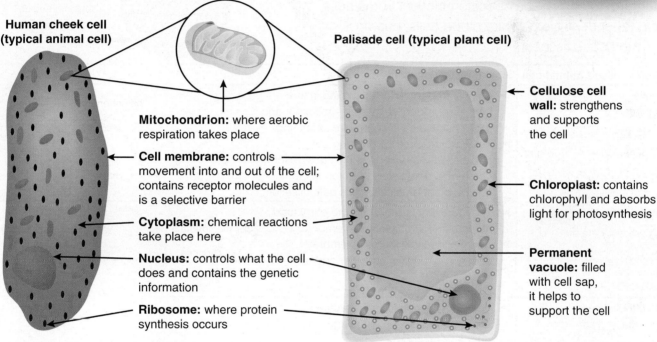

Human cheek cell (typical animal cell)

Palisade cell (typical plant cell)

Mitochondrion: where aerobic respiration takes place

Cell membrane: controls movement into and out of the cell; contains receptor molecules and is a selective barrier

Cytoplasm: chemical reactions take place here

Nucleus: controls what the cell does and contains the genetic information

Ribosome: where protein synthesis occurs

Cellulose cell wall: strengthens and supports the cell

Chloroplast: contains chlorophyll and absorbs light for photosynthesis

Permanent vacuole: filled with cell sap, it helps to support the cell

Plant cells tend to be more regular in shape than animal cells. They have additional structures: cell wall, sap vacuole and sometimes chloroplasts.

Keyword

Organelle ➤ A membrane-bound structure within a cell that carries out a particular function

Create a poster illustrating the main features of bacterial, plant and animal cells (i.e. prokaryotes and eukaryotes).

➤ Use different colours for the main organelles, e.g. blue for the nucleus, orange for cytoplasm.

➤ Add labels that describe the functions of the organelles.

1. List three examples of prokaryotes and three examples of eukaryotes.
2. How are prokaryotes and eukaryotes different in terms of genetic information?
3. All cells have a cell membrane. True or false?
4. Which organelle carries out the function of respiration?
5. Algae are a type of plant. Why do the cells contain chloroplasts?

Organisation and differentiation

Multicellular organisms need to have a coordinated system of structures so they can carry out vital processes, e.g. respiration, excretion, nutrition, etc.

Principles of organisation

Cells are the most basic unit of living organisms.

Tissues are collections of similar cells that work together to carry out the same function.

Organisation

An organ is formed when a group of tissues combine together and do a particular job.

Organs form organ systems, e.g. the intestines and the stomach are part of the digestive system.

Organ systems work together to make up a complex multicellular organism.

Cell specialisation

Animals and plants have many different types of cells. Each cell is adapted to carry out a specific function. Some cells can act independently, e.g. white blood cells, but most operate together as tissues.

Type of specialised animal cell	How they are adapted
Sperm cells	➤ They are adapted for swimming in the female reproductive system – mitochondria in the neck release energy for swimming. ➤ They are adapted for carrying out fertilisation with an egg cell – the acrosome contains enzymes for digestion of the ovum's outer protective cells at fertilisation. Mitochondria / Haploid nucleus / Acrosome / End piece
Egg cells (ovum)	➤ They are very large in order to carry food reserves for the developing embryo. ➤ After fertilisation, the cell membrane changes and locks out other sperm. Cell membrane / Cytoplasm / Mitochondria / Haploid nucleus
Ciliated epithelial cells	➤ They line the respiratory passages and help protect the lungs against dust and microorganisms. Mucus / Gland cells / Cilia / Movement of mucus
Nerve cells	➤ They have long, slender extensions called axons that carry nerve impulses.
Muscle cells	➤ They are able to contract (shorten) to bring about the movement of limbs.

Type of specialised plant cell	How they are adapted
Root hair cells	➤ They have tiny, hair-like extensions. These increase the surface area of roots to help with the absorption of water and minerals.
Xylem	➤ They are long, thin, hollow cells. Their shape helps with the transport of water through the stem, roots and leaves.
Phloem	➤ They are long, thin cells with pores in the end walls. Their structure helps the cell sap move from one phloem cell to the next.

Cell differentiation and stem cells

Stem cells are found in animals and plants. They are unspecialised or **undifferentiated**, which means that they have the potential to become almost any kind of cell. Once the cell is fully specialised, it will possess sub-cellular organelles specific to the function of that cell. Embryonic stem cells, compared with those found in adults' bone marrow, are more flexible in terms of what they can become.

Animal cells are mainly restricted to repair and replacement in later life. Plants retain their ability to **differentiate** (specialise) throughout life.

Using stem cells in humans

Therapeutic cloning treats conditions such as diabetes. Embryonic stem cells (that can specialise into any type of cell) are produced with the same genes as the patient. If these are introduced into the body, they are not usually rejected.

Treating paralysis is possible using stem cells that are capable of differentiating into new nerve cells. The brain uses these new cells to transmit nervous impulses to the patient's muscles.

There are benefits and objections to using stem cells.

Benefits	Risks and objections
➤ Stem cells left over from in vitro fertilisation (IVF) treatment (that would otherwise be destroyed) can be used to treat serious conditions. ➤ Stem cells are useful in studying how cell division goes wrong, e.g. cancer. ➤ In the future, stem cells could be used to grow new organs for transplantation.	➤ Some people believe that an embryo at any age is a human being and so should not be used to grow cells or be experimented on. ➤ One potential risk of using stem cells is transferring viral infections. ➤ If stem cells are used in an operation, they might act as a reservoir of cancer cells that spread to other parts of the body.

Using stem cells in plants

Plants have regions of rapid cell division called **meristems**. These growth regions contain stem cells that can be used to produce clones cheaply and quickly.

Meristems can be used for:
➤ growing and preserving rare varieties to protect them from extinction
➤ producing large numbers of disease-resistant crop plants.

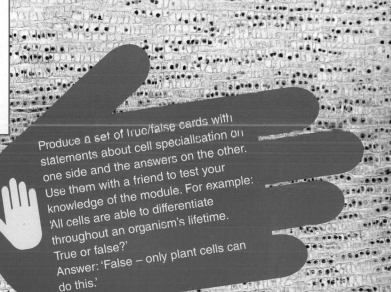

Produce a set of true/false cards with statements about cell specialisation on one side and the answers on the other. Use them with a friend to test your knowledge of the module. For example: 'All cells are able to differentiate throughout an organism's lifetime. True or false?'
Answer: 'False – only plant cells can do this.'

1. In the body, what do you call an arrangement of different tissues that carry out a particular job?
2. Describe how a muscle cell is specialised to perform its function.
3. Which type of specialised plant cell is used to transport the sugars made in photosynthesis?
4. Give one benefit of and one objection to the scientific use of stem cells.

Microscopy and microorganisms

Microscopes

Microscopes:

➤ observe objects that are too small to see with the naked eye

➤ are useful for showing detail at cellular and sub-cellular level.

There are two main types of microscope: the **light microscope** and the **electron microscope**.

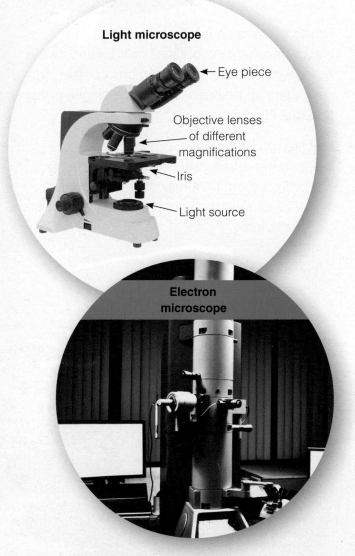

Light microscope

← Eye piece

Objective lenses of different magnifications

Iris

Light source

Electron microscope

You will probably use a light microscope in your school laboratory.

The electron microscope was invented in 1931. It has increased our understanding of sub-cellular structures because it has much higher magnifications and resolution than a light microscope.

These are white blood cells, as seen through a transmission electron microscope. The black structures are nuclei.

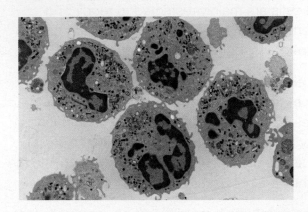

HT Here are some common units used in microscopy.

Measure	Scale	Symbol
1 metre		m
1 centimetre	$\frac{1}{100}$ th of a metre ($\times 10^{-2}$)	cm
1 millimetre	$\frac{1}{1000}$ (a thousandth) of a metre ($\times 10^{-3}$)	mm
1 micrometre	$\frac{1}{1\,000\,000}$ (a millionth) of a metre ($\times 10^{-6}$)	μm
1 nanometre	$\frac{1}{1\,000\,000\,000}$ (a thousand millionth or a billionth) of a metre ($\times 10^{-9}$)	nm

Keyword

Resolution ➤ The smallest distance between two points on a specimen that can still be told apart

Comparing light and electron microscopes

Light microscope	Electron microscope
Uses light waves to produce images	Uses electrons to produce images
Low resolution	High resolution
Magnification up to ×1500	Magnification up to ×500 000 (2D) and ×100 000 (3D)
Able to observe cells and larger organelles	Able to observe small organelles
2D images only	2D and 3D images produced

Magnification and resolution

Magnification measures how many times an object under a microscope has been made larger.

To calculate the magnifying power of a microscope, use this formula:

$$\text{magnification} = \frac{\text{size of image}}{\text{size of real object}}$$

You may be asked to carry out calculations using magnification.

Example: A light microscope produces an image of a cell which has a diameter of 1500 μm. The cell's actual diameter is 50 μm. Calculate the magnifying power of the microscope.

$$\text{magnification} = \frac{1500}{50} = \times 30$$

Resolution is the smallest distance between two points on a specimen that can still be told apart. The diagram below shows the limits of resolution for a light microscope. When looking through it you can see fine detail down to 200 nanometres. Electron microscopes can see detail down to 0.05 nanometres!

 200 nm

Staining techniques are used in light and electron microscopy to make organelles more visible.

➤ **Methylene blue** is used to stain the nuclei of animal cells for viewing under the light microscope.
➤ **Heavy metals** such as cadmium can be used to stain specimens for viewing under the electron microscope.

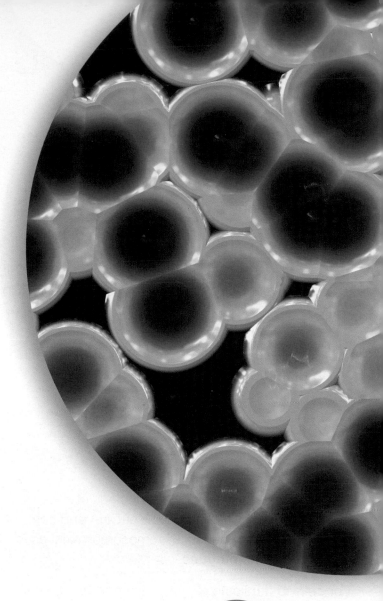

 3

Design a poster illustrating the differences between the light and electron microscopes for a science lab notice board. Your poster should include the advantages of each type of microscope and diagrams to show the functions of each part.
➤ For example, you could include: 'Focusing wheel – adjusts the clarity of the image so it can be seen clearly.'
If you design your poster using a word processing or desktop publishing package, you can use specimen clipart to show the different types of view obtained.

1. List two differences between light and electron microscopes.
2. A certain sub-cellular structure is 150 nm across. Why can't it be seen using a light microscope?

Cell division

Multicellular organisms grow and reproduce using cell division and cell enlargement. Plants can also grow via differentiation into leaves, branches, etc.

Cell division begins from the moment of fertilisation when the zygote replicates itself exactly through **mitosis**. Later in life, an organism may use cell division to produce sex cells (**gametes**) in a different type of division called **meiosis**.

The different stages of cell division make up the **cell cycle** of an organism.

Keywords

Gamete ➤ A sex cell, i.e. sperm or egg

Daughter cells ➤ Multiple cells arising from mitosis and meiosis

Polymer ➤ Large molecule, made of repeating units called monomers

Diploid ➤ A full set of chromosomes in a cell (twice the haploid number)

Haploid ➤ A half set of chromosomes in a cell; haploid cells are either eggs or sperm

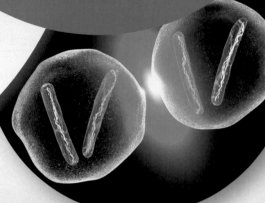

Chromosomes

Chromosomes are found in the nucleus of eukaryotic cells. They are made of DNA and carry a large number of genes. Chromosomes exist as pairs called **homologues**.

For cells to duplicate exactly, it is important that all of the genetic material is duplicated. Chromosomes take part in a sequence of events that ensures the genetic code is transmitted precisely and appears in the new **daughter cells**.

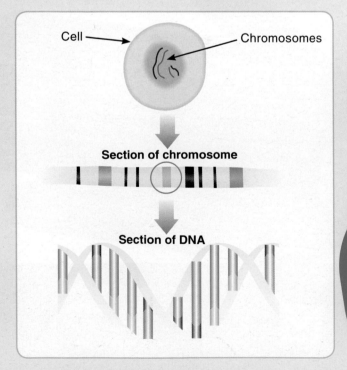

DNA replication

During the cell cycle, the genetic material (made of the **polymer** molecule, DNA) is doubled and then divided between the identical daughter cells. This process is called **DNA replication**.

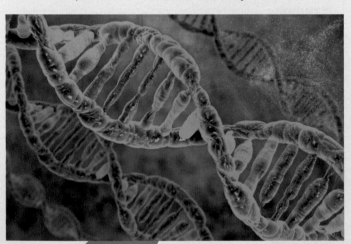

Use plasticine or playdough to create models showing mitosis and meiosis. Mitosis should show four stages and meiosis six stages. You could:
➤ use different colours for the chromosomes and the cytoplasm
➤ try mixing the stages up and then re-arranging them from memory
➤ explain to a friend what is happening at each stage in terms of the chromosomes and cytoplasm.

Mitosis

Mitosis is where a **diploid** cell (one that has a complete set of chromosomes) divides to produce two more diploid cells that are genetically identical. Most cells in the body are diploid.

Humans have a diploid number of 46.

Mitosis produces new cells:

➤ for growth
➤ to replace old cells
➤ to repair damaged tissue
➤ for asexual reproduction.

Before the cell divides, the DNA is duplicated and other organelles replicate, e.g. mitochondria and ribosomes. This ensures that there is an exact copy of all the cell's content.

Mitosis – the cell copies itself to produce two genetically identical cells

Parent cell with two pairs of chromosomes.

Each chromosome replicates (copies) itself.

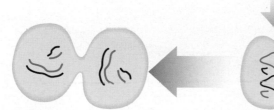

Each 'daughter' cell has the same number of chromosomes, and contains the same genes, as the parent cell.

Chromosomes line up along the centre of the cell, separate into chromatids and move to opposite poles.

Meiosis

Meiosis takes place in the testes and ovaries of sexually reproducing organisms and produces gametes (eggs or sperm). The gametes are called **haploid** cells because they contain half the number of chromosomes as a diploid cell. This chromosome number is restored during **fertilisation**.

Humans have a haploid number of 23.

Meiosis – the cell divides twice to produce four cells with genetically different sets of chromosomes

Cell with two pairs of chromosomes (diploid cell).

Each chromosome replicates itself.

Cell divides for the first time.

Chromosomes part company and move to opposite poles.

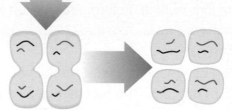

Copies now separate and the second cell division takes place.

Four haploid cells (gametes), each with half the number of chromosomes of the parent cell.

Cancer

Cancer is a non-infectious disease caused by **mutations** in living cells.

Cancerous cells:

➤ divide in an uncontrolled way
➤ form **tumours**.

Benign tumours do not spread from the original site of cancer in the body. **Malignant tumour cells** invade neighbouring tissues. They spread to other parts of the body and form **secondary tumours**.

Making healthy lifestyle choices is one way to reduce the likelihood of cancer. These include:

➤ not smoking tobacco products (cigarettes, cigars, etc.)
➤ not drinking too much alcohol (causes cancer of the liver, gut and mouth)
➤ avoiding exposure to UV rays (e.g. sunbathing, tanning salons)
➤ eating a healthy diet (high fibre reduces the risk of bowel cancer) and doing moderate exercise to reduce the risk of obesity.

Cancer cell

1. Why do multicellular organisms carry out cell division?
2. Name the structures in the nucleus that carry genetic information.
3. What are the purposes of mitosis and meiosis?
4. Which structures are replicated during cell division?

Metabolism – respiration

Keywords

Exothermic reaction ➤ A reaction that gives out heat

Energy demand ➤ Energy required by tissues (particularly muscle) to carry out their functions

Oxygen debt ➤ The oxygen needed to remove lactic acid after exercise

Metabolism

Metabolism is the sum of all the chemical reactions that take place in the body.

The two types of metabolic reaction are:
➤ building reactions (**anabolic**)
➤ breaking-down reactions (**catabolic**).

Anabolic reactions

Anabolic reactions require the input of energy. Examples include:
➤ converting glucose to starch in plants, or glucose to glycogen in animals
➤ the synthesis of lipid molecules

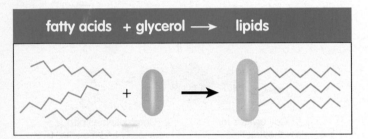

fatty acids + glycerol ⟶ lipids

➤ the formation of **amino acids** in plants (from glucose and nitrate ions) which, in turn, are built up into proteins.

Catabolic reactions

Catabolic reactions release energy. Examples include:
➤ breaking down amino acids to form **urea**, which is then excreted
➤ respiration.

Catabolic reactions produce waste energy in the form of heat (an **exothermic reaction**), which is transferred to the environment.

Respiration

Respiration continuously takes place in all organisms – the need to release energy is an essential life process. The reaction gives out energy and is therefore **exothermic**.

Aerobic respiration

Aerobic respiration takes place in cells. Oxygen and glucose molecules react and release energy. This energy is stored in a molecule called **ATP**.

glucose + oxygen ⟶ carbon dioxide + water

HT The symbol equation for aerobic respiration is:

$$C_6H_{12}O_6 + 6O_2 \longrightarrow 6CO_2 + 6H_2O + \text{energy released}$$

Energy is used in the body for many processes, including:
➤ muscle contraction (for movement)
➤ active transport
➤ transmitting nerve impulses
➤ synthesising new molecules
➤ maintaining a constant body temperature.

Anaerobic respiration

Anaerobic respiration takes place in the absence of oxygen and is common in muscle cells. It quickly releases a **smaller** amount of energy than aerobic respiration through the **incomplete breakdown** of glucose.

glucose ⟶ lactic acid + energy released

In plant and yeast cells, anaerobic respiration produces different products.

glucose ⟶ ethanol + carbon dioxide + energy released

HT The symbol equation for anaerobic respiration in plant and yeast cells is:

$$C_6H_{12}O_6 \longrightarrow 2C_2H_5OH + 2CO_2 + \text{energy released}$$

This reaction is used extensively in the brewing and wine-making industries. It is also the initial process in the manufacture of spirits in a distillery.

Response to exercise

In animals, anaerobic respiration takes place when muscles are working so hard that the lungs and circulatory system cannot deliver enough oxygen to break down all the available glucose through aerobic respiration. In these circumstances the **energy demand** of the muscles is high.

Anaerobic respiration and recovery

Anaerobic respiration releases energy much faster over short periods of time. It is useful when short, intense bursts of energy are required, e.g. a 100 m sprint.

However, the incomplete oxidation of glucose causes **lactic acid** to build up. Lactic acid is toxic and can cause pain, cramp and a sensation of fatigue.

The lactic acid must be broken down quickly and removed to avoid cell damage and prolonged muscle fatigue.

➤ During exercise the body's heart rate, breathing rate and breath volume increase so that sufficient oxygen and glucose is supplied to the muscles, and so that lactic acid can be removed.

➤ This continues after exercise when deep breathing or panting occurs until all the lactic acid is removed. This repayment of oxygen is called **oxygen debt**.

➤ Lactic acid is transported to the liver where it is converted back to glucose.
➤ Oxygen debt is the amount of **extra** oxygen that the body needs after exercise to react with the lactic acid and remove it from the cells.

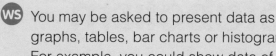 You may be asked to present data as graphs, tables, bar charts or histograms. For example, you could show data of breathing and heart rates on a line graph.

What does the line graph below tell you about breathing and pulse rates during recovery? Why is a line graph a good way to present the data?

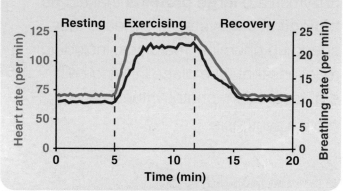

1. Give one example of a building reaction and one of a breaking-down reaction.
2. Which type of respiration releases most energy – aerobic or anaerobic?
3. Give two uses of energy release in the body.
4. Name the products of anaerobic respiration in humans and in yeast.
5. Why do athletes pant after a race?

Metabolism – enzymes

Enzymes are **large proteins** that act as **biological** catalysts. This means they speed up chemical reactions, including reactions that take place in living cells, e.g. respiration, photosynthesis and protein synthesis.

Enzyme facts

Enzymes:

➤ are specific, i.e. one enzyme catalyses one reaction

➤ have an **active site**, which is formed by the precise folding of the enzyme molecule

➤ can be **denatured** by high temperatures and extreme changes in pH

➤ have an **optimum temperature** at which they work – for many enzymes this is approximately 37°C (body temperature)

➤ have an optimum pH at which they work – this varies with the site of enzyme activity, e.g. pepsin works in the stomach and has an optimum pH of 1.5 (acid), salivary amylase works best at pH 7.3 (alkaline).

Keywords

Catalyst ➤ A substance that controls the rate of a chemical reaction without being chemically changed itself

Active site ➤ The place on an enzyme molecule into which a substrate molecule fits

Denaturation ➤ When a protein molecule such as an enzyme changes shape and makes it unable to function

Substrate ➤ The molecule acted on by an enzyme

Kinetic energy ➤ Energy possessed by moving objects, e.g. reactant molecules such as enzyme and substrate molecules

Enzyme activity

Enzyme molecules work by colliding with **substrate** molecules and forcing them to break up or to join with others in synthesis reactions. The theory of how this works is called the **lock and key theory**.

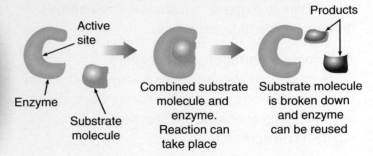

Enzyme — Active site

Substrate molecule

Combined substrate molecule and enzyme. Reaction can take place

Products

Substrate molecule is broken down and enzyme can be reused

High temperatures denature enzymes because excessive heat vibrates the atoms in the protein molecule, putting a strain on the bonds and breaking them. This changes the shape of the active site.

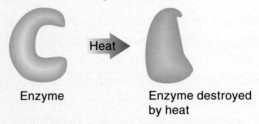

Enzyme   Heat   Enzyme destroyed by heat

In a similar way, an extreme pH alters the active site's shape and prevents it from functioning.

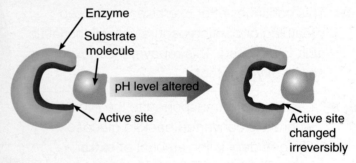

Enzyme

Substrate molecule

Active site

pH level altered

Active site changed irreversibly

At lower than the optimal temperature, an enzyme still works but much more slowly. This is because the low **kinetic energy** of the substrate and enzyme molecules lowers the number of collisions that take place. When they do collide, the energy is not always sufficient to create a bond between them.

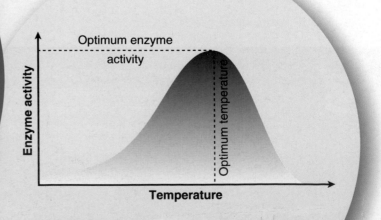

Optimum enzyme activity

Enzyme activity

Optimum temperature

Temperature

Enzymes in the digestive system

Enzymes in the digestive system help break down large nutrient molecules into smaller ones so they can be absorbed into the blood across the wall of the small intestine.

Enzyme types in the digestive system include carbohydrases, proteases and lipases.

Carbohydrases break down carbohydrates, e.g. **amylase**, which is produced in the mouth and small intestine.

starch ⟶ maltose

Other carbohydrases break down complex sugars into smaller sugars.

Proteases break down protein, e.g. **pepsin**, which is produced in the stomach.

protein ⟶ peptides ⟶ amino acids

Other enzymes in the small intestine complete protein breakdown with the production of amino acids.

Lipases, which are produced in the small intestine, break down lipids.

lipid ⟶ fatty acids + glycerol

Bile

Bile is a digestive chemical. It is produced in the liver and stored in the gall bladder.

➤ Its alkaline pH neutralises hydrochloric acid that has been produced in the stomach.

➤ It **emulsifies** fat, breaking it into small droplets with a large surface area.

➤ Its action enables lipase to break down fat more efficiently.

What happens to digested food?

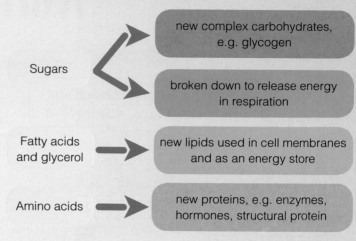

Sugars → new complex carbohydrates, e.g. glycogen

Sugars → broken down to release energy in respiration

Fatty acids and glycerol → new lipids used in cell membranes and as an energy store

Amino acids → new proteins, e.g. enzymes, hormones, structural protein

WS During your course you will investigate how certain factors affect the rate of enzyme activity. These include temperature, pH and substrate concentration.

Design an investigation to discover how temperature affects the activity of amylase. Here are some guidelines.

➤ Iodine solution turns from a red-brown colour to blue-black in the presence of starch.

➤ You can measure amylase activity by timing how long it takes for iodine solution to stop turning blue-black.

➤ A water bath can be set up with a thermometer. Add cold or hot water to regulate the temperature.

➤ Identify the independent, dependent and control variables in the investigation. Write out your method in clear steps.

1. Name two factors that affect the rate of enzyme activity.
2. Describe, in simple terms, how lock and key theory explains enzyme action.
3. State two ways in which bile aids in the digestion of lipids.
4. Which molecules act as building blocks for protein polymers?

Mind map

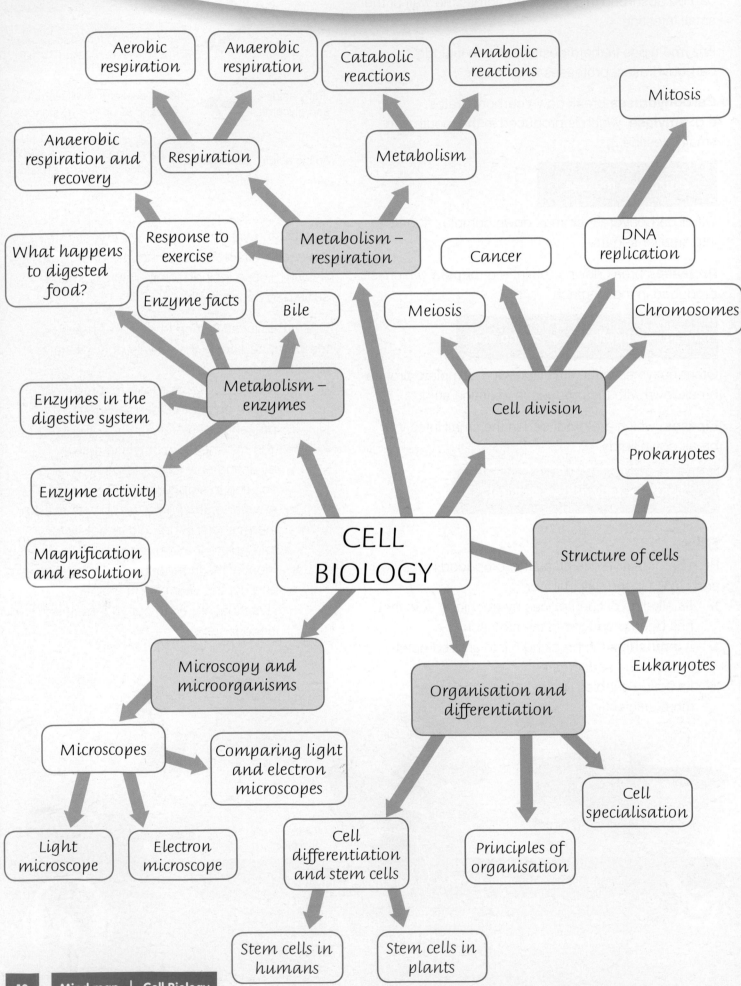

Aerobic respiration

Anaerobic respiration

Catabolic reactions

Anabolic reactions

Mitosis

Anaerobic respiration and recovery

Respiration

Metabolism

DNA replication

What happens to digested food?

Response to exercise

Metabolism – respiration

Cancer

Chromosomes

Enzyme facts

Bile

Meiosis

Enzymes in the digestive system

Metabolism – enzymes

Cell division

Prokaryotes

Enzyme activity

Magnification and resolution

CELL BIOLOGY

Structure of cells

Microscopy and microorganisms

Organisation and differentiation

Eukaryotes

Microscopes

Comparing light and electron microscopes

Cell specialisation

Light microscope

Electron microscope

Cell differentiation and stem cells

Principles of organisation

Stem cells in humans

Stem cells in plants

Practice questions

1. Name the parts of the bacterial cell (**A–D**). **(4 marks)**

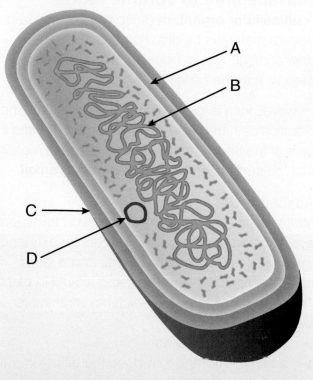

2. Lisa is playing football. She sprints the length of the pitch and scores a goal. However, she can barely celebrate because her legs have gone weak and she is panting heavily.

   a) Explain why Lisa's legs feel weak. **(2 marks)**

   b) Why would Lisa be unable to play the entire game at such a fast pace? **(1 mark)**

   c) Why does aerobic respiration yield more energy from glucose? **(1 mark)**

3. In 1894, the lock and key theory of enzyme action was put forward by Emil Fischer. The diagram shows the first stage in the reaction between an enzyme and a reactant.

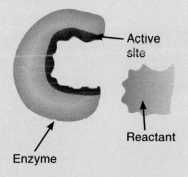

   a) What term describes the way that enzyme molecules change at high temperatures? **(1 mark)**

   b) Explain how a drop in pH will affect the structure of the enzyme shown in the diagram. **(2 marks)**

4. Red blood cells are one component of the human circulatory system. Explain why a human has these specialised cells but a paramecium (single-celled organism) does not. **(2 marks)**

Diffusion

Living cells need to obtain oxygen, glucose, water, mineral ions and other dissolved substances from their surroundings. They also need to excrete waste products, such as carbon dioxide or urea. These substances pass through the cell membrane by **diffusion**.

Diffusion:

➤ is the (net) movement of particles in a liquid or gas from a region of high concentration to one of low concentration (down a **concentration gradient**)

➤ happens due to the random motion of particles past each other

➤ stops once the particles have completely spread out

➤ is passive, i.e. requires no input of energy

➤ can be increased in terms of rate by making the concentration gradient steeper, the diffusion path shorter, increasing the temperature or increasing the surface area over which the process occurs, e.g. having a folded cell membrane.

A protist called amoeba can absorb oxygen through diffusion.

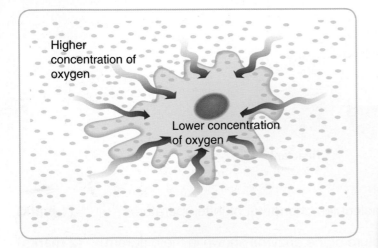

Higher concentration of oxygen

Lower concentration of oxygen

Surface area to volume ratios

A **unicellular organism** (such as a protist) can absorb materials by diffusion directly from the environment. This is because it has a **large surface area to volume ratio**.

However, for a large, **multicellular organism**, the diffusion path between the environment and the inner cells of the body is long. Its large size also means that the **surface area to volume ratio** is **small**.

Adaptations

Multicellular organisms therefore need transport systems and specialised structures for exchanging materials, e.g. mammalian lungs and a small intestine, fish gills, and roots and leaves in plants. These increase diffusion efficiency in animals because they have:

➤ a large surface area

➤ a thin membrane to reduce the diffusion path

➤ an extensive blood supply for transport (animals)

➤ a ventilation system for gaseous exchange, e.g. breathing in animals.

In mammals, the individual air sacs in the lungs increase their surface area by a factor of thousands. Ventilation moves air in and out of the alveoli and the heart moves blood through the capillaries. This maintains the diffusion gradient. The capillary and alveolar linings are very thin, decreasing the diffusion path.

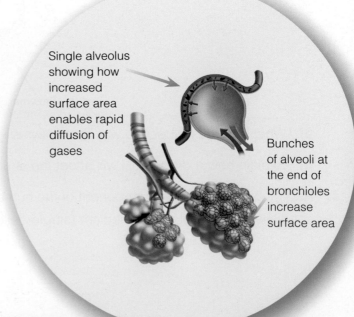

Single alveolus showing how increased surface area enables rapid diffusion of gases

Bunches of alveoli at the end of bronchioles increase surface area

Osmosis

Osmosis is a special case of diffusion that involves the movement of water only. There are two ways of describing osmosis.

1. The net movement of **water** from a region of **low** solute concentration to one of **high** concentration.
2. The movement down a **water potential gradient**.

> Osmosis:
> ➤ occurs across a **partially permeable membrane**, so solute molecules cannot pass through (only water molecules can)
> ➤ occurs in all organisms
> ➤ is passive (in other words, requires no input of energy)
> ➤ allows water movement into root hair cells from the soil and between cells inside the plant
> ➤ can be demonstrated and measured in plant cells using a variety of tissues, e.g. potato chips, daffodil stems.

Osmosis

| Dilute solution (high concentration of water) | → | Concentrated solution (low concentration of water) |

Partially permeable membrane

Net movement of water molecules

Active transport

Substances are sometimes absorbed **against** a concentration gradient, i.e. from a low to a high concentration.

Active transport:
➤ requires the release of energy from respiration
➤ takes place in the small intestine in humans, where sugar is absorbed into the bloodstream
➤ occurs via protein carrier molecules in the cell membrane
➤ allows plants to absorb mineral ions from the soil through root hair cells.

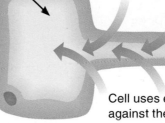

A cell absorbing ions by active transport

Root hair cell with high concentration of nitrate ions

Soil with lower concentration of nitrate ions

Cell uses energy to 'pull' ions in against the concentration gradient

WS During your course, you may investigate the effect of salt or sugar solutions on plant tissue.

Here is one experiment you could do.
1. Immerse raw potato cut into chips of equal length in sugar solutions of various concentration.
2. You will see the potato chips change in length depending on whether individual cells have lost or gained water.

Can you **predict** what would happen to the potato chips immersed in:
➤ concentrated sugar (e.g. 1 molar)
➤ medium concentration sugar (e.g. 0.5 molar)
➤ water (0 molar)?

Keywords

Surface area to volume ratio ➤ A number calculated by dividing the total surface area of an object by its volume. When the ratio is **high**, the efficiency of diffusion and other processes is **greater**

Water potential/diffusion gradient ➤ A higher concentration of particle numbers in one area than another; in living systems, these areas are often separated by a membrane or cell wall

Partially permeable membrane ➤ A membrane with microscopic holes that allows small particles through (e.g. water) but not large ones (e.g. sugar)

1. Which has the highest surface area to volume ratio – an elephant or a shrew?
2. Some plant tissue is placed in a highly concentrated salt solution. Explain why water leaves the cells.

A plant's system is made up of organs and tissues that enable it to be a **photosynthetic organism**.

These are the main plant structures and their functions.

➤ **Roots** absorb water and minerals. They anchor plants in the soil.

➤ The **stem** transports water and nutrients to leaves. It holds leaves up to the light for maximum absorption of energy.

➤ The **leaf** is the organ of photosynthesis.

➤ The **flower** makes sexual reproduction possible through pollination.

Plant tissues, organs and systems

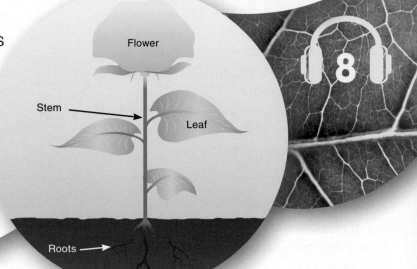

Leaves

As this cross-section of a leaf shows, leaf tissues are adapted for efficient photosynthesis. The epidermis covers the upper and lower surfaces of the leaf and protects the plant against pathogens.

Upper epidermis – cells are thin and flat to allow light to pass through

Palisade layer (mesophyll) – contains many chloroplasts for light absorption. It is positioned near the top of the leaf to be nearer to sunlight

Mesophyll layer

Spongy layer (mesophyll) – air spaces allow efficient diffusion of gases

Guard cells – they open and close to control gas exchange

Lower epidermis

Stem and roots

Veins in the stem, roots and leaves contain tissues that transport water, carbohydrate and minerals around the plant.

➤ **Xylem tissue** transports water and mineral ions from the roots to the rest of the plant.

➤ **Phloem tissue** transports dissolved sugars from the leaves to the rest of the plant.

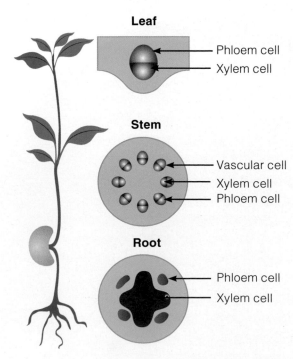

Meristem tissue is found at the growing tips of shoots and roots.

Xylem, phloem and root hair cells

Xylem, phloem and root hair cells are adapted to their function.

Part of plant	Appearance	Function	How they are adapted to their function
Xylem	Hollow tubes made from dead plant cells (the hollow centre is called a lumen)	Transport water and mineral ions from the roots to the rest of the plant in a process called **transpiration**	The cellulose cell walls are thickened and strengthened with a waterproof substance called **lignin**
Phloem	Columns of living cells	**Translocate** (move) cell sap containing sugars (particularly sucrose) from the leaves to the rest of the plant, where it is either used or stored	Phloem have pores in the end walls so that the cell sap can move from one phloem cell to the next
Root hair cells	Long and thin; have hair-like extensions	Absorb minerals and water from the soil	Large surface area

Keywords

Photosynthetic organism ➤ Able to absorb light energy and manufacture carbohydrate from carbon dioxide and water

Transpiration ➤ Flow of water through the plant ending in evaporation from leaves

Lignin ➤ Strengthening, waterproof material found in walls of xylem cells

Translocation ➤ Process in which sugars move through the phloem

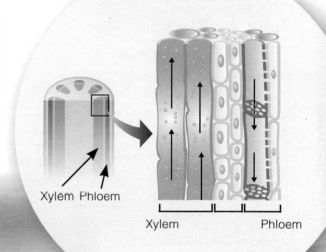

Xylem Phloem

Xylem Phloem

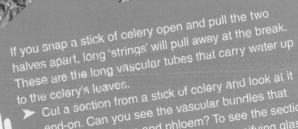

If you snap a stick of celery open and pull the two halves apart, long 'strings' will pull away at the break. These are the long vascular tubes that carry water up to the celery's leaves.

➤ Cut a section from a stick of celery and look at it end-on. Can you see the vascular bundles that contain the xylem and phloem? To see the section more clearly, use a hand lens or magnifying glass.

➤ Try putting a celery stick (bottom end down) in a cup of food colouring overnight. When you cut the stem open the next day, you will see the coloured dye in the vascular bundles.

1. What part of the plant organ system allows water to enter the plant?
2. Why are there gaps between cells in the spongy mesophyll?
3. Why do xylem cells not have end walls?

Transport in plants

Transpiration

The movement of water through a plant, from roots to leaves, takes place as a transpiration stream. Once water is in the leaves, it diffuses out of the stomata into the surrounding air. This is called **(evapo)transpiration**.

Water evaporates from the spongy mesophyll through the stomata.	Water passes by osmosis from the xylem vessels in the leaf into the spongy mesophyll cells to replace what has been lost.	This movement 'pulls' the column of water in that xylem vessel upwards.	Water enters root hair cells by osmosis to replace water that has entered the xylem.

Measuring rate of transpiration

A potometer

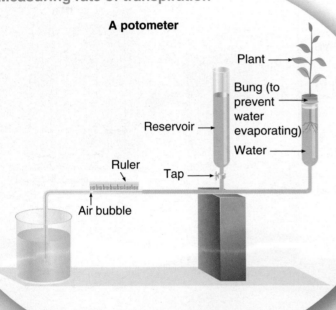

A leafy shoot's rate of transpiration can be measured using a **potometer**.

The shoot is held in a tube with a bung around the top to prevent any water from evaporating (this would give a false measurement of the water lost by transpiration).

As the plant transpires, it takes up water from the tube to replace what it has lost. All the water is then pulled up, moving the air bubble along.

The distance the air bubble moves can be used to calculate the plant's rate of transpiration for a given time period.

The experiment can be repeated, varying a different factor each time, to see how each factor affects the rate of transpiration.

Factors affecting rate of transpiration

Evaporation of water from the leaf is affected by **temperature**, **humidity**, **air movement** and **light intensity**.

➤ **Increased temperature** increases the kinetic energy of molecules and removes water vapour more quickly.

➤ **Increased air movement** removes water vapour molecules.

➤ **Increased light intensity** increases the rate of photosynthesis. This in turn draws up more water from the transpiration stream, which maintains high concentration of water in the spongy mesophyll.

➤ **Decreasing atmospheric humidity** lowers water vapour concentration outside of the stoma and so maintains the concentration gradient.

How water vapour exits the leaf

Opening and closing of stomata

Guard cells control the amount of water vapour that evaporates from the leaves and the amount of carbon dioxide that enters them.

➤ When light intensity is high and photosynthesis is taking place at a rapid rate, the sugar concentration rises in photosynthesising cells, e.g. palisade and guard cells.

➤ Guard cells respond to this by increasing the rate of water movement in the transpiration stream. This in turn provides more water for photosynthesis.

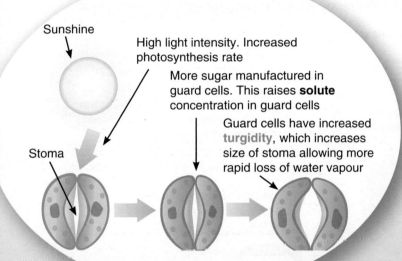

Sunshine

High light intensity. Increased photosynthesis rate

More sugar manufactured in guard cells. This raises **solute** concentration in guard cells

Guard cells have increased **turgidity**, which increases size of stoma allowing more rapid loss of water vapour

Stoma

Stomata

WS A **hypothesis** is an idea or explanation that you test through study and experiments. It should include a reason. For example: desert plants have fewer stomata than temperate plants **because** they need to minimise water loss.

➤ In an experiment investigating the factors that affect the rate of transpiration, a student plans to take measurements of weight loss or gain from a privet plant.

➤ Construct hypotheses for each of these factors: **temperature**, **humidity**, **air movement** and **light intensity**.

The first has been done for you: As temperature increases, the plant will lose mass/water more quickly **because** diffusion occurs more rapidly.

➤ Paint a thin layer of clear nail varnish onto the underside of a waxy leaf such as laurel – about 2 cm² should be sufficient.

➤ Allow the varnish to dry for at least 15 minutes. This will create a mould of the stomata as the liquid varnish fills the pores in the leaf.

➤ Peel the varnish strip off. Take care not to allow it to fold over or roll.

➤ Prepare it on a microscope slide with a drop of water and a cover slip.

➤ View it under medium power and you should see the stomata.

Compare different types of leaf, e.g. holly and privet, to see which leaves have most stomata. If you don't have a microscope at home, ask to use one at school.

Keywords

(Evapo)transpiration ➤ Evaporation of water from stomata in the leaf

Turgidity ➤ Where plant cells fill with water and swell as a result of osmosis

1. What effect would **decreasing** air humidity have on transpiration?
2. In what circumstances might it be beneficial for plants to **close** their stomata?
3. How does water pass from xylem vessels into the leaf?
4. Describe how water passes from roots to leaves.

Transport in humans 1

🎧 10

Blood circulation

Blood moves around the body in a **double circulatory system**. In other words, blood moves twice through the heart for every full circuit. This ensures maximum efficiency for absorbing oxygen and delivering materials to all living cells.

The layout of the system

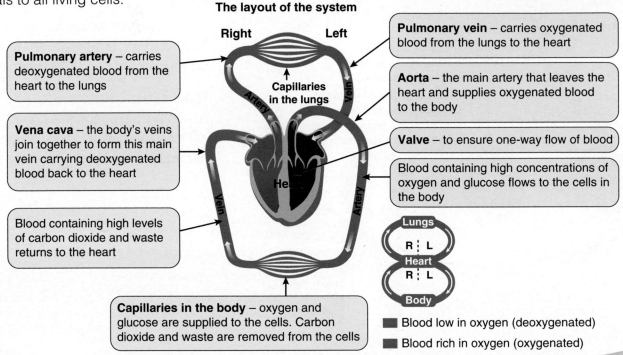

Right **Left**

Pulmonary artery – carries deoxygenated blood from the heart to the lungs

Capillaries in the lungs

Artery / Vein

Vena cava – the body's veins join together to form this main vein carrying deoxygenated blood back to the heart

Heart

Vein / Artery

Blood containing high levels of carbon dioxide and waste returns to the heart

Capillaries in the body – oxygen and glucose are supplied to the cells. Carbon dioxide and waste are removed from the cells

Pulmonary vein – carries oxygenated blood from the lungs to the heart

Aorta – the main artery that leaves the heart and supplies oxygenated blood to the body

Valve – to ensure one-way flow of blood

Blood containing high concentrations of oxygen and glucose flows to the cells in the body

Lungs
R : L
Heart
R : L
Body

■ Blood low in oxygen (deoxygenated)
■ Blood rich in oxygen (oxygenated)

The heart

The heart is made of powerful muscles that contract and relax rhythmically in order to continuously pump blood around the body. The **heart muscle** is supplied with food (particularly glucose) and oxygen through the coronary artery.

The sequence of events that takes place when the heart beats is called the **cardiac cycle**.

1. The heart relaxes and blood enters both atria from the veins.
2. The atria contract together to push blood into the ventricles, opening the atrioventricular valves.
3. The ventricles contract from the bottom, pushing blood upwards into the arteries. The backflow of blood into the ventricles is prevented by the **semilunar valves**.

The left side of the heart is more muscular than the right because it has to pump blood further round the body. The right side only has to pump blood to the lungs and back.

A useful measurement for scientists and doctors to take is **cardiac output**. This is calculated using:

> **cardiac output = stroke volume × heart rate**

So, for a person who pumps out 70 ml of blood in one heartbeat (stroke volume) and has a pulse of 70 beats per minute, the cardiac output would be 4900 ml per minute.

Keywords

Coronary artery ➤ The blood vessel delivering blood to the heart muscle
Non-communicable ➤ Disease or condition that cannot be spread from person to person via pathogen transfer
Plaque ➤ Fatty deposits that can build up in arteries

Controlling the heartbeat

The heart is stimulated to beat rhythmically by pacemaker cells. The pacemaker cells produce impulses that spread across the atria to make them contract. Impulses are spread from here down to the ventricles, making them contract, pushing blood up and out.

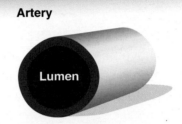

Pacemaker cells

Nerves connecting the heart to the brain can increase or decrease the pace of the pacemaker cells in order to regulate the heartbeat.

If a person has an irregular heartbeat, they can be fitted with an artificial, electrical pacemaker.

Blood vessels

Blood is carried through the body in three types of vessel.

➤ **Arteries** have thick walls made of elastic fibres and muscle fibres to cope with the high pressure. The **lumen** (space inside) is small compared to the thickness of the walls. There are no valves.

➤ **Veins** have thinner walls. The lumen is much bigger compared to the thickness of the walls and there are valves to prevent the backflow of blood.

➤ **Capillaries** are narrow vessels with walls only one cell thick. These microscopic vessels connect arteries to veins, forming dense networks or **beds**. They are the only blood vessels that have permeable walls to allow the exchange of materials.

Artery

Lumen

Vein

Valve

Lumen

Capillary

Note: capillaries are much smaller than veins or arteries

Coronary heart disease

Coronary heart disease (CHD) is a **non-communicable** disease. It results from the build-up of **cholesterol**, leading to **plaques** laid down in the coronary arteries. This restricts blood flow and the artery may become blocked with a blood clot or **thrombosis**. The heart muscle is deprived of glucose and oxygen, which causes a **heart attack**.

Coronary arteries

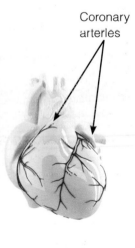

Healthy artery

Build-up of fatty material begins

Plaque forms

Plaque ruptures; blood clot forms

The likelihood of plaque developing increases if you have a high fat diet. The risk of having a heart attack can be reduced by:

➤ eating a balanced diet and not being overweight
➤ not smoking tobacco
➤ lowering alcohol intake
➤ reducing salt levels in your diet
➤ reducing stress levels.

1. What is the function of valves in veins?
2. Describe how eating a diet high in fat can lead to a heart attack.

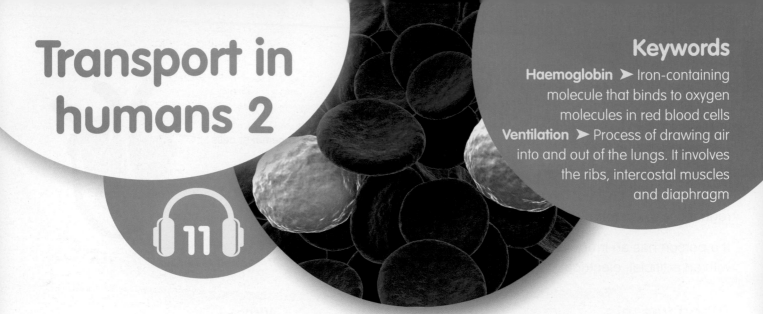

Transport in humans 2

🎧 11

Keywords

Haemoglobin ➤ Iron-containing molecule that binds to oxygen molecules in red blood cells

Ventilation ➤ Process of drawing air into and out of the lungs. It involves the ribs, intercostal muscles and diaphragm

Remedying heart disease

For patients who have heart disease, artificial implants called **stents** can be used to increase blood flow through the coronary artery.

Statins are a type of drug that can be taken to reduce blood cholesterol levels.

In some people, the heart valves may deteriorate, preventing them from opening properly. Alternatively, the valve may develop a leak.

This means that the supply of oxygenated blood to vital organs is reduced. The problem can be corrected by surgical replacement using a **biological** or **mechanical valve**.

When complete heart failure occurs, a heart transplant can be carried out. If a donor heart is unavailable, the patient may be kept alive by an artificial heart until one can be found. Mechanical hearts are also used to give the biological heart a rest while it recovers.

Blood as a tissue

Blood transports digested food and oxygen to cells and removes the cells' waste products. It also forms part of the body's defence mechanism.

The four components of blood are:
➤ platelets
➤ plasma
➤ white blood cells
➤ red blood cells.

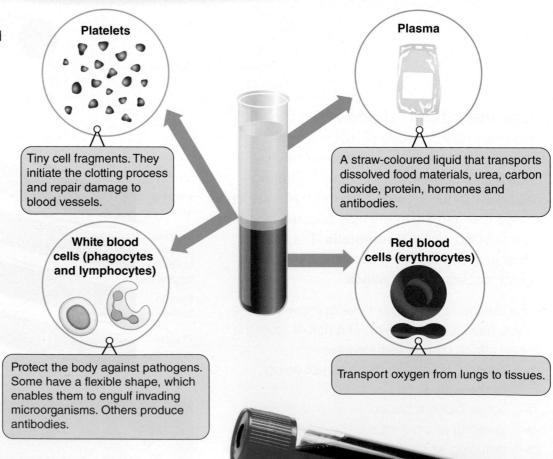

Platelets

Tiny cell fragments. They initiate the clotting process and repair damage to blood vessels.

Plasma

A straw-coloured liquid that transports dissolved food materials, urea, carbon dioxide, protein, hormones and antibodies.

White blood cells (phagocytes and lymphocytes)

Protect the body against pathogens. Some have a flexible shape, which enables them to engulf invading microorganisms. Others produce antibodies.

Red blood cells (erythrocytes)

Transport oxygen from lungs to tissues.

Oxygen transport

Red blood cells are small and have a biconcave shape. This gives them a large surface area to volume ratio for absorbing oxygen. When the cells reach the lungs, they absorb and bind to the oxygen in a molecule called **haemoglobin**.

> haemoglobin + oxygen ⇌ oxyhaemoglobin

Blood is then pumped around the body to the tissues, where the reverse of the reaction takes place. Oxygen diffuses out of the red blood cells and into the tissues.

Transport of oxygen in red blood cells

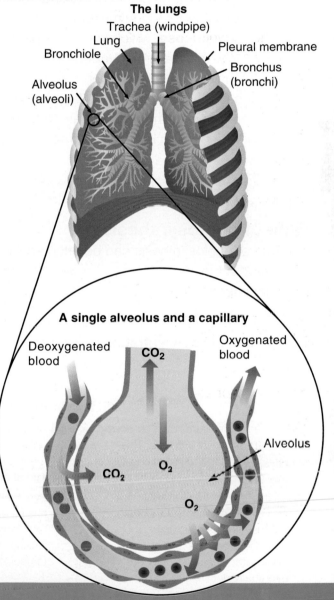

Oxygen from lungs bonds with hemoglobin molecules

Oxygen released to tissue cells

The lungs

Humans, like many vertebrates, have lungs to act as a **gaseous exchange surface**.

Other structures in the **thorax** enable air to enter and leave the lungs (**ventilation**).

➤ The **trachea** is a flexible tube, surrounded by rings of cartilage to stop it collapsing. Air is breathed in via the mouth and passes through here on its way to the lungs.

➤ **Bronchi** are branches of the trachea.

➤ The **alveoli** are small air sacs that provide a large surface area for the exchange of gases.

➤ **Capillaries** form a dense network to absorb maximum oxygen and release carbon dioxide.

In the alveoli, **oxygen** diffuses down a concentration gradient. It moves across the thin layers of cells in the alveolar and capillary walls, and into the red blood cells.

For **carbon dioxide**, the gradient operates in reverse. The carbon dioxide passes from the blood to the alveoli, and from there it travels back up the air passages to the mouth.

The lungs

Trachea (windpipe)
Lung
Bronchiole
Alveolus (alveoli)
Pleural membrane
Bronchus (bronchi)

A single alveolus and a capillary

Deoxygenated blood
CO_2
Oxygenated blood
CO_2
O_2
O_2
Alveolus

WS Scientists make observations, take measurements and gather data using a variety of instruments and techniques. Recording data is an important skill.

Create a table template that you could use to record data for the following experiment:

An investigation that involves measuring the resting and active pulse rates of 30 boys and 30 girls, together with their average breathing rates.

Make sure that:
➤ you have the correct number of columns and rows
➤ each variable is in a heading
➤ units are in the headings (so they don't need to be repeated in the body of the table).

1. What are the differences between lymphocytes and red blood cells?
2. Describe the route that would be travelled by a molecule of oxygen through the body until it reached a respiring muscle cell. State the cells, tissue, organs and processes that are involved.

Photosynthesis

Plants are **producers**. This means they can photosynthesise, i.e. make food molecules in the form of **carbohydrate** from the simple molecules, carbon dioxide and water. As such, they are the main producers of **biomass**. Sunlight energy is needed for photosynthesis.

Photosynthesis:

➤ is an **endothermic** reaction
➤ requires **chlorophyll** to absorb the sunlight; this is found in the **chloroplasts** of photosynthesising cells, e.g. palisade cells, guard cells and spongy mesophyll cells
➤ produces **glucose**, which is then respired for energy release or converted to other useful molecules for the plant
➤ produces **oxygen** that has built up in the atmosphere over millions of years; oxygen is vital for respiration in all organisms.

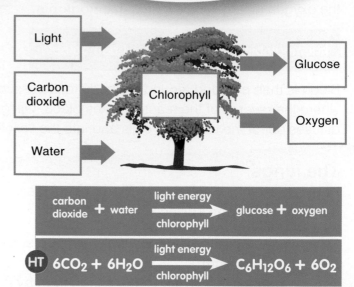

$$\text{carbon dioxide} + \text{water} \xrightarrow[\text{chlorophyll}]{\text{light energy}} \text{glucose} + \text{oxygen}$$

HT $$6CO_2 + 6H_2O \xrightarrow[\text{chlorophyll}]{\text{light energy}} C_6H_{12}O_6 + 6O_2$$

Rate of photosynthesis

The rate of photosynthesis can be affected by:

➤ temperature
➤ light intensity
➤ carbon dioxide concentration
➤ amount of chlorophyll.

In a given set of circumstances, **temperature**, **light intensity** and **carbon dioxide concentration** can act as **limiting factors**.

Temperature	Light intensity	Carbon dioxide concentration
① As the temperature rises, so does the rate of photosynthesis. This means temperature is limiting the rate of photosynthesis.	① As the light intensity increases, so does the rate of photosynthesis. This means light intensity is limiting the rate of photosynthesis.	① As carbon dioxide concentration increases, so does the rate of photosynthesis. Carbon dioxide concentration is the limiting factor.
② As the temperature approaches 45°C, the enzymes controlling photosynthesis start to be denatured. The rate of photosynthesis decreases and eventually declines to zero.	② Eventually, the rise in light intensity has no effect on photosynthesis rate. Light intensity is no longer the limiting factor; carbon dioxide or temperature must be.	② Eventually, the rise in carbon dioxide concentration has no effect – it is no longer the limiting factor.

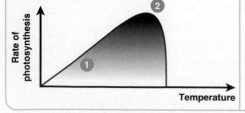

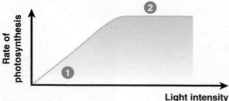

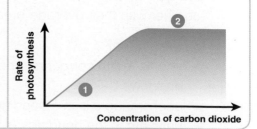

You need to understand that each factor has the potential to increase the rate of photosynthesis.

You also need to explain how these factors
HT interact in terms of which variable is acting as
the limiting factor.

The inverse law

The effect of light intensity on photosynthesis
can be investigated by placing a lamp at
varying distances from a plant. As the lamp
is moved further away from the plant the light
intensity decreases, as shown in the graph.

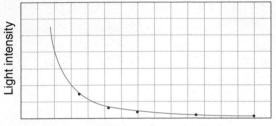

There is an **inverse relationship** between
the two variables. The graph can be used to
convert distances to light intensity, or light
intensity can be calculated using the formula:

$$\text{light intensity} = \frac{1}{d^2}$$

➤ *d* is the distance from the lamp.

There are no units of light intensity – it has an
arbitrary scale.

Commercial applications

Farmers and market gardeners can increase
their crop yields in greenhouses. They do
this by:

➤ making the temperature optimum for
growth using heaters
➤ increasing light intensity using lamps
➤ installing fossil-fuel burning stoves to
increase carbon dioxide concentration
(and increase temperature).

If applied carefully, the cost of adding these
features will be offset by increased profit from
the resulting crop.

Keywords

Biomass ➤ Mass of organisms calculated by multiplying
their individual mass by the number that exist
Endothermic ➤ A change that requires the input of energy
Chlorophyll ➤ A molecule that gives plants their green
colour and absorbs light energy
Limiting factor ➤ A variable that, if changed, will
influence the rate of reaction most
Cellulose ➤ Large carbohydrate molecule
found in all plants; an essential
constituent of cell walls

Uses of glucose in plants

The glucose produced from photosynthesis can be
used immediately in respiration, but some is used
to synthesise larger molecules: **starch**, **cellulose**,
protein and **lipids**.

Starch is insoluble. So it is suitable for storage in
leaves, stems or roots.

Cellulose is needed for cell walls.

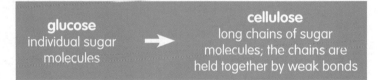

Protein is used for the growth and repair of plant
tissue, and also to synthesise enzyme molecules.

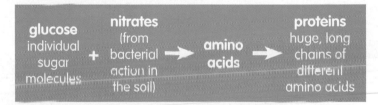

Lipids are needed in cell membranes, and for fat
and oil storage in seeds.

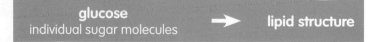

Use plasticine and coloured
paper / card to produce a
molecular model showing
the photosynthesis reaction.
Use ideas from the 'Uses of
glucose in plants' section to
help you.

1. Give two reasons why photosynthesis is
seen as the opposite of respiration.
HT 2. What **economic** factor must market
gardeners consider before installing wood-
burning stoves in their greenhouses?

Mind map

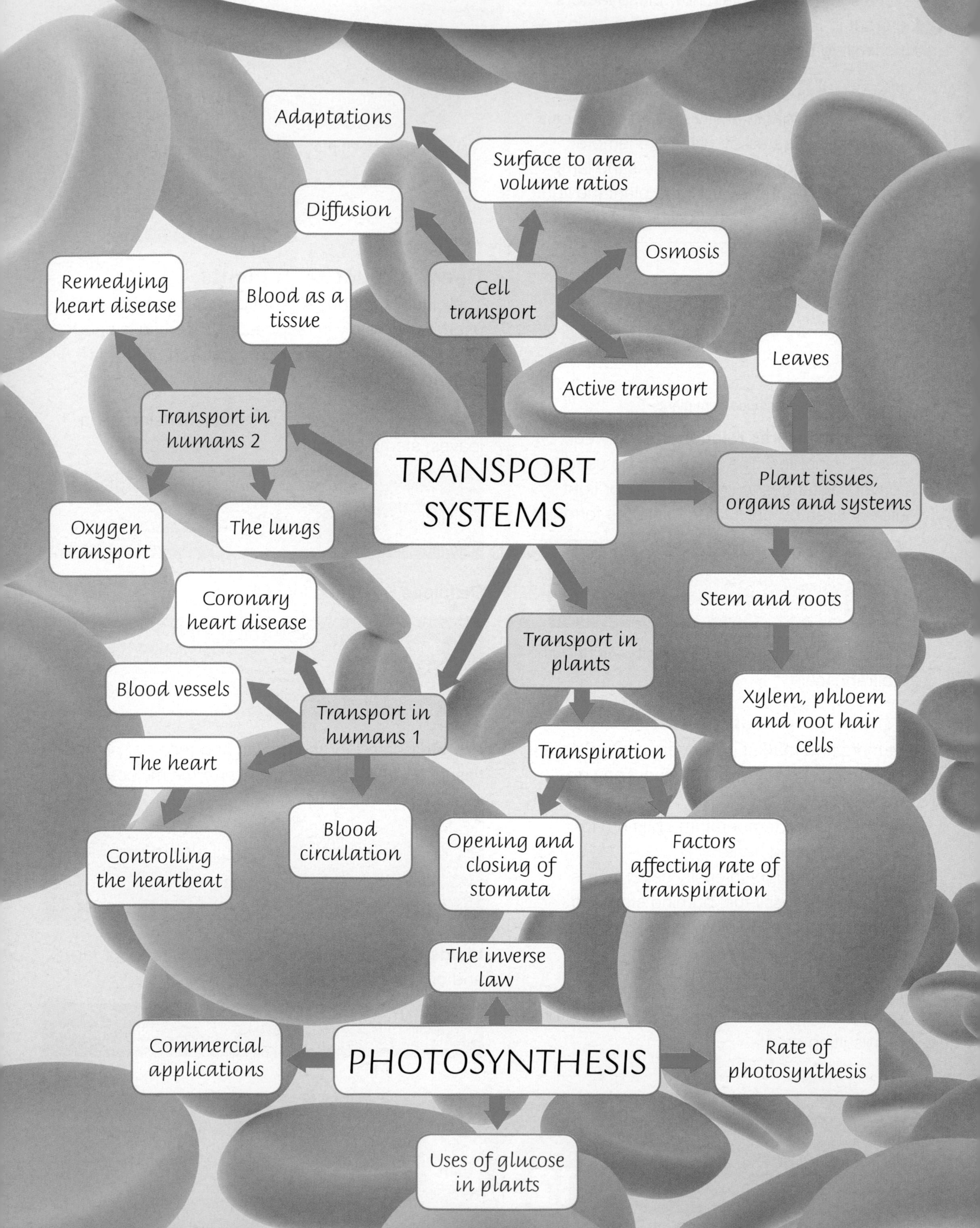

Adaptations

Surface to area volume ratios

Diffusion

Osmosis

Remedying heart disease

Blood as a tissue

Cell transport

Leaves

Active transport

Transport in humans 2

Plant tissues, organs and systems

Oxygen transport

The lungs

TRANSPORT SYSTEMS

Stem and roots

Coronary heart disease

Transport in plants

Xylem, phloem and root hair cells

Blood vessels

Transport in humans 1

Transpiration

The heart

Controlling the heartbeat

Blood circulation

Opening and closing of stomata

Factors affecting rate of transpiration

The inverse law

Commercial applications

PHOTOSYNTHESIS

Rate of photosynthesis

Uses of glucose in plants

Practice questions

1. Which of the following are examples of osmosis? Tick (✓) the three correct options. **(3 marks)**

   a) Water evaporating from leaves ☐

   b) Water moving from plant cell to plant cell and back again ☐

   c) Mixing pure water and sugar solution ☐

   d) A pear submerged in a concentrated sugar solution losing water ☐

   e) Water moving from blood plasma to body cells ☐

   f) Sugar being absorbed from the intestine into the blood ☐

2. Emphysema is a lung disease that increases the thickness of the surface of the lungs for gas exchange and reduces the total area available for gas exchange.

   Two men did the same amount of exercise. One man was in good health and the other man had emphysema.

   The results are shown in the table.

	Healthy man	Man with emphysema
Total air flowing into lungs (dm³/min)	89.5	38.9
Oxygen entering blood (dm³/min)	2.5	1.2

   a) Which man had more oxygen entering his blood? **(1 mark)**

   b) Explain why the man with emphysema struggled to carry out exercise. **(2 marks)**

3. The diagram shows two types of blood vessel.

   A   **B**

   a) Name each type of blood vessel. **(2 marks)**

   b) Explain why blood vessel A has a thick, elastic muscle wall. **(1 mark)**

   c) Why does blood vessel B have valves? **(1 mark)**

Non-communicable diseases

Communicable diseases are caused by **pathogens** such as bacteria and viruses. They can be transmitted from organism to organism in a variety of ways. Examples include cholera and tuberculosis.

Non-communicable diseases are not primarily caused by pathogens. Examples are diseases caused by a poor diet, diabetes, heart disease and smoking-related diseases.

Health is the state of physical, social and mental well-being. Many factors can have an effect on health, including stress and life situations.

Keywords

Pathogen ➤ A microorganism that causes disease

Symptoms ➤ Physical or mental features that indicate a condition or disease, e.g. rash, high temperature, vomiting

Immune system ➤ A system of cells and other components that protect the body from pathogens and other foreign substances

Malnutrition ➤ A diet lacking in one or more food groups

Risk factors

Non-communicable diseases often result from a combination of several **risk factors**.

➤ Risk factors produce an increased likelihood of developing that particular disease. They can be aspects of a person's lifestyle or substances found in the body or environment.

➤ Some of these factors are difficult to quantify or to establish as a definite **causal connection**. So scientists have to describe their effects in terms of probability or likelihood.

The **symptoms** observed in the body may result from communicable and non-communicable components interacting.

A lowered **immune system** may make a person more vulnerable to infection.

Immune reactions caused by pathogens can trigger allergies such as asthma and skin rashes.

Symptoms

Viruses inhabiting living cells can change them into cancer cells.

Serious physical health problems can lead to **mental illness** such as depression.

Poor diet

People need a **balanced diet**.

If a diet does not include enough of the main food groups, **malnutrition** might result. Lack of correct vitamins leads to diseases such as **scurvy** and **rickets**. Lack of the mineral, iron, results in **anaemia**.

A high fat diet contributes to cardiovascular disease and high levels of salt increase blood pressure.

Smoking tobacco

Chemicals in tobacco smoke affect health.

➤ **Carbon monoxide** decreases the blood's oxygen-carrying capacity.

➤ **Nicotine** raises the heart rate and therefore blood pressure.

➤ **Tar** triggers cancer.

➤ **Particulates** cause **emphysema** and increase the likelihood of **lung infections**.

Weight/lack of exercise

Obesity and lack of exercise both increase the risk of developing **type 2 diabetes** and cardiovascular disease.

One way to show whether someone is underweight or overweight for their height is to calculate their **body mass index (BMI)**, using the following formula:

$$BMI = \frac{mass\ (kg)}{height^2\ (m)}$$

Recommended BMI chart

BMI	What it means
<18.5	Underweight – too light for your height
18.5–25	Ideal – correct weight range for your height
25–30	Overweight – too heavy
30–40	Obese – much too heavy. Health risks!

Example:

Calculate a man's BMI if he is 1.65 m tall and weighs 68 kg.

$$BMI = \frac{mass\ (kg)}{height^2\ (m)} = \frac{68}{1.65^2} = \frac{68}{2.7} = \mathbf{25}$$

The recommended BMI for his height (1.65 m) is 18.5–25, so he is just a healthy weight.

There are drawbacks to using BMI as a way of assessing people's health. For example:

➤ teenagers go through a rapid growth phase
➤ a person could have a well-developed muscle system – this would increase their body mass but not make them obese.

Some scientists say a more accurate method is using the waist/hip ratio. A tape measure is used to measure the circumference of the hips and the waist (at its widest). The following chart can then be used.

Waist to hip ratio (WHR)		
Male	**Female**	**Health risk based solely on WHR**
0.95 or below	0.80 or below	Low
0.96 to 1.0	0.81 to 0.85	Moderate
1.0+	0.85+	High

Alcohol

Drinking excess alcohol can impair brain function and lead to **cirrhosis** of the liver. It also contributes to some types of cancer and cardiovascular disease.

Smoking and drinking alcohol during pregnancy

Unborn babies receive nutrition from the mother via the placenta. Substances from tobacco, alcohol and other drugs can pass to the baby and cause **lower birth weight**, **foetal alcohol syndrome** and **addiction**.

Carcinogens

Exposure to **ionising radiation** (for example, X-rays, gamma rays) can cause cancerous tumours. Overexposure to UV light can cause skin cancer. Certain chemicals such as mercury can also increase the likelihood of cancer.

WS Interpreting complex data in graphs doesn't need to be difficult. This line graph shows data about smoking and lung cancer. Look for different patterns in it. For example:

➤ males have higher smoking rates in all years
➤ female cancer rates have increased overall since 1972.

Can you see any other patterns?

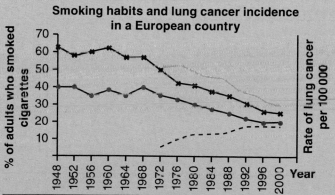

Smoking habits and lung cancer incidence in a European country

KEY
✗✗✗ Male smoking data .... Male incidence of lung cancer
●●● Female smoking data - - - Female incidence of lung cancer

1. State three factors that cause cancer.
2. Give one consequence of a lowered immune system.

Communicable diseases

How do pathogens spread?

Pathogens are disease-causing microorganisms from groups of bacteria, viruses, fungi and protists. All animals and plants can be affected by pathogens. They spread in many ways, including:

➤ **droplet infection** (sneezing and coughing), e.g. flu

➤ **physical contact**, such as touching a contaminated object or person

➤ **transmission** by transferral of or contact **with bodily fluids**, e.g. hepatitis B

➤ **sexual transmission**, e.g. HIV, gonorrhoea

➤ **contamination of food or water**, e.g. Salmonella, cholera

➤ **animal bites**, e.g. rabies.

How do pathogens cause harm?

➤ Bacteria and viruses reproduce rapidly in the body.

➤ Viruses cause cell damage.

➤ Bacteria produce toxins that damage tissues.

These effects produce **symptoms** in the body.

How can the spread of disease be prevented?

The spread of disease can be prevented by:

➤ good hygiene, e.g. washing hands/whole body, using soaps and disinfectants

➤ destroying **vectors**, e.g. disrupting the life cycle of mosquitoes can combat malaria

➤ the isolation or quarantine of individuals

➤ vaccination.

Bacterial diseases

Disease	Transmission	Symptoms	Treatment/prevention
Tuberculosis	Droplet infection	Persistent coughing, which may bring up blood; chest pain; weight loss; fatigue; fever; night sweats; chills	Long course of antibiotics
Cholera	Contaminated water/food	Diarrhoea; vomiting; dehydration	Rehydration salts
Chlamydia	Sexually transmitted	May not be present, but can include discharge and bleeding from sex organs	Antibiotics Using condoms during sexual intercourse can reduce chances of infection
Salmonella	Contaminated food containing toxins from pathogens – these could be introduced from unhygienic food preparation techniques	Vomiting; fever; diarrhoea, stomach cramps	Anti-diarrhoeals and antibiotics; vaccinations for chickens
Gonorrhoea	Sexually transmitted	Thick yellow or green discharge from vagina or penis; pain on urination	Antibiotic injection followed by antibiotic tablets; penicillin is no longer effective against gonorrhoea; prevention through use of condoms

Fungal diseases

Disease	Transmission	Symptoms	Treatment/prevention
Athlete's foot	Direct and indirect contact, e.g. skin-to-skin, bed sheets and towels (often spreads at swimming pools and in changing rooms)	Itchy, red, scaly, flaky and dry skin	Self-care and anti-fungal medication externally applied

Viral and protist diseases

Disease	Transmission	Symptoms and notes	Treatment/prevention
Measles (viral)	Droplets from sneezes and coughs	Fever; red skin rash; fatal if complications arise	No specific treatment; vaccine is a highly effective preventative measure
HIV (viral)	Sexually transmitted; exchange of body fluids; sharing of needles during drug use	Flu-like symptoms initially; late-stage AIDS produces complications due to compromised immune system	Anti-retroviral drugs
Malaria (protist)	Via mosquito vector	Headache; sweats; chills and vomiting; symptoms disappear and reappear on a cyclical basis; further life-threatening complications may arise	Various anti-malarial drugs are available for both prevention and cure; prevention of mosquito breeding and use of mosquito nets

Malarial parasite
The **plasmodium** is a **protist** that causes malaria. It can reproduce asexually in the human host but sexually in the mosquito.

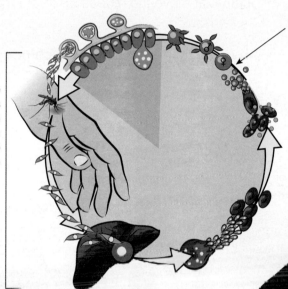

Parasite enters human from mosquito bite

Parasite re-enters mosquito when it feeds

Mosquito

> Create cards showing information about the disease-causing microorganisms in this module. Each card should have the name of the disease at the top and then list the symptoms, mode of transmission, etc.

> Use the cards with a revision buddy. You could give a score for each category of information, e.g. contagion factor (how easily the disease is transmitted), severity of symptoms, etc.

Keywords

Droplet infection ➤ Transmission of microorganisms through the aerosol (water droplets) produced through coughing and sneezing

Vectors ➤ Small organisms (such as mosquitoes or ticks) that pass on pathogens between people or places

1. Why is cholera transmitted rapidly in areas that have poor sanitation (sewage systems)?
2. Name two diseases that cause a rash or affect the skin in some way.

Human defences

15

Keywords

Epithelial ➤ A single layer of cells often found lining respiratory and digestive structures

Mucus ➤ Thick fluid produced in the lining of respiratory and digestive passages

Cilia ➤ Microscopic hairs found on the surface of epithelial cells; they 'waft' from side to side in a rhythmic manner

Antigen ➤ Molecular marker on a pathogen cell membrane that acts as a recognition point for antibodies

Antibodies ➤ Proteins produced by white blood cells (particularly lymphocytes). They lock on to antigens and neutralise them

Immunological memory ➤ The system of cells and cell products whose function is to prevent and destroy microbial infection

Non-specific defences

The body has a number of general or non-specific defences to stop pathogens multiplying inside it.

The skin covers most of the body – it is a **physical barrier** to pathogens. It also secretes antimicrobial peptides to kill microorganisms. If the skin is damaged, a clotting mechanism takes place in the blood preventing pathogens from entering the site of the wound.

Tears contain enzymes called **lysozymes**. Lysozymes break down pathogen cells that might otherwise gain entry to the body through tear ducts.

Hairs in the **nose** trap particles that may contain pathogens.

Tubes in the respiratory system (**trachea** and **bronchi**) are lined with special **epithelial** cells. These cells either produce a sticky, liquid **mucus** that traps microorganisms or have tiny hairs called **cilia** that move the mucus up to the mouth where it is swallowed.

The **stomach** produces **hydrochloric acid**, which kills microorganisms.

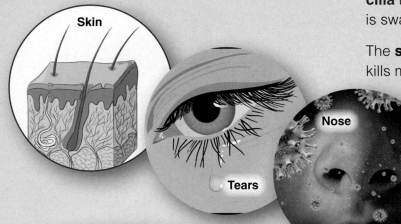

Skin

Tears

Nose

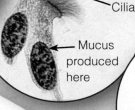

Epithelial cells

Cilia

Mucus produced here

Stomach

Phagocytes are a type of **white blood cell**. They move around in the bloodstream and body tissues searching for pathogens. When they find pathogens, they **engulf** and digest them in a process called **phagocytosis**.

White blood cell (phagocyte)

| Microorganisms invade the body | The white blood cell surrounds and ingests the microorganisms | The white blood cell starts to digest the microorganisms | The microorganisms have been digested by the white blood cell |

Specific defences

White blood cells called **lymphocytes** recognise molecular markers on pathogens called **antigens**. They produce **antibodies** that lock on to the antigens on the cell surface of the pathogen cell. The immobilised cells are clumped together and engulfed by phagocytes.

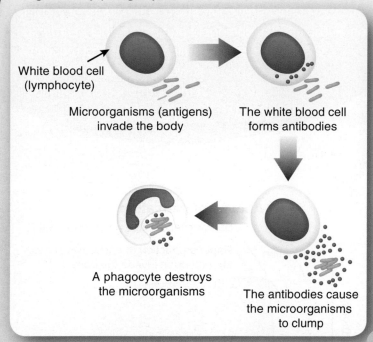

White blood cell (lymphocyte)

Microorganisms (antigens) invade the body

The white blood cell forms antibodies

A phagocyte destroys the microorganisms

The antibodies cause the microorganisms to clump

Some white blood cells produce **antitoxins** that neutralise the poisons produced from some pathogens.

Every pathogen has its own unique antigens. Lymphocytes make antibodies specifically for a particular antigen.

Example: Antibodies to fight TB will not fight cholera

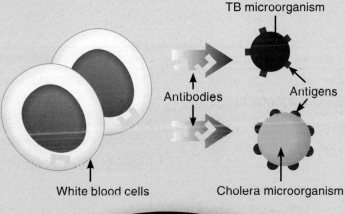

TB microorganism

Antibodies

Antigens

White blood cells

Cholera microorganism

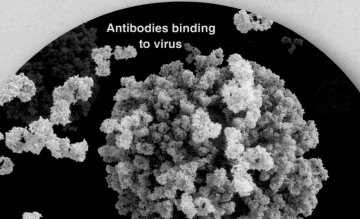

Antibodies binding to virus

Active immunity

Once lymphocytes recognise a particular pathogen, the interaction is stored as part of the body's **immunological memory** through **memory lymphocytes**. These memory cells can produce the right antibodies much quicker if the same pathogen is detected again, therefore providing future protection against the disease. The process is called the **secondary response** and is part of the body's **active immunity**. Active immunity can also be achieved through vaccination.

Memory lymphocytes and antibody production

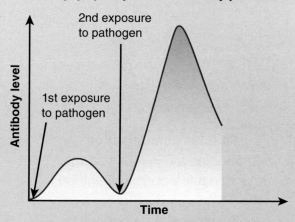

2nd exposure to pathogen

Antibody level

1st exposure to pathogen

Time

WS Investigating the growth of pathogens in the laboratory involves culturing microorganisms. This presents hazards that require a **risk assessment**. A risk assessment involves taking into account the severity of each hazard and the likelihood that it will occur.

Any experiment of this type involves thinking about risks in advance. Here is an example of a risk assessment table for this investigation.

Hazard	Infection from pathogen	Scald from autoclave (a specialised pressure cooker for superheating its contents)
Risk	High	High
How to lower the risk	➤ Observe **aseptic technique**. ➤ Wash hands thoroughly before and after experiment. ➤ Store plates at a maximum temperature of 25°C.	➤ Ensure lid is tightly secured. ➤ Adjust heat to prevent too high a pressure. ➤ Wait for autoclave to cool down before removing lid.

1. Describe the process of phagocytosis.
2. Explain how active immunity can be developed in the body.

Fighting disease

🎧 16

Keywords

Sensitisation ➤ Cells in the immune system are able to 'recognise' antigens or foreign cells and respond by attacking them or producing antibodies

Herd immunity ➤ Vaccination of a significant portion of a population (or herd) makes it hard for a disease to spread because there are so few people left to infect. This gives protection to susceptible individuals such as the elderly or infants

Inhibition ➤ The effect of one agent against another in order to slow down or stop activity, e.g. chemical reactions can be slowed down using inhibitors. Some hormones are inhibitors

Vaccination

There are two types of vaccination.

Passive immunisation

Antibodies are introduced into an individual's body, rather than the person producing them on their own. Some pathogens or toxins (e.g. snake venom) act very quickly and a person's immune system cannot produce antibodies quickly enough. So the person must be injected with the antibodies. However, this does not give long-term protection.

Active immunisation

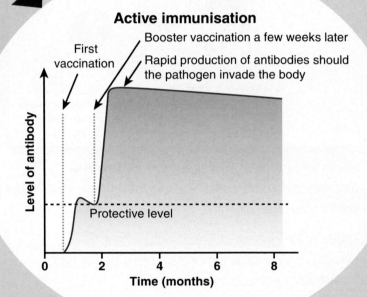

First vaccination

Booster vaccination a few weeks later

Rapid production of antibodies should the pathogen invade the body

Protective level

Level of antibody

Time (months)

Immunisation gives a person immunity to a disease without the pathogens multiplying in the body, or the person having symptoms.

1 A weakened or inactive strain of the pathogen is injected. The pathogen is heat-treated so it cannot multiply. The antigen molecules remain intact.

2 Even though they are harmless, the antigens on the pathogen trigger the white blood cells to produce specific antibodies.

3 As with natural immunity, **memory lymphocytes** remain **sensitised**. This means they can produce more antibodies very quickly if the same pathogen is detected again.

Benefits of immunisation	Risks of immunisation
➤ It protects against diseases that could kill or cause disability (e.g. polio, measles).	➤ A person could have an allergic reaction to the vaccine (small risk).
➤ If everybody is vaccinated and **herd immunity** is established, the disease eventually dies out (this is what happened to smallpox).	

HT

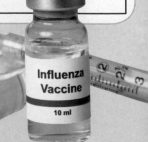

Influenza Vaccine
10 ml

Antibiotics and painkillers

Diseases caused by bacteria (not viruses) can be treated using **antibiotics**, e.g. penicillin. Antibiotics are drugs that destroy the pathogen. Some bacteria need to be treated with antibiotics specific to them.

Antibiotics work because they **inhibit** cell processes in the bacteria but not the body of the host.

Viral diseases can be treated with **antiviral drugs**, e.g. swine flu can be treated with 'Tamiflu' tablets. It is a challenge to develop drugs that destroy viruses without harming body tissues.

Antibiotic resistance

Antibiotics are very effective at killing bacteria. However, some bacteria are **naturally resistant** to particular antibiotics. It is important for patients to follow instructions carefully and take the full course of antibiotics so that all the harmful bacteria are killed.

If doctors over-prescribe antibiotics, there is more chance of resistant bacteria surviving. These multiply and spread, making the antibiotic useless. **MRSA** is a bacterium that has become resistant to most antibiotics. These bacteria have been called 'superbugs'.

Painkillers

Painkillers or **analgesics** are given to patients to relieve symptoms of a disease, but they do not kill pathogens. Types of painkiller include paracetamol and ibuprofen. Morphine is another painkiller – it is a medicinal form of heroin used to treat extreme pain.

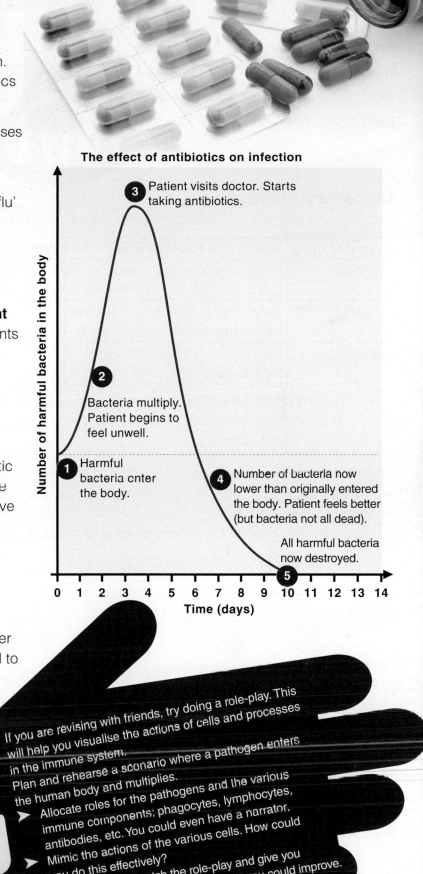

The effect of antibiotics on infection

(y-axis: Number of harmful bacteria in the body; x-axis: Time (days), 0 to 14)

3 Patient visits doctor. Starts taking antibiotics.

2 Bacteria multiply. Patient begins to feel unwell.

1 Harmful bacteria enter the body.

4 Number of bacteria now lower than originally entered the body. Patient feels better (but bacteria not all dead).

5 All harmful bacteria now destroyed.

If you are revising with friends, try doing a role-play. This will help you visualise the actions of cells and processes in the immune system.

Plan and rehearse a scenario where a pathogen enters the human body and multiplies.

➤ *Allocate roles for the pathogens and the various immune components: phagocytes, lymphocytes, antibodies, etc. You could even have a narrator.*

➤ *Mimic the actions of the various cells. How could you do this effectively?*

➤ *Ask someone to watch the role-play and give you feedback on what went well and what you could improve.*

1. What is the difference between an antibiotic and an antibody?
2. What is the difference between an antiviral and an analgesic?
3. What can doctors and patients do to reduce the risk of antibiotic-resistant bacteria developing?

Drugs used for treating illnesses and health conditions include antibiotics, analgesics and other chemicals that modify body processes and chemical reactions. In the past, these drugs were obtained from plants and microorganisms.

Discovery and development of drugs

17

Discovery of drugs

The following drugs are obtained from plants and microorganisms.

Name of drug	Where it is found/origin	Use
Digitalis	Foxgloves (common garden plants that are found in the wild)	Slows down the heartbeat; can be used to treat heart conditions
Aspirin	Willow trees (aspirin contains the **active ingredient** salicylic acid)	Mild painkiller
Penicillin	Penicillium mould (discovered by Alexander Fleming)	Antibiotic

Modern **pharmaceutical drugs** are synthesised by chemists in laboratories, usually at great cost. The starting point might still be a chemical extracted from a plant.

New drugs have to be developed all the time to combat new and different diseases. This is a lengthy process, taking up to ten years. During this time the drugs are tested to determine:
➤ that they work
➤ that they are safe
➤ that they are given at the correct **dose** (early tests usually involve low doses).

New drugs made in laboratory

⬇

Drugs tested in laboratory for toxicity using cells, tissues and live animals

⬇

Clinical trials involving healthy volunteers and patients to check for side-effects

⬇

In addition to testing, **computer models** are used to predict how the drug will affect cells, based on knowledge about how the body works and the effects of similar drugs. There are many who believe this type of testing should be extended and that animal testing should be phased out.

Keywords

Active ingredient ➤ Chemical in a drug that has a therapeutic effect (other chemicals in the drug simply enhance flavour or act as bulking agents)

Pharmaceutical drug ➤ Chemicals that are developed artificially and taken by a patient to relieve symptoms of a disease or treat a condition

Placebo ➤ A substitute for the medication that does not contain the active ingredient

Clinical trials

Clinical trials are carried out on healthy volunteers and patients who have the disease. Some are given the new drug and others are given a **placebo**. The effects of the drug can then be compared to the effects of taking the placebo.

Blind trials involve volunteers who do not know if they have been given the new drug or a placebo. This eliminates any psychological factors and helps to provide a fair comparison. (Blind trials are not normally used in modern clinical trials.)

Double blind trials involve volunteers who are randomly allocated to groups. **Neither they nor the doctors/scientists** know if they have been given the new drug or a placebo. This eliminates **all** bias from the test.

New drugs must also be tested against the best existing treatments.

 When studies involving new drugs are published, there is a **peer review**. This is where scientists with appropriate knowledge read the scientific study and examine the data to see if it is **valid**. Sometimes the trials are duplicated by others to see if similar results are obtained. This increases the **reliability** of the findings and filters out false or exaggerated claims.

Once a **consensus** is agreed, the paper is published. This allows others to hear about the work and to develop it further.

In the case of pharmaceutical drugs, clinical bodies have to decide if the drug can be **licensed** (allowed to be used) and whether it is **cost-effective**. This can be controversial because a potentially life-saving drug may not be used widely simply because it costs too much and/or would benefit too few people.

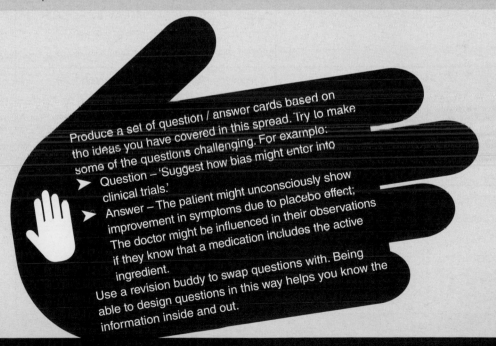

Produce a set of question / answer cards based on the ideas you have covered in this spread. Try to make some of the questions challenging. For example:

➤ Question – 'Suggest how bias might enter into clinical trials.'

➤ Answer – The patient might unconsciously show improvement in symptoms due to placebo effect; The doctor might be influenced in their observations if they know that a medication includes the active ingredient.

Use a revision buddy to swap questions with. Being able to design questions in this way helps you know the information inside and out.

1. What are the alternatives to testing drugs on animals?
2. Give two reasons why newly developed drugs need to be tested in clinical trials.

Plant diseases

Pathogens and pests that affect plants

Disease	Pathogen	Appearance/effect on plants	Treatment
Rose black spot	Fungal disease – the fungal spores are spread by water and wind	Purple/black spots on leaves; these then turn yellow and drop early, leading to a lack of photosynthesis and poor growth	Apply a fungicide and/or remove affected leaves Don't plant roses too close together. Avoid wetting leaves
Tobacco mosaic virus (TMV)	Widespread disease that affects many plants (including tomatoes)	'Mosaic' pattern of discolouration; can lead to lack of photosynthesis and poor growth	Remove infected plants Crop rotation Wash hands after treating plant
Ash dieback	Caused by the fungus *Chalara*	Leaf loss and bark lesions	Cut back or remove diseased trees to reduce chance of airborne spores
Barley powdery mildew	*Erysiphe graminis*	Causes powdery mildew to appear on grasses, including cereals	Fungicides and careful application of nitrogen fertilisers
Crown gall disease	*Agrobacterium tumefaciens*	Tumours or 'galls' at the crown of plants such as apple, raspberry and rose	Use of copper and methods of biological control

Pests	What they do	Appearance/effect on plants	Control
Invertebrates and particularly insects, e.g. many species of aphids	Feed on sap, leaves and storage organs; transmit pathogenic viruses		Chemical pesticides or biological control methods

Mineral ion deficiencies

Plants need **mineral ions** to build complex molecules. The ions are obtained from the soil via the roots in an active manner (requiring energy). In particular, plants need:

➤ **nitrates** to form **amino acids**, the building blocks of **proteins**. They are also needed to make nucleic acids such as **DNA**. Lack of nitrates in a plant leads to yellow leaves and stunted growth

➤ **magnesium** to form chlorophyll, which absorbs light energy for photosynthesis. Lack of magnesium results in **chlorosis**, which is a discolouration of the leaves.

Keyword

Chlorosis ➤ Where leaves lose their colour as a result of mineral deficiency

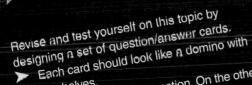

Revise and test yourself on this topic by designing a set of question/answer cards.

➤ Each card should look like a domino with two halves.

➤ On one side, write a question. On the other, write the answer to a question from the next card. The last card's answer should loop back to the first card's question.

➤ Then shuffle and re-organise the cards and start playing!

1. Name two control methods for Rose black spot.
2. Why is the tobacco mosaic virus so damaging to plants?

🎧 18

Mind map

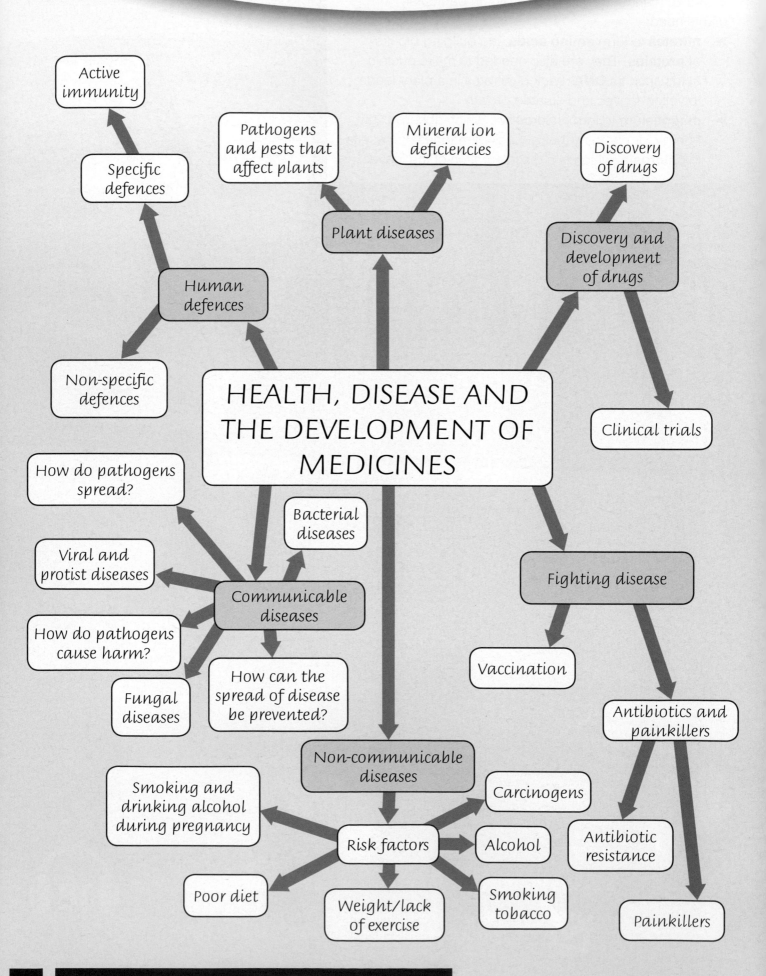

Active immunity

Specific defences

Pathogens and pests that affect plants

Mineral ion deficiencies

Discovery of drugs

Plant diseases

Discovery and development of drugs

Human defences

Non-specific defences

HEALTH, DISEASE AND THE DEVELOPMENT OF MEDICINES

Clinical trials

How do pathogens spread?

Viral and protist diseases

Bacterial diseases

How do pathogens cause harm?

Communicable diseases

Fighting disease

Fungal diseases

How can the spread of disease be prevented?

Vaccination

Antibiotics and painkillers

Non-communicable diseases

Smoking and drinking alcohol during pregnancy

Carcinogens

Risk factors

Alcohol

Antibiotic resistance

Poor diet

Weight/lack of exercise

Smoking tobacco

Painkillers

Practice questions

1. Draw lines to link the name of the microorganism to the disease it causes. **(3 marks)**

Bacterium		HIV
Fungus		Malaria
Virus		Cholera
Protist		Athlete's foot

2. Rani has caught flu and has been confined to bed for several days. Her mother is a health worker and was immunised against flu the previous month.

   a) Describe how the different types of blood component deal with the viruses in Rani's body.

       i) phagocytes **(1 mark)**

       ii) antibodies **(1 mark)**

   b) Describe how the cells in Rani's mother's body responded to the vaccination she was given. In your answer, state what was in the vaccine and use the words **antigen**, **antibody** and **memory cells**. **(4 marks)**

   c) After four days Rani is still unwell and she goes to the doctor. The doctor advises plenty of rest, regular intake of fluids and painkillers when necessary. Explain why the doctor doesn't prescribe antibiotics. **(2 marks)**

   d) If Rani's symptoms continued, which other type of drug might she be prescribed? **(1 mark)**

3. Two drugs called 'Redu' and 'DDD' have been developed to help obese people lose weight. Clinical trials are carried out on the two drugs. The results are shown in the table.

Drug	Number of volunteers in trial	Average weight loss in 6 weeks (kg)
Redu	3250	3.2
DDD	700	5.8
Placebo	2800	2.6

   a) The scientific team concluded that DDD was a more effective weight loss drug. Do you agree? Use the data in the table to give a reason for your answer. **(2 marks)**

   b) The trial carried out was 'double blind'. Explain what this term means and why it is used. **(2 marks)**

Homeostasis and negative feedback

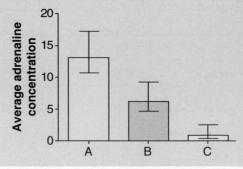

Keywords

Endocrine system ➤ System of ductless organs that release hormones

Stimuli ➤ Changes in the internal or external environment that affect receptors

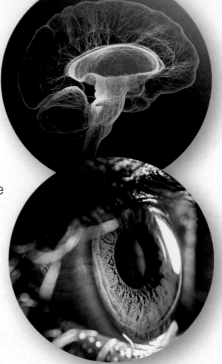

Homeostasis

The body has automatic control systems to maintain a constant internal environment (**homeostasis**). These systems make sure that cells function efficiently.

Homeostasis balances inputs and outputs to ensure that optimal levels of temperature, pH, water, oxygen and carbon dioxide are maintained. For example, even in the cold, homeostasis ensures that body temperature is regulated at about 37°C.

Control systems in the body may involve the nervous system, the **endocrine system**, or both. There are three components of control.

➤ **Effectors** cause responses that restore optimum levels, e.g. muscles and glands.

➤ **Coordination centres** receive and process information from the receptors, e.g. brain, spinal cord and pancreas.

➤ **Receptors** detect **stimuli** from the environment, e.g. taste buds, nasal receptors, the inner ear, touch receptors and receptors on retina cells.

WS When taking measurements, the quality of the measuring instrument and a scientist's skill is very important to achieve **accuracy**, **precision** and **minimal error**.

Adrenaline levels in blood plasma are measured by a chromatography method called HPLC. This is often coupled to a detector that gives a digital readout.

This digital readout displays the concentration of adrenaline as 6.32. This means that the instrument is precise up to $\frac{1}{100}$ of a unit.

A less precise instrument might only measure down to $\frac{1}{10}$ of a unit, e.g. 6.3 (one decimal place).

A bar graph of some data generated from HPLC is shown below. The graph shows the **average concentration** of three different samples of blood. The average is taken from many individual measurements. The vertical error bars indicate the range of measurements (the difference between highest and lowest) obtained for each sample.

Sample C shows **the greatest precision** as the individual readings do not vary as much as the others. There is less error so we can be more confident that the average is closer to the **true value** and therefore more **accurate**.

Negative feedback

Negative feedback occurs frequently in homeostasis. It involves the automatic reversal of a change in the body's condition.

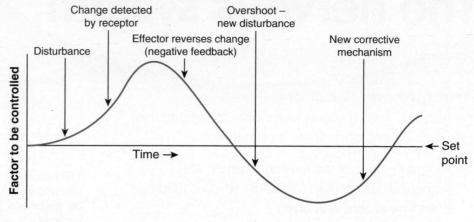

In the body, examples of negative feedback include osmoregulation/water balance, balancing blood sugar levels, maintaining a constant body temperature and controlling metabolic rate.

Metabolism needs to be controlled so that chemical reactions in the body take place at an optimal rate. Negative feedback controls metabolic rate by using the hormones **thyroxine** and **adrenaline**.

Thyroxine

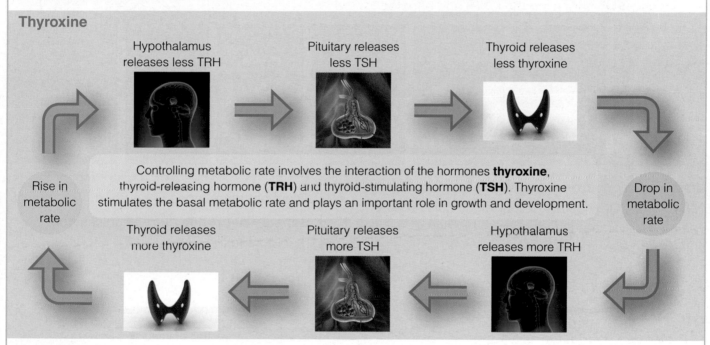

Controlling metabolic rate involves the interaction of the hormones **thyroxine**, thyroid-releasing hormone (**TRH**) and thyroid-stimulating hormone (**TSH**). Thyroxine stimulates the basal metabolic rate and plays an important role in growth and development.

Adrenaline

Adrenaline is sometimes called the 'flight or fight' hormone. During times of stress the adrenal glands produce adrenaline. It has a direct effect on muscles, the liver, intestines and many other organs to prepare the body for sudden bursts of energy. Specifically, adrenaline increases the heart rate so that the brain and muscles receive oxygen and glucose more rapidly.

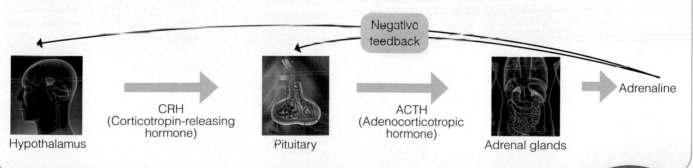

HT **1.** Give two examples of negative feedback in the human body.

HT **2.** What is the target organ for the hormone CRH?

The nervous system

Structure and function

The nervous system allows organisms to react to their surroundings and coordinate their behaviour.

The two main parts of the nervous system are:
➤ the central nervous system (**CNS**), which is made up of the **spinal cord** and **brain**
➤ the **peripheral nervous system**.

The flow of **impulses** in the nervous system is carried out by nerve cells linking the receptor, coordinator (neurones and synapses in the CNS) and effector.

The main components of the nervous system

Brain

Spinal cord

The neurones that make up the peripheral nervous system

CNS (brain and spinal cord)

Sense organ	Sensory neurone	Synapse	Relay neurone	Synapse	Motor neurone	Muscle
In the sense organ, receptors detect a change – either inside or outside the body. The change is a stimulus.	Conducts the impulse from the sense organ towards the CNS.	The gap between the sensory and relay neurones.	Passes the impulse on to a motor neurone.	The gap between the relay neurone and the motor neurone.	Passes the impulse on to the muscle (or gland).	The muscle responds by contracting, which results in a movement. Muscles and glands are examples of effectors.

Nerve cells or **neurones** are specially adapted to carry nerve impulses, which are electrical in nature. The impulse is carried in the long, thin part of the cell called the **axon**.

Motor neurone

Fatty sheath

Axon

There are three types of neurone.

Sensory neurones carry impulses from receptors to the CNS.

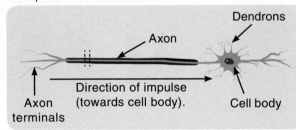

Dendrons

Axon

Direction of impulse (towards cell body).

Axon terminals

Cell body

Relay neurones make connections between neurones inside the CNS.

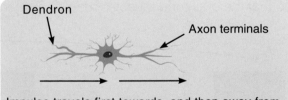

Dendron

Axon terminals

Impulse travels first towards, and then away from, cell body.

Motor neurones carry impulses from the CNS to muscles and glands.

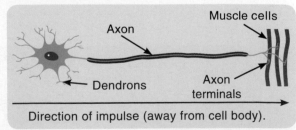

Muscle cells

Axon

Dendrons

Axon terminals

Direction of impulse (away from cell body).

🎧 20

Synapses

Synapses are junctions between neurones. They play an important part in regulating the way impulses are transmitted. Synapses can be found between different neurones, neurones and muscles, and between dendrites (the root-like outgrowths from the cell body).

When an impulse reaches a synapse, a **neurotransmitter** is released by the neurone ('A' in the diagram) into the gap that lies between the neurones. It travels by diffusion and binds to **receptor molecules** on the next neurone. This triggers a new electrical impulse to be released.

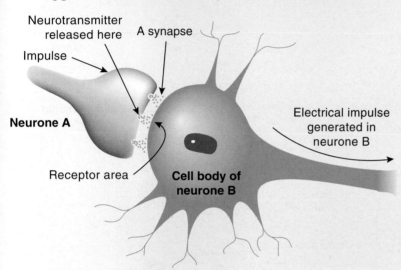

Neurotransmitter released here · A synapse

Impulse

Neurone A

Electrical impulse generated in neurone B

Receptor area · **Cell body of neurone B**

Keywords

Spinal cord ➤ Nervous tissue running down the centre of the vertebral column; millions of nerves branch out from it

Impulses ➤ Electrical signals sent down neurones that trigger responses in the nervous system

Receptor molecule ➤ Protein on the outer membrane of a cell that binds to a specific molecule, such as transmitter substance

Reflex arcs

Reflex actions:
➤ are involuntary/automatic
➤ are very rapid
➤ protect the body from harm
➤ bypass conscious thought.

The pathway taken by impulses around the body is called a **reflex arc**. Examples include:
➤ opening and closing the pupil in the eye
➤ the knee-jerk response
➤ withdrawing your hand from a hot plate.

Here is the arc pathway for a pain response.

WS You may have to investigate the effect of factors on human reaction time.

For example, you could be asked to investigate a learned reflex by measuring how far up a ruler someone can catch it. The nearer to the zero the ruler is caught, the faster the reflex.

You could investigate factors such as:
➤ experience/practice at catching
➤ sound   ➤ touch   ➤ sight.

Can you design experiments to test these variables? Which factors will need to be kept the same?

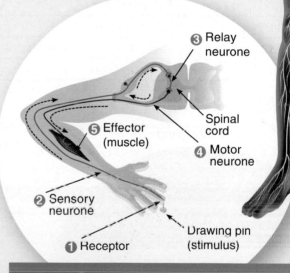

❸ Relay neurone

Spinal cord

❹ Motor neurone

❺ Effector (muscle)

❷ Sensory neurone

Drawing pin (stimulus)

❶ Receptor

1. Name the long, thin extensions of nerve cells.
2. How do reflex arcs aid survival of an organism?
3. Design and draw a flow diagram to represent the pathway followed by impulses in the knee-jerk reflex. (The flow diagram at the beginning of this module should help you.)

The endocrine system

Keywords

Ductless gland ➤ A gland that does not secrete its chemicals through a tube. The pancreas is an exception to this rule as it contains a duct for delivering enzymes, but its hormones are released directly into the bloodstream

HT Glucagon ➤ Hormone released by the pancreas that stimulates the conversion of glycogen to glucose

Glycogen ➤ Storage carbohydrate found in animals

Structure and function

The endocrine system is made up of glands that are **ductless** and secrete **hormones** directly into the bloodstream. The blood carries these chemical messengers to **target organs** around the body, where they cause an effect.

Hormones:

➤ are large, protein molecules

➤ interact with the nervous system to exert control over essential biological processes

➤ act over a longer time period than nervous responses but their effects are slower to establish.

Endocrine gland	Hormone(s) produced
Pituitary gland	TSH, ADH, FSH, LH, etc.
Pancreas	Insulin, glucagon HT
Thyroid	Thyroxine
Adrenal gland	Adrenaline
Ovaries (female)	Oestrogen, progesterone
Testes (male)	Testosterone

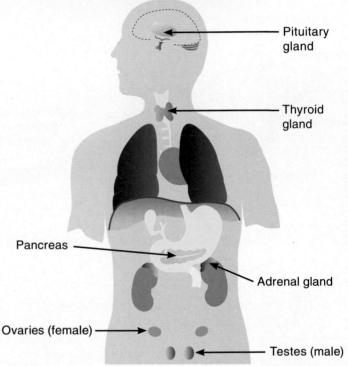

The endocrine system

- Pituitary gland
- Thyroid gland
- Pancreas
- Adrenal gland
- Ovaries (female)
- Testes (male)

Pituitary gland

The pituitary gland

The pituitary is often referred to as the **master gland** because it secretes many hormones that control other processes in the body. Pituitary hormones often trigger other hormones to be released.

➤ Create a series of flashcards about controlling blood glucose levels. On each one, write a hormone, organ or effect relating to the control system.

➤ Shuffle the cards and put them face down. With a revision buddy, or on your own, pick up each card and explain how the particular component is involved in the control process.

Controlling blood glucose concentration

The control system for balancing blood glucose levels involves the **pancreas**.

The pancreas monitors the blood glucose concentration and releases hormones to restore the balance. When the concentration is too high, the pancreas produces insulin that causes glucose to be absorbed from the blood by all body cells, but particularly those in the liver and muscles. These organs convert glucose to **glycogen** for storage until required.

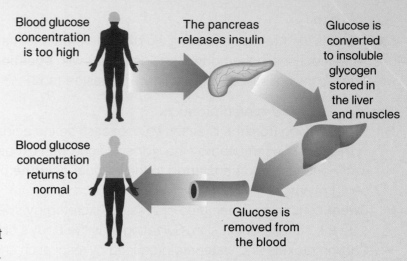

Blood glucose concentration is too high → The pancreas releases insulin → Glucose is converted to insoluble glycogen stored in the liver and muscles → Glucose is removed from the blood → Blood glucose concentration returns to normal

HT If blood glucose concentration is too low, the pancreas secretes glucagon. This stimulates the conversion of glycogen to glucose via enzymic systems. It is then released into the blood.

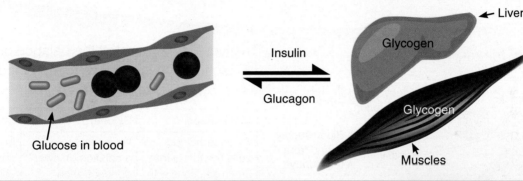

Glucose in blood — Insulin ⇌ Glucagon — Liver, Glycogen, Glycogen, Muscles

Diabetes

There are two types of diabetes.

Type I diabetes:
- is caused by the pancreas' inability to produce insulin
- results in dangerously high levels of blood glucose
- is controlled by delivery of insulin into the bloodstream via injection or a 'patch' worn on the skin
- is more likely to occur in people under 40
- is the most common type of diabetes in childhood
- is thought to be triggered by an auto-immune response where cells in the pancreas are destroyed.

Type II diabetes:
- is caused by fatty deposits preventing body cells from absorbing insulin; the pancreas tries to compensate by producing more and more insulin until it is unable to produce any more
- results in dangerously high levels of blood glucose
- is controlled by a low carbohydrate diet and exercise initially; it may require insulin in the later stages
- is more common in people over 40
- is a risk factor if you are obese.

1. Why is the pituitary called the master gland?
2. Where are the sex hormones of the body produced?
3. What effects does type II diabetes have on the body?

Excretion

Excretion is the process of getting rid of waste products made by chemical reactions in the body. Don't confuse it with **egestion**, which is the loss of solid waste (mainly undigested food).

The following are excreted products.

➤ **Urea** is made from the breakdown of excess amino acids in the liver. It is removed by the kidneys along with excess water and ions and transferred to the bladder as **urine** before being released.

➤ **Sweat** containing water, urea and salt is excreted by sweat glands onto the surface of the skin. Sweating aids the body's cooling process.

➤ **Carbon dioxide** and **water** are produced by respiration and leave the body from the lungs during exhalation.

The lungs and skin don't control the loss of substances. They are simply the organs by which these substances are removed.

Water & nitrogen balance

The kidneys

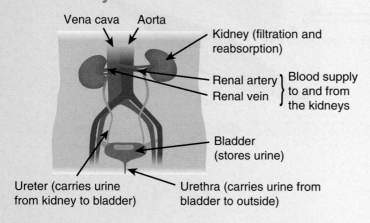

Vena cava   Aorta

Kidney (filtration and reabsorption)

Renal artery ⎫ Blood supply
Renal vein ⎭ to and from the kidneys

Bladder (stores urine)

Ureter (carries urine from kidney to bladder)

Urethra (carries urine from bladder to outside)

The kidneys filter the blood, allowing urea to pass to the bladder. The filtering is carried out within the kidney by thousands of tiny **kidney tubules**.

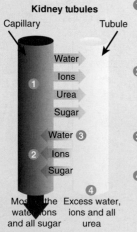

Kidney tubules

Capillary   Tubule

Water
Ions
Urea
Sugar

Water ❸
Ions
Sugar

Most of the water, ions and all sugar

Excess water, ions and all urea

❶ **Filtration**
Lots of water plus all the small molecules are squeezed out of the blood, under pressure, into the tubules.

❷ **Selective reabsorption**
Useful substances, including glucose, ions and water, are reabsorbed into the blood from the tubules.

❸ **Osmoregulation**
Amount of water in the blood and urine is adjusted here.

❹ **Excretion of waste**
Excess water, ions and all the urea now pass to the bladder in the form of urine and are eventually released from the body.

Other useful substances (glucose, amino acids, fatty acids, glycerol and some water) are **selectively re-absorbed** early in the process.

The kidneys also control the balance of water in the blood. Damage occurs to red blood cells if water content is not balanced.

Ideal shape	Swollen	Shrivelled
When red blood cells (erythrocytes) are in solutions with equal concentration to their cytoplasm, they have an ideal, biconcave shape. This is because there is no net movement of water in or out.	When immersed in a solution of lower concentration (higher water concentration), the cells absorb water by osmosis. The weak cell membrane cannot resist the added water pressure and may burst.	In a more concentrated solution (lower water concentration), cells lose water by osmosis. They shrivel up and become **crenated** (have scalloped edges).

Kidney tubules (nephrons)

In terms of nephron structure, filtration, selective reabsorption and excretion of waste occur in the following regions.

Structure of the nephron

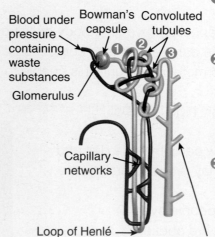

Blood under pressure containing waste substances

Bowman's capsule

Convoluted tubules

Glomerulus

Capillary networks

Loop of Henlé

Collecting ducts (lead to the ureter)

❶ Filtration, where all small molecules and lots of water are squeezed out of the blood and into the tubules.

❷ Selective reabsorption of useful substances (water, ions, glucose) back into the blood from the convoluted tubules. This may take energy in the case of glucose and ions.

❸ Excretion of waste in the form of excess water, excess ions and all urea. These drain into the collecting tubules and pass to the bladder as urine.

Kidney failure

Kidneys may fail due to accidents or disease. A patient can survive with one kidney. If both kidneys are affected, two treatments are available.

> **Kidney transplant** – involves a healthy person donating one kidney to replace two failed kidneys in another person.

> **Dialysis** – offered to patients while they wait for the possibility of a kidney transplant. A dialysis machine removes urea and maintains levels of sodium and glucose in the blood.

This is what happens during dialysis.

1. Blood is taken from a person's vein and run into the dialysis machine, where it comes into close contact with a **partially permeable membrane**.
2. This separates the blood from the dialysis fluid.
3. The urea and other waste diffuse from the blood into the dialysis fluid. The useful substances remain and are transferred back to the body.

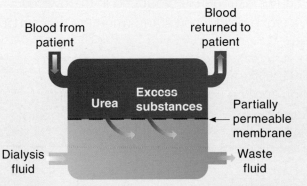

Keywords

Urea ➤ Nitrogenous waste product
Selective re-absorption ➤ Occurs in the kidney tubules and allows useful substances to pass from the kidneys back into the blood
Partially permeable membrane ➤ Artificial or organic layer that only allows small molecules through
HT Deamination ➤ Process in the liver in which nitrogen is removed from an amino acid molecule
HT Ammonia ➤ Nitrogenous waste product

HT How urea is formed

Proteins obtained from the diet may produce a surplus of **amino acids** that need to be excreted safely.

1. First, the amino acids are **deaminated** in the **liver** to form **ammonia**.
2. Ammonia is toxic so is immediately converted to urea, which is then filtered out in the kidney.

Controlling water content

The osmotic balance of the body's fluids needs to be tightly controlled because if cells gain or lose too much water they do not function efficiently.

The amount of water re-absorbed by the kidneys is controlled by **anti-diuretic hormone (ADH)**. This is produced in the pituitary.

1. ADH directly increases the permeability of the kidney tubules to water.
2. When the water content of the blood is low (higher blood concentration), **negative feedback** operates to restore normal levels.

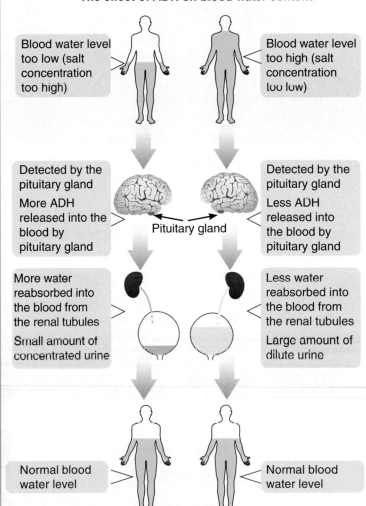

The effect of ADH on blood water content

---

1. List three substances that are selectively re-absorbed back into the bloodstream from the kidney.
2. **HT** What effect does producing **more** ADH have on the concentration of urine?
3. Describe what happens to a urea molecule as it passes through a dialysis machine.

Hormones in human reproduction

Hormones play a vital role in regulating human reproduction, especially in the female **menstrual** cycle.

Puberty

During **puberty** (approximately 10–16 in girls and 12–17 in boys), the sex organs begin to produce **sex hormones**. This causes the development of **secondary sexual characteristics**.

In **males**, the primary sex hormone is **testosterone**.

During puberty, testosterone is produced from the testes and causes:
➤ production of sperm in testes
➤ development of muscles and penis
➤ deepening of the voice
➤ growth of pubic, facial and body hair.

In **females**, the primary sex hormone is **oestrogen**. Other sex hormones are **progesterone**, **FSH** and **LH**.

During puberty, oestrogen is produced in the ovaries and progesterone production starts when the menstrual cycle begins.

The secondary sexual characteristics are:
➤ ovulation and the menstrual cycle
➤ breast growth
➤ widening of hips
➤ growth of pubic and armpit hair.

The menstrual cycle

A woman is fertile between the ages of approximately 13 and 50.

During this time, an egg is released from one of her ovaries each month and the lining of her uterus is replaced each month (approximately 28 days) to prepare for pregnancy.

The menstrual cycle

Ovary

Follicle with egg gradually develops

Ovulation (egg released)

Empty follicle gradually disappears

Thickness of uterus wall

Uterus wall rich in blood vessels

0 7 14 21 28 7
Day of cycle

1. Uterus lining breaks down (i.e. a period).
2. Repair of the uterus wall. Oestrogen causes the uterus lining to gradually thicken.
3. Egg released by the ovary.
4. Progesterone and oestrogen make the lining stay thick, waiting for a fertilised egg.
5. No fertilised egg so cycle restarts.

Concentration of hormones in the blood

Oestrogen

Progesterone

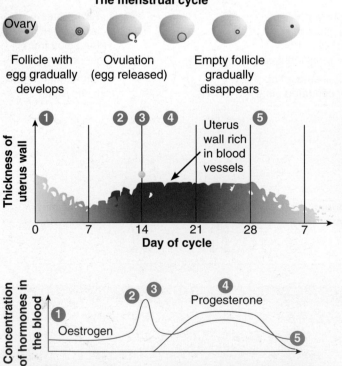

As well as oestrogen and progesterone, the two other hormones involved in the cycle are:

➤ **FSH** or **follicle stimulating hormone**, which causes maturation of an egg in the ovary

➤ **LH** or **luteinising hormone**, which stimulates release of an egg.

Negative feedback in the menstrual cycle

The four female hormones interact in a complex manner to regulate the cycle.

➤ **FSH** is produced in the pituitary and acts on the ovaries, causing an egg to mature. It **stimulates** the ovaries to produce oestrogen.

➤ **Oestrogen** is secreted in the ovaries and **inhibits** further production of FSH. It also **stimulates** the release of LH and promotes repair of the uterus wall after menstruation.

➤ **LH** is produced in the pituitary. It also **stimulates** release of an egg.

➤ **Progesterone** is secreted by the empty **follicle** in the ovary (left by the egg). It **maintains** the lining of the uterus after ovulation has occurred. It also **inhibits** FSH and LH.

HT

Female reproductive system

Low progesterone levels allow FSH from the pituitary gland to stimulate the maturation of an egg (in a follicle). This in turn stimulates oestrogen production.

High levels of oestrogen stimulate a surge in LH from the pituitary gland. This triggers ovulation in the middle of the cycle.

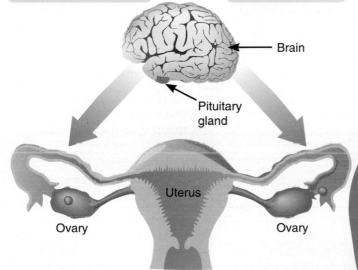

Brain

Pituitary gland

Uterus

Ovary   Ovary

23

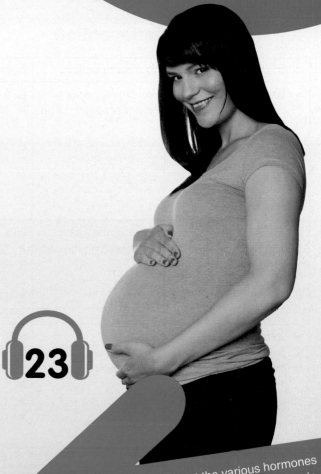

Keywords

Menstruation ➤ Loss of blood and muscle tissue from the uterus wall during the monthly cycle

Follicle stimulating hormone ➤ A hormone produced by the pituitary gland that controls oestrogen production by the ovaries

HT **Inhibition** ➤ Negative effect in negative feedback, where the increase in one factor brings a **decrease** in another

To familiarise yourself with what the various hormones do in the menstrual cycle, you may find it helpful to do the following.

➤ On a computer, create a series of text boxes listing the organs, hormones and effects relating to the menstrual cycle. You could also include diagrams of the organs.

➤ Re-arrange the text boxes/diagrams so they are out of order.

➤ Test yourself or ask a revision buddy to put them back in the correct position/order. Alternatively, you could draw or write the organs, hormones and effects on paper and re-arrange them manually.

1. Name the four hormones involved in the menstrual cycle. What are their functions?
2. At approximately what stage in the menstrual cycle does the uterus lining repair itself?
3. Name one effect of testosterone in puberty.

Contraception and infertility

Fertility and the possibility of pregnancy can be controlled using non-hormonal and hormonal methods of **contraception**.

Keywords

Contraception ➤ Literally means 'against conception'; any method that reduces the likelihood of a sperm meeting an egg
Intrauterine ➤ Inside the uterus
Implantation ➤ Process in which an embryo embeds itself in the uterine wall
Oral contraceptive ➤ Hormonal contraceptive taken in tablet form

Non-hormonal contraception

Contraceptive method	Method of action	Advantages	Disadvantages
➤ Barrier method – condom (male + female)	Prevents the sperm from reaching the egg	82% effective ➤ Most effective against STIs	➤ Can only be used once ➤ May interrupt sexual activity ➤ Can break ➤ Women may be allergic to latex
➤ Barrier method – diaphragm	Prevents the sperm from reaching the egg	88% effective ➤ Can be put in place right before intercourse or 2–3 hours before ➤ Don't need to take out between acts of sexual intercourse	➤ Increases urinary tract infections ➤ Doesn't protect against STIs
➤ **Intrauterine** device	Prevents **implantation** – some release hormones	99% effective ➤ Very effective against pregnancy ➤ Doesn't need daily attention ➤ Comfortable ➤ Can be removed at any time	➤ Doesn't protect against STIs ➤ Needs to be inserted by a medical practitioner ➤ Higher risk of infection when first inserted ➤ Can have side effects such as menstrual cramping ➤ Can fall out and puncture the uterus (rare)
➤ Spermicidal agent	Kills or disables sperm	72% effective ➤ Cheap	➤ Doesn't protect against STIs ➤ Needs to be reapplied after one hour ➤ Increases urinary tract infections ➤ Some people are allergic to spermicidal agents
➤ Abstinence ➤ Calendar method	Refraining from sexual intercourse when an egg is likely to be in the oviduct	76% effective ➤ Natural ➤ Approved by many religions ➤ Woman gets to know her body and menstrual cycles	➤ Doesn't protect against STIs ➤ Calculating the ovulation period each month requires careful monitoring and instruction ➤ Can't have sexual intercourse for at least a week each month
➤ Surgical method	Vasectomy and female sterilisation	99% effective ➤ Very effective against pregnancy ➤ One-time decision providing permanent protection	➤ No protection against STIs ➤ Need to have minor surgery ➤ Permanent

Hormonal contraception

Contraceptive method	Method of action	Advantages	Disadvantages
➤ Oral contraceptive	Contains hormones that inhibit FSH production, so eggs fail to mature	91% effectiveness ➤ Very effective against pregnancy if used correctly ➤ Makes menstrual periods lighter and more regular ➤ Lowers risk of ovarian and uterine cancer, and other conditions ➤ Doesn't interrupt sexual activity	➤ Doesn't protect against STIs ➤ Need to remember to take it every day at the same time ➤ Can't be used by women with certain medical problems or by women taking certain medications ➤ Can occasionally cause side effects
➤ Hormone injection ➤ Skin patch ➤ Implant	Provides slow release of progesterone; this inhibits maturation and release of eggs	91–99% effectiveness depending on method used ➤ Lasts over many months or years ➤ Light or no menstrual periods ➤ Doesn't interrupt sexual activity	➤ Doesn't protect against STIs ➤ May require minor surgery (for implant) ➤ Can cause side effects

The percentage figures in the contraception tables are based on users in a whole population, regardless of whether they use the method correctly. If consistently used correctly, the percentage effectiveness of each method is usually higher. Some methods, such as the calendar method, are more prone to error than others.

Infertility treatment

Infertility treatment is used by couples who have problems conceiving.

Reasons for infertility

No eggs being released from the ovaries.
Endometriosis, which occurs when the tissue that lines the inside of the uterus enters other organs of the body, such as the abdomen and fallopian tubes; this reduces the maturation rate and release of eggs.
Male infertility/low sperm count.
Uterine fibroids.
Complete or partial blocking and/or scarring of the fallopian tubes.
Reduced number and quality of eggs.

Methods of treatment

Treating infertility is known as ART (assisted reproductive technology). There are a number of methods of treatment.

➤ **Fertility drugs** containing FSH and LH are given to women who do not produce enough FSH themselves. They may then become pregnant naturally.

➤ **Clomifene therapy** prevents the production of oestrogen and so inhibits negative feedback.

➤ **In vitro fertilisation (IVF)** is a method in which the potential mother is given FSH and LH to stimulate the production of several eggs. Sperm is collected from the father. The sperm and eggs are then introduced together outside the body in a petri dish. One or two growing embryos can then be transplanted into the woman's uterus.

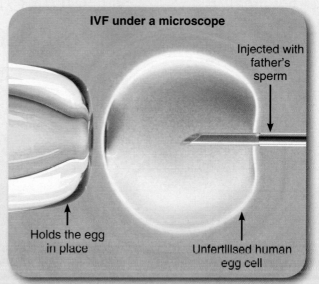

IVF under a microscope

Injected with father's sperm

Holds the egg in place

Unfertilised human egg cell

Disadvantages of IVF

It is very expensive.
It can be mentally and physically stressful.
Success rates are only approximately 40% (at the time of writing).
There is an increased risk of multiple births.

1. Which contraceptives might not be suitable for a woman suffering from high blood pressure?
2. Why are condoms effective against the spread of HIV?
3. How has the development of microscopy helped couples with infertility problems?

Mind map

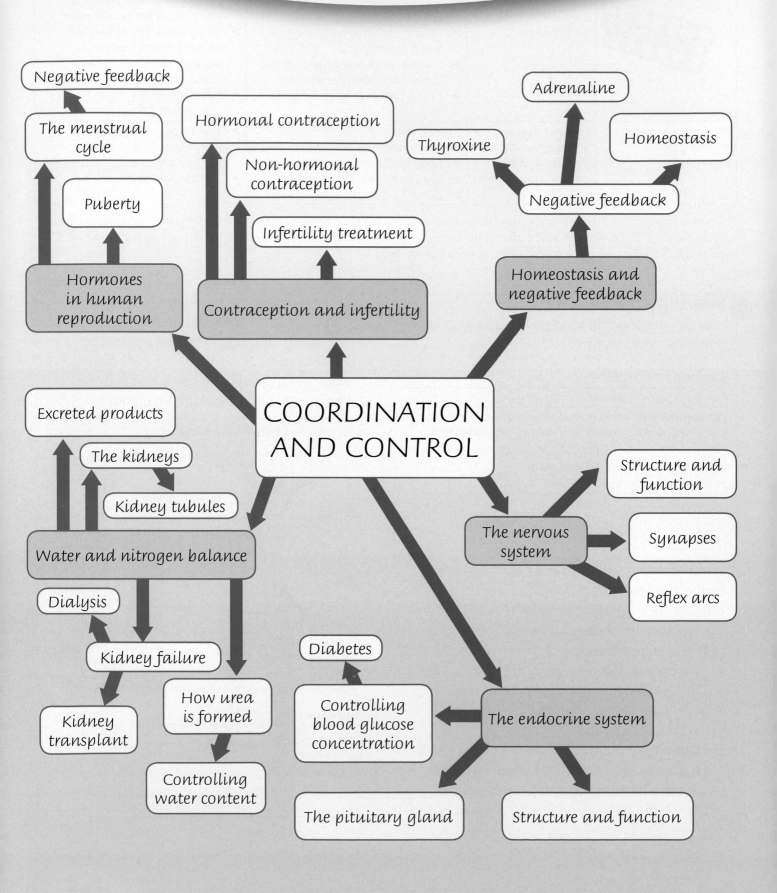

Negative feedback

The menstrual cycle

Puberty

Hormones in human reproduction

Hormonal contraception

Non-hormonal contraception

Infertility treatment

Contraception and infertility

Adrenaline

Thyroxine

Homeostasis

Negative feedback

Homeostasis and negative feedback

COORDINATION AND CONTROL

Excreted products

The kidneys

Kidney tubules

Water and nitrogen balance

Dialysis

Kidney failure

Kidney transplant

How urea is formed

Controlling water content

Diabetes

Controlling blood glucose concentration

The endocrine system

The pituitary gland

Structure and function

The nervous system

Structure and function

Synapses

Reflex arcs

Practice questions

1. The flow chart shows the events that occur during a reflex action.

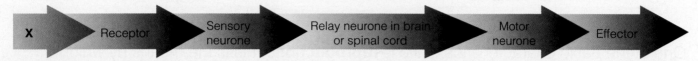

| X | → | Receptor | → | Sensory neurone | → | Relay neurone in brain or spinal cord | → | Motor neurone | → | Effector | → |

Paul accidentally puts his hand on a pin. Without thinking, he immediately pulls his hand away.

a) Which component of a reflex arc is represented by the letter X? **(1 mark)**

b) Give **two** reasons why this can be described as a reflex action. **(2 marks)**

c) Use the flow chart to describe what happens in this reflex action. **(4 marks)**

2. Look at the graph showing a person's blood sugar levels.

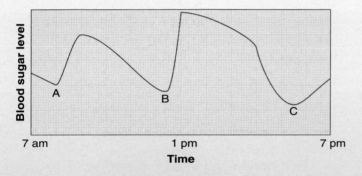

a) How can we tell from the graph that this person has diabetes? **(2 marks)**

b) Explain why the person's blood sugar level rises rapidly just after points A and B. **(1 mark)**

c) Describe what would happen after points A and B if the person did not have diabetes. **(1 mark)**

d) Explain why the person needed to eat a chocolate at point C. **(1 mark)**

3. Penny is exercising. Many changes are happening in her body. Sweat glands help to control her temperature.

a) Explain how the sweat glands help to control the temperature of her body. **(2 marks)**

b) As Penny exercises, she produces carbon dioxide in her cells. What name is given to the process that converts substances into waste products? **(1 mark)**

c) Penny's liver produces urea. Which substances are changed to form urea? **(1 mark)**

d) Penny's kidneys process the urea. The route the urea follows is shown below. Write down the missing stages. **(2 marks)**

| Urea produced in liver | → | | → | Urea filtered in the kidneys |
| Urea in urine passes out of body | ← | | ← | Urine passes down ureter |

Sexual and asexual reproduction

One of the basic characteristics of life is **reproduction**. This is the means by which a species continues. If sufficient offspring are not produced, the species becomes **extinct**.

Sexual reproduction

Sexual reproduction is where a male **gamete** (e.g. sperm) meets a female gamete (e.g. egg). This **fusion** of the two gametes is called **fertilisation** and may be **internal** or **external**.

Gametes are produced by **meiosis** in the sex organs.

Asexual reproduction

Asexual reproduction does not require different male and female cells. Instead, genetically identical clones are produced from mitosis. These may just be individual cells, as in the case of yeast, or whole multicellular organisms, e.g. **aphids**.

Many organisms can reproduce using both methods, depending on the environmental conditions.

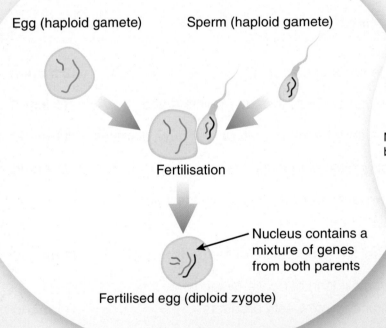

Egg (haploid gamete)   Sperm (haploid gamete)

Fertilisation

Nucleus contains a mixture of genes from both parents

Fertilised egg (diploid zygote)

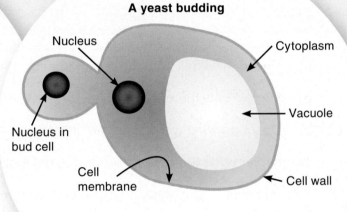

A yeast budding

Nucleus

Cytoplasm

Nucleus in bud cell

Vacuole

Cell membrane

Cell wall

Comparing sexual and asexual reproduction

Advantages of sexual reproduction

➤ Produces **variation** in offspring through the process of meiosis, where genes are 'shuffled.' Variation is increased by **random fusion of gametes**.
➤ Survival advantage gained when the environment changes because different genetic types have more chance of producing well-adapted offspring.
➤ Humans can make use of sexual reproduction through **selective breeding**. This enhances food production.

Disadvantages of sexual reproduction

➤ Relatively slow process.
➤ Variation can be a disadvantage in stable environments.
➤ More resources required than for asexual reproduction, e.g. energy, time.
➤ Results of selective breeding are unpredictable and might lead to genetic abnormalities from 'in-breeding'.

Advantages of asexual reproduction

➤ Only one parent required.
➤ Fewer resources (energy and time) need to be devoted to finding a mate.
➤ Faster than sexual reproduction – survival advantage of producing many offspring in a short period of time.
➤ Many identical offspring of a well-adapted individual can be produced to take advantage of favourable conditions.

Disadvantages of asexual reproduction

➤ Offspring may not be well adapted in a changing environment.

Keywords

Fusion ➤ Joining together; in biology the term is used to describe fertilisation
Internal fertilisation ➤ Gametes join **inside** the body of the female
External fertilisation ➤ Gametes join **outside** the body of the female
Aphid ➤ A type of sap-sucking insect

Asexual reproduction

Sexual reproduction

1. Sexual reproduction requires a greater devotion of resources by an organism. So why do so many organisms use it?
2. State one advantage of asexual reproduction.

25

DNA

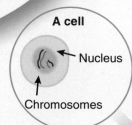

A cell

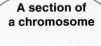
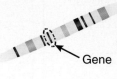

Nucleus

Chromosomes

DNA and the genome

The nucleus of each cell contains a complete set of genetic instructions called the **genetic code**. The information is carried as genes, which are small sections of DNA found on **chromosomes**. The genetic code controls cell activity and, consequently, characteristics of the whole organism.

A section of a chromosome

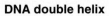

Gene

DNA facts

➤ DNA is a **polymer**.

➤ It is made of two strands coiled around each other called a **double helix**.

➤ The genetic code is in the form of nitrogenous **bases**.

➤ Bases bond together in pairs forming **hydrogen bond** cross-links.

➤ The structure of DNA was discovered in 1953 by **James Watson** and **Francis Crick**, using experimental data from **Rosalind Franklin** and **Maurice Wilkins**.

➤ A single gene codes for a particular sequence of **amino acids**, which, in turn, makes up a single **protein**.

DNA double helix

A section of the double helix

Bases

A —— T

C —— G

G —— C

➤ Construct part of a DNA molecule using plasticine. Use different colours to represent bases, sugar and phosphate molecules. Use the model to illustrate how changes in the base sequence can result in new proteins. You could use different colours to represent different amino acids. Make appropriate shapes to represent each component. The diagrams used in this module are a good starting point.

➤ Use your model as a way of learning the names of the different components.

Keywords

Polymer ➤ A long chain molecule made up of individual units called **monomers**

Hydrogen bond ➤ A bond formed between hydrogen and oxygen atoms on different molecules close to each other

Anthropologists ➤ Scientists who study the human race and its evolution

The human genome

The **genome** of an organism is the entire genetic material present in an adult cell of an organism.

The Human Genome Project (HGP)

The HGP was an international study. Its purpose was to map the complete set of genes in the human body.

HGP scientists worked out the code of the human genome in three ways. They:

➤ determined the sequence of all the bases in the genome

➤ drew up maps showing the locations of the genes on chromosomes

➤ produced linkage maps that could be used for tracking inherited traits from generation to generation, e.g. for genetic diseases. This could then lead to targeted treatments for these conditions.

The results of the project, which involved collaboration between UK and US scientists, were published in 2003. Three billion base pairs were determined.

DNA structure and base sequences

The four bases in DNA are A, T, C and G. The code is 'read' on one strand of DNA. Three consecutive bases (a **triplet**) code for one particular amino acid. The sequence of these triplets determines the structure of a whole protein.

The bases are attached to a sugar phosphate **backbone**. These form a basic unit called a nucleotide.

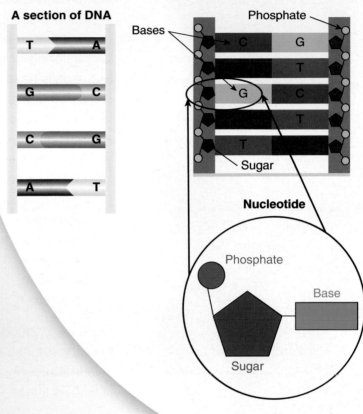

A section of DNA

Nucleotide

The mapping of the human genome has enabled **anthropologists** to work out historical human migration patterns. This has been achieved by collecting and analysing DNA samples from many people across the globe. The study is called the **Genographic Project**.

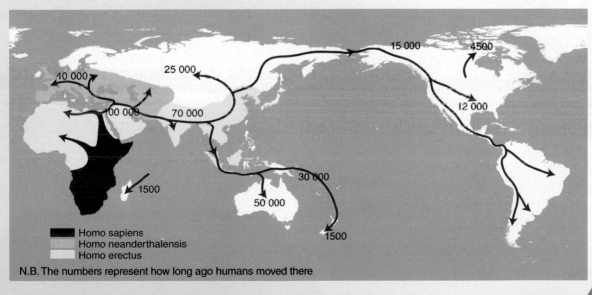

World map showing suggested migration patterns of early hominids

- Homo sapiens
- Homo neanderthalensis
- Homo erectus

N.B. The numbers represent how long ago humans moved there

1. How has the Human Genome Project advanced medical science?
2. What do genes code for?

The genetic code

27

HT Mutations

Mutations (genetic variants):

➤ are changes to the structure of a DNA molecule

➤ occur continuously during the cell division process or as a result of external influences, e.g. exposure to radioactive materials or emissions such as X-rays or UV light

➤ usually have a neutral effect as amino acids may still be produced or the proteins produced work in the same way

➤ may result in harmful conditions or, more rarely, beneficial traits

➤ result in a change in base sequence and therefore changes in the amino acid sequence and protein structure.

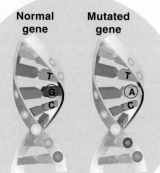

Normal gene   **Mutated gene**

The G base is substituted for an A base

Proteins produced as a result of mutation may no longer be able to carry out their function. This is because they have a different 3D structure. For example, an enzyme's active site may no longer fit with its substrate, or a structural protein may lose its strength.

Changes in the base sequence may be passed on to daughter cells when cell division occurs. This in turn may lead to offspring having genetic conditions.

WS During your course, you will be expected to recognise, draw and interpret scientific diagrams.

The way complementary strands of DNA are arranged can be worked out once you know that base T bonds with A and base C bonds with G.

Can you write out the complementary (DNA) strand to this sequence?

_____

A T T A C G T G A G C C

Keywords

Alleles ➤ Alternative forms of a gene on a homologous pair of chromosomes

Homologous chromosomes ➤ A pair of chromosomes carrying alleles that code for the same characteristics

Monohybrid crosses

Most characteristics or **traits** are the result of multiple alleles interacting but some are controlled by a single gene. Examples include fur colour in mice and the shape of ear lobes in humans. These genes exist as pairs called **alleles** on **homologous chromosomes**.

Alleles are described as being **dominant** or **recessive**.

➤ A **dominant** allele controls the development of a characteristic even if it is present on only one chromosome in a pair.

➤ A **recessive** allele controls the development of a characteristic only if a dominant allele is not present, i.e. if the recessive allele is present on both chromosomes in a pair.

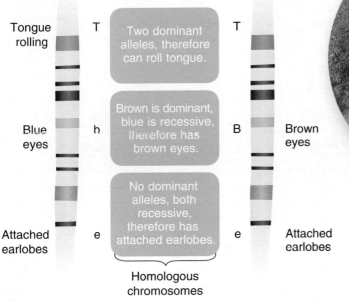

Tongue rolling	T	T
	Two dominant alleles, therefore can roll tongue.	
Blue eyes	h	B	Brown eyes
	Brown is dominant, blue is recessive, therefore has brown eyes.	
	No dominant alleles, both recessive, therefore has attached earlobes.	
Attached earlobes	e	e	Attached earlobes

Homologous chromosomes

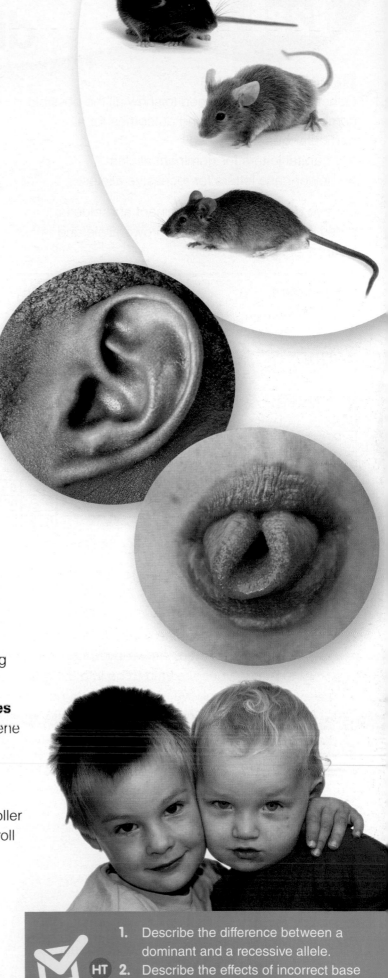

If **both chromosomes** in a pair contain the **same allele** of a gene, the individual is described as being **homozygous** for that gene or condition.

If the chromosomes in a pair contain **different alleles** of a gene, the individual is **heterozygous** for that gene or condition.

The combination of alleles for a particular characteristic is called the **genotype**. For example, the genotype for a homozygous dominant tongue-roller would be **TT**. The fact that this individual is able to roll their tongue is termed their **phenotype**.

Other examples are:

➤ **bb** (genotype), blue eyes (phenotype)

➤ **EE** or **Ee** (genotype), unattached/pendulous ear lobes (phenotype).

When a characteristic is determined by just one pair of alleles, as with eye colour and tongue rolling, it is called **monohybrid inheritance**.

1. Describe the difference between a dominant and a recessive allele.

HT 2. Describe the effects of incorrect base sequences on protein manufacture.

28

Inheritance and genetic disorders

Genetic diagrams

Genetic diagrams are used to show all the possible combinations of alleles and outcomes for a particular gene. They use:

➤ capital letters for dominant alleles
➤ lower-case letters for recessive alleles.

For eye colour, brown is dominant and blue is recessive. So B represents a brown allele and b represents a blue allele.

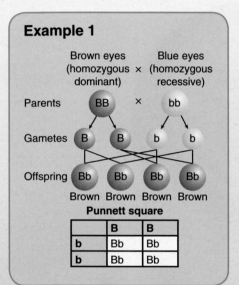

Example 1

Brown eyes (homozygous dominant) × Blue eyes (homozygous recessive)

Parents: BB × bb
Gametes: B B b b
Offspring: Bb Bb Bb Bb
Brown Brown Brown Brown

Punnett square

	B	B
b	Bb	Bb
b	Bb	Bb

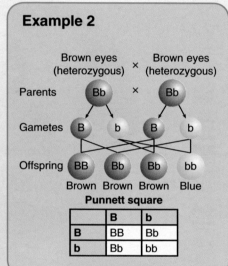

Example 2

Brown eyes (heterozygous) × Brown eyes (heterozygous)

Parents: Bb × Bb
Gametes: B b B b
Offspring: BB Bb Bb bb
Brown Brown Brown Blue

Punnett square

	B	b
B	BB	Bb
b	Bb	bb

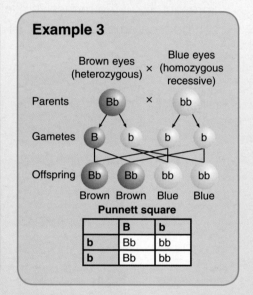

Example 3

Brown eyes (heterozygous) × Blue eyes (homozygous recessive)

Parents: Bb × bb
Gametes: B b b b
Offspring: Bb Bb bb bb
Brown Brown Blue Blue

Punnett square

	B	b
b	Bb	bb
b	Bb	bb

(WS) You need to be able to interpret genetic diagrams and work out ratios of offspring.

➤ In Example 2 above, the phenotypes of the offspring are 'brown eyes' and 'blue eyes'. As there are potentially three times as many brown-eyed children as blue-eyed, the phenotypes are said to be in a 3:1 ratio.

➤ In Example 3 above, the ratio would be 1:1 because half of the theoretical offspring are brown-eyed and half blue-eyed. Another way of saying this is that the probability of parents producing a brown-eyed child is 50%, or ½, or 0.5.

Most traits result not from one pair of alleles but from multiple genes interacting, e.g. inheritance of blood groups in the **ABO** system.

(HT) In exams, you may be asked to construct your own punnett squares to solve genetic cross problems like the ones above.

Family trees

Family trees are another way of showing how genetic traits can be passed on. Here is an example.

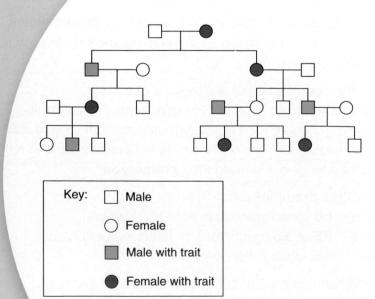

Key:
☐ Male
○ Female
■ Male with trait
● Female with trait

Inheritance of sex

Sex in humans/mammals is determined by whole chromosomes. These are the 23rd pair and are called sex chromosomes. There is an 'X' chromosome and a smaller 'Y' chromosome. The other 22 chromosome pairs carry the remainder of genes coding for the rest of the body's characteristics.

All egg cells carry X chromosomes. Half the sperm carry X chromosomes and half carry Y chromosomes. The sex of an individual depends on whether the egg is fertilised by an X-carrying sperm or a Y-carrying sperm.

If an X sperm fertilises the egg it will become a girl. If a Y sperm fertilises the egg it will become a boy. The chances of these events are equal, which results in approximately equal numbers of male and female offspring.

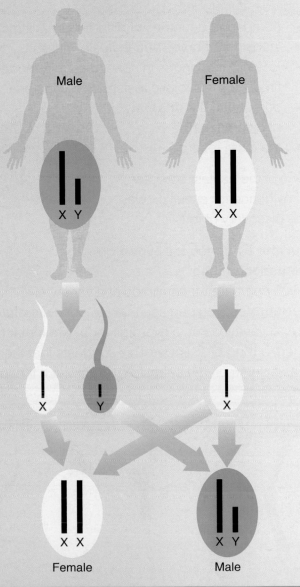

Inherited diseases

Some disorders are caused by a 'faulty' gene, which means they can be **inherited**. One example is **polydactyly**, which is caused by a dominant allele and results in extra fingers or toes. The condition is not life-threatening.

Cystic fibrosis, on the other hand, can limit life expectancy. It causes the mucus in respiratory passages and the gut lining to be very thick, leading to build-up of phlegm and difficulty in producing correct digestive enzymes.

Cystic fibrosis is caused by a recessive allele. This means that an individual will only exhibit symptoms if both recessive alleles are present in the genotype. Those carrying just one allele will not show symptoms, but could potentially pass the condition on to offspring. Such people are called **carriers**.

Conditions such as cystic fibrosis are mostly caused by **faulty alleles** that are **recessive**.

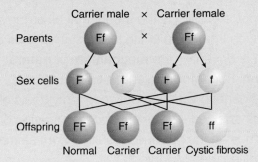

Knowing that there is a 1 in 4 chance that their child might have cystic fibrosis gives parents the opportunity to make decisions about whether to take the risk and have a child. This is a very difficult decision to make.

Technology has advanced and it is now possible to screen embryos for genetic disorders.

➤ If an embryo has a life-threatening condition it could be destroyed, or simply not be implanted if IVF was being applied.

➤ Alternatively, new gene therapy techniques might be able to reverse the effects of the condition, resulting in a healthy baby.

As yet, these possibilities have to gain approval from ethics committees – some people think that this type of 'interference with nature' could have harmful consequences.

1. If a homozygous brown-eyed individual is crossed with a homozygous blue-eyed individual, what is the probability of them producing a blue-eyed child?
2. What is the genotype of a human female?
3. How does the combination of two faulty, cystic fibrosis genes affect the phenotype of the person who possesses them?

Variation and evolution

Keywords

Anatomy ➤ The study of structures within the bodies of organisms

Vertebrate ➤ Animal with a backbone

Compress ➤ Squash or squeeze. In geology, this is usually due to Earth movements or laying down sediments

Extinction ➤ When there are no more members of a species left living

Variation

The two major factors that contribute to the appearance and function of an organism are:

➤ **genetic information** passed on from parents to offspring

➤ **environment** – the conditions that affect that organism during its lifetime, e.g. climate, diet, etc.

These two factors account for the large variation we see **within** and **between** species. In most cases, both of these factors play a part.

Evolution

Put simply, evolution is the theory that all organisms have arisen from simpler life forms over billions of years. It is driven by the **mechanism** of **natural selection**. For natural selection to occur, there must be genetic variation between individuals of the same species. This is caused by mutation or new combinations of genes resulting from sexual reproduction (see Module 27).

Most mutations have no effect on the phenotype of an organism. Where they do, and if the environment is changing, this can lead to relatively rapid change.

Evidence for evolution

Evidence for evolution comes from many sources. It includes:

➤ comparing genomes of different organisms

➤ studying embryos and their similarities

➤ looking at changes in species during modern times, e.g. antibiotic resistance in bacteria

➤ comparing the **anatomy** of different forms

➤ the fossil record.

One of the earliest sources of evidence for evolution was the discovery of fossils.

Further evidence for evolution – the pentadactyl limb

If you compare the forelimbs of a variety of **vertebrates**, you can see that the bone structures are all variations on a five-digit form, whether it be a leg, a wing or a flipper. This suggests that there was a common ancestral form from which these organisms developed.

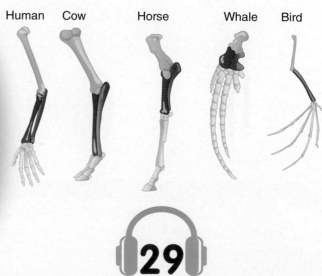

Human   Cow   Horse   Whale   Bird

29

How fossils are formed

1. When an animal or plant dies, the processes of decay usually cause all the body tissues to break down. In rare circumstances, the organism's body is rapidly **covered** and oxygen is prevented from reaching it. Instead of decay, fossilisation occurs.

2. Over hundreds of thousands of years, further sediments are laid down and **compress** the organism's remains.
3. Parts of the organism, such as bones and teeth, are **replaced by minerals** from solutions in the rock.

4. Earth upheavals, e.g. **tectonic plate movement**, bring sediments containing the fossils nearer the Earth's surface.

5. Erosion of the rock by wind, rain and rivers exposes the fossil. At this stage, the remains might be found and excavated by **paleontologists**.

Fossils can also be formed from footprints, burrows and traces of tree roots.

By comparing different fossils and where they are found in the rock layers, paleontologists can gain insights into how one form may have developed into another.

Difficulties occur with earlier life forms because many were **soft-bodied** and therefore not as well-preserved as organisms with bones or shells. Any that *are* formed are easily destroyed by Earth movements. As a result of this, scientists cannot be certain about exactly how life began.

Extinction

The fossil record provides evidence that most organisms that once existed have become **extinct**. In fact, there have been at least five **mass extinctions** in geological history where most organisms died out. One of these coincides with the disappearance of dinosaurs.

Causes of extinction include:
➤ **catastrophic events**, e.g. volcanic eruptions, asteroid collisions
➤ changes to the environment over geological time
➤ new **predators**
➤ new **diseases**
➤ new, more successful **competitors**.

Use different coloured pieces of card to depict one of the ideas covered in this module. Keep the design simple. For example, you could:
➤ show different forms of the pentadactyl limb and how they have evolved from a common ancestor
➤ produce five scenes showing the different stages of fossilisation.

When you have completed your design, explain the process/idea to a revision buddy.

1. State two pieces of evidence that support the theory of evolution through natural selection.
2. Why are fossils so rare?

Darwin and evolution

30

Keywords

Fittest ➤ The most adapted individual or species

Competition ➤ When two individuals or populations seek to exploit a resource, e.g. food. One individual/population will eventually replace the other

Human evolution

Modern man has evolved from a common ancestor that gave rise to all the primates: gorillas, chimpanzees and orangutans. DNA comparisons have shown we are most closely related to the chimpanzee.

The evolution of man can be traced back over the last four to five million years. Over this period of time, the **human form** (hominid) has developed:

➤ a more upright, bipedal stance
➤ less body hair
➤ a smaller and less 'domed' forehead
➤ greater intelligence and use of tools, initially from stone. These tools can be dated using scientific techniques, e.g. radiometric dating and carbon dating.

There have been significant finds of fossils that give clues to human evolution.

1. **Ardi** – at 4.4 million years old, this is the oldest, most complete hominid skeleton.
2. **Lucy** – from 3.2 million years ago, this is one of the first fossils to show an upright walking stance.
3. **Proconsul skull** – discovered by **Mary Leakey** and her husband; the hominid is thought to be from about 1.6 million years ago.

Darwin's theory of evolution through natural selection

Charles Darwin

Within a population of organisms there is a range of variation among individuals. This is caused by genes. Some differences will be beneficial; some will not.

Beneficial characteristics make an organism more likely to survive and pass on their genes to the next generation. This is especially true if the environment is changing. This ability to be successful is called **survival of the fittest**.

Species that are not well adapted to their environment may become extinct. This process of change is summed up in the theory of evolution through **natural selection**, put forward by **Charles Darwin** in the nineteenth century.

Many theories have tried to explain how life might have come about in its present form.

However, Darwin's theory is accepted by most scientists today. This is because it explains a wide range of observations and has been discussed and tested by many scientists.

Darwin's theory can be reduced to five ideas. They are:

➤ variation
➤ survival of the fittest
➤ competition
➤ inheritance
➤ extinction.

This activity should help you memorise Darwin's theory and learn how to apply the features using different scenarios.

➤ Arrange pieces of coloured paper into sets of five. About three lots will do – so fifteen altogether.
➤ On each set, write out the headings for the theory of evolution through natural selection: variation, competition, survival of the fittest, inheritance and extinction.
➤ Now research three case studies relating to natural selection, e.g. warfarin resistance in rats or the shape of shells in Galapagos tortoises. As you read, write down information on each of the five cards.

Darwin's ideas are illustrated in the following two examples.

Example 1: peppered moths

Variation – most peppered moths are pale and speckled. They are easily camouflaged amongst the lichens on silver birch tree bark. There are some rare, dark-coloured varieties (that originally arose from genetic mutation). They are easily seen and eaten by birds.

Competition – in areas with high levels of air pollution, lichens die and the bark becomes discoloured by soot. The lighter peppered moths are now put at a competitive disadvantage.

Survival of the fittest – the dark (melanic) moths are now more likely to avoid detection by predators.

Inheritance – the genes for dark colour are passed on to offspring and gradually become more common in the general population.

Extinction – if the environment remains polluted, the lighter form is more likely to become extinct.

Dark peppered moth

Peppered moth

Example 2: methicillin-resistant bacteria

The resistance of some bacteria to antibiotics is an increasing problem. MRSA bacteria have become more common in hospital wards and are difficult to eradicate.

Variation – bacteria mutate by chance, giving them a resistance to antibiotics.

Competition – the non-resistant bacteria are more likely to be killed by the antibiotic and become less competitive.

Survival of the fittest – the antibiotic-resistant bacteria survive and reproduce more often.

Inheritance – resistant bacteria pass on their genes to a new generation; the gene becomes more common in the general population.

Extinction – non-resistant bacteria are replaced by the newer, resistant strain.

To slow down the rate at which new, resistant strains of bacteria can develop:

➤ doctors are urged not to prescribe antibiotics for obvious viral infections or for mild bacterial infections

➤ patients should complete the full course of antibiotics to ensure that **all** bacteria are destroyed (so that none will survive to mutate into resistant strains).

Species become more and more specialised as they evolve and adapt to their environmental conditions.

The point at which a new species is formed occurs when the original population can no longer interbreed with the newer, 'mutant' population. For this to occur, **isolation** needs to happen.

Speciation

➤ Groups of the same species that are separated from each other by physical boundaries (like mountains or seas) will not be able to breed and share their genes. This is called **geographical isolation**.

➤ Over long periods of time, separate groups may specialise so much that they cannot successfully breed any longer and so two new species are formed – this is **reproductive isolation**.

1. Define evolution and natural selection.
2. State two examples where natural selection has been observed by scientists in recent times.
3. What has to happen to the beneficial genes for a helpful phenotype to spread through a population?

Selective breeding and genetic engineering

Keywords

Herbicide ➤ A chemical applied to crops to kill weeds

HT Vector ➤ Organism, cell or molecule that can be used to transfer DNA from one organism to another

HT Plasmid ➤ A ring of DNA found in bacteria

Selective breeding

Farmers and dog breeders have used the principles of selective breeding for thousands of years by keeping the best animals and plants for breeding.

For example, to breed Dalmatian dogs, the spottiest dogs have been bred through the generations to eventually get Dalmatians. The factor most affected by selective breeding in dogs is probably temperament. Most breeds are either naturally obedient to humans or are trained to be so.

This is the process of selective breeding.

| Select the desired characteristics in parents. | ➤ | Allow the individuals to breed (or cross-pollinate if you are dealing with plants). | ➤ | Select the desired offspring and allow them to become parents of the next generation. |

This process has to be repeated many times to get the desired results.

Advantages of selective breeding
➤ It results in an organism with the 'right' characteristics for a particular function.
➤ In farming and horticulture, it is a more efficient and economically viable process than natural selection.

Disadvantages of selective breeding
➤ Intensive selective breeding reduces the gene pool – the range of alleles in the population decreases so there is **less variation**.
➤ Lower variation reduces a species' ability to respond to environmental change.
➤ It can lead to an accumulation of harmful recessive characteristics (in-breeding), e.g. restriction of respiratory pathways and dislocatable joints in bulldogs.

Examples of selective breeding
Modern food plants

Three of our modern vegetables have come from a single ancestor by selective breeding. (Remember, it can take many, many generations to get the desired results.)

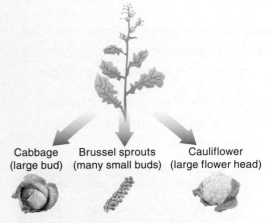

| Cabbage (large bud) | Brussel sprouts (many small buds) | Cauliflower (large flower head) |

Selective breeding in plants has also been undertaken to produce:
➤ disease resistance in crops
➤ large, unusual flowers in garden plants.

Modern cattle

Selective breeding can contribute to improved yields in cattle. Here are some examples.
➤ **Quantity of milk** – years of selecting and breeding cattle that produce larger than average quantities of milk has produced herds of cows that produce high daily volumes of milk.
➤ **Quality of milk** – as a result of selective breeding, Jersey cows produce milk that is rich and creamy, and can therefore be sold at a higher price.
➤ **Beef production** – the characteristics of the Hereford and Angus varieties have been selected for beef production over the past 200 years or more. They include hardiness, early maturity, high numbers of offspring and the swift, efficient conversion of grass into body mass (meat).

Genetic engineering

All living organisms use the same basic genetic code (DNA). So genes can be transferred from one organism to another in order to deliberately change the recipient's characteristics. This process is called genetic engineering or genetic modification (GM).

Altering the genetic make-up of an organism can be done for many reasons.

➤ **To improve resistance to** herbicides: for example, soya plants are genetically modified by inserting a gene that makes them resistant to a herbicide. When the crop fields are sprayed with the herbicide only the weeds die, leaving the soya plants without competition so they can grow better. Resistance to frost or disease can also be genetically engineered. Bigger yields result.

➤ **To improve the quality of food**: for example, bigger and more tasty fruit.

➤ **To produce a substance you require**: for example, the gene for human insulin can be inserted into bacteria or fungi, to make human insulin on a large scale to treat diabetes.

➤ **Disease resistance**: crop plants receive genes that give them resistance to the bacterium *Bacillus thuringiensis*.

Advantages of genetic engineering
➤ It allows organisms with new features to be produced rapidly.
➤ It can be used to make biochemical processes cheaper and more efficient.
➤ In the future, it may be possible to use genetic engineering to change a person's genes and cure certain disorders, e.g. cystic fibrosis. This is an area of research called gene therapy.

Disadvantages of genetic engineering
➤ Transplanted genes may have unexpected harmful effects on human health.
➤ Some people are worried that GM plants may cross-breed with wild plants and release their new genes into the environment.

HT Producing insulin

The following method is used to produce insulin.

1. The human gene for insulin production is identified and removed using a **restriction enzyme**, which cuts through the DNA strands in precise places.
2. The same restriction enzyme is used to cut open a ring of bacterial **vector** DNA (a **plasmid**).
3. Other enzymes called **ligases** are then used to insert the section of human DNA into the plasmid. The DNA can be 'spliced' in this way because the ends of the strands are 'sticky'.
4. The plasmid is reinserted into a bacterium, which starts to divide rapidly. As it divides, it replicates the plasmid.
5. The bacteria are cultivated on a large scale in fermenters. Each bacterium carries the instructions to make insulin. When the bacteria make the protein, commercial quantities of insulin are produced.

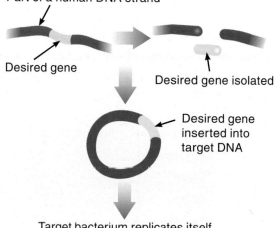

Part of a human DNA strand

Desired gene

Desired gene isolated

Desired gene inserted into target DNA

Target bacterium replicates itself

Bacterium

Sometimes, other vectors are used to introduce human DNA into organisms, e.g. viruses. It is important that the hybrid genes are transferred to the host organism at an early stage of its development, e.g. the egg or the embryo stage. As the cells are quite undifferentiated, the desired characteristics from the inserted DNA are more likely to develop.

Design a poster describing the stages of selective breeding.

1. What advantages does genetic engineering have over selective breeding?
2. Should we be expanding the range of GM foods we eat? Give one reason **for** this proposal and one reason **against**.

There is a huge variety of living organisms. Scientists group or classify them using shared characteristics. This is important because it helps to:

➤ work out how organisms evolved on Earth
➤ understand how organisms coexist in ecological communities
➤ identify and monitor rare organisms that are at risk from extinction.

Classification

Carl Linnaeus

The origins of classification

In the past, observable characteristics were used to place organisms into categories.

In the eighteenth century, **Carl Linnaeus** produced the first classification system. He developed a hierarchical arrangement where larger groups were subdivided into smaller ones.

Kingdom	Largest group
Phylum	
Class	
Order	
Family	
Genus	
Species	Smallest group

Linnaeus also developed a **binomial system** for naming organisms according to their genus and species. For example, the common domestic cat is *Felis catus*. Its full classification would be:

➤ Kingdom: *Animalia*
➤ Phylum: *Chordata*
➤ Class: *Mammalia*
➤ Order: *Carnivora*
➤ Family: *Felidae*
➤ Genus: *Felis*
➤ Species: *Catus*.

Linnaeus' system was built on and resulted in a **five-kingdom system**. Developments that contributed to the introduction of this system included improvements in microscopes and a more thorough understanding of the biochemical processes that occur in all living things. For example, the presence of particular chemical pathways in a range of organisms indicated that they probably had a **common ancestor** and so were more closely related than organisms that didn't share these pathways.

Kingdom	Features	Examples
Plants	Cellulose cell wall Use light energy to produce food	Flowering plants Trees Ferns Mosses
Animals	Multicellular Feed on other organisms	Vertebrates Invertebrates
Fungi	Cell wall of chitin Produce spores	Toadstools Mushrooms Yeasts Moulds
Protoctista Protozoa	Mostly single-celled organisms	Amoeba Paramecium
Prokaryotes	No nucleus	Bacteria Blue–green algae

The classification diagram below illustrates how different lines of evidence can be used. The classes of vertebrates share a common ancestor and so are quite closely related. Evidence for this lies in comparative anatomy (e.g. the pentadactyl limb) and similarities in biochemical pathways.

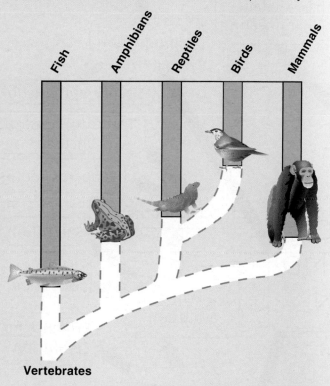

Fish Amphibians Reptiles Birds Mammals

Vertebrates

In more recent times, improvements in science have led to a **three-domain system** developed by **Carl Woese**. In this system organisms are split into:

➤ **archaea** (primitive bacteria)
➤ **bacteria** (true bacteria)
➤ **eukaryota** (including Protista, fungi, plants and animals).

Further improvements in science include chemical analysis and further refinements in comparisons between non-coding sections of DNA.

Evolutionary trees

Tree diagrams are useful for depicting relationships between similar groups of organisms and determining how they may have developed from common ancestors. Fossil evidence can be invaluable in establishing these relationships.

Here, two species are shown to have evolved from a common ancestor.

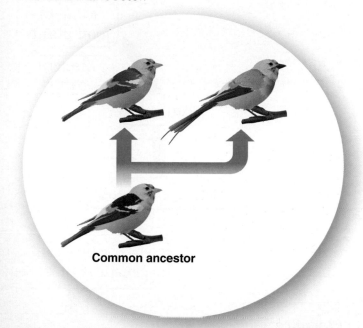

Common ancestor

WS You need to understand how new evidence and data leads to changes in models and theories.

In the case of the three-domain system, a more accurate and cohesive classification structure was proposed as a result of improvements in microscopy and increasing knowledge of organisms' internal structures.

These apes share a common ancestor

1. What do the first and second words in the binomial name of an organism mean?
2. Name four groups of organisms found in the domain *Eukaryota*.
3. It is thought that chimpanzees and humans evolved from a now extinct ape. What term describes this animal?

 **32**

Mind map

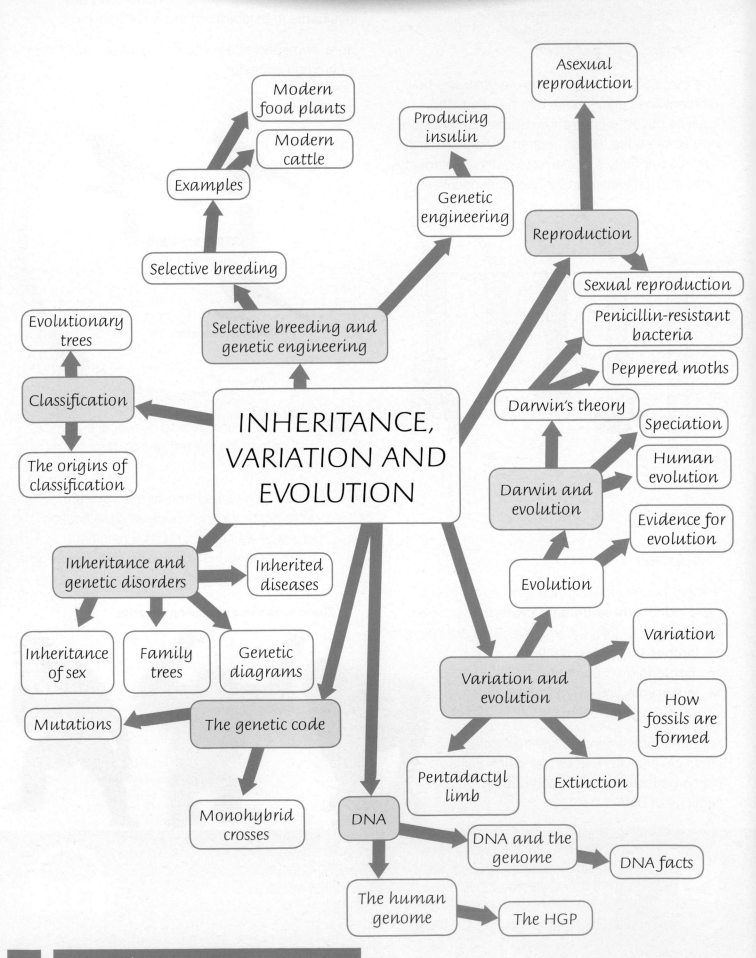

Modern
food plants

Modern
cattle

Examples

Producing
insulin

Asexual
reproduction

Selective breeding

Genetic
engineering

Reproduction

Evolutionary
trees

Selective breeding and
genetic engineering

Sexual reproduction

Classification

Penicillin-resistant
bacteria

Peppered moths

The origins of
classification

INHERITANCE,
VARIATION AND
EVOLUTION

Darwin's theory

Speciation

Human
evolution

Darwin and
evolution

Evidence for
evolution

Inheritance and
genetic disorders

Inherited
diseases

Evolution

Inheritance
of sex

Family
trees

Genetic
diagrams

Variation

Mutations

The genetic code

Variation and
evolution

How
fossils are
formed

Monohybrid
crosses

Pentadactyl
limb

Extinction

DNA

DNA and the
genome

DNA facts

The human
genome

The HGP

Practice questions

1. Scientists believe that the whale may have evolved from a horse-like ancestor that lived in swampy regions millions of years ago. Suggest how whales could have evolved from a horse-like mammal. In your answer, use Darwin's theory of natural selection. **(4 marks)**

2. The diagram below shows the inheritance of cystic fibrosis in a family.

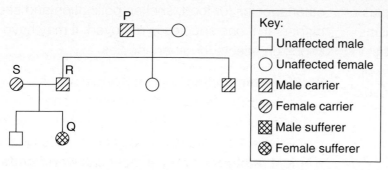

Key:
- ☐ Unaffected male
- ◯ Unaffected female
- ▨ Male carrier
- ◉ Female carrier
- ⊠ Male sufferer
- ⊛ Female sufferer

Cystic fibrosis is caused by a recessive allele, f. The dominant allele of the gene is represented by F.

   a) Give the alleles for person P. **(1 mark)**

   b) Give the alleles for person Q. **(1 mark)**

HT 3. The schematic below shows how insulin can be genetically engineered.

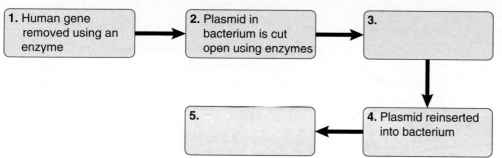

1. Human gene removed using an enzyme → 2. Plasmid in bacterium is cut open using enzymes → 3.

3. → 4. Plasmid reinserted into bacterium

5. ← 4. Plasmid reinserted into bacterium

   a) Write the missing steps **3** and **5**. **(2 marks)**

   b) Name the type of enzyme used in steps **1** and **2**. **(1 mark)**

4. The diagram shows a molecule of DNA.

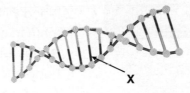

X

   a) Name the part labelled **X** in the DNA diagram. **(1 mark)**

   b) The 'backbone' of the molecule is arranged in such a way as to make it very stable. Name the term used to describe the shape of DNA. **(1 mark)**

Organisms and ecosystems

33

Keyword

Environmental resources ➤ Materials or factors that organisms need to survive, e.g. high oxygen concentration, living space or a particular food supply

Communities

Ecosystems are physical environments with a particular set of conditions (**abiotic** factors), plus all the organisms that live in them. The organisms interact through competition and predation. An ecosystem can support itself without any influx of other factors or materials. Its energy source (usually the Sun) is the only external factor.

Other terms help to describe aspects of the environment.

➤ The **habitat** of an animal or plant is the part of the physical environment where it lives. There are many types of habitat, each with particular characteristics, e.g. pond, hedgerow, coral reef.
➤ A **population** is the number of individuals of a species in a defined area.
➤ A **community** is the total number of individuals of all the different populations of organisms that live together in a habitat at any one time.

An organism must be well-suited to its habitat to be able to compete with other species for limited **environmental resources**. Even organisms within the same species may compete in order to survive and breed. Organisms that are specialised in this way are restricted to that type of habitat because their adaptations are unsuitable elsewhere.

Resources that plants compete over include:
➤ light
➤ space
➤ water
➤ minerals.

Animals compete over:
➤ food
➤ mates.
➤ territory.

Interdependence

In communities, each species may depend on other species for food, shelter, pollination and seed dispersal. If one species is removed, it may have knock-on effects for other species.

Stable communities contain species whose numbers fluctuate very little over time. The populations are in balance with the physical factors that exist in that habitat. Stable communities include **tropical rainforests** and ancient oak **woodlands**.

Adaptations

Adaptations:

➤ are special features or behaviours that make an organism particularly well-suited to its environment and better able to compete with other organisms for limited resources
➤ can be thought of as a biological solution to an environmental challenge – evolution provides the solution and makes species fit their environment.

Animals have developed in many different ways to become well adapted to their environment and to help them survive. Adaptations are usually of three types:

➤ **Structural** – for example, skin colouration in chameleons provides camouflage to hide them from predators.
➤ **Functional** – for example, some worms have blood with a high affinity for oxygen; this helps them to survive in anaerobic environments.
➤ **Behavioural** – for example, penguins huddle together to conserve body heat in the Antarctic habitat.

Look at the **polar bear** and its life in a very cold climate. It has:

➤ small ears and large bulk to reduce its surface area to volume ratio and so reduce heat loss
➤ a large amount of insulating fat (blubber)
➤ thick white fur for insulation and camouflage
➤ large feet to spread its weight on snow and ice
➤ fur on the soles of its paws for insulation and grip
➤ powerful legs so it is a good swimmer and runner, which enables it to catch its food
➤ sharp claws and teeth to capture prey.

The **cactus** is well adapted to living in a desert habitat. It:

➤ has a rounded shape, which gives a small surface area to volume ratio and therefore reduces water loss
➤ has a thick waxy cuticle to reduce water loss
➤ stores water in a spongy layer inside its stem to resist drought
➤ has sunken stomata, meaning that air movement is reduced, minimising loss of water vapour through them
➤ has leaves that take the form of spines to reduce water loss and to protect the cactus from predators.

Some organisms have biochemical adaptations. **Extremophiles** can survive extreme environmental conditions. For example:

➤ bacteria living in deep sea vents have optimum temperatures for enzymes that are much higher than 37°C
➤ icefish have antifreeze chemicals in their bodies, which lower the freezing point of body fluids
➤ some organisms can resist high salt concentrations or pressure.

WS During your course you will be asked to suggest explanations for observations made in the field or laboratory. These include:

➤ suggesting factors for which organisms are competing in a certain habitat
➤ giving possible adaptations for organisms in a habitat.

For example, low-lying plants in forest ecosystems often have specific adaptations for maximising light absorption as they are shaded by taller plants. Adaptations might include leaves with a large surface area and higher concentrations of photosynthetic pigments to absorb the correct wavelengths and lower intensities of light.

1. How is an ecosystem different from a habitat?
2. Which is the more stable community – a mixed-leaf woodland or a dry river bed in Africa? What is the reason for this?
3. How is a community different from a population?
4. Give two examples of extremophiles.
5. Why is it important for organisms to be well adapted?

Studying ecosystems

Testing soil pH

Taking measurements in ecosystems

Ecosystems involve the interaction between **non-living (abiotic)** and **living (biotic)** parts of the environment. So it is important to identify which factors need to be measured in a particular habitat.

Abiotic factors include:
➤ light intensity
➤ temperature
➤ moisture levels
➤ soil pH and mineral content
➤ wind intensity and direction
➤ carbon dioxide levels for plants
➤ oxygen levels for aquatic animals.

Biotic factors include:
➤ availability of food
➤ new predators arriving
➤ new pathogens
➤ one species out-competing another.

Measuring biotic factors – sampling methods

It is usually impossible to count all the species living in a particular area, so a **sample** is taken.

When sampling, make sure you:
➤ **take a big enough sample** to make the estimate good and reliable – the larger the sample, the more accurate the results.
➤ **sample randomly** – the more random the sample, the more likely it is to be representative of the population.

Quadrats

Quadrats are square frames that typically have sides of length 0.5 m. They provide excellent results as long as they are placed randomly. The population of a certain species can then be estimated.

For example, if an average of 4 dandelion plants are found in a 0.25 m² quadrat, a scientist would estimate that 16 dandelion plants would be found in each 1 m² and 16 000 dandelion plants in a 1000 m² field.

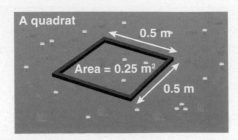

A quadrat
0.5 m
Area = 0.25 m²
0.5 m

Transects

Sometimes an environmental scientist may want to look at how species change across a habitat, or the boundary between two different habitats – for example, the plants found in a field as you move away from a hedgerow.

This needs a different approach that is systematic rather than random.

1 Lay down a line such as a tape measure. Mark regular intervals on it.

2 Next to the line, lay down a small quadrat. Estimate or count the number of plants of the different species. This can sometimes be done by estimating the percentage cover.

3 Move the quadrat along at regular intervals. Estimate and record the plant populations at each point until the end of the line.

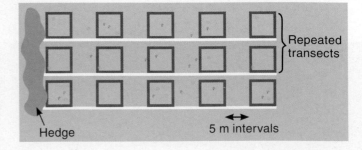

Repeated transects

Hedge

5 m intervals

Sampling methods

Sampling animal populations is more problematic as they are mobile and well adapted to evade capture. Here are three of the main techniques used.

Pooters	
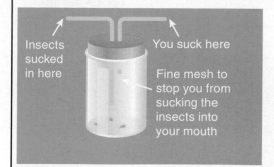	This is a simple technique in which insects are gathered up easily without harm. With this method, you get to find out which species are actually present, although you have to be systematic about your sampling in order to get representative results and it is difficult to get ideas of numbers.
Sweepnets	
	Sweepnets are used in long grass or moderately dense woodland where there are lots of shrubs. Again, it is difficult to get truly representative samples, particularly in terms of the relative numbers of organisms.
Pitfall traps	
	Pitfall traps are set into the ground and used to catch small insects, e.g. beetles. Sometimes a mixture of ethanol or detergent and water is placed in the bottom of the trap to kill the samples, and prevent them from escaping. This method can give an indication of the relative numbers of organisms in a given area if enough traps are used to give a representative sample.

Design a poster showing the different sampling methods.

1. In what situation would you use a transect? What information would it give you?

Feeding relationships

Predator–prey relationships

Animals that kill and eat other animals are called **predators** (e.g. foxes, lynx). The animals that are eaten are called **prey** (e.g. rabbits, snowshoe hares).

Many animals can be both predator and prey. For instance, a stoat is a predator when it hunts rabbits and it is the prey when it is hunted by a fox.

Predator – stoat

Predator – fox

Prey – rabbit

Prey – stoat

In nature there is a delicate balance between the population of a predator (e.g. lynx) and its prey (e.g. snowshoe hare). However, the prey will always outnumber the predators.

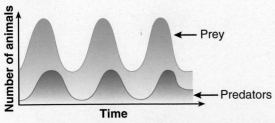

The number of predators and prey follow a classic population cycle. There will always be more hares than lynx and the population peak for the lynx will always come after the population peak for the hare. As the population cycle is cause and effect, they will always be out of phase.

Normal prey population (they outnumber predators)

Predator population increases as plenty of food is available

Decrease in prey population as more are being eaten by increased number of predators

Decrease in predator population as there is now not enough food

Trophic levels

Communities of organisms are organised in an ecosystem according to their feeding habits.

Food chains show:
➤ the organisms that consume other organisms
➤ the transfer of **energy** and **materials** from organism to organism.

Energy from the Sun enters most food chains when green plants absorb sunlight to **photosynthesise**. Photosynthetic and chemosynthetic organisms are the producers of **biomass** for the Earth. Feeding passes this energy and biomass from one organism to the next along the food chain.

A food chain

Green plant:
producer

Rabbit:
primary consumer

Stoat:
secondary consumer

Fox:
tertiary consumer

The arrow shows the flow of energy and biomass along the food chain.
➤ All food chains start with a **producer**.
➤ The rabbit is a herbivore (plant eater), also known as the **primary consumer**.
➤ The stoat is a carnivore (meat eater), also known as the **secondary consumer**.
➤ The fox is the top carnivore in this food chain, the **tertiary consumer**.

Each consumer or producer occupies a **trophic level** (feeding level).
➤ Level 1 are producers.
➤ Level 2 are primary consumers.
➤ Level 3 are secondary consumers.
➤ Level 4 are tertiary consumers.

Excretory products and uneaten parts of organisms can be the starting points for other food chains, especially those involving **decomposers**.

Decomposers

Keyword

Decomposers ➤ Microorganisms that break down dead plant and animal material by secreting enzymes into the environment. Small, soluble molecules can then be absorbed back into the microorganism by the process of diffusion

To demonstrate predator/prey cycles, do the following.
➤ Cut out multiple pictures of the animals in a particular predator–prey relationship (e.g. foxes and rabbits).
➤ Show these animals grouped together – try 5 foxes and 15 rabbits.
Add 3 foxes. How will this affect the number of rabbits?
➤ Explain this to a revision buddy.
Now show the changes in number of both rabbits and foxes as time goes by. Ask your buddy to rate your explanation.
➤ Swap roles.

1. What is meant by a trophic level?
2. Explain how a population of foxes might rise and fall with a population of rabbits.

Environmental change & biodiversity

Environmental change

Waste management

The human population is increasing exponentially (i.e. at a rapidly increasing rate). This is because birth rates exceed death rates by a large margin.

So the use of finite resources like fossil fuels and minerals is accelerating. In addition, waste production is going up:

➤ **on land**, from domestic waste in landfill, toxic chemical waste, **pesticides** and **herbicides**
➤ **in water**, from sewage fertiliser and toxic chemicals
➤ **in the air**, from smoke, carbon dioxide and sulfur dioxide.

Acid rain

When coal or oils are burned, sulfur dioxide is produced. Sulfur dioxide and nitrogen dioxide dissolve in water to produce acid rain.

Acid rain can:

➤ damage trees, stonework and metals
➤ make rivers and lakes acidic, which means some organisms can no longer survive.

The acids can be carried a long way away from the factories where they are produced. Acid rain falling in one country could be the result of fossil fuels being burned in another country.

The greenhouse effect and global warming

The diagram explains how global warming can lead to climate change. This in turn leads to lower biodiversity.

Small amount of infrared radiation transmitted to space

CO_2 and CH_4 in the atmosphere absorb some of the energy and radiate it back to Earth

Rays from the Sun reach Earth and are reflected back towards the atmosphere

The consequences of global warming are:

➤ a rise in sea levels leading to flooding in low-lying areas and loss of habitat
➤ the migration of species and changes in their distribution due to more extreme temperature and rainfall patterns; some organisms won't survive being displaced into new habitats, or newly migrated species may outcompete native species. The overall effect is a loss of biodiversity.

 You may be asked to evaluate methods used to address problems caused by human impact on the environment.

For example, here are some figures relating to quotas and numbers of haddock in the North Sea in two successive years.

	2009	2010
Haddock quota (tonnes)	27 507	23 381
Estimated population (thousands)	102	101

What conclusions could you draw from this data? What additional information would you need to give a more accurate picture?

Create a board game called 'Conservation' that has 100 squares. The object of the game is to improve the quality and quantity of the world's ecosystems. The winner is the first person to reach square 100.

Here is an idea for a **bonus** square.
➤ Establish a breeding programme for endangered snow-leopards. (Throw the dice again.)

Here is an idea for a penalty square.
➤ Deforestation of Brazilian rainforest lowers biodiversity. (Go back three spaces.)

Try to grade bonuses and penalties according to their impact.

Keywords

Pesticide ➤ Chemical sprayed on crops to kill invertebrate pests

Herbicide ➤ Chemical sprayed on crops to kill weeds

Carbon sinks ➤ Resources that lock up carbon in their structure rather than allowing them to form carbon dioxide, e.g. peat bogs, oceans, limestone deposits

Endangered ➤ Category of risk attached to rare species of plants and animals. This usually triggers efforts to preserve the species' numbers

Emissions ➤ Gaseous products usually connected with pollution, e.g. carbon dioxide emissions from exhausts

Regeneration ➤ Rebuilding or regrowth of a habitat, e.g. flooding peatland to encourage regrowth of mosses and other plants

Biodiversity

Biodiversity is a measure of the number and variety of species within an ecosystem. A healthy ecosystem:

➤ has a large biodiversity
➤ has a large degree of interdependence between species
➤ is stable.

Species depend on each other for food, shelter and keeping the external physical environment maintained. Humans have had a negative impact on biodiversity due to:

➤ pollution killing plants and animals
➤ degrading the environment through deforestation and removing resources such as minerals and fossil fuels
➤ over-exploiting habitats and organisms.

Only recently have humans made efforts to reduce their impact on the environment. It is recognised that maintaining biodiversity is important to ensure the continued survival of the human race.

Impact of land use

As humans increase their economic activity, they use land that would otherwise be inhabited by living organisms. Examples of habitat destruction include:

A marble quarry

➤ farming
➤ quarrying
➤ dumping waste in landfill.

Peat bogs

Peat bogs are important habitats. They support a wide variety of organisms and act as **carbon sinks**.

If peat is burned it releases carbon dioxide into the atmosphere and contributes to global warming. Removing peat for use as compost in gardens takes away the habitat for specialised animals and plants that aren't found in other habitats.

Peat cut and left to dry

Deforestation

Deforestation is a particular problem in tropical regions. Tropical rainforests are removed to:

➤ **release land for cattle and rice fields** – these are needed to feed the world's growing population and for increasingly Western-style diets
➤ **grow crops for biofuel** – the crops are converted to **ethanol-based** fuels for use in petrol and diesel engines. Some specialised engines can run off pure ethanol.

The consequences of deforestation are:

➤ There are fewer plants, particularly trees, to absorb carbon dioxide. This leads to increased carbon dioxide in the atmosphere and accelerated global warming.
➤ Combustion and decay of the wood from deforestation releases more carbon dioxide into the atmosphere.
➤ There is reduced biodiversity as animals lose their habitats and food sources.

Maintaining biodiversity

To prevent further losses in biodiversity and to improve the balance of ecosystems, scientists, the government and environmental organisations can take action.

➤ Scientists establish **breeding programmes** for **endangered species**. These may be captive methods where animals are enclosed, or protection schemes that allow rare species to breed without being poached or killed illegally.
➤ The government sets **limits** on **deforestation** and **greenhouse gas emissions**.

Environmental organisations:

➤ **protect and regenerate** shrinking habitats such as mangrove swamps, heathlands and coral reefs
➤ **conserve and replant** hedgerows around the margins of fields used for crop growth
➤ introduce and encourage **recycling** initiatives that reduce the volume of landfill.

1. Name one pollutant gas that contributes to acid rain.
2. The human population is increasing exponentially – what does this term mean?
3. Why is high biodiversity seen as a good thing?
4. What steps could you take to maintain the biodiversity of a British mixed woodland?

36

Recycling

Materials within ecosystems are constantly being recycled and used to provide the substances that make up future organisms. Two of these substances are water and carbon.

Keyword

Biosphere ➤ Area on the Earth's crust that is inhabited by living things

The water cycle

Water is a vital part of the **biosphere**. Most organisms consist of over 50% water.

The two key processes that drive the water cycle are **evaporation** and **condensation**.

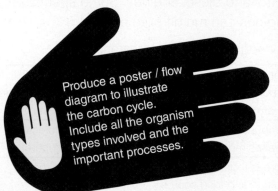

Produce a poster / flow diagram to illustrate the carbon cycle. Include all the organism types involved and the important processes.

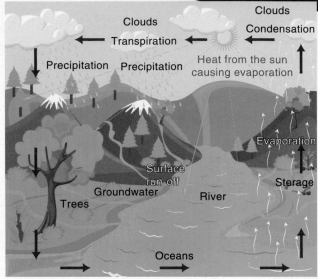

The carbon cycle

The constant recycling of carbon is called the carbon cycle.

➤ Carbon dioxide is removed from the atmosphere by green plants for photosynthesis.
➤ Plants and animals respire, releasing carbon dioxide into the atmosphere.
➤ Animals eat plants and other animals, which incorporates carbon into their bodies. In this way, carbon is passed along food chains and webs.
➤ Microorganisms such as fungi and bacteria feed on dead plants and animals, causing them to decay. The microorganisms respire and release carbon dioxide gas into the air. Mineral ions are returned to the soil through decay. This extraction and return of nutrients to the soil is called the decay cycle.
➤ Some organisms' bodies are turned into fossil fuels over millions of years, trapping the carbon as coal, peat, oil and gas.
➤ When fossil fuels are burned (combustion), the carbon dioxide is returned to the atmosphere.

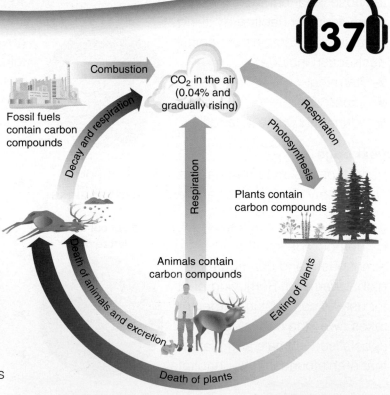

1. Which two processes drive the water cycle?
2. How can carbon be stored in rocks?
3. Name two processes that add carbon dioxide to the atmosphere.

Farming and sustainability

Keywords

Eutrophication ➤ A process where nitrates and phosphates enrich waterways, causing massive growth of algae and loss of oxygen

Sustainability ➤ Carrying out human activity, e.g. farming, fishing and extraction of resources from the ground, so that damage to the environment is minimised or removed

Eutrophication

Overusing fertilisers in intensive farming can lead to **eutrophication**.

1 Fertilisers or sewage can run into the water and pollute it. As a result, there are a lot of nitrates and phosphates, which leads to rapid growth of algae.

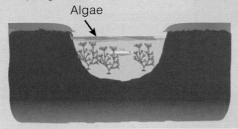

Algae

2 The algal blooms reproduce quickly, then die and rot. They also block off sunlight, which causes underwater plants to die and rot.

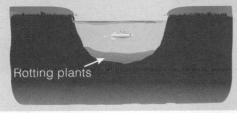

Rotting plants

3 The number of aerobic bacteria increase. As they feed on the dead organisms they use up oxygen. This causes larger organisms and plants to die because they are unable to respire.

Sustainable fishing

Fish stocks are declining across the globe. The problem is so big that unless methods are used to halt the decline, some species (such as the northwest Atlantic cod) might disappear.

Methods to make fishing **sustainable** include:
➤ governments imposing **quotas** that limit the weight of fish that can be taken from the oceans on a yearly basis – this practice is not always followed and illegal fishing is difficult to combat
➤ increasing the mesh size of nets to allow smaller fish to escape and reach adulthood, so that they can breed.

Carry out a role-play exercise that mimics a debate between two opposing groups, such as conservationists versus the fishing industry.
➤ Ideally, this activity works best with at least four people (two people representing each group).
➤ Draw up the points you want to make. Include the science you have learned in this topic.
➤ Allow each side to make their case. Then ask an independent 'judge' to make a ruling.
➤ Evaluate the exercise – ask the judge what factors led them to make their decision.

38

1. Explain why the activity of bacteria during eutrophication causes the death of other aquatic animals.
2. State two measures that can help to increase fish stocks.

Mind map

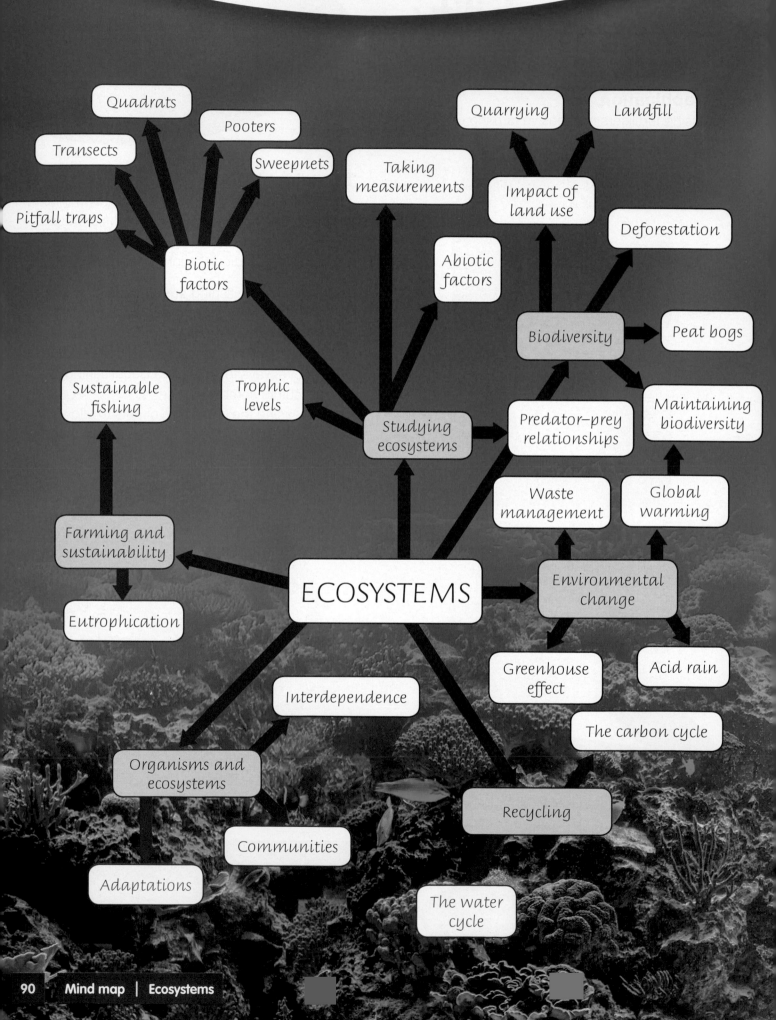

Quadrats

Pooters

Transects

Sweepnets

Pitfall traps

Biotic factors

Taking measurements

Quarrying

Landfill

Impact of land use

Abiotic factors

Deforestation

Biodiversity

Peat bogs

Sustainable fishing

Trophic levels

Studying ecosystems

Predator–prey relationships

Maintaining biodiversity

Waste management

Global warming

Farming and sustainability

ECOSYSTEMS

Environmental change

Eutrophication

Greenhouse effect

Acid rain

Interdependence

The carbon cycle

Organisms and ecosystems

Recycling

Communities

Adaptations

The water cycle

Practice questions

1. Carbon is recycled in the environment in a process called the **carbon cycle**. The main processes of the carbon cycle are shown on the right.

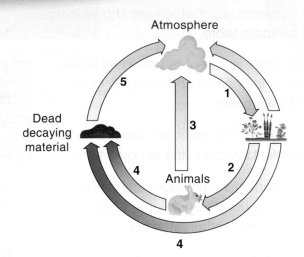

   a) Name the process that occurs at stage **3** in the diagram. **(1 mark)**

   b) The UK government is planning to use fewer fossil-fuel-burning power stations in the future. How might this affect the carbon cycle? Use ideas about **combustion** and **fossil fuel formation** in your answer. **(2 marks)**

2. An environmental scientist observed and measured a kingfisher and fish population in a county's rivers over 10 years. She recorded her results as a graph.

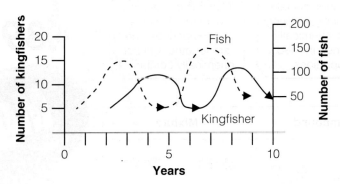

   a) How many fish were recorded in the third year? **(1 mark)**

   b) Describe how the size of the kingfisher population affected the size of the fish population. **(1 mark)**

   HT c) The scientist took her measurements by ringing and observing kingfishers on three rivers in the county. Fish numbers were estimated by counting the different species that anglers landed along the banks of the three rivers. Describe the limitations of these methods and suggest two ways in which the methods could be improved. **(6 marks)**

3. Choose the correct words to complete the following passage about adaptations. **(3 marks)**

environment	population	features	community
characteristics	survival	evolutionary	predatory	suited

   Adaptations are special .... or .... that make a

   living organism particularly well .... to its ....

   Adaptations are part of an .... process that increases a living organism's

   chance of ....

ⓦⓢ Scientific models of the atom

Scientists had originally thought that atoms were tiny spheres that could not be divided.

John Dalton conducted experiments in the early 19th century and concluded that…

➤ all matter is made of indestructible atoms
➤ atoms of a particular element are identical
➤ atoms are rearranged during chemical reactions
➤ compounds are formed when two or more different types of atom join together.

Upon discovery of the electron by **J. J. Thomson** in 1897, the 'plum pudding' model suggested that the atom was a ball of positive charge with negative electrons embedded throughout.

The results from **Rutherford**, **Geiger** and **Marsden's** alpha scattering experiments (1911–1913) led to the plum pudding model being replaced by the nuclear model.

In this experiment, alpha particles (which are positive) are fired at a thin piece of gold. A few of the alpha particles do not pass through the gold and are deflected. Most went straight through the thin piece of gold. This led Rutherford, Geiger and Marsden to suggest that this is because the positive charge of the atom is confined in a small volume (now called the nucleus).

Niels Bohr adapted the nuclear model in 1913, by suggesting that electrons orbit the nucleus at specific distances. Bohr's theoretical calculations were backed up by experimental results.

Later experiments led to the idea that the positive charge of the nucleus was subdivided into smaller particles (now called protons), with each particle having the same amount of positive charge.

The work of **James Chadwick** suggested in 1932 that the nucleus also contained neutral particles that we now call neutrons.

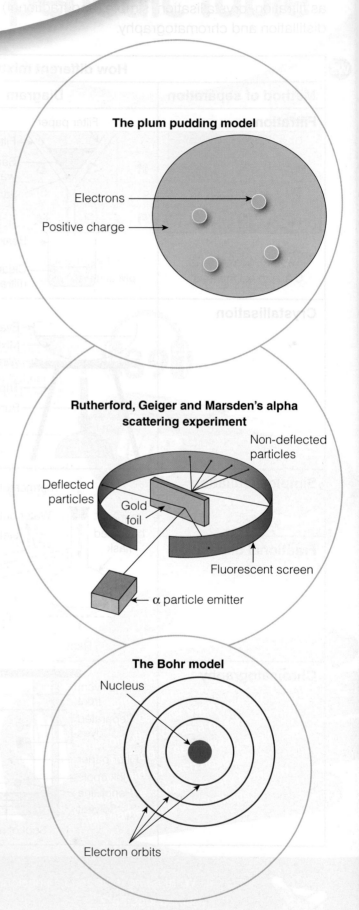

The plum pudding model

Electrons

Positive charge

Rutherford, Geiger and Marsden's alpha scattering experiment

Non-deflected particles

Deflected particles

Gold foil

Fluorescent screen

α particle emitter

The Bohr model

Nucleus

Electron orbits

Properties of atoms

Particle	Relative charge	Relative mass
Proton	+1	1
Neutron	0	1
Electron	−1	negligible

➤ Atoms are neutral. This is because the number of protons is equal to the number of electrons.

➤ Atoms of different elements have different numbers of protons. This number is called the atomic number.

➤ Atoms are very small, having a radius of approximately 0.1 nm (1×10^{-10} m).

➤ The radius of the nucleus is approximately $\frac{1}{10\,000}$ of the size of the atom.

> The **mass number** tells you the total number of protons and neutrons in an atom

$$^{23}_{11}Na$$

> The **atomic number** tells you the number of protons in an atom

mass number − atomic number = number of neutrons

Some atoms can have different numbers of neutrons. These atoms are called **isotopes**. The existence of isotopes results in the relative atomic mass of some elements, e.g. chlorine, not being whole numbers.

HT Chlorine exists as two isotopes. Chlorine-35 makes up 75% of all chlorine atoms. Chlorine-37 makes up the other 25%. We say that the abundance of chlorine-35 is 75%.

The relative atomic mass of chlorine can be calculated as follows:

$$\frac{(\text{mass of isotope 1} \times \text{abundance}) + (\text{mass of isotope 2} \times \text{abundance})}{100}$$

$$= \frac{(35 \times 75) + (37 \times 25)}{100} = 35.5$$

Make models of atoms using different coloured paper to represent the protons, neutrons and electrons.

1. What is the difference between the plum pudding model of the atom and the nuclear model of the atom?

2. Why did Rutherford, Geiger and Marsden's alpha scattering experiment lead them to suggest that the positive charge in an atom was contained within a small volume?

3. How many protons, neutrons and electrons are present in the following atom?

$$^{13}_{6}C$$

4. What name is given to atoms of the same element which have the same number of protons but different numbers of neutrons?

Electronic structure & the periodic table

Keywords

Energy level ➤ A region in an atom where electrons are found

Shell ➤ Another word for an energy level

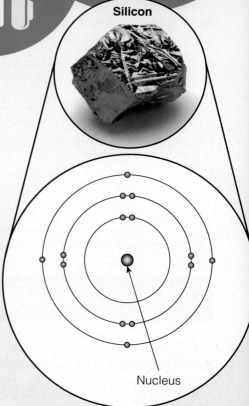

Silicon

Nucleus

Electronic structures

Electrons in an atom occupy the lowest available **energy level** (**shell**). The first energy level (closest to the nucleus) can hold up to two electrons. The second and third energy levels can hold up to eight electrons.

For example, silicon has the atomic number 14. This means that there are 14 protons in the nucleus of a silicon atom and therefore there must be 14 electrons (so that the atom is neutral).

The electronic structure of silicon can be written as 2, 8, 4 or shown in a diagram like the one on the right.

Silicon is in group 4 of the periodic table. This is because it has four electrons in its outer shell. The chemical properties (reactions) of an element are related to the number of electrons in the outer shell of the atom.

The electronic structure of the first 20 elements are shown here.

Group 8

Helium, He
Atomic No. = 2
No. of electrons = 2

2

Group 1	**Group 2**		**Group 3**	**Group 4**	**Group 5**	**Group 6**	**Group 7**

Hydrogen, H
Atomic No. = 1
No. of electrons = 1

1

Lithium, Li
Atomic No. = 3
No. of electrons = 3

2, 1

Beryllium, Be
Atomic No. = 4
No. of electrons = 4

2, 2

Boron, B
Atomic No. = 5
No. of electrons = 5

2, 3

Carbon, C
Atomic No. = 6
No. of electrons = 6

2, 4

Nitrogen, N
Atomic No. = 7
No. of electrons = 7

2, 5

Oxygen, O
Atomic No. = 8
No. of electrons = 8

2, 6

Fluorine, F
Atomic No. = 9
No. of electrons = 9

2, 7

Neon, Ne
Atomic No. = 10
No. of electrons = 10

2, 8

Sodium, Na
Atomic No. = 11
No. of electrons = 11

2, 8, 1

Magnesium, Mg
Atomic No. = 12
No. of electrons = 12

2, 8, 2

Aluminium, Al
Atomic No. = 13
No. of electrons = 13

2, 8, 3

Silicon, Si
Atomic No. = 14
No. of electrons = 14

2, 8, 4

Phosphorus, P
Atomic No. = 15
No. of electrons = 15

2, 8, 5

Sulfur, S
Atomic No. = 16
No. of electrons = 16

2, 8, 6

Chlorine, Cl
Atomic No. = 17
No. of electrons = 17

2, 8, 7

Argon, Ar
Atomic No. = 18
No. of electrons = 18

2, 8, 8

Potassium, K
Atomic No. = 19
No. of electrons = 19

2, 8, 8, 1

Calcium, Ca
Atomic No. = 20
No. of electrons = 20

2, 8, 8, 2

THE TRANSITION METALS

This table is arranged in order of atomic (proton) numbers, placing the elements in groups. Elements in the same group have the same number of electrons in their highest occupied energy level (outer shell).

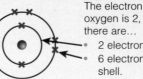

The electron configuration of oxygen is 2, 6 because there are...
• 2 electrons in the first shell
• 6 electrons in the second shell.

The periodic table

The elements in the periodic table are arranged in order of increasing atomic (proton) number. The table is called a **periodic table** because similar properties occur at regular intervals.

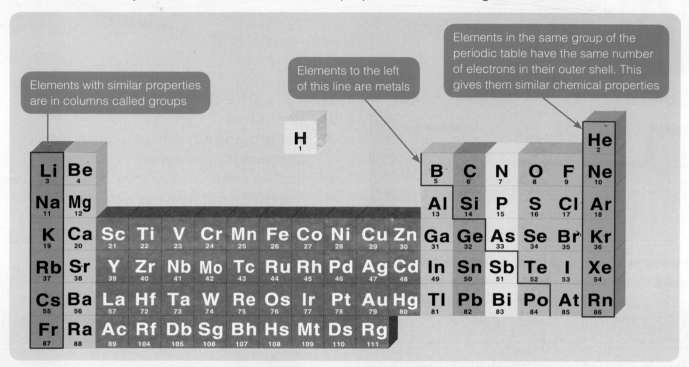

Elements with similar properties are in columns called groups

Elements to the left of this line are metals

Elements in the same group of the periodic table have the same number of electrons in their outer shell. This gives them similar chemical properties

Development of the periodic table

Before the discovery of protons, neutrons and electrons, early attempts to classify the elements involved placing them in order of their atomic weights. These early attempts resulted in incomplete tables and the placing of some elements in appropriate groups based on their chemical properties.

Dmitri Mendeleev overcame some of these problems by leaving gaps for elements that he predicted were yet to be discovered. He also changed the order for some elements based on atomic weights. Knowledge of isotopes made it possible to explain why the order based on atomic weights was not always correct.

Metals and non-metals

➤ Metals are elements that react to form positive ions.
➤ Elements that do not form positive ions are non-metals.

Typical properties of metals and non-metals	
Metals	**Non-metals**
Have high melting / boiling points	Have low melting / boiling points
Conduct heat and electricity	Thermal and electrical insulators
React with oxygen to form alkalis	React with oxygen to form acids
Shiny	Dull
Malleable and ductile	Brittle

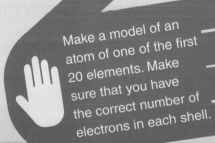

Make a model of an atom of one of the first 20 elements. Make sure that you have the correct number of electrons in each shell.

1. Sodium has the atomic number 11. What is the electronic structure of sodium?
2. Why did Mendeleev leave gaps in his periodic table?
3. Element X has a high melting point, is malleable and conducts electricity. Is X a metal or a non-metal?

Groups 0, 1 and 7

42

Group 0

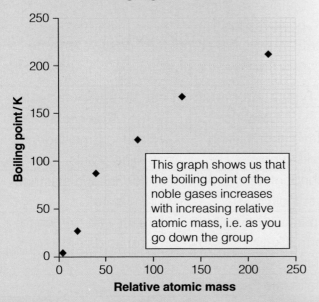

The elements in group 0 are called the **noble gases**. They are chemically inert (unreactive) and do not easily form molecules because their atoms have full outer shells (energy levels) of electrons. The inertness of the noble gases, combined with their low density and non-flammability, mean that they can be used in airships, balloons, light bulbs, lasers and advertising signs.

This graph shows us that the boiling point of the noble gases increases with increasing relative atomic mass, i.e. as you go down the group

Write each property of the alkali metals and the halogens on separate cards. Shuffle the cards. Now try to place them into the correct two piles: **alkali metals** and **halogens**.

Group 1 (the alkali metals)

The alkali metals…

➤ have a low density (lithium, sodium and potassium float on water)
➤ react with non-metals to form ionic compounds in which the metal ion has a charge of +1
➤ form compounds that are white solids and dissolve in water to form colourless solutions.

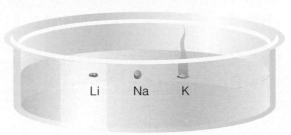

The alkali metals react with water forming metal hydroxides which dissolve in water to form alkaline solutions and hydrogen gas. For example, for the reaction between sodium and water:

$$2Na_{(s)} + 2H_2O_{(l)} \rightarrow 2NaOH_{(aq)} + H_{2(g)}$$

The alkali metals become more reactive as you go down the group because the outer shell gets further away from the positive attraction of the nucleus. This makes it easier for an atom to lose an electron from its outer shell.

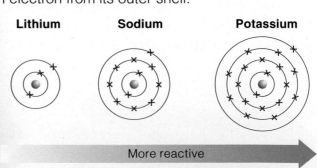

More reactive

Keywords

Halogen ➤ One of the five non-metals in group 7 of the periodic table
Displacement reaction ➤ A reaction in which a more reactive element takes the place of a less reactive element in a compound

Group 7 (the halogens)

The **halogens**…

➤ are non-metals

➤ consist of diatomic molecules (molecules made up of two atoms)

➤ react with metals to form ionic compounds where the halide ion has a charge of –1

➤ form molecular compounds with other non-metals

➤ form hydrogen halides (e.g. HCl), which dissolve in water, forming acidic solutions.

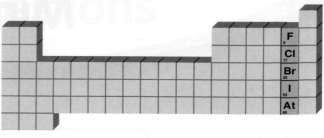

Crystals of natural fluorite

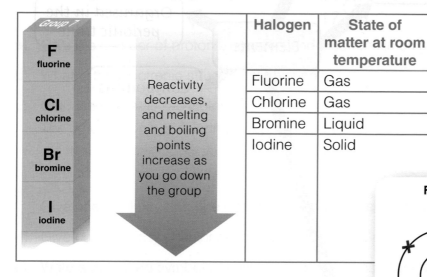

Halogen	State of matter at room temperature	Colour
Fluorine	Gas	Yellow
Chlorine	Gas	Green
Bromine	Liquid	Red / orange
Iodine	Solid	Grey / black

Reactivity decreases, and melting and boiling points increase as you go down the group

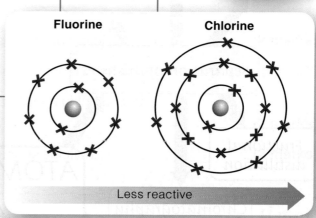

Fluorine   Chlorine

Less reactive

Halogens become less reactive as you go down the group because the outer electron shell gets further away from the attraction of the nucleus, and so an electron is gained less easily.

Displacement reactions of halogens

A more reactive halogen will **displace** a less reactive halogen from an aqueous solution of its metal halide.

For example:

chlorine + potassium bromide → potassium chloride + bromine
$$Cl_2 + 2KBr \rightarrow 2KCl + Br_2$$

The products of reactions between halogens and aqueous solutions of halide ion salts are as follows.

		Halide salts		
		Potassium chloride, KCl	Potassium bromide, KBr	Potassium iodide, KI
Halogens	Chlorine, Cl_2	No reaction	Potassium chloride + bromine	Potassium chloride + iodine
	Bromine, Br_2	No reaction	No reaction	Potassium bromide + iodine
	Iodine, I_2	No reaction	No reaction	No reaction

1. Why are the noble gases so unreactive?
2. What are the products of the reaction between lithium and water?
3. What is the trend in reactivity of the halogens as you go down the group?
4. What are the products of the reaction between bromine and potassium iodide?

There are three types of chemical bond:

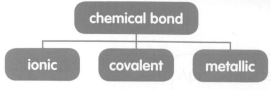

Ionic bonding

Ionic bonds occur between metals and non-metals. An ionic bond is the electrostatic force of attraction between two oppositely charged **ions** (called **cations** and **anions**).

Ionic bonds are formed when metal atoms transfer electrons to non-metal atoms. This is done so that each atom forms an ion with a full outer shell of electrons.

Example 1: The formation of an ionic bond between sodium and chlorine

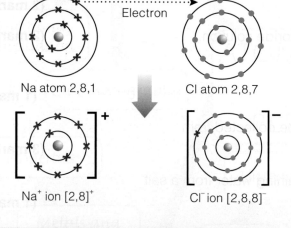

Na atom 2,8,1   Cl atom 2,8,7

Na^+ ion $[2,8]^+$ Cl^- ion $[2,8,8]^-$

Example 2: The formation of the ionic bond between magnesium and oxygen

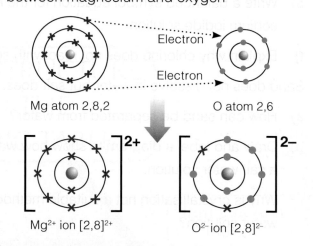

Mg atom 2,8,2   O atom 2,6

Mg^{2+} ion $[2,8]^{2+}$ O^{2-} ion $[2,8]^{2-}$

Covalent bonding

Covalent bonds occur between two non-metal atoms. Atoms share a pair of electrons so that each atom ends up with a full outer shell of electrons, such as:

➤ the formation of a covalent bond between two hydrogen atoms

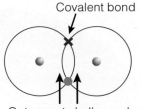

Hydrogen atoms   **A hydrogen molecule**

Covalent bond

Outermost shells overlap

➤ the covalent bonding in methane, CH_4.

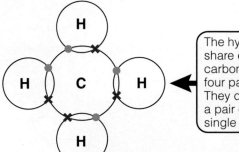

The hydrogen atoms share electrons. The carbon atom shares four pairs of electrons. They do this by sharing a pair of electrons in a single bond

Double covalent bonds occur when two pairs of electrons are shared between atoms, for example in carbon dioxide.

Carbon dioxide

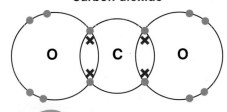

Keywords

Ion ➤ An atom or group of atoms that has gained or lost one or more electrons in order to gain a full outer shell
Cation ➤ A positive ion
Anion ➤ A negative ion
Delocalised electrons ➤ Free-moving electrons

Metallic bonding

Metals consist of giant structures. Each atom loses its outer shell electrons and these electrons become **delocalised**, i.e. they are free to move through the structure. The metal cations are arranged in a regular pattern called a lattice (see below).

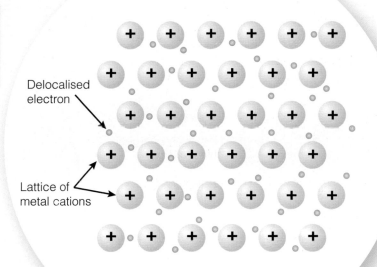

Delocalised electron

Lattice of metal cations

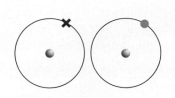

Use the models of atoms you have previously made to try to work out what happens when different atoms bond together. Make sure that each atom ends up with a full outer shell. Remember that you might need more than one of each type of atom.

1. What type of bonding occurs between a metal and non-metal atom?
2. How many electrons are present in every covalent bond?
3. Describe the structure of a metal.

Ionic and covalent structures

Structure of ionic compounds

Compounds containing ionic bonds form giant structures. These are held together by strong electrostatic forces of attraction between the oppositely charged ions. These forces act in all directions throughout the lattice.

The diagram below represents a typical giant ionic structure, sodium chloride.

Sodium chloride

— Negatively charged chloride ions

+ Positively charged sodium ions

The ratio of each ion present in the structure allows the **empirical formula** of the compound to be worked out. In the diagram above, there are equal numbers of sodium ions and chloride ions. This means that the empirical formula is NaCl.

Structure of covalent compounds

Covalently bonded substances may consist of....
➤ small molecules / simple molecular structures (e.g. Cl_2, H_2O and CH_4)
➤ large molecules, called **polymers**
➤ giant covalent structures (e.g. diamond, graphite and silicon dioxide).

Small molecular structures

The bonding between hydrogen and carbon in methane can be represented in several ways, as shown here.

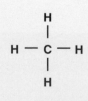

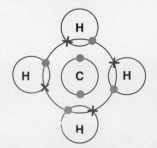

Large molecules

Polymers can be represented in the form:

$$\left[\begin{array}{cc} V & W \\ | & | \\ -C-C- \\ | & | \\ Y & X \end{array}\right]_n$$

where *n* is a large number

V, W, X and Y represent the atoms bonded to the carbon atoms

For example, poly(ethene) can be represented as:

$$\left[\begin{array}{cc} H & H \\ | & | \\ -C-C- \\ | & | \\ H & H \end{array}\right]_n$$

Keywords

Empirical formula ➤ The simplest whole number ratio of each kind of atom present in a compound

Polymer ➤ A large, long-chained molecule

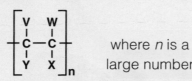

Make a model that represents sodium chloride or silicon dioxide. Count the number of each particle and then work out the simplest whole number ratio of each particle present. This is the empirical formula.

Giant covalent structures

This is the giant covalent structure of silicon dioxide.

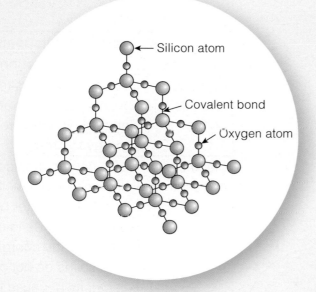

- ← Silicon atom
- ← Covalent bond
- ← Oxygen atom

Diamond

The formula of silicon dioxide is SiO_2 – this can be deduced by looking at the ratio of Si to O atoms in the diagram above.

Models, such as dot-and-cross diagrams, ball-and-stick diagrams and two- / three-dimensional diagrams to represent structures, are limited in value, as they do not accurately represent the structures of materials. For example, a chemical bond is not a solid object as depicted in some models, it is actually an attraction between particles. The relative size of different atoms is often not shown when drawing diagrams.

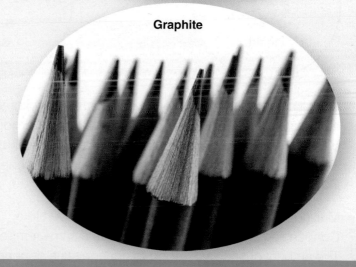

Graphite

1. What forces hold ionic structures together?
2. What are the three types of covalent substance?
3. Draw a diagram to show the structure of sodium chloride.

States of matter: properties of compounds

States of matter

The three main states of matter are **solids**, **liquids** and **gases**. Individual atoms do not have the same properties as these bulk substances. The diagram below shows how they can be interconverted and also how the particles in the different states of matter are arranged.

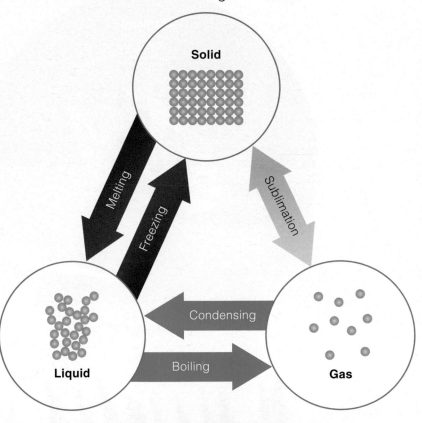

These are physical changes because the particles are either gaining or losing energy and are not undergoing a chemical reaction. Particles in a gas have more energy than in a liquid; particles in a liquid would have more energy than in a solid.

Melting and freezing occur at the same temperature. Condensing and boiling also occur at the same temperature. The amount of energy needed to change state depends on the strength of the forces between the particles of the substance.

The stronger the forces between the particles, the higher the melting and boiling points of the substance.

Properties of ionic compounds	
Property	**Explanation**
High melting and boiling points	There are lots of strong bonds throughout an ionic lattice which require lots of energy to break.
Electrical conductivity	Ionic compounds conduct electricity when molten or dissolved in water because the ions are free to move and carry the charge. Ionic solids do not conduct electricity because the ions are in a fixed position and are unable to move.

HT The model on the left is limited in value because….
  ➤ it does not indicate that there are forces between the spheres
  ➤ all particles are represented as spheres
  ➤ the spheres are solid.

Keyword

Intermolecular forces ➤ The weak forces of attraction that occur between molecules

Properties of small molecules

Substances made up of small molecules are usually gases or liquids at room temperature. They have relatively low melting and boiling points because there are weak (intermolecular) forces that act between the molecules. It is these weak forces and not the strong covalent bonds that are broken when the substance melts or boils.

Substances made up of small molecules do not normally conduct electricity. This is because the molecules do not have an overall electric charge or delocalised electrons.

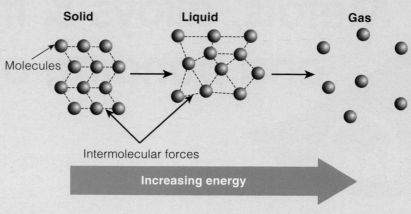

Solid   Liquid   Gas

Molecules

Intermolecular forces

Increasing energy

Polymers

Polymers are very large molecules made up of atoms joined together by strong covalent bonds. The **intermolecular forces** between polymer molecules are much stronger than in small molecules because the molecules are larger. This is why most polymers are solid at room temperature.

Giant covalent structures

Substances with a giant covalent structure are solids at room temperature. They have relatively high melting and boiling points. This is because there are lots of strong covalent bonds that need to be broken.

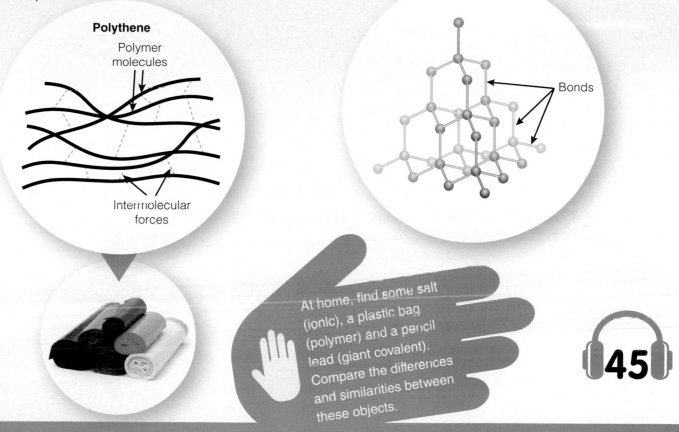

Polythene

Polymer molecules

Intermolecular forces

Bonds

At home, find some salt (ionic), a plastic bag (polymer) and a pencil lead (giant covalent). Compare the differences and similarities between these objects.

45

1. What is the main factor that determines the melting point of a solid?
2. Why do ionic compounds have relatively high melting points?
3. What needs to be broken in order to melt a substance made up of small molecules such as water?
4. Why do polymers have higher melting points than substances made up of small molecules?
5. Why do substances with giant covalent structures have relatively high melting points?

Metals, alloys & the structure and bonding of carbon

Structure and properties of metals

Metals have giant structures. Metallic bonding (the attraction between the cations and the delocalised electrons) is strong meaning that most metals have high melting and boiling points.

The layers are able to slide over each other, which means that metals can be bent and shaped.

Metals are good conductors of electricity because the delocalised electrons are able to move.

The delocalised electrons also transfer energy meaning that they are good thermal conductors.

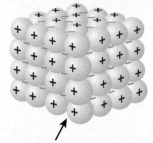

High melting point

Strong forces of attraction between cations and electrons

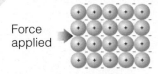

Malleable

Force applied

Force applied

Rows of ions slide over each other

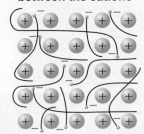

Electrons moving between the cations

Alloys

Most metals we use are **alloys**. Many pure metals (such as gold, iron and aluminium) are too soft for many uses and so are mixed with other materials (usually metals) to make alloys.

The different sizes of atoms in alloys make it difficult for the layers to slide over each other. This is why alloys are harder than pure metals.

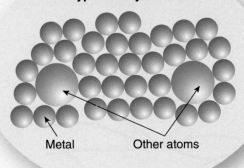

Typical alloy structure

Metal   Other atoms

Structure and bonding of carbon

Carbon has four different structures.

carbon
- diamond
- graphite
- graphene
- fullerenes

Keywords

Alloy ➤ A mixture of two or more metals, or a mixture of a metal and a non-metal

Fullerene ➤ A molecule made of carbon atoms arranged as a hollow sphere

Nanotube ➤ A molecule made of carbon atoms arranged in a tubular structure

High tensile strength ➤ Does not break easily when stretched

Diamond

Diamond is a giant covalent structure (or macromolecule) where each carbon atom is bonded to four others.

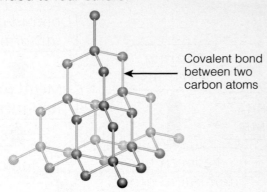

Covalent bond between two carbon atoms

In diamond, there are lots of very strong covalent bonds so diamond…

➤ is hard
➤ has a high melting point.

For these reasons, diamond is used in making cutting tools.

There are no free electrons in diamond so it does not conduct electricity.

Graphite

Graphite is also a giant covalent structure, with each carbon atom forming three covalent bonds, resulting in layers of hexagonal rings of carbon atoms. Carbon has four electrons in its outer shell and as only three are used for bonding the other one is delocalised.

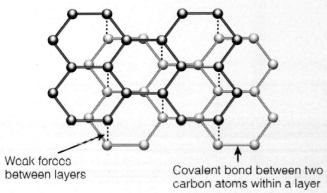

Weak forces between layers

Covalent bond between two carbon atoms within a layer

The layers in graphite are able to slide over each other because there are only weak intermolecular forces holding them together. This is why graphite is soft and slippery. These properties make graphite suitable for use as a lubricant.

Like diamond, there are lots of strong covalent bonds in graphite so it has a high melting point.

The delocalised electrons allow graphite to conduct electricity and heat.

Graphene and fullerenes

Graphene is a single layer of graphite and so it is one atom thick.

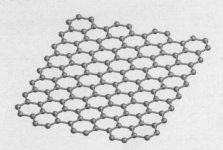

Fullerenes are molecules made up of carbon atoms and they have hollow shapes. The structure of fullerenes is based on hexagonal rings of carbon atoms but they may also contain rings with five or seven carbon atoms.

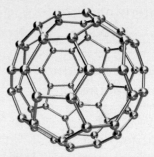

buckminsterfullerene (C_{60}) was the first fullerene to be discovered

Carbon **nanotubes** are cylindrical fullerenes.

Fullerenes have **high**…

➤ **tensile strength**
➤ electrical conductivity
➤ thermal conductivity.

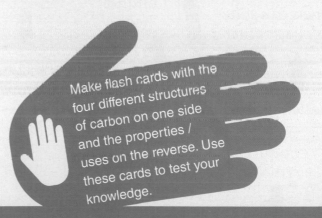

Fullerenes can be used…

➤ for drug delivery into the body
➤ as lubricants
➤ for reinforcing materials, e.g. tennis rackets.

Make flash cards with the four different structures of carbon on one side and the properties / uses on the reverse. Use these cards to test your knowledge.

1. Why do metals generally have high melting points?
2. Why are alloys harder than pure metals?
3. Why does graphite conduct electricity?
4. State two properties of fullerenes.
5. Give two uses of fullerenes.

Mind map

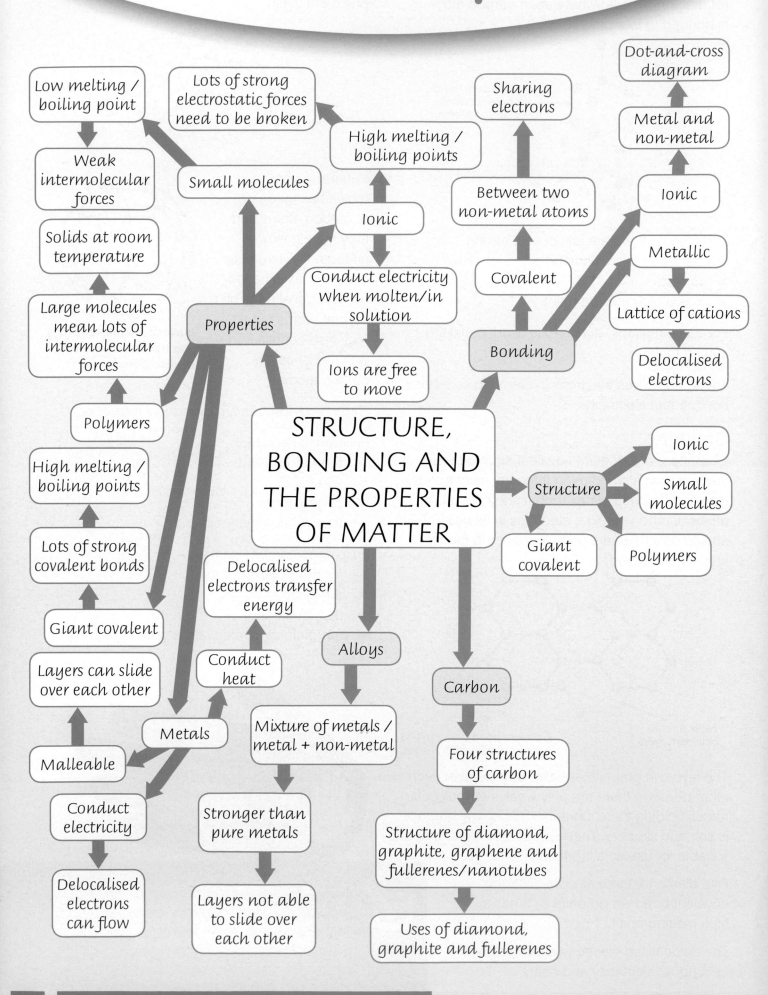

STRUCTURE, BONDING AND THE PROPERTIES OF MATTER

Low melting / boiling point

Weak intermolecular forces

Solids at room temperature

Large molecules mean lots of intermolecular forces

Polymers

High melting / boiling points

Lots of strong covalent bonds

Giant covalent

Layers can slide over each other

Malleable

Conduct electricity

Delocalised electrons can flow

Metals

Conduct heat

Delocalised electrons transfer energy

Mixture of metals / metal + non-metal

Stronger than pure metals

Layers not able to slide over each other

Alloys

Lots of strong electrostatic forces need to be broken

Small molecules

High melting / boiling points

Ionic

Conduct electricity when molten/in solution

Ions are free to move

Properties

Sharing electrons

Between two non-metal atoms

Covalent

Bonding

Carbon

Four structures of carbon

Structure of diamond, graphite, graphene and fullerenes/nanotubes

Uses of diamond, graphite and fullerenes

Dot-and-cross diagram

Metal and non-metal

Ionic

Metallic

Lattice of cations

Delocalised electrons

Structure

Ionic

Small molecules

Giant covalent

Polymers

Practice questions

1. This question is about the structure and bonding of sodium chloride and the properties that it has.

   a) What type of bonding is present in sodium chloride? **(1 mark)**

   b) Draw a dot-and-cross diagram to show the formation of the bond in sodium chloride. Draw the electronic structure of the atoms before the bond has formed and the ions after the bond has formed. **(3 marks)**

   c) Explain how the ions in sodium chloride are held together. **(2 marks)**

   d) Does sodium chloride have a high or a low boiling point? Explain your answer. **(2 marks)**

   e) Draw a diagram showing the positions of the ions in a crystal of sodium chloride. **(1 mark)**

2. Carbon dioxide and silicon dioxide have different structures.

   a) What type of bonding is present in both carbon dioxide and silicon dioxide? **(1 mark)**

   b) The diagram below shows the bonding in carbon dioxide.

   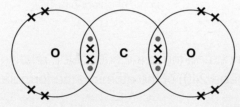

   i) How many covalent bonds are there between the carbon atom and each oxygen atom? **(1 mark)**

   ii) Does carbon dioxide have a simple molecular or giant covalent (macromolecular) structure? **(1 mark)**

   c) The structure of silicon dioxide is shown below.

   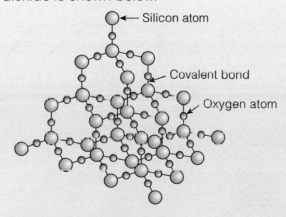

   i) Does silicon dioxide have a simple molecular or a giant covalent (macromolecular) structure? **(1 mark)**

   ii) In terms of structure, what is the difference between a simple molecular structure and a giant covalent (macromolecular) structure? **(2 marks)**

   d) Would you expect silicon dioxide to have a higher or lower boiling point than carbon dioxide? Explain your answer. **(2 marks)**

Mass and equations

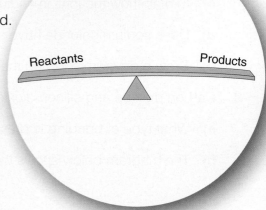

47

Keywords

Relative formula mass ➤ The sum of the atomic masses of the atoms in a formula

Thermal decomposition ➤ The breakdown of a chemical substance due to the action of heat

Conservation of mass

The total mass of reactants in a chemical reaction is equal to the total mass of the products because atoms are not created or destroyed.

Chemical reactions are represented by balanced symbol equations.

For example:

This means there are four atoms of Na

➤ $4Na + TiCl_4 \rightarrow 4NaCl + Ti$

This means there are four atoms of chlorine in $TiCl_4$

Reactants   Products

Relative formula mass

The **relative formula mass** (M_r) of a compound is the sum of the relative atomic masses (see the periodic table on page 240) of the atoms in the formula.

For example:
➤ The M_r of MgO is 40   (24 + 16)
➤ The M_r of H_2SO_4 is 98   [(2 × 1) + 32 + (4 × 16)]

In a balanced symbol equation, the sum of the relative formula masses of the reactants equals the sum of the relative formula masses of the products.

Example:

$$CaCO_3 + 2HCl \rightarrow CaCl_2 + H_2O + CO_2$$

Sum of relative formula masses: 100 + (2 × 36.5) = 173   111 + 18 + 44 = 173

Mass changes when a reactant or product is a gas

During some chemical reactions, there can appear to be a change in mass. When copper is heated its mass actually increases because oxygen is being added to it.

Copper

copper + oxygen → copper oxide

The mass of copper oxide formed is equal to the starting mass of copper plus the mass of the oxygen that has been added to it.

During a **thermal decomposition** reaction of a metal carbonate, the final mass of remaining metal oxide solid is less than the starting mass. This is because when the metal carbonate thermally decomposes it releases carbon dioxide gas into the atmosphere.

copper carbonate → copper oxide + carbon dioxide

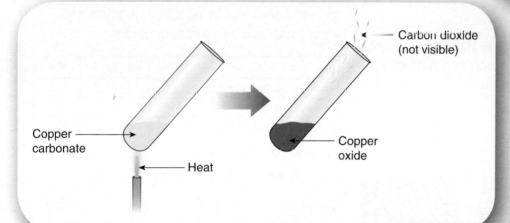

Copper carbonate

Heat

Carbon dioxide (not visible)

Copper oxide

Example:

Starting mass of copper carbonate = 8.00 g
Final mass of copper oxide = 5.15 g

Therefore, mass of carbon dioxide
released to the atmosphere = 2.85 g (8.00 g – 5.15 g)

Make cards with the symbol of the element on one side and the relative atomic mass on the reverse. Use these cards to work out the relative formula mass of the compounds you find in this book.

1. In a chemical reaction the total mass of reactants is 13.60 g. Will the expected mass of all the products be lower, higher or the same as 13.60 g?
2. With reference to the periodic table on page 240 work out the relative formula mass of the following compounds.
   a) NH_4NO_3
   b) $Mg(OH)_2$
3. When 5.0 g of zinc carbonate is heated will the mass of remaining metal oxide be lower, higher or the same as 5.0 g?

Moles, masses, empirical and molecular formula

48

Keywords
HT Mole ➤ The amount of material containing 6×10^{23} particles
HT Avogadro's constant ➤ 6×10^{23} (the number of particles in one mole)

HT Moles and Avogadro's constant

Amounts of chemicals are measured in **moles** (mol). The number of atoms, molecules or ions in a mole of a given substance is 6.02×10^{23}. This value is known as **Avogadro's constant**.

Avogadro's constant = 602 000 000 000 000 000 000 000

For example:
➤ 1 mole of carbon contains 6.02×10^{23} carbon atoms
➤ 1 mole of sulfur dioxide (SO_2) contains 6.02×10^{23} sulfur dioxide molecules.

Moles and relative formula mass

The mass of one mole of a substance in grams is equal to its relative formula mass (M_r).

For example:
➤ The mass of one mole of carbon is 12 g.
➤ The mass of one mole of sulfur dioxide is 64 g.

The number of moles can be calculated using the following formula: $\text{moles} = \dfrac{\text{mass}}{M_r}$

For example, the number of moles of carbon in 48 g $= \dfrac{48}{12} = 4$

By rearranging the above equation, the relative formula mass of a compound can be worked out from the number of moles and mass.

Example: Calculate the relative formula mass of the compound given that 0.23 moles has a mass of 36.8 g.

$$M_r = \dfrac{\text{mass}}{\text{moles}} \qquad M_r = \dfrac{36.8}{0.23} = 160$$

Amounts of substances in equations

Balanced symbol equations give information about the number of moles of reactants and products. For example:

$$2Mg + O_2 \rightarrow 2MgO$$

This equation tells us that 2 moles of magnesium react with one mole of oxygen to form 2 moles of magnesium oxide.

This means that 48 g of Mg (the mass of 2 moles of Mg) reacts with 32 g of oxygen to form 2 moles of magnesium oxide.

	2Mg	+	O_2	→	2MgO
Number of moles reacting	2		1		2
Relative formula mass	24		32		40
Mass reacting/formed (g)	48		32		80

We can use this relationship between mass and moles to calculate reacting masses.

Example: Calculate the mass of magnesium oxide formed when 12 g of magnesium reacts with an excess of oxygen.

	2Mg	+	O_2	→	2MgO
Number of moles reacting	2		1		2
Relative formula mass	24		32		40
Mass reacting/formed (g)	48		32		80
Reacting mass (g)	12				

To get from 48 to 12 we divide by 4

Therefore to find the mass of magnesium oxide formed we divide 80 by 4

The mass of magnesium oxide formed is therefore 20 g.

Empirical formula

The empirical formula is the simplest whole number ratio of each type of atom present in a compound. For example, hexene (C_6H_{12}) has the empirical formula CH_2.

You can work out the empirical formula of a substance from its chemical formula. For example, the empirical formula of ethanoic acid (CH_3COOH) is CH_2O.

The empirical formula of a compound can be calculated from either:

➤ the percentage composition of the compound by mass

or

➤ the mass of each element in the compound.

To calculate the empirical formula:

1 List all the elements in a compound.

2 Divide the data for each element by the relative atomic mass (A_r) of the element (to find the number of moles).

3 Select the smallest answer from step 2 and divide each answer by that result to obtain a ratio.

4 The ratio may need to be scaled up to give whole numbers.

Example 1: What is the empirical formula of a hydrocarbon containing 75% carbon? (Hydrogen = 25%)

1   Carbon : Hydrogen

2 $\dfrac{75}{12}$: $\dfrac{25}{1}$

      6.25 : 25

3 $\div 6.25$ $\div 6.25$

4   1 : 4

So the empirical formula is C_1H_4 or CH_4.

Example 2: What is the empirical formula of a compound containing 24 g of carbon, 8 g of hydrogen and 32 g of oxygen?

1   Carbon : Hydrogen   Oxygen

2 $\dfrac{24}{12}$: $\dfrac{8}{1}$ $\dfrac{32}{16}$

      2 : 8   2

3 $\div 2$: $\div 2$ $\div 2$

4   1 : 4   1

So the empirical formula is CH_4O.

Molecular formula

The molecular formula is the actual whole number ratio of each type of atom in a compound. It can be the same as the empirical formula or a multiple of the empirical formula. To convert an empirical formula into a molecular formula, you also need to know the relative formula mass of the compound.

Example: A compound has an empirical formula of CH_2 and an M_r of 42. What is its molecular formula?
(A_r for C = 12 and A_r for H = 1)

Work out the relative formula mass of the empirical formula $= 12 + (2 \times 1) = 14$

Then divide the actual M_r by the empirical formula M_r $= \dfrac{42}{14} = 3$

This gives the multiple.

The molecular formula is C_3H_6.

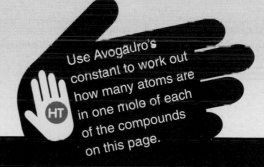

Use Avogadro's constant to work out how many atoms are in one mole of each of the compounds on this page.

HT 1. What is the mass of one mole of $CaCO_3$?

HT 2. Using the equation below, calculate the mass of sodium oxide formed when 92 g of sodium reacts with an excess of oxygen.

$$4Na + O_2 \rightarrow 2Na_2O$$

3. Calculate the empirical formula of a compound containing 0.35 g of lithium and 0.40 g of oxygen.

4. An oxide of phosphorus has the empirical formula P_2O_5 and an M_r of 284. What is its molecular formula?

Moles, solutions and equations

(HT)

Keyword

Solute ➤ A solid that dissolves in a liquid to form a solution

Concentration of solutions in g/dm³

Many chemical reactions take place in solutions. The concentration of a solution can be measured in mass of **solute** per given volume of solution, e.g. grams per dm³ (1 dm³ = 1000 cm³).

For example, a solution of 5 g/dm³ has 5 g of solute dissolved in 1 dm³ of water. It has half the concentration of a 10 g/dm³ solution of the same solute.

The mass of solute in a solution can be calculated if the concentration and volume of solution are known.

> **Example:** Calculate the mass of solute in 250 cm³ of a solution whose concentration is 8 g/dm³.
>
> **Step 1:** Divide the mass by 1000 (this gives you the mass of solute in 1 cm³).
>
> $8 \div 1000 = 0.008$ g/cm³
>
> **Step 2:** Multiply this value by the volume specified.
>
> $0.008 \times 250 = 2$ g

Using moles to balance equations

The masses of reactants / products in an equation and the M_r values can be used to work out the balancing numbers in a symbol equation.

Example: Balance the equation below given that 8 g of CH_4 reacts with 32 g of oxygen to form 22 g of CO_2 and 18 g of H_2O

$$...CH_4 + ...O_2 \rightarrow ...CO_2 + ...H_2O$$

Chemical	CH_4	O_2	CO_2	H_2O
Mass (from question)	8	32	22	18
M_r	16	32	44	18
Moles = $\dfrac{mass}{M_r}$	$\dfrac{8}{16} = 0.5$	$\dfrac{32}{32} = 1$	$\dfrac{22}{44} = 0.5$	$\dfrac{18}{18} = 1$

We can make this a whole number ratio by dividing all answers by the smallest answer

$\div 0.5$		$\dfrac{0.5}{0.5} = 1$	$\dfrac{1}{0.5} = 2$	$\dfrac{0.5}{0.5} = 1$	$\dfrac{1}{0.5} = 2$

The balanced equation is therefore:

$$.......CH_4 + ..2...O_2 \rightarrow ....CO_2 + ..2...H_2O$$

49

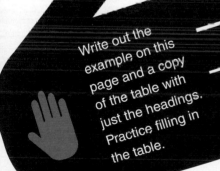

Write out the example on this page and a copy of the table with just the headings. Practice filling in the table.

1. Calculate the mass of solute in 125 cm^3 of a solution whose concentration is 18.4 g/dm^3.
2. Balance the equation below for the reaction that occurs when 7 g of silicon reacts with 35.5 g of chlorine to form 42.5 g of silicon chloride.

$$..........Si + ...Cl_2 \rightarrow ....SiCl_4$$

Reactivity of metals and metal extraction

50

Keywords
Oxidation ➤ A reaction involving the gain of oxygen **HT** or the loss of electrons

Reduction ➤ A reaction involving the loss of oxygen **HT** or the gain of electrons

Reaction of metals with oxygen

Many metals react with oxygen to form metal oxides, for example:

> copper + oxygen ⟶ copper oxide

These reactions are called **oxidation** reactions. Oxidation reactions take place when a chemical gains oxygen.

When a substance loses oxygen it is called a **reduction** reaction.

The reactivity series

When metals react they form positive ions. The more easily the metal forms a positive ion the more reactive the metal.

Calcium and magnesium are both in group 2 of the periodic table so will form 2^+ ions when they react. Calcium is more reactive than magnesium so it has a greater tendency/is more likely to form the 2^+ ion.

Metal	Reaction with water	Reaction with acid
Potassium	Very vigorous	Explosive
Sodium	Vigorous	Dangerous
Lithium	Steady	Very vigorous
Calcium	Steady fizzing and bubbling	Vigorous
Magnesium	Slow reaction	Steady fizzing and bubbling
Aluminium	Slow reaction	Steady fizzing and bubbling
*Carbon		
Zinc	Very slow reaction	Gentle fizzing and bubbling
Iron	Extremely slow	Slight fizzing and bubbling
*Hydrogen		
Copper	No reaction	No reaction
Silver	No reaction	No reaction
Gold	No reaction	No reaction

Decreasing reactivity

* included for comparison

The reactivity series can also be used to predict displacement reactions.

> zinc + copper oxide ⟶ zinc oxide + copper

In this reaction…
➤ zinc displaces (i.e. takes the place of) copper
➤ zinc is oxidised (i.e. it gains oxygen)
➤ copper oxide is reduced (i.e. it loses oxygen).

Gold

Extraction of metals and reduction

Unreactive metals, such as gold, are found in the Earth's crust as pure metals. Most metals are found as compounds and chemical reactions are required to extract the metal. The method of extraction depends on the position of the metal in the reactivity series.

Position of metal in the reactivity series

above carbon | below carbon

metal extracted by electrolysis | metal extracted by reduction with carbon

For example, iron is found in the earth as iron(III) oxide, Fe_2O_3. The iron(III) oxide can be reduced by reacting it with carbon.

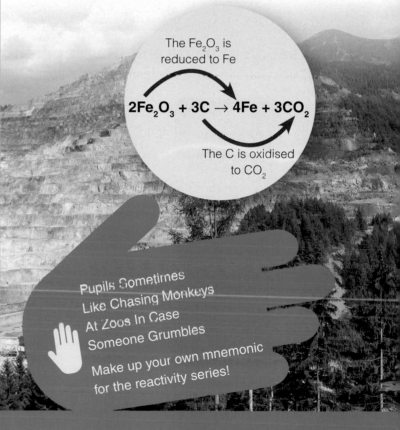

The Fe_2O_3 is reduced to Fe

$$2Fe_2O_3 + 3C \rightarrow 4Fe + 3CO_2$$

The C is oxidised to CO_2

Pupils Sometimes
Like Chasing Monkeys
At Zoos In Case
Someone Grumbles

Make up your own mnemonic for the reactivity series!

HT Oxidation and reduction in terms of electrons

Oxidation and reduction can also be defined in terms of electrons:

O oxidation
I is
L loss (of electrons)
R reduction
I is
G gain (of electrons)

This mnemonic can be useful to work out what is being oxidised and reduced in displacement reactions, for example:

magnesium +	copper sulfate	→	magnesium sulfate	+ copper
Mg	+ CuSO$_4$	→	MgSO$_4$	+ Cu

The ionic equation for this reaction is:

Mg **loses electrons** to become Mg^{2+}

Oxidation

$$Mg + Cu^{2+} \rightarrow Mg^{2+} + Cu$$

Reduction

Cu^{2+} **gains electrons** to become Cu

1. Write a word equation for the oxidation of magnesium to form magnesium oxide.
2. Both sodium and lithium react to form 1+ ions. Which one of these metals has a greater tendency / is more likely to form this ion?
3. Name two metals from the reactivity series that are extracted by reduction with carbon.

HT 4. In the equation below, which species is oxidised and which one is reduced?

$$Mg + Zn^{2+} \rightarrow Mg^{2+} + Zn$$

Reactions of acids

Reactions of acids with metals

Acids react with metals that are above hydrogen in the reactivity series to make **salts** and hydrogen, for example:

magnesium + hydrochloric acid → magnesium chloride + hydrogen

This is a salt

 The reactions of metals with acids are **redox** reactions. The ionic equation for the reaction of magnesium with hydrochloric acid is:

$$Mg + 2H^+ \rightarrow Mg^{2+} + H_2$$

The metal (in this case magnesium) is oxidised, i.e. it loses electrons.

The hydrogen ions are reduced, i.e. they gain electrons.

Mg is **oxidised**, i.e. it loses electrons (to form Mg^{2+})

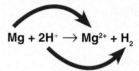

$$Mg + 2H^+ \rightarrow Mg^{2+} + H_2$$

H^+ is **reduced**, i.e. it gains electrons (to form H_2)

Neutralisation of acids and the preparation of salts

Acids can be neutralised by the following reactions.

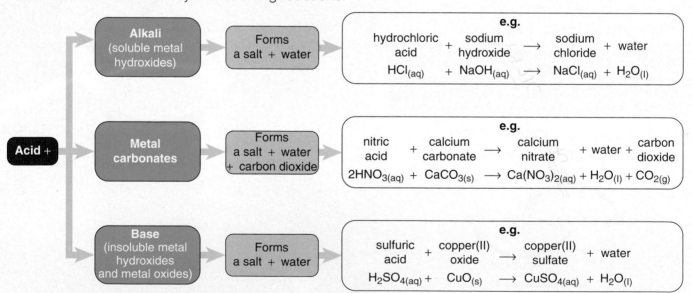

The first part of the salt formed contains the positive ion (usually the metal) from the alkali, base or carbonate followed by...

➤ chloride if hydrochloric acid was used
➤ sulfate if sulfuric acid was used
➤ nitrate if nitric acid was used.

For example, when calcium hydroxide is reacted with sulfuric acid, the salt formed is calcium sulfate.

Write examples of neutralisation reactions on pieces of paper or card. Stick them on a wall near where you study, so that you regularly see them.

Making salts

Salts can be either soluble or insoluble. The majority of salts are soluble.

The general rules for deciding whether a salt will be soluble are as follows.

➤ All common sodium, potassium and ammonium salts are soluble.

➤ All nitrates are soluble.

➤ All common chlorides, except silver chloride, are soluble.

➤ All common sulfates, except barium and calcium, are soluble.

➤ All common carbonates are insoluble, except potassium, sodium and ammonium.

(ws) Preparation of soluble salts

Soluble salts can be prepared by the following method.

| Add solid to the acid until no more reacts | → | Filter off the excess solid | → | Obtain the solid salt by **crystallisation** |

For example, copper(II) sulfate crystals can be made by reacting copper(II) oxide with sulfuric acid.

Copper(II) oxide

Sulfuric acid

| Add copper(II) oxide to sulfuric acid | → | Filter to remove any unreacted copper(II) oxide | → | Evaporate to leave behind blue crystals of the 'salt' copper(II) sulfate |

Keywords

Salt ➤ A product of the reaction that occurs when an acid is neutralised

HT **Redox** ➤ A reaction in which both oxidation and reduction occur

Crystallisation ➤ A method used to separate a soluble solid from its solution when you want to collect the solid

Copper(II) sulfate

---

1. Write a word equation for the reaction that occurs when zinc reacts with sulfuric acid.

HT **2.** Identify the species that is oxidised in the following reaction.

$$Fe + 2H^+ \longrightarrow Fe^{2+} + H_2$$

3. Other than an alkali, name a substance that can neutralise an acid.

4. Name the salt formed when lithium oxide reacts with nitric acid.

5. What are the three main steps in preparing a soluble salt from an acid and a metal oxide?

6. Which one of the following salts is insoluble?

ammonium carbonate

barium sulfate

copper(II) nitrate

pH, neutralisation, acid strength and electrolysis

Indicators, the pH scale and neutralisation reactions

Indicators are useful dyes that become different colours in acids and alkalis.

Indicator	Colour in acid	Colour in alkali
Litmus	Red	Blue
Phenolphthalein	Colourless	Pink
Methyl orange	Pink	Yellow

The pH scale measures the acidity or alkalinity of a solution. The pH scale runs from 0 to 14 and the pH of a solution can be measured using universal indicator or a pH probe.

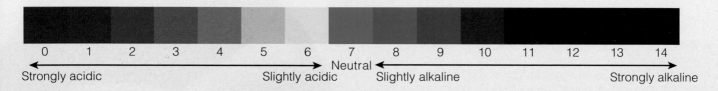

| 0 | 1 | 2 | 3 | 4 | 5 | 6 | 7 | 8 | 9 | 10 | 11 | 12 | 13 | 14 |

Neutral

Strongly acidic   Slightly acidic   Slightly alkaline   Strongly alkaline

Acids are solutions that contain hydrogen ions (H^+). The higher the concentration of hydrogen ions, the more acidic the solution (i.e. the lower the pH).

Alkalis are solutions that contain hydroxide ions (OH^-). The higher the concentration of hydroxide ions, the more alkaline the solution (i.e. the higher the pH).

When an acid is neutralised by an alkali, the hydrogen ions from the acid react with the hydroxide ions in the alkali to form water.

$$H^+_{(aq)} + OH^-_{(aq)} \rightarrow H_2O_{(l)}$$

HT **Strong acids**, such as hydrochloric, sulfuric and nitric acids, are those that completely ionise in aqueous solution. For example:

$$HCl_{(aq)} \rightarrow H^+_{(aq)} + Cl^-_{(aq)}$$

This means dissolved in water

Weak acids, such as ethanoic, citric and carbonic acids, only partially ionise in water. For example:

$$CH_3COOH_{(aq)} \rightleftharpoons CH_3COO^-_{(aq)} + H^+_{(aq)}$$

This sign means that the reaction is reversible, i.e. that the acid does not fully ionise

The pH of an acid is a measure of the concentration of hydrogen ions. When two different acids of the same concentration have different pH values the strongest acid will have the lowest pH.

The pH scale is a logarithmic scale. As the pH decreases by 1 unit (e.g. from 3 to 2) the hydrogen ion concentration increases by a factor of 10.

Electrolysis

An electric current is the flow of electrons through a conductor but it can also flow by the movement of ions through a solution or a liquid.

Covalent compounds do not contain free electrons or ions that can move. So they will not conduct electricity when solid, liquid, gas or in solution.

The ions in:

➤ an **ionic solid** are fixed and cannot move
➤ an **ionic substance** that is **molten** or in **solution** are free to move.

Electrolysis is a chemical reaction that involves passing electricity through an **electrolyte**. An electrolyte is a liquid that conducts electricity. Electrolytes are either molten ionic compounds or solutions of ionic compounds. Electrolytes are decomposed during electrolysis.

➤ The positive ions (**cations**) move to, and discharge at, the negative electrode (**cathode**).
➤ The negative ions (**anions**) move to, and discharge at, the positive electrode (**anode**).

Electrons are removed from the anions at the anode. These electrons then flow around the circuit to the cathode and are transferred to the cations.

Keywords

HT Strong acid ➤ An acid that fully ionises when dissolved
HT Weak acid ➤ An acid that partially ionises when dissolved in water
Electrolyte ➤ A liquid or solution containing ions that is broken down during electrolysis

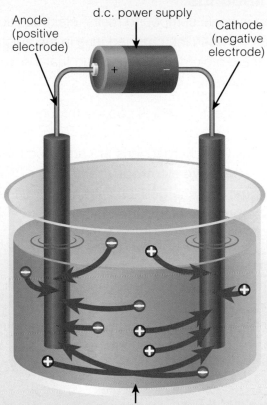

Anode (positive electrode)
d.c. power supply
Cathode (negative electrode)

Electrolyte (liquid that conducts electricity and decomposes in electrolysis)

Colour pieces of paper in different colours on the pH scale. On the back of each, write the pH number that each colour corresponds to. Mix up the pieces of paper, then practise putting them into the right order.

1. What type of substance has a pH of less than 7?
2. Which ion is responsible for solutions being alkaline?
3. Write an ionic equation for the reaction that takes place when an acid is neutralised by an alkali.
HT 4. What is the difference between a strong acid and a weak acid?
5. Why must electrolytes be in the liquid state?

Applications of electrolysis

Keywords
Cathode ➤ The negative electrode
Anode ➤ The positive electrode

Electrolysis of molten ionic compounds

When an ionic compound melts, electrostatic forces between the charged ions in the crystal lattice are broken down, meaning that the ions are free to move.

When a direct current is passed through a molten ionic compound:

➤ positively charged ions are attracted towards the **negative electrode** (cathode)
➤ negatively charged ions are attracted towards the **positive electrode** (anode).

For example, in the electrolysis of molten lead bromide:

➤ positively charged lead ions are attracted towards the **cathode**, forming lead
➤ negatively charged bromide ions are attracted towards the **anode**, forming bromine.

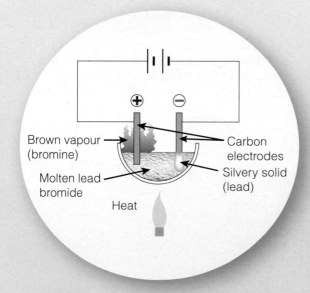

Brown vapour (bromine)
Carbon electrodes
Molten lead bromide
Silvery solid (lead)
Heat

When ions get to the oppositely charged electrode they are **discharged** – they lose their charge. For example, in the electrolysis of molten lead bromide, the non-metal ion loses electrons to the positive electrode to form a bromine atom. The bromine atom then bonds with a second atom to form a bromine molecule.

ⓦⓢ Using electrolysis to extract metals

Aluminium is the most abundant metal in the Earth's crust. It must be obtained from its ore by electrolysis because it is too reactive to be extracted by heating with carbon. The electrodes are made of graphite (a type of carbon). The aluminium ore (bauxite) is purified to leave aluminium oxide, which is then melted so that the ions can move. Cryolite is added to increase the conductivity and lower the melting point.

When a current passes through the molten mixture:

➤ positively charged aluminium ions move towards the negative electrode (**cathode**) and form aluminium
➤ negatively charged oxygen ions move towards the positive electrode (**anode**) and form oxygen.

The positive electrodes gradually wear away (because the graphite electrodes react with the oxygen to form carbon dioxide gas). This means they have to be replaced every so often. Extracting aluminium can be quite an expensive process because of the cost of the large amounts of electrical energy needed to carry it out.

Bauxite

Aluminium rods

Electrolysis of aqueous solutions

When a solution undergoes electrolysis, there is also water present. During electrolysis water molecules break down into hydrogen ions and hydroxide ions.

$$H_2O_{(l)} \rightarrow H^+_{(aq)} + OH^-_{(aq)}$$

This means that when an aqueous compound is electrolysed there are two cations present (H^+ from water and the metal cation from the compound) and two anions present (OH^- from water and the anion from the compound).

Solution	Product at cathode	Product at anode
copper chloride	copper	chlorine
sodium sulfate	hydrogen	oxygen
water (diluted with sulfuric acid to aid conductivity)	hydrogen	oxygen

For example, in copper(II) sulfate solution…
➤ cations present: Cu^{2+} and H^+
➤ anions present: SO_4^{2-} and OH^-

At the positive electrode (anode): *Oxygen is produced unless the solution contains halide ions*. In this case the oxygen is produced.

At the negative electrode (cathode): *The least reactive element is formed*. The reactivity series in Module 50 will be helpful here. In this case, hydrogen is formed.

Example:

What are the three products of the electrolysis of sodium chloride solution?

Cations present: Na^+ and H^+
Q. What happens at the cathode?
A. Hydrogen is less reactive than sodium therefore hydrogen gas is formed.

Anions present: Cl^- and OH^-
Q. What happens at the anode?
A. A halide ion (Cl^-) is present therefore chlorine will be formed.

The sodium ions and hydroxide ions stay in solution (i.e. sodium hydroxide solution remains).

HT Half-equations

During electrolysis, the cation that is discharged at the cathode gains electrons (is reduced) to form the element. For example:

$$Cu^{2+} + 2e^- \rightarrow Cu$$

$$2H^+ + 2e^- \rightarrow H_2$$

At the anode the anion loses electrons (is oxidised). For example:

$$2Cl^- \rightarrow Cl_2 + 2e^-$$ ← this can also be written as $2Cl^- - 2e^- \rightarrow Cl_2$

$$4OH^- \rightarrow O_2 + 2H_2O + 4e^-$$

or $4OH^- - 4e^- \rightarrow O_2 + 2H_2O$

Try making a model to show how the ions move during electrolysis.

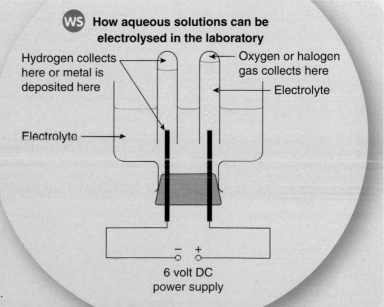

WS How aqueous solutions can be electrolysed in the laboratory

Hydrogen collects here or metal is deposited here

Oxygen or halogen gas collects here

Electrolyte

Electrolyte

6 volt DC power supply

---

1. When molten potassium iodide is electrolysed, what will be formed at the cathode and anode?
2. When aqueous potassium iodide is electrolysed, what will be formed at the cathode and anode?
HT 3. When aqueous copper(II) sulfate is electrolysed, oxygen gas is formed at the anode. Write a half-equation for this oxidation reaction.

Energy changes in reactions

54

Keywords
Exothermic ➤ A reaction in which energy is given out
Endothermic ➤ A reaction in which energy is taken in

Exothermic and endothermic reactions

Energy is not created or destroyed during chemical reactions, i.e. the amount of energy in the universe at the end of a chemical reaction is the same as before the reaction takes place.

Type of reaction	Is energy given out or taken in?	What happens to the temperature of the surroundings?
Exothermic	out	increases
Endothermic	in	decreases

Examples of **exothermic** reactions include…
➤ combustion
➤ neutralisation
➤ many oxidation reactions
➤ precipitation reactions
➤ displacement reactions.

Everyday applications of exothermic reactions include self-heating cans and hand warmers.

Examples of **endothermic** reactions include…
➤ thermal decomposition
➤ the reaction between citric acid and sodium hydrogen carbonate.

Some changes, such as dissolving salts in water, can be either exothermic or endothermic. Some sports injury packs are based on endothermic reactions.

Reaction profiles

For a chemical reaction to occur, the reacting particles must collide together with sufficient energy. The minimum amount of energy that the particles must have in order to react is known as the 'activation energy'.

Reaction profiles can be used to show the relative energies of reactants and products, the activation energy and the overall energy change of a reaction.

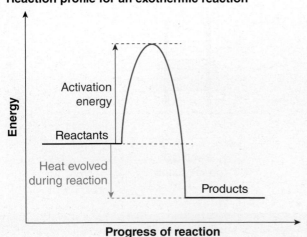

Reaction profile for an exothermic reaction

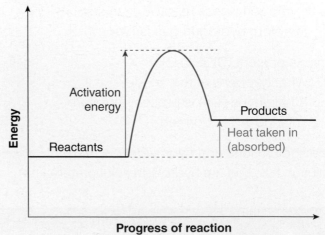

Reaction profile for an endothermic reaction

Chemical reactions in which more energy is made when new bonds are made than was used to break the existing bonds are **exothermic**.

Chemical reactions in which more energy is used to break the existing bonds than is released in making the new bonds are **endothermic**.

The energy change of reactions

HT

During a chemical reaction:

➤ bonds are broken in the reactant molecules – this is an endothermic process

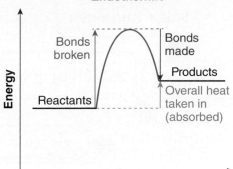

Endothermic

Bonds broken

Bonds made

Products

Reactants

Overall heat taken in (absorbed)

Energy

Progress of reaction

➤ bonds are made to form the product molecules – this is an exothermic process.

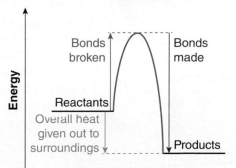

Exothermic

Bonds broken

Bonds made

Reactants

Overall heat given out to surroundings

Products

Energy

Progress of reaction

Example:

Hydrogen is burned in oxygen to produce water:

hydrogen + oxygen → water

$2H_{2(g)}$ + $O_{2(g)}$ → $2H_2O_{(l)}$

2H–H + O=O → 2H–O–H

The following are **bond energies** for the **reactants** and **products**:

H–H is 436 kJ   O=O is 496 kJ   O–H is 463 kJ

Calculate the energy change.

You can calculate the energy change using this method:

1 Calculate the energy used to break bonds:

$(2 \times H–H) + O=O = (2 \times 436) + 496 =$ **1368 kJ**

2 Calculate the energy released when new bonds are made:

(Water is made up of 2 × O–H bonds.)
$2 \times H–O–H = 2 \times (2 \times 463) =$ **1852 kJ**

Enthalpy change (ΔH) = energy used to break bonds – energy released when new bonds are made

$\Delta H = 1368 – 1852$
$\Delta H =$ **−484 kJ**

The reaction is **exothermic** because the energy from making the bonds is **more than** the energy needed to break the bonds.

Pull apart 'things' that are 'bonded' together, such as a pen from its lid. You have to use energy to separate the pen from the lid just like you have to use energy to break chemical 'things' that are 'bonded' together!

1. What happens to the temperature of the surroundings when an endothermic reaction takes place?
2. Draw and label a reaction profile for an exothermic reaction.
   HT 3. The energy required to break the bonds in a reaction is 2314 kJ. The energy released when the new bonds are made is 3613 kJ. What is the energy change for this reaction?
   HT 4. Is the reaction in question 3 exothermic or endothermic? Explain your answer.

Mind map

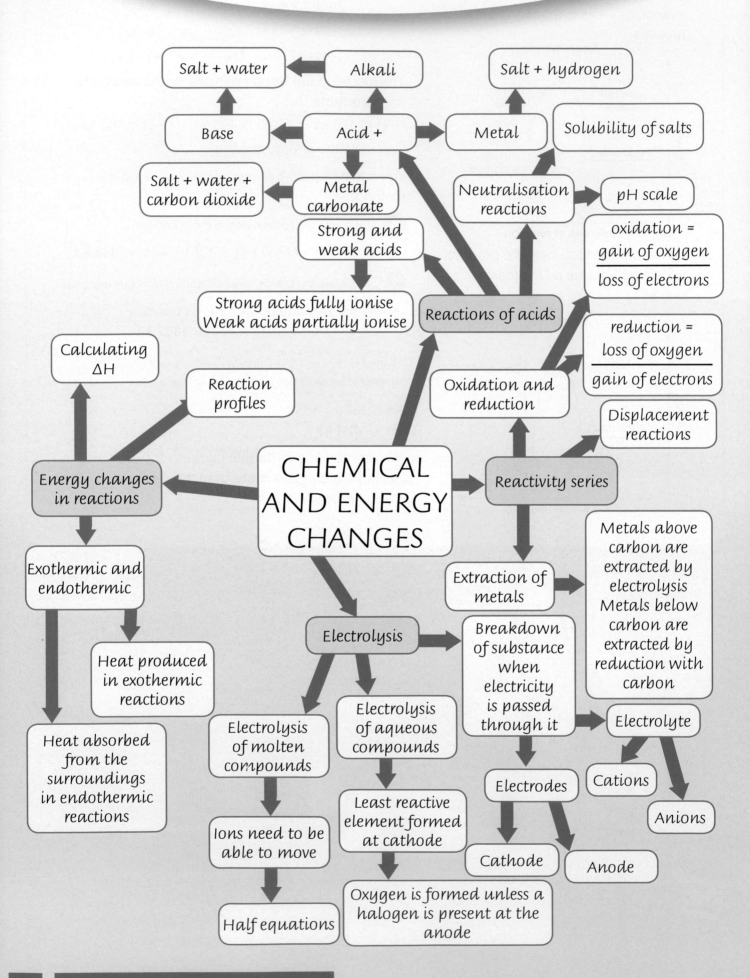

Salt + water ← Alkali

Salt + hydrogen

Base ← Acid + → Metal

Solubility of salts

Salt + water + carbon dioxide ← Metal carbonate

Neutralisation reactions → pH scale

Strong and weak acids

oxidation = gain of oxygen / loss of electrons

Strong acids fully ionise
Weak acids partially ionise

Reactions of acids

reduction = loss of oxygen / gain of electrons

Calculating ΔH

Reaction profiles

Oxidation and reduction

Displacement reactions

Energy changes in reactions ← **CHEMICAL AND ENERGY CHANGES** → Reactivity series

Exothermic and endothermic

Extraction of metals

Metals above carbon are extracted by electrolysis
Metals below carbon are extracted by reduction with carbon

Heat produced in exothermic reactions

Electrolysis → Breakdown of substance when electricity is passed through it

Heat absorbed from the surroundings in endothermic reactions

Electrolysis of molten compounds

Electrolysis of aqueous compounds

Electrolyte

Electrodes

Cations

Ions need to be able to move

Least reactive element formed at cathode

Cathode

Anode

Anions

Half equations

Oxygen is formed unless a halogen is present at the anode

Practice questions

1. Zinc is found in the Earth's crust as zinc oxide.

   a) Write a balanced symbol equation for the reaction between zinc and oxygen to form zinc oxide. **(1 mark)**

   b) Zinc can be extracted by reacting the zinc oxide with magnesium, as shown in the equation below.

   $Mg + ZnO \rightarrow MgO + Zn$

   Which species has been reduced in this reaction?
   Explain your answer. **(2 marks)**

   c) Is zinc more or less reactive than magnesium?
   Explain your answer with reference to the above equation. **(2 marks)**

   d) Would you expect zinc metal to normally be extracted from its ore by electrolysis or by reduction with carbon? Explain your answer. **(2 marks)**

   e) Zinc will react with copper solutions according to the ionic equation below.

   $Zn_{(s)} + Cu^{2+}_{(aq)} \rightarrow Zn^{2+}_{(aq)} + Cu_{(s)}$

   Which species is oxidised in this reaction?
   Explain your answer. **(2 marks)**

2. When methane burns in air the equation for the reaction is:

$$\begin{array}{c} H \\ | \\ H-C-H \\ | \\ H \end{array} + 2\,O{=}O \rightarrow O{=}C{=}O + 2\,H{-}O{-}H$$

   a) The reaction between methane and oxygen is exothermic. Draw and label a reaction profile for this reaction. **(3 marks)**

   HT b) Use the bond energy values in the table below to calculate the value of ΔH for the reaction between methane and oxygen. **(3 marks)**

Bond	Energy kJ/mol
C–H	413
O=O	498
C=O	805
O–H	464

   c) During an exothermic reaction, what happens to the temperature of the surroundings? **(1 mark)**

Rates of reaction

55

WS Calculating rates of reactions

The **rate** of a chemical reaction can be determined by measuring the quantity of a reactant used or (more commonly) the quantity of a product formed over time.

$$\text{mean rate of reaction} = \frac{\text{quantity of reactant used}}{\text{time taken}}$$

$$\text{mean rate of reaction} = \frac{\text{quantity of product formed}}{\text{time taken}}$$

For example, if 46 cm³ of gas is produced in 23 seconds then the mean rate of reaction is 2 cm³/s.

Rates of reaction can also be determined from graphs.

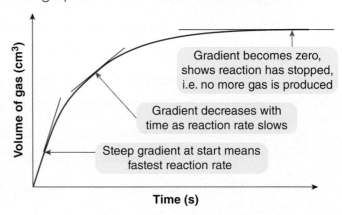

Gradient becomes zero, shows reaction has stopped, i.e. no more gas is produced

Gradient decreases with time as reaction rate slows

Steep gradient at start means fastest reaction rate

HT If the gradient of the tangent is calculated, this gives a numerical measure of the rate of reaction. For example:

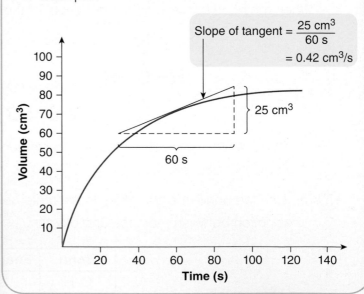

Slope of tangent = $\frac{25 \text{ cm}^3}{60 \text{ s}}$

= 0.42 cm³/s

25 cm³

60 s

Keywords

Rate ➤ A measure of the speed of a chemical reaction

Catalyst ➤ A species that alters the rate of a reaction without being used up or chemically changed at the end

Factors affecting the rates of reactions

There are five factors that affect the rate of chemical reactions:
➤ concentrations of the reactants in solution
➤ pressure of reacting gases
➤ surface area of any solid reactants
➤ temperature
➤ presence of a **catalyst**.

During experiments the rate of a chemical reaction can be found by...
➤ measuring the mass of the reaction mixture (e.g. if a gas is lost during a reaction)
➤ measuring the volume of gas produced
➤ observing a solution becoming opaque or changing colour.

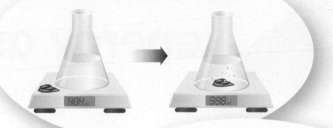

Weighing the reaction mixture

Measuring the volume of gas produced

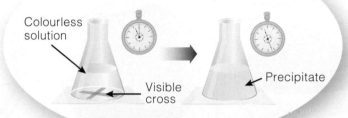

Observing the formation of a precipitate

Colourless solution

Visible cross

Precipitate

| As particle size decreases | The surface area to volume ratio increases | and the rate of reaction increases |

Add a teaspoon of sugar to a cup of tea or coffee and stir.
Time how long it takes for the sugar to dissolve.
Occasionally, lift the teaspoon to check that the sugar has all dissolved.
Make another cup of tea or coffee and repeat the experiment but using a cube of sugar instead.
Does sugar dissolve more quickly as a cube or as individual granules?
Dissolving is a physical process rather than a chemical reaction but the principle is the same!

1. What is the rate of the reaction in which 12 g of reactant is used up over 16 seconds?
2. State two factors that affect the rate of reaction.
3. How would you measure the rate of a reaction where one of the products is hydrogen gas?
4. What is the effect on the rate of a reaction as the surface area to volume ratio of a solid reactant increases?

Collision theory, activation energy and catalysts

56

Factors affecting rates of reaction

Collision theory explains how various factors affect rates of reaction.
It states that, for a chemical reaction to occur…

1 The reactant particles must collide with each other.

AND

2 They must collide with sufficient energy – this amount of energy is known as the **activation energy**.

Surface area	Temperature	Pressure	Concentration
			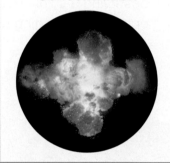
A smaller particle size means a higher surface area to volume ratio. With smaller particles, more collisions can take place, meaning a greater rate of reaction.	Increasing the temperature increases the rate of reaction because the particles are moving more quickly and so will collide more often. Also, more particles will possess the activation energy, so a greater proportion of collisions will result in a reaction.	At a higher pressure, the gas particles are closer together, so there is a greater chance of them colliding, resulting in a higher rate of reaction.	At a higher concentration, there are more reactant particles in the same volume of solution, which increases the chance of collisions and increases the rate of reaction.
Large pieces – small surface area to volume ratio  **Small pieces** – large surface area to volume ratio	**Low temperature** 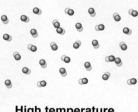 **High temperature**	**Low pressure**  **High pressure** 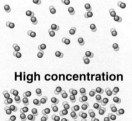	**Low concentration** **High concentration**

Enzyme (biological catalyst)

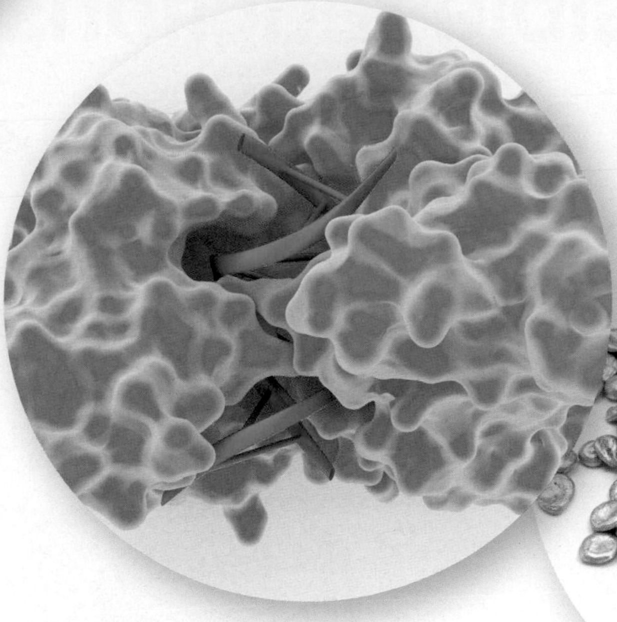

Zinc catalyst

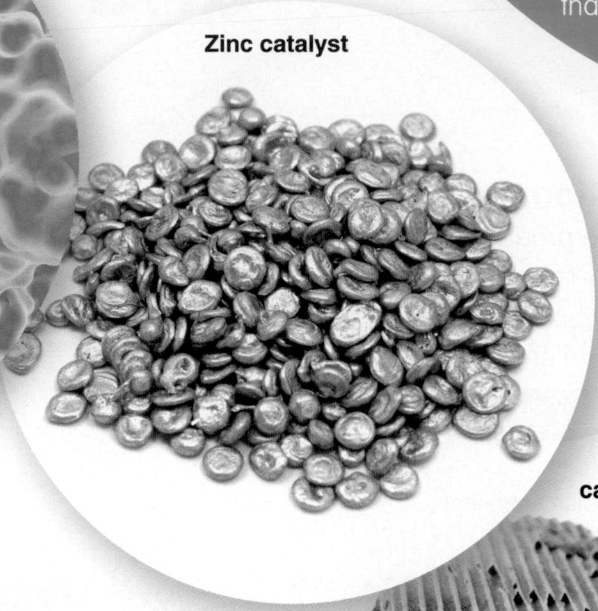

Part of car catalytic converter

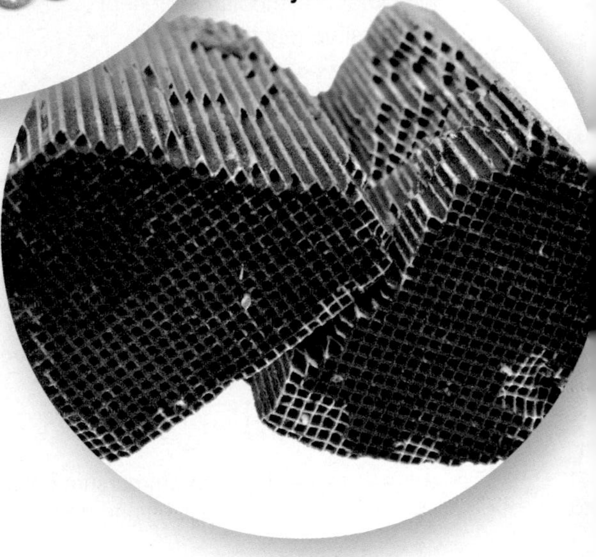

Keyword

Activation energy ➤ The minimum amount of energy that particles must collide with in order to react

Catalysts

Catalysts are chemicals that change the rate of chemical reactions but are not used up during the reaction. Different chemical reactions need different catalysts. In biological systems enzymes act as catalysts.

Catalysts work by providing an alternative reaction pathway of lower activation energy. This can be shown on a reaction profile.

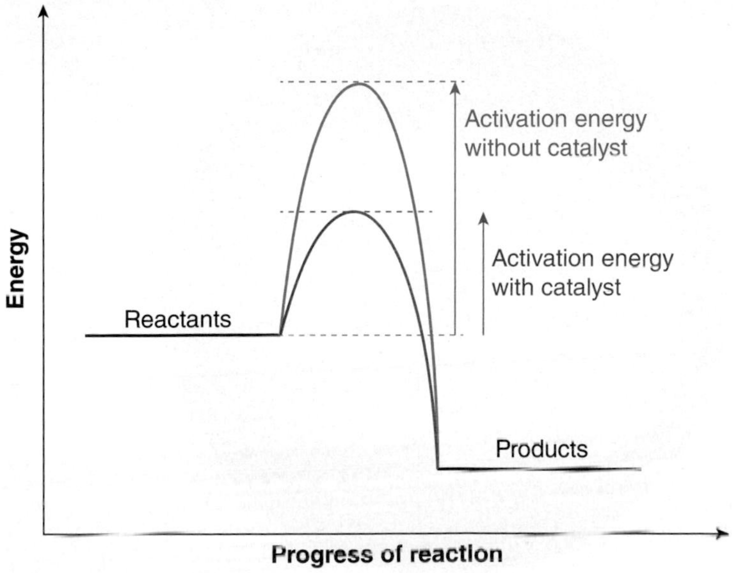
Energy
Activation energy without catalyst
Activation energy with catalyst
Reactants
Products
Progress of reaction

Catalysts are not reactants and so they are not included in the chemical equation.

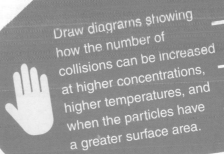

Draw diagrams showing how the number of collisions can be increased at higher concentrations, higher temperatures, and when the particles have a greater surface area.

1. What is collision theory?
2. What is meant by the term 'activation energy'?
3. Why does a higher concentration of solution increase the rate of a chemical reaction?
4. What is a catalyst?
5. Explain how catalysts increase the rate of chemical reactions.

Keyword

Equilibrium ➤ A reversible reaction where the rate of the forward reaction is the same as the rate of the reverse reaction

Reversible reactions and equilibrium

57

Reversible reactions

In some reactions, the products of the reaction can react to produce the original reactants. These reactions are called reversible reactions. For example:

➤ Heating ammonium chloride:

$$NH_4Cl_{(s)} \rightleftharpoons NH_{3(g)} + HCl_{(g)}$$

we use this symbol to represent a reversible reaction

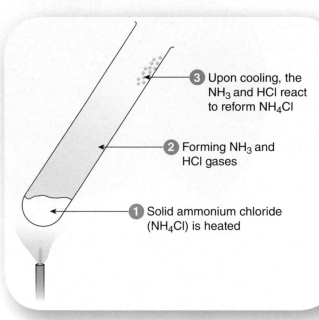

③ Upon cooling, the NH_3 and HCl react to reform NH_4Cl

② Forming NH_3 and HCl gases

① Solid ammonium chloride (NH_4Cl) is heated

➤ Heating hydrated copper(II) sulfate:

Heat
$$CuSO_4 \cdot 5H_2O_{(s)} \rightleftharpoons CuSO_{4(s)} + 5H_2O_{(g)}$$
blue   white

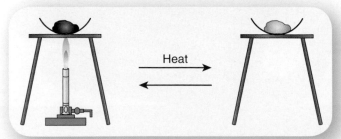

Heat

If the forward reaction is endothermic (absorbs heat) then the reverse reaction must be exothermic (releases heat).

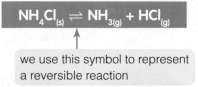

Write out the column and row headings from the table in the 'changing temperature' section on page 137. Write out all of the four effects on separate pieces of paper and practise placing them in the right box.

HT

Equilibrium

When a reversible reaction is carried out in a closed system (nothing enters or leaves) and the rate of the forward reaction is equal to the rate of the reverse reaction, the reaction is said to have reached **equilibrium**.

HT Equilibrium conditions

The relative amounts of reactants and products at equilibrium depend on the **reaction conditions**. The effect of changing conditions on reactions at equilibrium can be predicted by Le Chatelier's principle, which states that 'for a reversible reaction, if changes are made to the concentration, temperature or pressure (for gaseous reactions) then the system responds to counteract the change'.

Changing concentration

If the concentration of one of the reactants is increased, more products will be formed (to use up the extra reactant) until equilibrium is established again (i.e. the equilibrium moves to the right until a new equilibrium is established). Similarly, if the concentration of one of the products is increased, more reactants will be formed (i.e. the equilibrium moves to the left until a new equilibrium is established).

Changing temperature

Forward reaction	Effect of increasing temperature	Effect of decreasing temperature
Endothermic	Equilibrium moves to right-hand side (i.e. forward reaction)	Equilibrium moves to left-hand side (i.e. reverse reaction)
Exothermic	Equilibrium moves to left-hand side	Equilibrium moves to right-hand side

Changing pressure

In order to predict the effect of changing pressure, the number of molecules of gas on each side of the equation needs to be known:

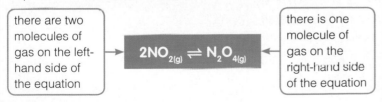

there are two molecules of gas on the left-hand side of the equation

$$2NO_{2(g)} \rightleftharpoons N_2O_{4(g)}$$

there is one molecule of gas on the right-hand side of the equation

If the pressure on a reaction at equilibrium is **increased**, the equilibrium shifts to the side of the equation with the **fewer** molecules of gas. In this case, increasing the pressure will shift the reaction to the right-hand side (i.e. producing more N_2O_4).

1. Which symbol is used to represent a reversible reaction?
2. The forward reaction in a reversible reaction is exothermic. Is the reverse reaction exothermic or endothermic?
HT 3. Consider the following reaction at equilibrium.

$$N_{2(g)} + 3H_{2(g)} \rightleftharpoons 2NH_{3(g)}$$

What is the effect on the amount of nitrogen at equilibrium of...
   a) Increasing the concentration of hydrogen?
   b) Increasing the pressure?

Mind map

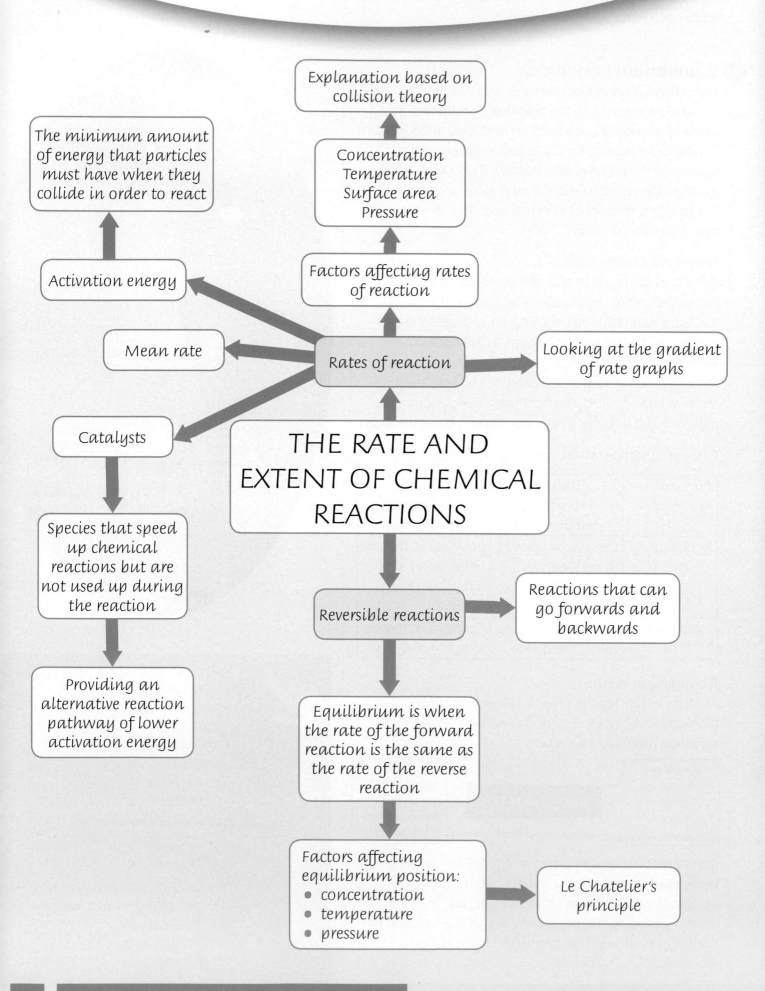

Explanation based on collision theory

The minimum amount of energy that particles must have when they collide in order to react

Concentration
Temperature
Surface area
Pressure

Activation energy

Factors affecting rates of reaction

Mean rate

Rates of reaction

Looking at the gradient of rate graphs

Catalysts

THE RATE AND EXTENT OF CHEMICAL REACTIONS

Species that speed up chemical reactions but are not used up during the reaction

Reversible reactions

Reactions that can go forwards and backwards

Providing an alternative reaction pathway of lower activation energy

Equilibrium is when the rate of the forward reaction is the same as the rate of the reverse reaction

Factors affecting equilibrium position:
- concentration
- temperature
- pressure

Le Chatelier's principle

Practice questions

1. A student was investigating the rate of reaction between magnesium and hydrochloric acid. He measured out a 0.25 g strip of magnesium metal and then added it to 25 cm³ of acid in a conical flask. A gas syringe was attached as shown in the diagram.

   The volume of hydrogen collected was recorded every 10 seconds. A graph of the student's results is shown below.

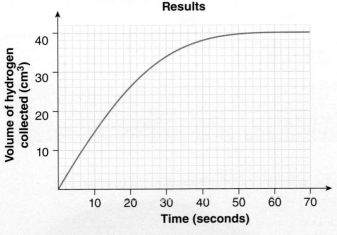

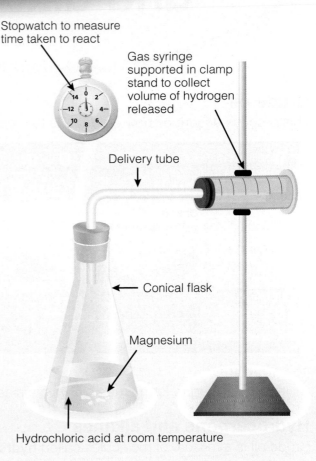

Stopwatch to measure time taken to react

Gas syringe supported in clamp stand to collect volume of hydrogen released

Delivery tube

Conical flask

Magnesium

Hydrochloric acid at room temperature

   a) How long did the reaction take to finish? Explain your answer. **(2 marks)**

   b) Using your answer to part **a**, calculate the mean rate of reaction. **(2 marks)**

   c) How can you tell from the graph that the rate of reaction was faster after 10 seconds than it was after 40 seconds? **(1 mark)**

   d) The student then repeated the experiment using 0.25 g of magnesium powder instead of magnesium ribbon. Everything else was kept the same. Sketch on the graph the curve that the results from this experiment would have produced. **(2 marks)**

   e) The student predicted that carrying out the experiment with a higher concentration of acid would have increased the rate of reaction. Explain why he is correct. **(2 marks)**

2. Hydrogen for use in the Haber process or in fuel cells can be produced from methane and water according to the equation below.

$$CH_{4(g)} + H_2O_{(g)} \rightleftharpoons CO_{(g)} + 3H_{2(g)}$$

   The forward reaction is endothermic.

   a) How can you tell that this process is carried out at a temperature above 100°C? **(1 mark)**

   b) What does the $\rightleftharpoons$ symbol tell you about the reaction? **(1 mark)**

   c) Explain why increasing the pressure on the equilibrium mixture will decrease the yield of hydrogen. **(1 mark)**

   d) State and explain the effect on the yield of hydrogen of increasing the temperature of the equilibrium mixture. **(2 marks)**

Crude oil, hydrocarbons and alkanes

Keywords

Hydrocarbon ➤ A molecule containing hydrogen and carbon atoms only

Fractional distillation ➤ A method used to separate mixtures of liquids

Crude oil

This process describes how crude oil is formed.

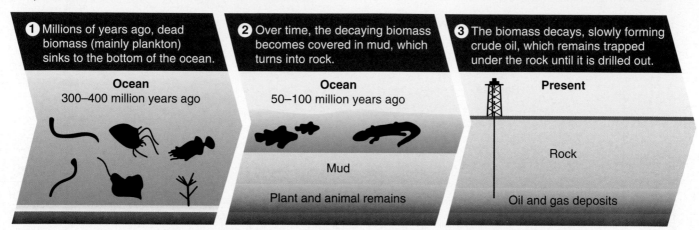

1 Millions of years ago, dead biomass (mainly plankton) sinks to the bottom of the ocean.

Ocean
300–400 million years ago

2 Over time, the decaying biomass becomes covered in mud, which turns into rock.

Ocean
50–100 million years ago

Mud

Plant and animal remains

3 The biomass decays, slowly forming crude oil, which remains trapped under the rock until it is drilled out.

Present

Rock

Oil and gas deposits

As it takes so long to form crude oil, we consider it to be a finite or non-renewable resource.

Hydrocarbons and alkanes

Crude oil is a mixture of molecules called **hydrocarbons**. Most hydrocarbons are members of a homologous series of molecules called alkanes.

Members of an homologous series…

➤ have the same general formula
➤ differ by CH_2 in their molecular formula from neighbouring compounds
➤ show a gradual trend in physical properties, e.g. boiling point
➤ have similar chemical properties.

Alkanes are hydrocarbons that have the general formula C_nH_{2n+2}.

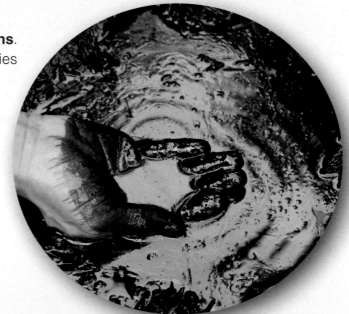

Alkane	Methane, CH_4	Ethane, C_2H_6	Propane, C_3H_8	Butane, C_4H_{10}
Displayed formula	H | H – C – H | H	H H | | H – C – C – H | | H H	H H H | | | H – C – C – C – H | | | H H H	H H H H | | | | H – C – C – C – C – H | | | | H H H H

Make up your own mnemonic to remember the different fractions in a fractionating column.

Fractional distillation

Crude oil on its own is relatively useless. It is separated into more useful components (called fractions) by **fractional distillation**. The larger the molecule, the stronger the intermolecular forces and so the higher the boiling point.

Crude oil is heated until it evaporates.

It then enters a fractionating column which is hotter at the bottom than at the top

where the molecules condense at different temperatures.

Groups of molecules with similar boiling points are collected together. They are called fractions.

The fractions are sent for processing to produce fuels and feedstock (raw materials) for the petrochemical industry

which produces many useful materials, e.g. solvents, lubricants, detergents and polymers (plastics).

Fractionating column

Cool (approximately 25°C)

Refinery gases / LPG (bottled gas)

Petrol (fuel for cars)

Naphtha (making other chemicals)

Kerosene / paraffin (aircraft fuel)

Diesel (fuel for cars / lorries / buses)

Heated crude oil

Fuel oil (fuel for power stations / ships)

Bitumen (tar for roofs and roads)

Hot (approximately 350°C)

Small molecules

Low boiling point

Low viscosity

Burn easily

Large molecules

High boiling point

High viscosity

Don't burn easily

1. What is crude oil formed from?
2. What are hydrocarbons?
3. What is the molecular formula of propane?
4. By what process is crude oil separated?

Combustion and cracking of hydrocarbons

Combustion of hydrocarbons

Some of the fractions of crude oil (e.g. petrol and kerosene) are used as fuels. Burning these fuels releases energy. Combustion (burning) reactions are oxidation reactions. When the fuel is fully combusted, the carbon in the hydrocarbons is oxidised to carbon dioxide and the hydrogen is oxidised to water.

For example, the combustion of methane:

$$CH_{4(g)} + 2O_{2(g)} \rightarrow CO_{2(g)} + 2H_2O_{(l)}$$

Cracking and alkenes

Many of the long-chain hydrocarbons found in crude oil are not very useful. **Cracking** is the process of turning a long-chain hydrocarbon into shorter, more useful ones.

Cracking is done by passing hydrocarbon vapour over a hot catalyst or mixing the hydrocarbon vapour with steam before heating it to a very high temperature.

The diagram shows how cracking can be carried out in the laboratory.

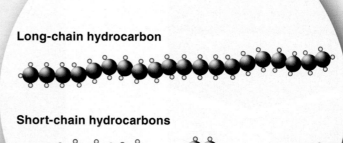

Long-chain hydrocarbon

Short-chain hydrocarbons

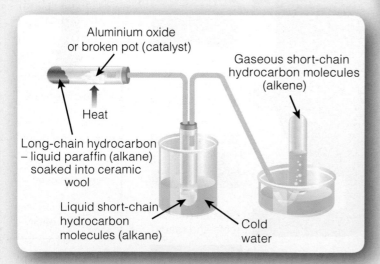

Aluminium oxide or broken pot (catalyst)

Gaseous short-chain hydrocarbon molecules (alkene)

Heat

Long-chain hydrocarbon – liquid paraffin (alkane) soaked into ceramic wool

Liquid short-chain hydrocarbon molecules (alkane)

Cold water

Cracking produces **alkanes** and **alkenes**. The small-molecule alkanes that are formed during cracking are in high demand as fuels. The alkenes (which are more reactive than alkanes) are mostly used to make plastics by the process of polymerisation and as starting materials for the production of many other chemicals.

Keywords

Cracking ➤ A process used to break up large hydrocarbon molecules into smaller, more useful molecules.
Alkane ➤ Hydrocarbons that have the general formula C_nH_{2n+2}
Alkene ➤ Hydrocarbons that contain a carbon–carbon double bond

There are many different equations that can represent cracking. This is because the long hydrocarbon can break in many different places.
A typical equation for the cracking of the hydrocarbon decane ($C_{10}H_{22}$) is:

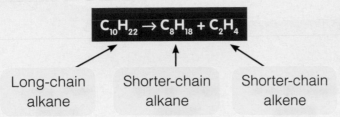

$$C_{10}H_{22} \rightarrow C_8H_{18} + C_2H_4$$

Long-chain alkane | Shorter-chain alkane | Shorter-chain alkene

Example: The cracking of dodecane ($C_{12}H_{26}$) forms one molecule of ethene (C_2H_4), one molecule of butane (C_4H_{10}) and two molecules of another hydrocarbon, as shown in the equation below:

$$C_{12}H_{26} \rightarrow C_2H_4 + C_4H_{10} + 2 \ldots\ldots\ldots\ldots$$

Complete the equation for the cracking of dodecane ($C_{12}H_{26}$) by working out the molecular formula of the other hydrocarbon formed.

There are 12 carbon atoms on the left-hand side of the equation and only 6 on the right (2 + 4). Therefore, the two molecules of hydrocarbon must contain 6 carbon atoms in total, i.e. 3 carbon atoms per molecule.

There are 26 hydrogen atoms on the left-hand side of the equation and only 14 on the right (4 + 10). Therefore, the two molecules of hydrocarbon must contain 12 hydrogen atoms in total, i.e. 6 hydrogen atoms per molecule.

Therefore, the molecular formula of the missing hydrocarbon is C_3H_6 and the completed equation is:

$$C_{12}H_{26} \rightarrow C_2H_4 + C_4H_{10} + 2C_3H_6$$

The presence of alkenes can be detected using bromine water. Alkenes decolourise bromine water but when it is mixed with alkanes, the bromine water stays orange.

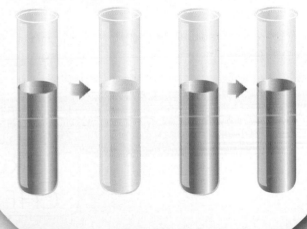

Unsaturated alkene (C=C) + bromine water   Saturated alkane (C–C) + bromine water

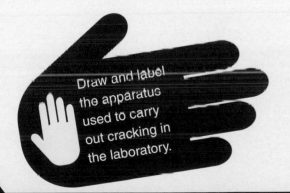

Draw and label the apparatus used to carry out cracking in the laboratory.

1. Write a balanced symbol equation for the complete combustion of ethane, C_2H_6.
2. In this equation, give the formula for the missing hydrocarbon formed by the cracking of octane: $C_8H_{18\,(g)} \rightarrow 2C_2H_{4\,(g)} +$ _____
3. As well as using a catalyst, how else can cracking be carried out?
4. What is the chemical test and observation for alkenes?
5. What is the main use of alkenes?

Mind map

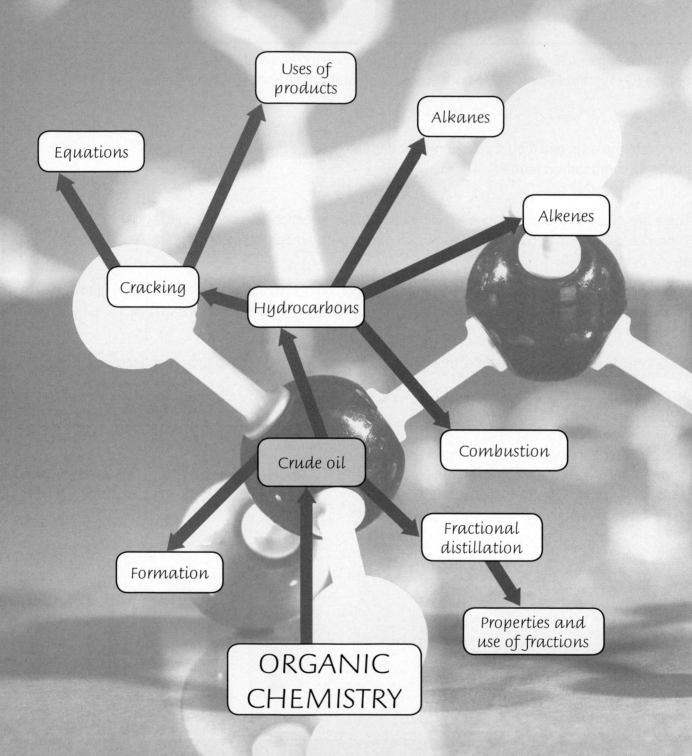

Uses of products

Equations

Alkanes

Alkenes

Cracking

Hydrocarbons

Combustion

Crude oil

Formation

Fractional distillation

Properties and use of fractions

ORGANIC CHEMISTRY

Practice questions

1. Crude oil is extracted from the earth by drilling and then it is separated into useful components. Some of the alkanes found in crude oil undergo further processing to make them more useful in a process called cracking.

   a) Describe the stages in the formation of crude oil. **(3 marks)**

   b) What is the name of the process by which crude oil is separated and by what property are the molecules in crude oil separated? **(2 marks)**

   c) What are alkanes? **(2 marks)**

   d) Why is cracking an important process? **(2 marks)**

   e) State one way in which cracking can be carried out. **(1 mark)**

   f) The hydrocarbon dodecane ($C_{12}H_{26}$) can be cracked to produce two molecules of ethene (C_2H_4) and one other molecule. Complete the equation below stating the formula of this other product.

   $$C_{12}H_{26} \rightarrow 2C_2H_4 + \text{.............................}$$ **(1 mark)**

2. Kerosene and bitumen are two fractions found in crude oil. Molecules in the kerosene fraction typically have between 11 and 18 carbon atoms. Molecules in the bitumen fraction typically have more than 35 carbon atoms.

   a) State a use for kerosene and bitumen. **(2 marks)**

   b) Which fraction, kerosene or bitumen, would you expect to be the most viscous? **(1 mark)**

   c) Which fraction, kerosene or bitumen, would you expect to be the most flammable? **(1 mark)**

   d) Which fraction, kerosene or bitumen, would you expect to have the highest boiling temperature? Explain your answer. **(2 marks)**

3. Alkanes are a homologous series of hydrocarbons with the general formula C_nH_{2n+2}.

   a) What are hydrocarbons? **(2 marks)**

   b) Other than the same general formula, give two other characteristics of members of the same homologous series. **(2 marks)**

   c) How many carbon atoms are there in the alkane containing 36 hydrogen atoms? **(1 mark)**

   d) Draw the displayed formula of the alkane containing 3 carbon atoms. **(1 mark)**

   e) Write a balanced symbol equation for the complete combustion of butane (C_4H_{10}). **(2 marks)**

   f) Another homologous series of hydrocarbons are the alkenes. Describe how you could chemically distinguish between an alkane and an alkene. **(3 marks)**

Purity, formulations and chromatography

Keywords

Formulation ➤ A mixture that has been designed as a useful product

Chromatography ➤ A method of separating mixtures of dyes

Purity

In everyday language, a pure substance can mean a substance that has had nothing added to it (i.e. in its natural state), such as milk.

In chemistry, a pure substance is a single element or compound (i.e. not mixed with any other substance).

Pure elements and compounds melt and boil at specific temperatures. For example, pure water freezes at 0°C and boils at 100°C. However, if something is added to water (e.g. salt) then the freezing point decreases (i.e. goes below 0°C) and the boiling point rises above 100°C.

Formulations

A **formulation** is a mixture that has been designed as a useful product. Many formulations are complex mixtures in which each ingredient has a specific purpose.

Formulations are made by mixing the individual components in carefully measured quantities to ensure that the product has the correct properties.

Fuels

Cleaning materials

Fertilisers

Examples of formulations

Paints

Foods

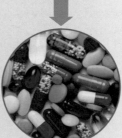
Medicines

Find five items at home or in a supermarket that are described as 'pure'. Look at their composition (e.g. from a food label) and decide whether they are chemically pure.

Chromatography

Chromatography is used to separate mixtures of dyes. It is used to help identify substances.

In paper chromatography, a solvent (the mobile phase) moves up the paper (the stationary phase) carrying different components of the mixture different distances, depending on their attraction for the paper and the solvent. In thin layer chromatography (TLC), the stationary phase is a thin layer of an inert substance (e.g. silica) supported on a flat, unreactive surface (e.g. a glass plate).

In the chromatogram on the right, substance X is being analysed and compared with samples A, B, C, D and E.

It can be seen from the chromatogram that substance X has the same pattern of spots as sample D. This means that sample X and sample D are the same substance. Pure compounds (e.g. compound A) will only produce one spot on a chromatogram.

The ratio of the distance moved by the compound to the distance moved by the solvent is known as its R_f value.

$$R_f = \frac{\text{distance moved by substance}}{\text{distance moved by solvent}}$$

Different compounds have different R_f values in different solvents. This can be used to help identify unknown compounds by comparing R_f values with known substances.

In this case, the R_f value is $0.73 \left(\frac{4.0}{5.5}\right)$ →

In **gas chromatography** (GC), the mobile phase is an inert gas (e.g. helium). The stationary phase is a very thin layer of an inert liquid on a solid support, such as beads of silica packed into a long thin tube. GC is a more sensitive method than TLC for separating mixtures, and it allows you to determine the amount of each chemical in the mixture.

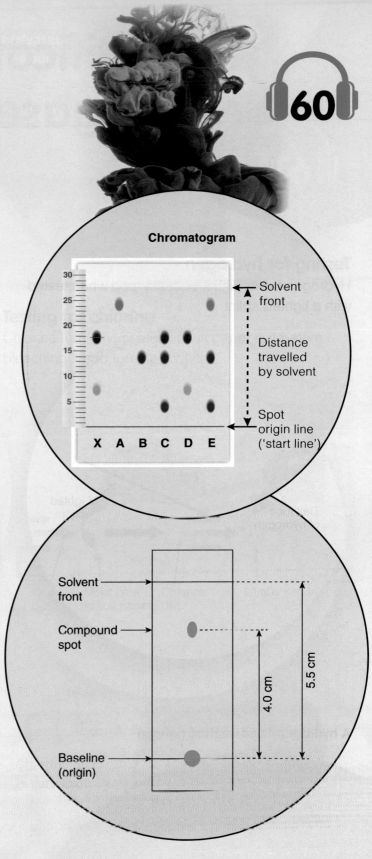

Chromatogram

1. In chemistry what is meant by the term 'pure substance'?
2. What is a formulation?
3. Give two examples of substances that are formulations.
4. In a chromatogram, the solvent travelled 6 cm and a dye travelled 3.3 cm. What is the R_f value of the dye?

Mind map

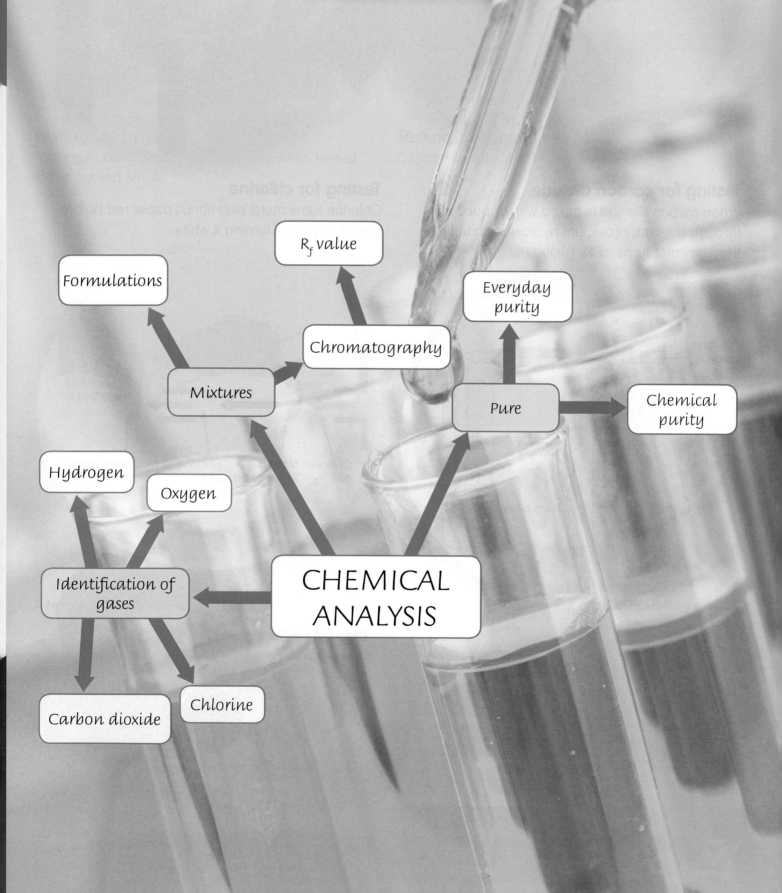

Formulations

R$_f$ value

Everyday purity

Chromatography

Mixtures

Pure

Chemical purity

Hydrogen

Oxygen

Identification of gases

CHEMICAL ANALYSIS

Carbon dioxide

Chlorine

Practice questions

1. Shown below is a chromatogram for four dyes (W, X, Y and Z) and three coloured inks (blue, red and yellow). Each ink is made up of a single compound.

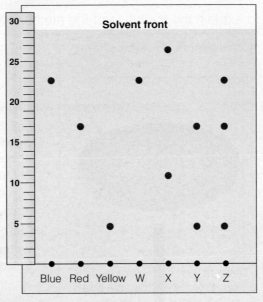

a) Which one of the dyes contains three colours?
   Explain your answer. **(2 marks)**

b) Which dyes contain blue ink? **(1 mark)**

c) Which two coloured inks are present in dye Y? **(1 mark)**

d) Which dye doesn't contain blue, red or yellow ink?
   Explain your answer. **(2 marks)**

e) Calculate the R_f value for the blue ink. **(2 marks)**

f) Which dye is chemically pure?
   Explain your answer. **(2 marks)**

g) Many industrial dyes are formulations. What is meant by the term 'formulation'? **(1 mark)**

2. Complete the table below **(8 marks)**

Gas	Test	Observation
		A 'squeaky pop' is heard
Oxygen		
	Add moist blue litmus paper	
	Add limewater	

Evolution of the atmosphere

The Earth's early atmosphere

Theories about the composition of Earth's early atmosphere and how the atmosphere was formed have changed over time. Evidence for the early atmosphere is limited because the Earth is approximately 4.6 billion years old.

The table below gives one theory to explain the evolution of the atmosphere.

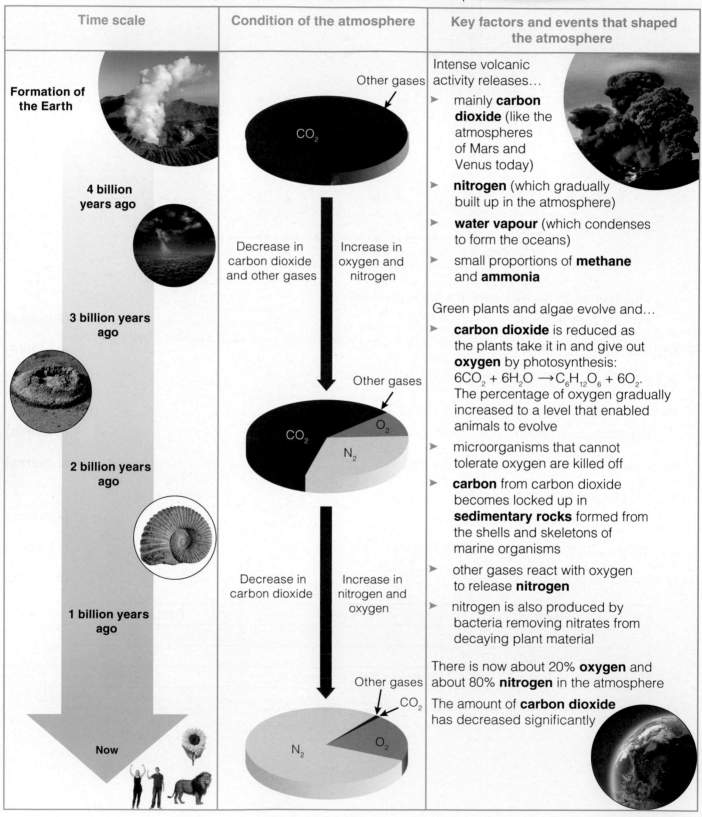

Time scale	Condition of the atmosphere	Key factors and events that shaped the atmosphere
Formation of the Earth	Other gases — CO_2	Intense volcanic activity releases…
4 billion years ago	Decrease in carbon dioxide and other gases / Increase in oxygen and nitrogen	▶ mainly **carbon dioxide** (like the atmospheres of Mars and Venus today) ▶ **nitrogen** (which gradually built up in the atmosphere) ▶ **water vapour** (which condenses to form the oceans) ▶ small proportions of **methane** and **ammonia**
3 billion years ago	Other gases — O_2, CO_2, N_2	Green plants and algae evolve and… ▶ **carbon dioxide** is reduced as the plants take it in and give out **oxygen** by photosynthesis: $6CO_2 + 6H_2O \rightarrow C_6H_{12}O_6 + 6O_2$. The percentage of oxygen gradually increased to a level that enabled animals to evolve ▶ microorganisms that cannot tolerate oxygen are killed off
2 billion years ago	Decrease in carbon dioxide / Increase in nitrogen and oxygen	▶ **carbon** from carbon dioxide becomes locked up in **sedimentary rocks** formed from the shells and skeletons of marine organisms ▶ other gases react with oxygen to release **nitrogen** ▶ nitrogen is also produced by bacteria removing nitrates from decaying plant material
1 billion years ago	Other gases — CO_2, N_2, O_2	There is now about 20% **oxygen** and about 80% **nitrogen** in the atmosphere The amount of **carbon dioxide** has decreased significantly
Now		

Composition of the atmosphere today

The proportions of gases in the atmosphere have been more or less the same for about 200 million years. **Water vapour** may also be present in varying quantities (0–3%).

Mainly argon, plus other noble gases (1%)

Carbon dioxide, CO_2 (0.03%)

Oxygen, O_2 (21%)

Nitrogen, N_2 (78%)

Keyword

Photosynthesis ➤ The process by which green plants and algae use water and carbon dioxide to make glucose and oxygen

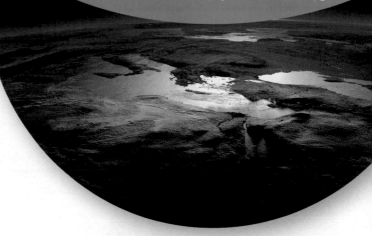

How carbon dioxide decreased

The amount of carbon dioxide in the atmosphere today is much less than it was when the atmosphere first formed. This is because…

➤ green plants and algae use carbon dioxide for **photosynthesis**

Make a timeline showing the key changes in the evolution of the Earth's atmosphere.

➤ carbon dioxide is used to form sedimentary rocks, e.g. limestone

➤ fossil fuels such as oil (see Module 58) and coal (a sedimentary rock made from thick plant deposits that were buried and compressed over millions of years) have captured CO_2.

1. Name two gases that volcanoes released into the early atmosphere.
2. How did oxygen become present in the atmosphere?
3. How much of the atmosphere today is nitrogen gas?
4. State two ways that the amount of carbon dioxide present in the early atmosphere decreased.

Climate change

ⓌⓈ Human activity and global warming

Some human activities increase the amounts of greenhouse gases in the atmosphere including…

Combustion of fossil fuels releases carbon dioxide into the atmosphere

Increased animal farming releases more methane into the atmosphere, e.g. as a by-product of digestion and decomposition of waste

Deforestation reduces the amount of carbon dioxide removed from the atmosphere by photosynthesis

Decomposition of rubbish in landfill sites also releases methane into the atmosphere

Greenhouse gases

The temperature on Earth is maintained at a level to support life by the greenhouse gases in the atmosphere. These gases allow short wavelength radiation from the Sun to pass through but absorb the long wavelength radiation reflected back from the ground trapping heat and causing an increase in temperature. Common greenhouse gases are water vapour, carbon dioxide and methane.

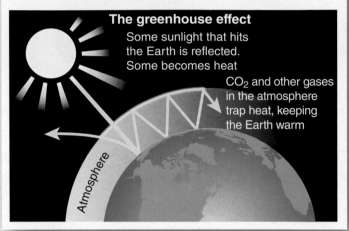

The greenhouse effect

Some sunlight that hits the Earth is reflected. Some becomes heat

CO_2 and other gases in the atmosphere trap heat, keeping the Earth warm

Atmosphere

The increase in carbon dioxide levels in the last century or so correlates with the increased use of fossil fuels by humans.

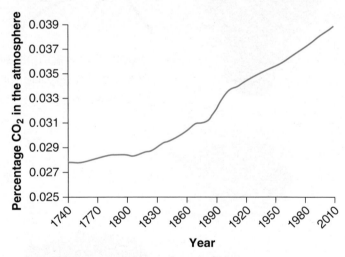

Based on **peer-reviewed evidence**, many scientists believe that increasing these human activities will lead to global climate change.

Predicting the impact of changes on global climate change is not easy because of the many different contributing factors involved. This can lead to simplified models and speculation often presented in the media that may not be based on all of the evidence. This means that the information could be biased.

Increased human activity resulting in more release of fossil fuels ➤ Increased temperatures ➤ Global climate change

Global climate change

Increasing average global temperature is a major cause of climate change. Potential effects of climate change include:

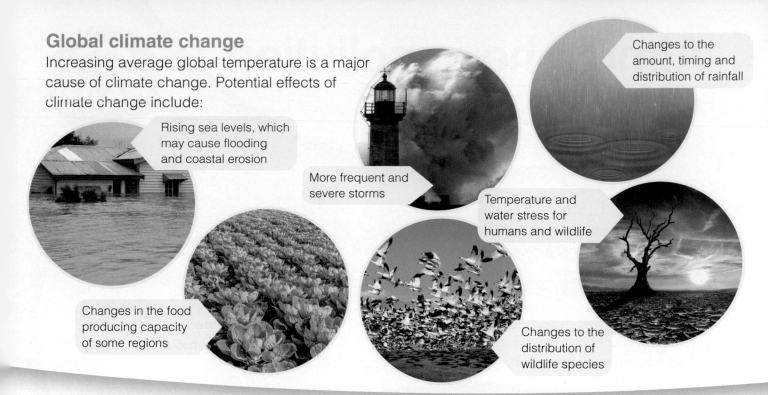

Rising sea levels, which may cause flooding and coastal erosion

Changes to the amount, timing and distribution of rainfall

More frequent and severe storms

Temperature and water stress for humans and wildlife

Changes in the food producing capacity of some regions

Changes to the distribution of wildlife species

(ws) Reducing the carbon footprint

The **carbon footprint** is a measure of the total amount of carbon dioxide (and other greenhouse gases) emitted over the life cycle of a product, service or event.

Problems of trying to reduce the carbon footprint include…

➤ disagreement over the causes and consequences of global climate change
➤ lack of public information and education
➤ lifestyle changes, e.g. greater use of cars / aeroplanes
➤ economic considerations, i.e. the financial costs of reducing the carbon footprint
➤ incomplete international co-operation.

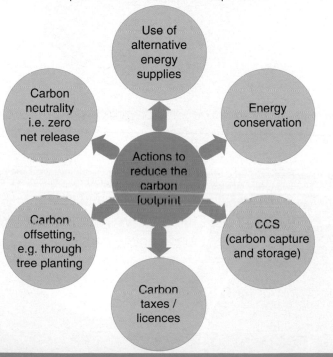

Use of alternative energy supplies

Carbon neutrality i.e. zero net release

Energy conservation

Actions to reduce the carbon footprint

Carbon offsetting, e.g. through tree planting

CCS (carbon capture and storage)

Carbon taxes / licences

Produce a leaflet informing members of the public about how they can reduce their own carbon footprint.

Keywords

Peer-reviewed evidence ➤ Work (evidence) of scientists that has been checked by other scientists to ensure that it is accurate and scientifically valid
Carbon footprint ➤ The total amount of carbon dioxide (and other greenhouse gases) emitted over the full life cycle of a product, service or event

1. Name two greenhouse gases.
2. State one way that human activity leads to an increased amount of methane in the atmosphere.
3. Give two potential effects of global climate change.
4. Give an example of one problem of trying to reduce the carbon footprint.

63

Atmospheric pollution

Pollutants from fuels

The combustion of **fossil fuels** is a major source of atmospheric pollutants. Most fuels contain carbon and often sulfur is present as an impurity. Many different gases are released into the atmosphere when a fuel is burned.

Solid particles and unburned hydrocarbons can also be released forming **particulates** in the air.

Gases produced by burning fuels

- carbon monoxide
- carbon dioxide
- oxides of nitrogen
- water vapour
- sulfur dioxide

Sulfur dioxide is produced by the oxidation of sulfur present in fuels – often from coal-burning power stations

Carbon monoxide and soot (carbon) are produced by incomplete combustion of fuels

Oxides of nitrogen are formed from the reaction between nitrogen and oxygen from the air – often from the high temperatures and sparks in the engines of motor vehicles

Keywords

Fossil fuel ➤ Fuel formed in the ground over millions of years from the remains of dead plants and animal

Particulates ➤ Small solid particles present in the air

Properties and effects of atmospheric pollutants

Carbon monoxide is a colourless, odourless toxic gas and so it is difficult to detect. It combines with haemoglobin in the blood, which reduces the oxygen-carrying capacity of blood.

Sulfur dioxide and **oxides of nitrogen** cause respiratory problems in humans and can form acid rain in the atmosphere. Acid rain damages plants and buildings.

Particulates in the atmosphere can cause global dimming, which reduces the amount of sunlight that reaches the Earth's surface. Breathing in particulates can also damage lungs, which can cause health problems.

Make a list of all of the ways in one day that you see waste gases being released into the atmosphere.

1. Name two gases produced by burning fuels.
2. How is carbon monoxide formed?
3. What problems do atmospheric sulfur dioxide and oxides of nitrogen cause?

Using the Earth's resources and obtaining potable water

Keywords

Sustainable development ➤ Living in a way that meets the needs of the current generation without compromising the potential of future generations to meet their own needs

Potable water ➤ Water that is safe to drink

Earth's resources

We use the Earth's **resources** to provide us with warmth, shelter, food and transport. These needs are met from natural resources which, supplemented by agriculture, provide food, timber, clothing and fuels. Resources from the earth, atmosphere and oceans are processed to provide energy and materials.

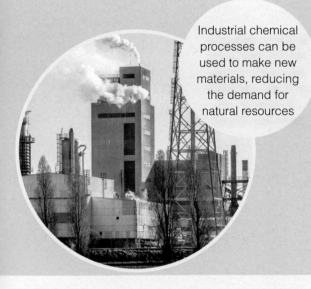

Industrial chemical processes can be used to make new materials, reducing the demand for natural resources

Chemistry plays a role in providing **sustainable development**. This means that the needs of the current generation are met without compromising the potential of future generations to meet their own needs. For example…

Chemistry plays an important role in improving agricultural processes, e.g. by developing fertilisers

Drinking water

Water that is safe to drink is called **potable water**. It is not pure in the chemical sense (see Module 60) because it contains dissolved minerals and ions.

Water of appropriate quality is essential for life. This means that it contains sufficiently low levels of dissolved salts and microbes.

In the UK, most potable water comes from rainwater. To turn rainwater into potable water, water companies carry out a number of processes.

1. An appropriate source of fresh water is selected

2. It is then passed through filter beds to remove any solid impurities

3. Finally it is sterilised (suitable sterilising agents include chlorine, ozone and ultraviolet light) to kill microbes, making it safe to drink

Waste water

Urban lifestyles and industrial processes generate large quantities of waste water, which requires treatment before being released into the environment. Sewage and agricultural waste water require removal of organic matter and harmful microbes. Industrial waste water may require removal of organic matter and harmful chemicals.

Sewage treatment includes...
➤ screening and grit removal
➤ sedimentation to produce sewage sludge and effluent
➤ anaerobic digestion of sewage sludge
➤ aerobic biological treatment of effluent.

When supplies of fresh water are limited, removal of salt (desalination) of salty water / seawater can be used.

This is done in two ways:

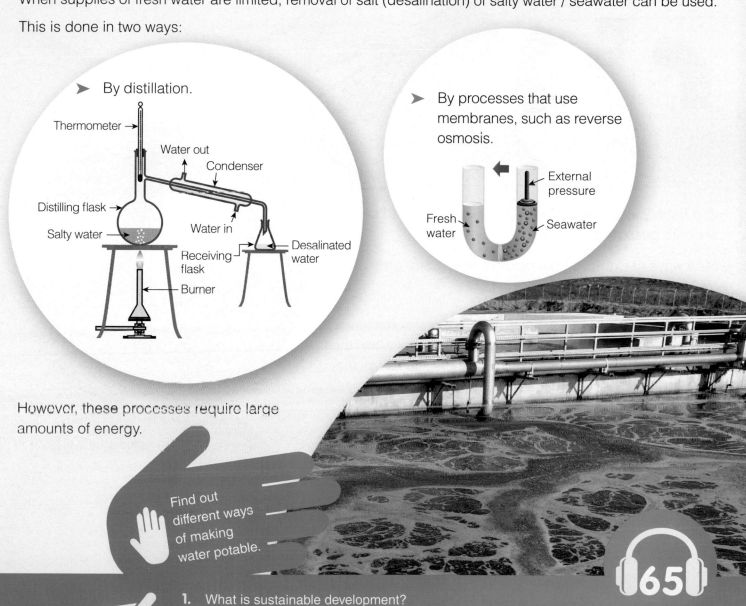

➤ By distillation.

Thermometer
Water out
Condenser
Distilling flask
Salty water
Water in
Receiving flask
Desalinated water
Burner

➤ By processes that use membranes, such as reverse osmosis.

External pressure
Fresh water
Seawater

However, these processes require large amounts of energy.

Find out different ways of making water potable.

1. What is sustainable development?
2. State the difference between pure water and potable water.
3. What are the two main stages in turning rainwater into potable water?
4. Name one way of desalinating salty water.

Alternative methods of extracting metals

HT

copper ore

Extracting copper

Copper is an important metal with lots of uses. It is used in electrical wiring because it is an excellent conductor of electricity. It is also used in water pipes because it conducts heat and does not corrode or react with the water.

The Earth's resources of metal **ores** are limited and copper ores are becoming scarce.

New ways of extracting copper from **low-grade ores** include…

➤ **phytomining**
Phytomining uses plants to absorb metal compounds. This means that the plants accumulate metal within them. Harvesting and then burning the plants leaves ash that is rich in the metal compounds.

➤ **bioleaching**
Bioleaching uses bacteria to extract metals from low-grade ores. A solution containing bacteria is mixed with a low-grade ore. The bacteria release the metals into solution (known as a leachate) where they can be easily extracted.

These new extraction methods reduce the impact on the Earth of mining, moving and disposing of large amounts of rock.

Processing metal compounds

The metal compounds from phytomining and bioleaching are processed to obtain the metal. Copper can be obtained from solutions of copper compounds by…

➤ **displacement** using scrap iron – iron is more reactive than copper, so placing iron into a solution of copper will result in copper metal being displaced.

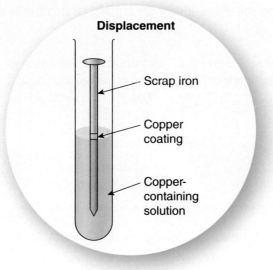

Displacement

- Scrap iron
- Copper coating
- Copper-containing solution

➤ **electrolysis**.

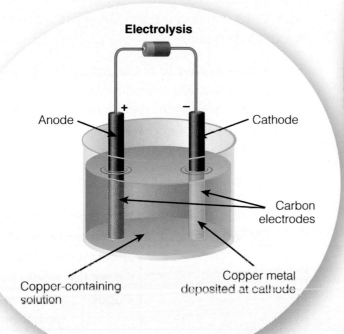

Electrolysis

- Anode
- Cathode
- Carbon electrodes
- Copper-containing solution
- Copper metal deposited at cathode

Keywords

Ore ➤ A naturally occurring mineral from which it is economically viable to extract a metal

Low-grade ores ➤ Ores that contain small amounts of metal

Phytomining ➤ A method of metal extraction that involves growing plants in metal solutions so that they accumulate metal; the plants are then burnt and the metal extracted from the ash

Bioleaching ➤ An extraction method that uses bacteria to extract metals from low-grade ores

Find examples of copper being used in your home.
Think what properties of copper make it suitable for that use.

66

1. State one use of copper.
2. Why is it important to develop new ways of extracting metals?
3. Which biological method of extracting metals involves bacteria?
4. Give one way that metal can be extracted from a metal containing solution.

Life-cycle assessment and recycling

Life-cycle assessments

Life-cycle assessments (LCAs) are carried out to evaluate the environmental impact of products in each of the following stages.

| Extracting and processing raw materials | Manufacturing and packaging | Disposal at the end of useful life | Transport and distribution at each of the previous stages |

The following steps are considered when carrying out an LCA.

- How much energy is needed?
- How much water is used?
- How much pollution is produced?
- What resources are required?
- How much waste is produced?

Life-cycle assessment

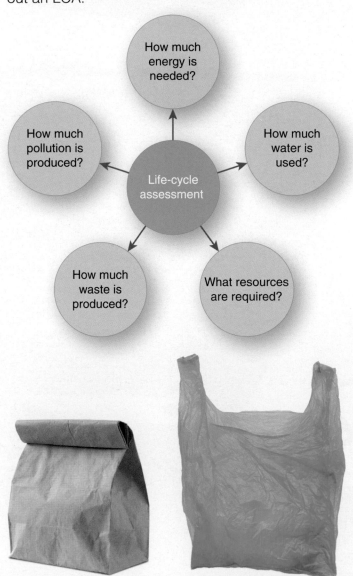

Many of these values are relatively easy to quantify. However, some values, such as the amount of pollution, are often difficult to measure and so value judgements have to be made. This means that carrying out an LCA is not a purely objective process.

It is not always easy to obtain accurate figures. This means that selective or abbreviated LCAs, which are open to bias or misuse, can be devised to evaluate a product, to reinforce predetermined conclusions or to support claims for advertising purposes.

For example, look at the LCA below.

Example of an LCA for the use of plastic (polythene) and paper shopping bags		
	Amount per 1000 bags over the whole LCA	
	Paper	**Plastic (polythene)**
Energy use (MJ)	2590	713
Fossil fuel use (Kg)	28	13
Solid waste (Kg)	34	6
Greenhouse gas emissions (kg CO_2)	72	36
Freshwater use (litres)	3387	198

This LCA provides evidence supporting the argument that using polythene bags is better for the environment than paper bags!

Ways of reducing the use of resources

- Re-use
- Reduction in use
- Recycling
- Reduces use of resources
- Use and limited resources
- Waste and environmental impacts
- Energy consumption

Keywords

Life-cycle assessment ➤ An evaluation of the environmental impact of a product over the whole of its lifespan
Blast furnace ➤ Industrial method of extracting iron from iron ore

Quarrying

Many materials such as glass, metals, building materials, plastics and clay ceramics are produced from limited raw materials. Most of the energy used in their production comes from limited resources, such as fossil fuels. Obtaining raw materials from the earth by quarrying and mining has a detrimental environmental impact.

Some products, like glass, can be **reused** (e.g. washing and then using again for the same purpose). Recycled glass is crushed, melted and remade into glass products.

Recycling

Other products cannot be reused and so they are **recycled** for a different use.

Metals are recycled by sorting them, followed by melting them and recasting / reforming them into different products. The amount of separation required for recycling depends on the material (e.g. whether they are magnetic or not) and the properties required of the final product. For example, some scrap steel can be added to iron from a **blast furnace** to reduce the amount of iron that needs to be extracted from iron ore.

Blast furnace

Try to identify the environmental impact of this book by considering the effects of all of the stages of its life cycle.

1. What does a life-cycle assessment measure?
2. State two factors that a life-cycle assessment tries to evaluate.
3. Why are life-cycle assessments not always totally objective?
4. State one way in which we can reduce the use of resources.

Mind map

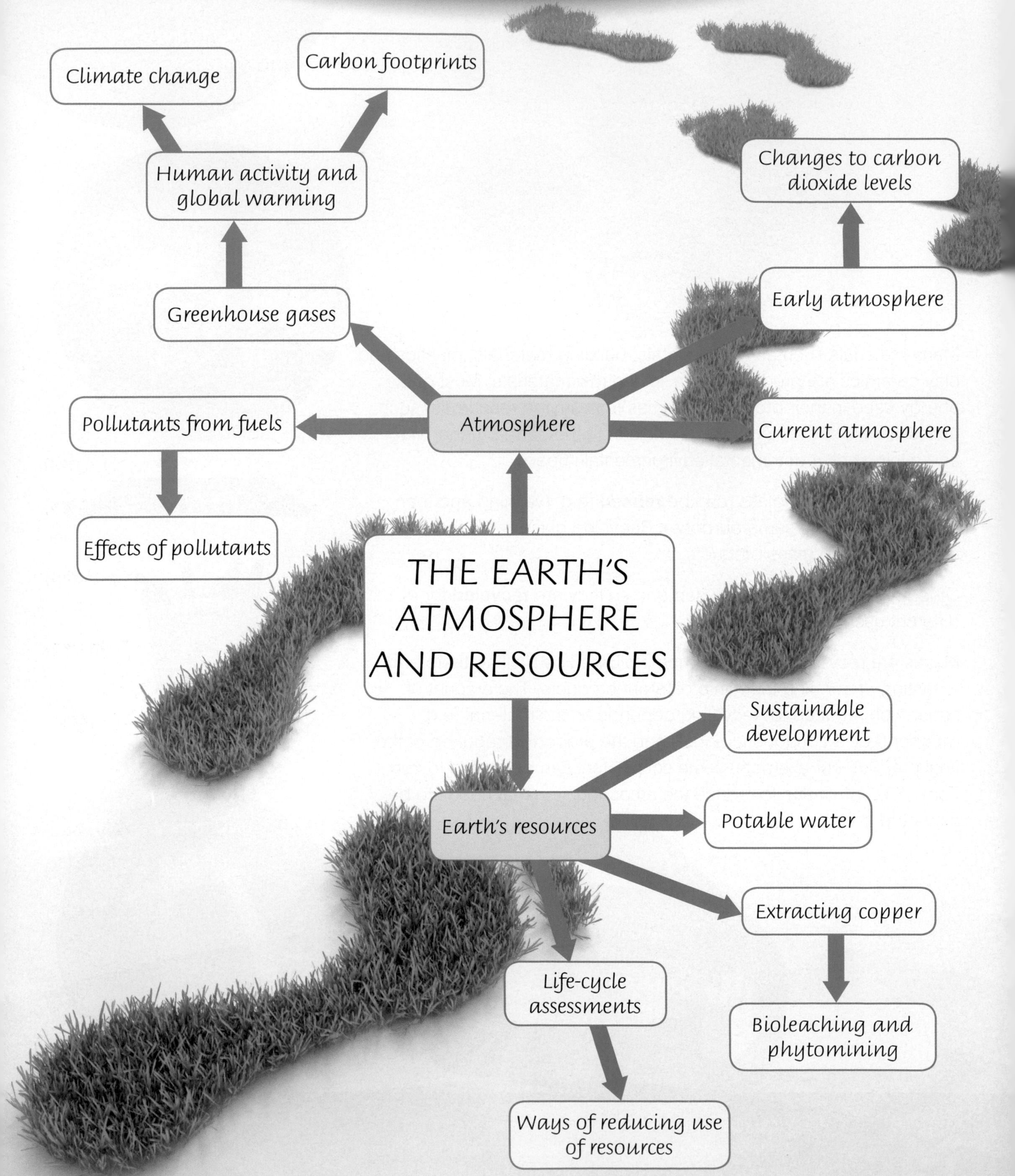

Climate change

Carbon footprints

Human activity and global warming

Changes to carbon dioxide levels

Greenhouse gases

Early atmosphere

Pollutants from fuels

Atmosphere

Current atmosphere

Effects of pollutants

THE EARTH'S ATMOSPHERE AND RESOURCES

Sustainable development

Earth's resources

Potable water

Extracting copper

Life-cycle assessments

Bioleaching and phytomining

Ways of reducing use of resources

Practice questions

1. The composition of the Earth's atmosphere today is very different from how it was 4.6 million years ago. The pie charts below show the composition of the atmosphere today compared with millions of years ago.

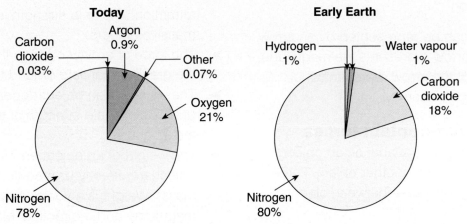

   a) When the Earth was formed, where did many of the gases in the early atmosphere come from? **(1 mark)**

   b) Name one gas whose composition has remained fairly constant over time. **(1 mark)**

   c) Explain why oxygen is now present in the atmosphere and why it has not always been there. **(2 marks)**

   d) Why is the amount of carbon dioxide in the atmosphere much lower today than in the early atmosphere? **(2 marks)**

   e) Explain why the level of carbon dioxide in the atmosphere has been steadily increasing over the last couple of centuries. **(2 marks)**

2. This question is about climate change and the carbon footprint.

   a) Other than combustion of fossil fuels, describe **two** ways that human activity increases the amount of greenhouse gases in the atmosphere. **(2 marks)**

   b) What is meant by 'carbon footprint'? **(2 marks)**

   c) Outline **two** actions that can be taken to reduce the carbon footprint. **(2 marks)**

   d) As well as carbon dioxide and water vapour, the combustion of fossil fuels produces many other atmospheric pollutants.

   i) Other than carbon dioxide, name one other gas produced by the combustion of fossil fuels. **(2 marks)**

   ii) Outline the effect on the environment that the gas you have named in part i) has on the environment. **(1 mark)**

Forces

Forces

Scalar quantities have magnitude only.

Vector quantities have magnitude and an associated direction.

A vector quantity can be represented by an arrow. The length of the arrow represents the magnitude, and the direction of the arrow represents the direction of the vector quantity.

Contact and non-contact forces

A force is a push or pull that acts on an object due to the interaction with another object. Force is a vector quantity. All forces between objects are either:

➤ contact forces – the objects are physically touching, for example:
   friction, air resistance, tension and normal contact force
   or

➤ non-contact forces – the objects are physically separated, for example:
   gravitational force, electrostatic force and magnetic force.

Friction

Air resistance

Gravity

➤ **Weight** is the force acting on an object due to gravity.

➤ All matter has a gravitational field that causes attraction. The field strength is much greater for massive objects.

➤ The force of gravity close to the Earth is due to the gravitational field around the Earth.

➤ The weight of an object depends on the gravitational field strength at the point where the object is.

➤ The weight of an object and the mass of an object are directly proportional (weight ∝ mass). Weight is a vector quantity as it has a magnitude and a direction. Mass is a scalar quantity as it only has a magnitude.

Weight is measured using a calibrated spring-balance – a **newtonmeter**.

Weight can be calculated using the following equation:

weight = mass × gravitational field strength
$$W = mg$$
➤ weight, W, in newtons, N
➤ mass, m, in kilograms, kg
➤ gravitational field strength, g, in newtons per kilogram, N/kg

Example:
What is the weight of an object with a mass of 54 kg in a gravitational field strength of 10 N/kg?

weight = mass × gravitational field strength
   = 54 kg × 10 N/kg
   = 540 N

Resultant force

The resultant force equals the total effect of all the different forces acting on an object.

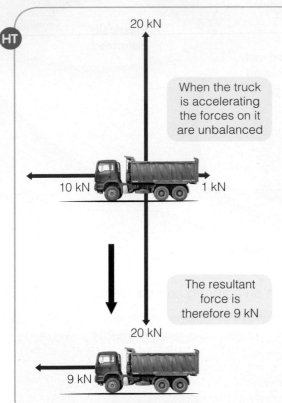

20 kN

When the truck is accelerating the forces on it are unbalanced

10 kN   1 kN

The resultant force is therefore 9 kN

20 kN

9 kN

If the forces on an object are balanced, the resultant force is zero. If the object is stationary it remains stationary and if it is moving it continues moving at a constant speed.

A single force can be resolved into two components acting at right angles to each other. The two component forces together have the same effect as the single force.

Keywords

Scalar ➤ A quantity that only has a magnitude

Vector ➤ A quantity that has both a magnitude and a direction

Weight ➤ Force acting on an object due to gravity

Work done and energy transfer

Work is done when a force causes an object to move. The force causes a displacement.

The work done by a force on an object can be calculated using the following equation:

> **work done = force × distance moved along the line of action of the force**
>
> $$W = Fs$$
>
> ➤ **work done, W, in joules, J**
> ➤ **force, F, in newtons, N**
> ➤ **distance, s, in metres, m (s represents displacement, commonly called distance)**

Example:

What work is done when a force of 90 N moves an object 14 m?

work done = force × distance moved along the line of action of the force

work done = 90 × 14 = 1260 J

One joule of work is done when a force of one newton causes a displacement of one metre.

1 joule = 1 newton metre

Work done against the frictional forces acting on an object causes a rise in the temperature of the object.

Draw two more large diagrams of the truck shown at the top of the page. Alter the force arrows to represent the truck decelerating and the truck stationary.

1. What is the difference between a vector quantity and a scalar quantity?
2. Give two examples of contact forces.
3. What is the weight of a 67 g object in a gravitational field strength of 10 N/kg?
4. What is 78 Nm in joules?

Forces and elasticity

Elastically deformed

Inelastically deformed

When an object is stretched and returns to its original length after the force is removed, it is **elastically deformed**.

When an object does not return to its original length after the force has been removed, it is **inelastically deformed**. This is **plastic deformation**.

Extension

The extension of an elastic object, such as a spring, is directly proportional to the force applied (extension ∝ force applied), if the limit of proportionality is not exceeded.

> **Stretching** – when a spring is stretched, the force pulling it exceeds the force of the spring.
> **Bending** – when a shelf bends under the weight of too many books, the downward force is from the weight of the books, and the shelf is resisting this weight.
> **Compressing** – when a car goes over a bump in the road, the force upwards is opposed by the springs in the car's suspension.

In order for any of these processes to occur, there must be more than one force applied to the object to bring about the change.

The force on a spring can be calculated using the following equation:

---

force = spring constant × extension

$F = ke$

> force, F, in newtons, N
> spring constant, k, in newtons per metre, N/m
> extension, e, in metres, m

Example:

A spring with spring constant 35 N/m is extended by 0.3 m. What is the force on the spring?

$F = ke$

$= 35 \times 0.3$

$= 10.5$ N

This relationship also applies to the compression of an elastic object, where the extension e would be the compression of the object.

A force that stretches (or compresses) a spring does **work** and **elastic potential energy** is stored in the spring. Provided the spring does not go past the limit of proportionality, the work done on the spring equals the stored elastic potential energy.

Spring balance

Force and extension

Force and extension have a linear relationship.

If force and extension are plotted on a graph, the points can be connected with a straight line (see Graph 1).

The points in a non-linear relationship cannot be connected by a straight line (see Graph 2).

Keywords

Elastically deformed ➤ Stretched object that returns to its original length after the force is removed

Inelastically deformed ➤ Stretched object that does not return to its original length after the force is removed

Graph 1 – Linear relationship

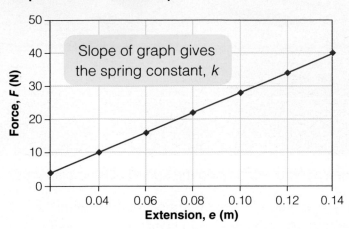

Slope of graph gives the spring constant, k

Graph 2 – Non-linear relationship

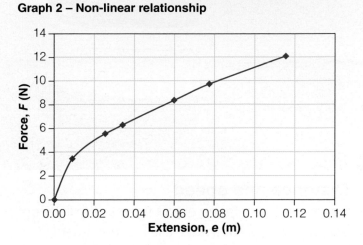

In order to calculate the spring constant in Graph 1, take two points and apply the equation.

$$\text{So, spring constant} = \frac{\text{force}}{\text{extension}}$$

$$= \frac{10}{0.04}$$

$$= 250 \text{ N/m}$$

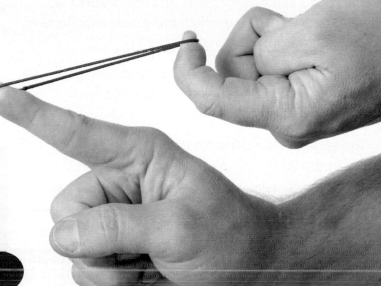

Attach a number of objects of different masses to an elastic band and measure how far the band extends. Repeat the investigation again using an plastic bag instead of a rubber band. How do your results compare?

1. What is the force of a spring with an extension of 0.1 m and a spring constant of 2 N/m?
2. When is the extension of an elastic object, such as a spring, directly proportional to the force applied?
3. What type of energy is stored in a spring?

Speed and velocity

70

Distance and speed

Distance is how far an object moves. As distance does not involve direction, it is a scalar quantity.

Displacement includes both the distance an object moves, measured in a straight line from the start point to the finish point, and the direction of that straight line. As displacement has magnitude and a direction, it is a vector quantity.

The speed of a moving object is rarely constant. When people walk, run or travel in a car, their speed is constantly changing.

The speed that a person can walk, run or cycle depends on:

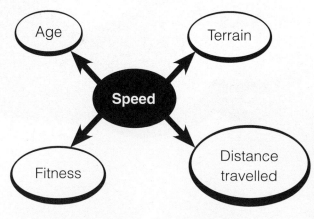

Some typical speeds are:
➤ walking – 1.5 m/s
➤ running – 3 m/s
➤ cycling – 6 m/s
➤ car – 20 m/s
➤ train – 35 m/s

The speed of sound and the speed of wind also vary.

A typical value for the speed of sound in air is 330 m/s. A gale force wind is one with a speed above 14 m/s.

Speed can be investigated in labs using equipment such as light gates.

For an object travelling at a constant speed, distance travelled can be calculated by the following equation:

distance travelled = speed × time

$$s = vt$$

➤ distance, s, in metres, m
➤ speed, v, in metres per second, m/s
➤ time, t, in seconds, s

Example:
What distance is covered by a runner with a speed of 3 m/s in 6000 seconds?

distance travelled = speed × time
$$= 3 \times 6000$$
$$= 18\,000 \text{ m}$$
$$= 1.8 \text{ km}$$

Velocity

The **velocity** of an object is its speed in a given direction. As velocity has a magnitude and a direction, it is a vector quantity.

Keywords

Displacement ➤ Distance travelled in a given direction

Velocity ➤ Speed in a given direction

HT A car travelling at a constant speed around a bend would have a varying velocity because it is changing direction.

When an object moves in a circle, the direction of the object is continually changing. This means that an object moving in a circle at constant speed, such as an orbiting satellite, has a continually changing velocity. For motion in a circle, there is a resultant centripetal force that acts towards the centre of the circle.

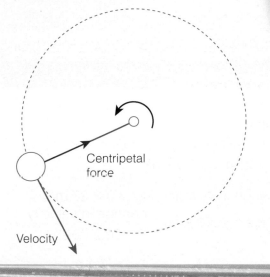

Centripetal force

Velocity

Time how long it takes to travel to school. Use a mapping website to calculate the distance. Now calculate the average speed of your journey. Replicate this investigation on different days. Is there much variation in your average speed?

1. Why is distance a scalar quantity?
2. What is the speed of a walker who covers 10 km in 2.5 hours?
3. What is the difference between speed and velocity?

Distance–time and velocity–time graphs

71

Distance and time

The distance an object moves in a straight line can be represented by a distance–time graph.

The speed of an object can be calculated from the gradient of its distance–time graph.

The graph below shows a person jogging.

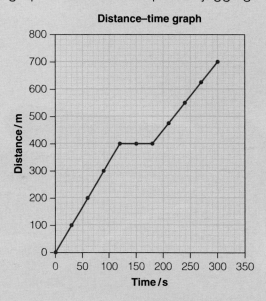

Distance–time graph

The average speed of this jogger between 0–120 seconds can be worked out as follows:

$$\text{speed} = \frac{\text{distance}}{\text{time}} = \frac{400}{120} = 3.33 \text{ m/s}$$

The speed of an accelerating object can be determined by using a tangent to measure the gradient of the distance–time graph.

Measure out a short distance and roll a ball. Time how long it takes the ball to travel the distance you've measured. Plot the distance travelled and the time taken on a graph. Repeat the investigation, but this time roll the ball harder. Again, plot the result on the same speed–time graph. Compare the gradients of the two lines. What do you notice? Use your graph to calculate the average speed of the two balls.

Acceleration

Acceleration can be calculated using the following equation:

$$\text{average acceleration} = \frac{\text{change in velocity}}{\text{time taken}}$$

$$\left[a = \frac{\Delta v}{t} \right]$$

➤ acceleration, a, in metres per second squared, m/s²
➤ change in velocity, Δv, in metres per second, m/s
➤ time, t, in seconds, s

Example:
A car travels from 0 to 27 m/s in 3.8 seconds. What is its acceleration?

$$\text{change in velocity} = 27 - 0 = 27 \text{ m/s}$$
$$\text{average acceleration} = \frac{\text{change in velocity}}{\text{time taken}}$$
$$= \frac{27}{3.8} = 7.1 \text{ m/s}^2$$

An object that slows down (decelerates) has a negative acceleration.

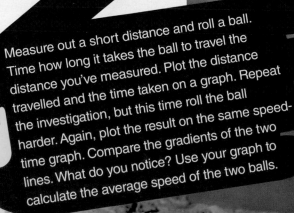

Velocity–time graph

Acceleration can be calculated from the gradient of a velocity–time graph.

HT Distance travelled can be calculated from the area under a velocity–time graph.

Keyword

Acceleration ➤ Change in velocity over time

The graph below shows the movement of a car.

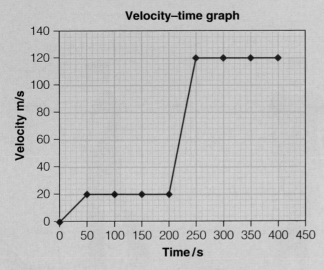

Velocity–time graph

(y-axis: Velocity m/s, 0 to 140; x-axis: Time/s, 0 to 450)

The acceleration between 0–50 seconds can be worked out as follows:

$$\text{gradient of line} = \frac{\text{velocity}}{\text{time}}$$

$$= \frac{20}{50} = 0.4 \text{ m/s}^2$$

As the gradient of the line is steeper between 200–250 seconds than it is between 0–50 seconds, the acceleration must have been greater between 200–250 seconds.

HT The distance travelled between 0–200 seconds can be worked out as follows:

Area from 0–50s

$$= \left(20 \times \frac{50}{2}\right) = 500 \text{ m}$$

Area from 50–200s

$$= 20 \times 150 = 3000 \text{ m}$$

Total distance travelled $= 3500$ m

The equation below applies to uniform motion:

final velocity² – initial velocity² = 2 × acceleration × distance

$$v^2 - u^2 = 2\,as$$

➤ final velocity, *v*, in metres per second, m/s
➤ initial velocity, *u*, in metres per second, m/s
➤ acceleration, *a*, in metres per second squared, m/s²
➤ distance, *s*, in metres, m

Falling objects

Near the Earth's surface, any object falling freely under gravity has an acceleration of about 10 m/s². This is the gravitational field strength, or acceleration due to gravity, and is used to calculate weight.

An object falling through a fluid initially accelerates due to the force of gravity. Eventually the resultant force will be zero and the object will move at its terminal velocity.

1. What does the gradient of a distance–time graph represent?
2. What type of acceleration will an object which is slowing down have?
HT 3. What does the area under a velocity–time graph represent?

Newton's laws

Newton's first law

Newton's first law deals with the effect of resultant forces.

➤ If the resultant force acting on an object is zero and the object is stationary, the object remains stationary.

➤ If the resultant force acting on an object is zero and the object is moving, the object continues to move at the same speed and in the same direction (its velocity will stay the same).

Newton's first law means that the velocity of an object will only change if a resultant force is acting on the object.

Stationary object – zero resultant force

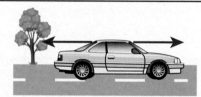

Object moving at constant speed – zero resultant force

Examples of resultant force:

A car is stationary. At this point the resultant force is zero.	The car starts to move and accelerates. As it is accelerating, the resultant force on the car is no longer zero.	The car travels at a constant velocity. The resultant force is zero again.

HT The tendency of objects to continue in their state of rest or of uniform motion is called **inertia**.

Newton's second law

The acceleration of an object is proportional to the resultant force acting on the object, and inversely proportional to the mass of the object.

Therefore:

> acceleration ∝ resultant force
>
> resultant force = mass × acceleration
> ➤ force, F, in newtons, N
> ➤ mass, m, in kilograms, kg
> ➤ acceleration, a, in metres per second squared, m/s^2

Example:

A motorbike and rider of mass 270 kg accelerate at 6.7 m/s^2. What is the resultant force on the motorbike?

$$270 \times 6.7 = 1809 \text{ N}$$

If the motorbike slows to a constant speed, the resultant force would now be 0 (as acceleration = 0, $270 \times 0 = 0$).

HT **Inertial mass** is a measure of how difficult it is to change the velocity of an object. It is defined by the ratio of force over acceleration.

Keyword

HT **Inertia** ➤ The tendency of objects to continue in their state of rest or uniform motion

Newton's third law

Whenever two objects interact, the forces they exert on each other are equal and opposite.

When a fish swims it exerts a force on the water, pushing it backwards. The water exerts an equal and opposite force on the fish, pushing it forwards.

Make a revision poster with a drawing illustrating each of Newton's laws and the resultant force equation.

1. A book of weight 67 N is on a desk. What force is the desk exerting on the book?
2. A sprinter of mass 89 kg accelerates at 10 m/s^2. What is the resultant force?
3. What happens to the speed of a moving object that has a resultant force of 0 acting on it?

Mind map

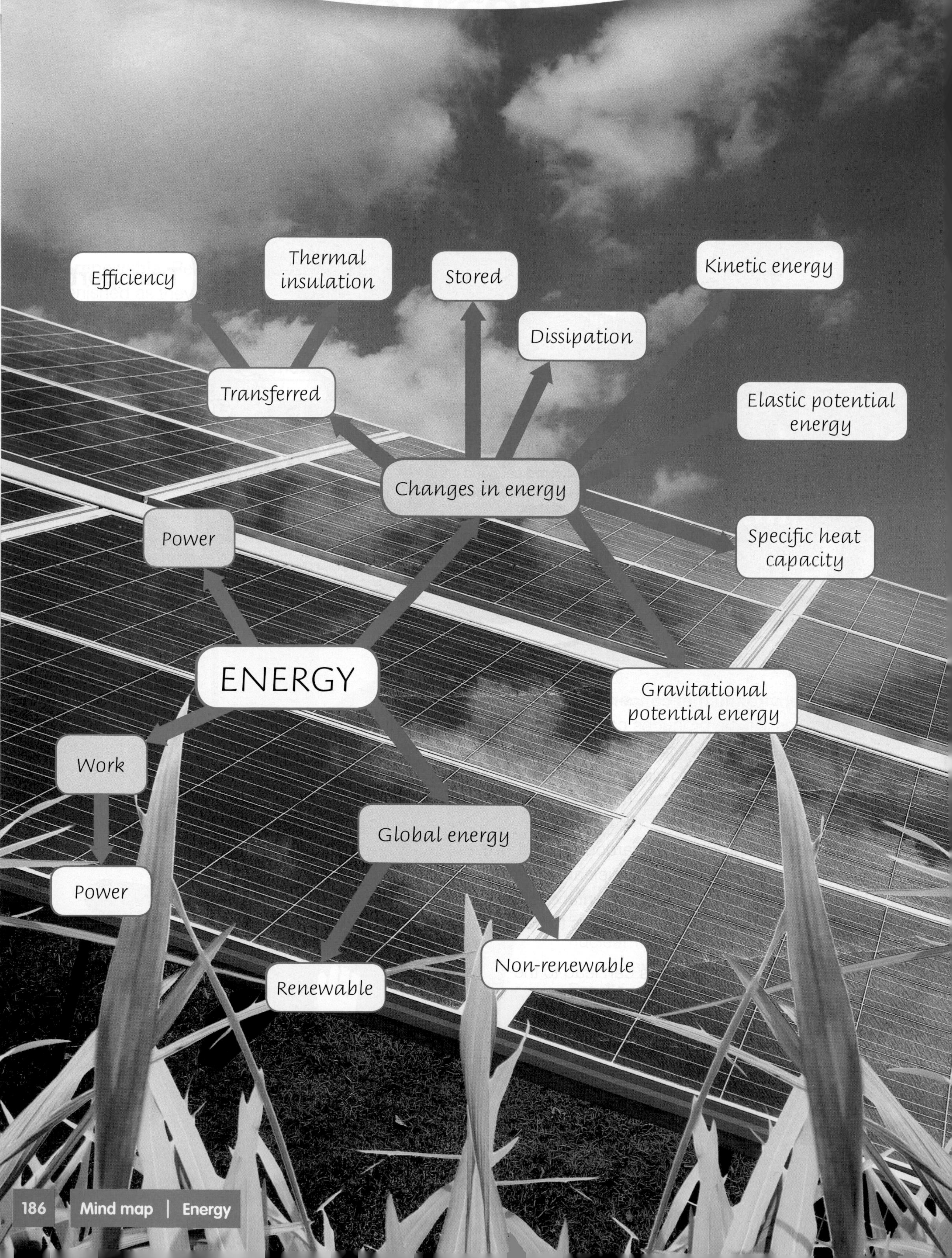

Efficiency

Thermal insulation

Stored

Kinetic energy

Dissipation

Transferred

Elastic potential energy

Changes in energy

Specific heat capacity

Power

ENERGY

Gravitational potential energy

Work

Power

Global energy

Renewable

Non-renewable

Practice questions

1. **a)** Explain the difference between a renewable and a non-renewable energy resource. **(2 marks)**

   b) Nuclear power is a very reliable source of energy but some environmentalists protest against it.
   Explain why. **(2 marks)**

   c) Many environmentalists would rather use wind or tidal power stations.
   What are the potential disadvantages of using these energy resources? **(2 marks)**

2. A car has a mass of 1600 kg and moves at 32 m/s.

   a) What is the kinetic energy of the car? **(2 marks)**

   b) If the fuel burnt by the car to reach this speed contained 1500 kJ, what was the efficiency of this transfer of energy? **(2 marks)**

   c) Give two ways energy was transferred into less useful forms by the car's engine. **(2 marks)**

   d) Give one feature of the car's engine that reduced the energy dissipated. **(1 mark)**

3. A bungee jumper of mass 77 kg stands on a bridge 150 m high.

   a) What is their gravitational potential energy? (Assume gravitational field strength = 10 N/kg) **(2 marks)**

   b) The bungee jumper jumps off and quickly reaches a speed of 20 m/s.
   What is their kinetic energy at this point? **(2 marks)**

   c) Explain the energy transfers that occur from when the bungee jumper jumps to when they reach their lowest height. **(2 marks)**

Circuits, charge and current

Circuit symbols

The diagram below shows the standard symbols used for components in a circuit.

Here is an example of a circuit diagram:

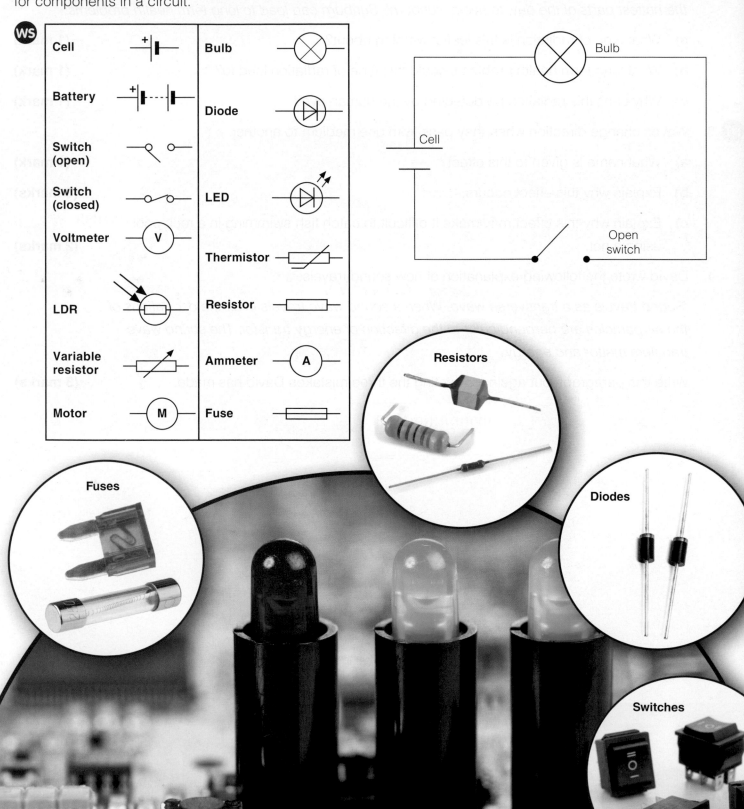

AMPERES

Electrical charge and current

For electrical charge to flow through a closed circuit, the circuit must include a source of energy that produces a potential difference, such as a battery, cell or powerpack.

Electric current is a flow of electrical charge. The size of the electric current is the rate of flow of electrical charge. Charge flow, current and time are linked by the following equation:

> **charge flow = current × time**
>
> $$Q = It$$
>
> ➤ charge flow, **Q**, in coulombs, **C**
> ➤ current, **I**, in amperes or amps A
> ➤ time, **t**, in seconds, s

Example:
A current of 6 A flows through a circuit for 14 seconds. What is the charge flow?

charge flow = current × time
= 6 × 14
= 84 C

The current at any point in a single closed loop of a circuit has the same value as the current at any other point in the same closed loop.

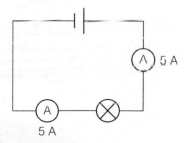

Both ammeters in the circuit above show the same current of 5 amps.

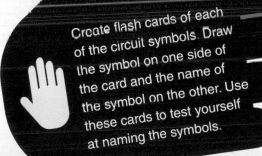

Create flash cards of each of the circuit symbols. Draw the symbol on one side of the card and the name of the symbol on the other. Use these cards to test yourself at naming the symbols.

1. What is the difference between the symbol for a resistor and the symbol for a variable resistor?
2. What charge flows through a circuit per second if the current is 4.2 A?
3. What is the current of a charge flow of 450 C in five seconds?

Current, resistance and potential difference

Current, resistance and potential difference

The current through a component depends on both the resistance of the component and the potential difference (p.d.) across the component. Potential difference is the energy transferred per unit charge passed.

The greater the resistance of the component, the smaller the current for a given potential difference across the component.

Current, potential difference or resistance can be calculated using the following equation:

> **potential difference = current × resistance**
> $$V = IR$$
> ➤ **potential difference, V, in volts, V**
> ➤ **current, I, in amperes or amps, A**
> ➤ **resistance, R, in ohms, Ω**

Example:
A 5 ohm resistor has a current of 2 A flowing through it. What is the potential difference across the resistor?

potential difference = current × resistance
$$= 5 \times 2$$
$$= 10 \text{ V}$$

By measuring the current through, and potential difference across a component, it's possible to calculate the resistance of a component.

The circuit diagram below would allow you to determine the resistance of the filament lamp.

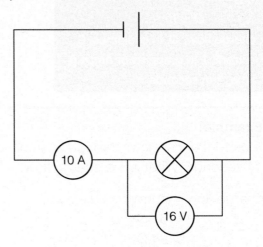

potential difference = current × resistance

$$\text{resistance} = \frac{\text{potential difference}}{\text{current}}$$

$$= \frac{16}{10}$$

$$= 1.6 \text{ ohms}$$

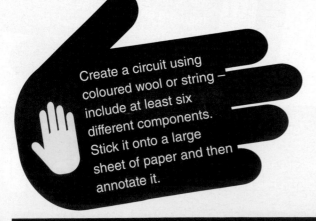
Create a circuit using coloured wool or string – include at least six different components. Stick it onto a large sheet of paper and then annotate it.

Resistors

In an **ohmic conductor**, at a constant temperature the current is directly proportional to the potential difference across the resistor. This means that the resistance remains constant as the current changes.

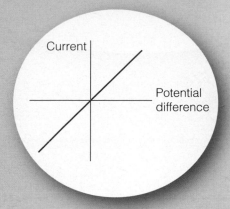

The resistance of components such as lamps, diodes, thermistors and LDRs is not constant; it changes with the current through the component. They are not ohmic conductors.

When a current flows through a resistor, the energy transfer causes the resistor to heat up. This is due to collisions between electrons and the ions in the lattice of the resistor.

This heating can be an advantage, such as in an electrical heater. It is also a disadvantage as it can lead to electrical devices being damaged due to overheating. Thicker wires have a lower resistance as there is a larger cross-sectional area for the current to pass through.

Filament lamps

The resistance of a filament lamp increases as the temperature of the filament increases.

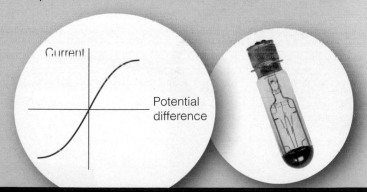

Diodes

The current through a diode flows in one direction only. This means the diode has a very high resistance in the reverse direction.

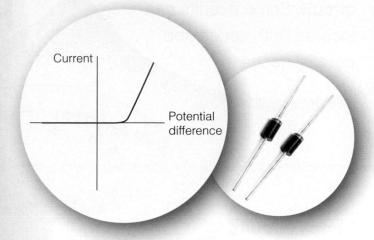

Light dependent resistors (LDR)

The resistance of an LDR decreases as light intensity increases. LDRs are used in circuits where lights are required to switch on when it gets dark, such as floodlights. When the resistance decreases due to the lack of light, sufficient current flows through the LDR to activate the light.

Thermistors

The resistance of a thermistor decreases as the temperature increases. Thermistors are used in thermostats to control heating systems.

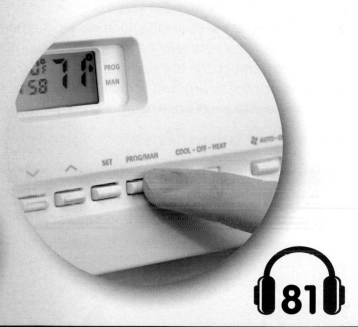

81

---

1. Explain why an LDR is not an ohmic conductor.
2. What two pieces of equipment need to be wired into a circuit in order to determine the resistance of a component in the circuit?
3. What is the potential difference if the current is 4 A and the resistance is 2 ohms?
4. Calculate the resistance of a component that has a current of 3 A flowing through it and a potential difference of 6 V.

Components can be joined together in either a **series circuit** or a **parallel circuit**. Some circuits can include both series and parallel sections.

Series and parallel circuits

Voltmeter

Series circuits

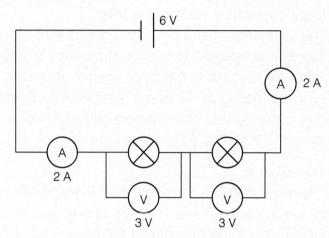

6 V

A) 2 A

A
2 A

V
3 V

V
3 V

For components connected in series:

➤ there is the same current through each component
➤ the total potential difference of the power supply is shared between the components
➤ the total resistance of two components is the sum of the resistance of each component.

Total resistance is given by the following equation:

R total = R1 + R2
➤ **resistance, R, in ohms, Ω**

Example:
What is the total resistance of the two resistors in the series circuit below?

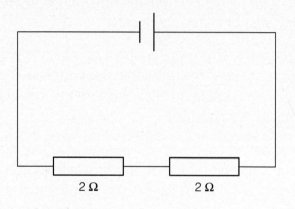

2 Ω   2 Ω

Total = R1 + R2
= 2 Ω + 2 Ω
= 4 Ω

Keywords
Series circuit ➤ Circuit where all components are connected along a single path
Parallel circuit ➤ Circuit which contains branches and where all the components will have the same voltage

Parallel circuits

6 V

A 2 A

A 1 A

⊗

V 6 V

A 1 A

⊗

V 6 V

For components connected in parallel:

- ➤ the potential difference across each component is the same
- ➤ the total current through the whole circuit is the sum of the currents through the separate components. The current splits between the branches of the circuit and combines when the branches meet
- ➤ the total resistance of two resistors is less than the resistance of the smallest individual resistor. This is due to the potential difference across the resistors being the same but the current splitting.

82

Draw a parallel circuit of your own design, making sure that you include at least two resistors.

$I = V/R$

1. If the current through one component in a series circuit is 5 A, what is the current through the rest of the components?
2. How do you calculate the total resistance of two resistors in series?
3. A 3 Ω resistor and a 2 Ω resistor are connected in parallel. Would the resistance be higher or lower than 2 Ω?

Domestic uses and safety

Direct and alternating current

Cells and batteries supply current that always passes in the same direction. This is direct current (**dc**).

Alternating current (**ac**) changes direction at a frequency of fifty times a second. Mains electricity is an ac supply. In the UK it has a frequency of 50 Hz and is about 230 V.

Mains electricity

WS Most electrical appliances are connected to the mains using a three-core cable with a three-pin plug.

Live wire	Brown	Carries the alternating potential difference from the supply.
Neutral wire	Blue	Completes the circuit. The neutral wire is at, or close to, earth potential (0 V).
Earth wire	Green and yellow stripes	The earth wire is at 0 V. It only carries a current if there is a fault.

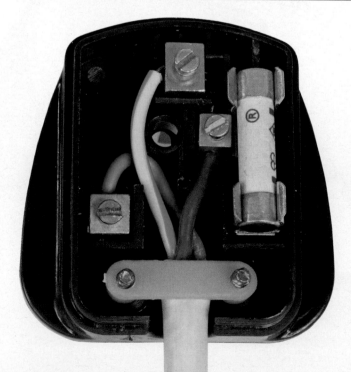

The potential difference between the live wire and earth (0 V) is about 230 V.

Our bodies are at earth potential (0 V). Touching a live wire produces a large potential difference across our body. This causes a current to flow through our body, resulting in an electric shock that could cause serious injury or death.

Insulation, fuses and circuit breakers

If an electrical fault causes too great a current, the circuit is disconnected by a fuse or a circuit breaker connected to the live wire.

The current will cause the fuse to overheat and melt or the circuit breaker to switch off (trip). A circuit breaker operates much faster than a fuse and can be reset.

Appliances with metal cases are usually earthed. If a fault occurs, a large current flows from the live wire to earth. This melts the fuse and disconnects the live wire.

Some appliances are double insulated meaning it is impossible for the case to become live. (Either the case is plastic or it is impossible for the live wire to come into contact with the casing). Double insulated appliances have no earth connection.

Electric drills are examples of appliances that are double insulated.

Keywords

dc ➤ Direct current that always passes in the same direction

ac ➤ Alternating current that changes direction

Circuit breaker

Fuses

Make small cards of the colours, names and functions of the wires in a three-pin plug. Mix the cards up and then arrange them to show the correct colours, functions and names of the wires.

1. Why don't double insulated appliances have an earth connection?
2. What are the advantages of a circuit breaker over a conventional fuse?
3. Why is it dangerous to touch a live wire?

Energy transfers

Keyword

National Grid ➤ System of transformers and cables linking power stations to consumers

Power

The power of a device is related to the potential difference across it and the current through it by the following equations:

power = potential difference × current

$$P = VI$$

or

power = current² × resistance

$$P = I^2 R$$

➤ power, *P*, in watts, W
➤ potential difference, *V*, in volts, V
➤ current, *I*, in amperes or amps, A
➤ resistance, *R*, in ohms, Ω

Example:

A bulb has a potential difference of 240 V and a current flowing through it of 0.6 A. What is the power of the bulb?

power = potential difference × current
    = 240 × 0.6
    = 144 W

Energy transfers in everyday appliances

Everyday electrical appliances are designed to bring about energy transfers.

The amount of energy an appliance transfers depends on how long the appliance is switched on for and the power of the appliance.

Here are some examples of everyday energy transfer in appliances:

➤ A hairdryer transfers electrical energy from the ac mains to kinetic energy (in an electric motor to drive a fan) and heat energy (in a heating element).
➤ A torch transfers electrical energy from batteries into light energy from a bulb.

Work done

Work is done when charge flows in a circuit.

The amount of energy transferred by electrical work can be calculated using the following equation:

> **energy transferred = power × time**
>
> $$E = Pt$$
>
> **and**
>
> $$\frac{\text{energy transferred}}{} = \text{charge flow} \times \text{potential difference}$$
>
> $$E = QV$$
>
> ➤ energy transferred, *E*, in joules, J
> ➤ power, *P*, in watts, W
> ➤ time, *t*, in seconds, s,
> ➤ charge flow, *Q*, in coulombs, C
> ➤ potential difference, *V*, in volts, V

The National Grid

The **National Grid** is a system of cables and transformers linking power stations to consumers.

Electrical power is transferred from power stations to consumers using the National Grid.

Step-up transformers **increase** the potential difference from the power station to the transmission cables.

Step-down transformers **decrease** the potential difference to a much lower and safer level for domestic use.

Increasing the potential difference reduces the current so reduces the energy loss due to heating in the transmission cables. Reducing the loss of energy through heat makes the transfer of energy much more efficient. Also, the wires would glow and be more likely to break over time if the current through them was high.

Make a flow chart showing the transfer of electrical energy into other forms of energy that occur during your day (TV, computer, mobile, hairdryer and so on).

1. What is the power of a device that has a current flowing through it of 5 A and a resistance of 2 Ω?
2. What is the energy transferred by a charge flow of 60 C and a potential difference of 12 V?
3. Why are step-down transformers important in the National Grid?

Mind map

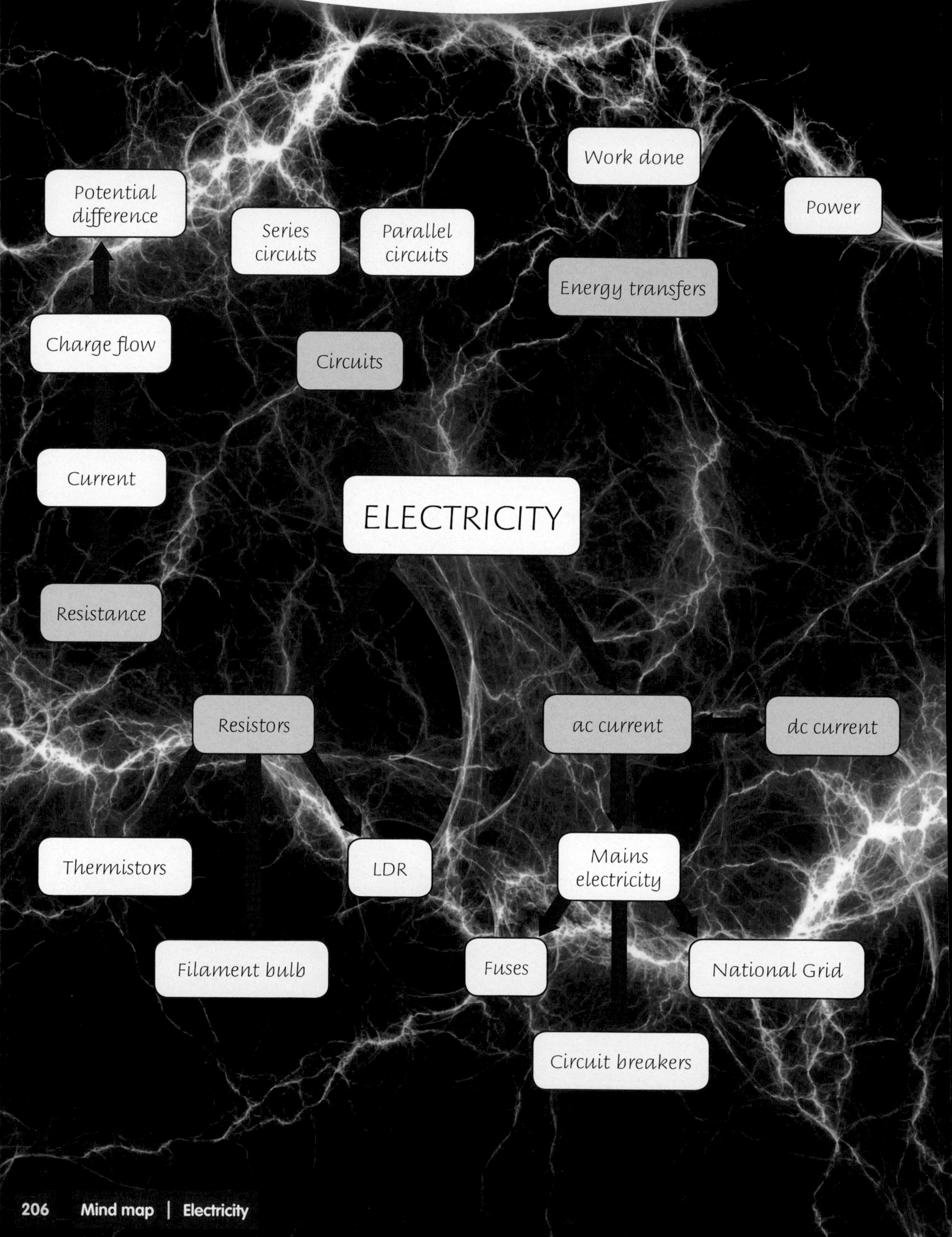

Work done

Power

Potential difference

Series circuits

Parallel circuits

Energy transfers

Charge flow

Circuits

Current

ELECTRICITY

Resistance

Resistors

ac current

dc current

Thermistors

LDR

Mains electricity

Filament bulb

Fuses

National Grid

Circuit breakers

Practice questions

1. Look at the parallel circuit below.

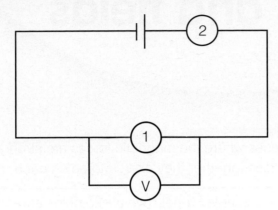

   a) Component 1 has a resistance of 3 Ω and has a potential difference of 15 V across it.
   What is the current through it? **(3 marks)**

   b) What is the current at point 2 in the circuit?
   Explain how you arrived at your answer. **(2 marks)**

   c) Sketch a graph to show the relationship between potential difference and current in an ohmic conductor. **(3 marks)**

   d) Give an example of a component that would show a non-linear relationship between potential difference and current. **(1 mark)**

2. **a)** **I)** What colour is the live wire in an electrical plug? **(1 mark)**

   ii) Explain the importance of this wire being a different colour to the neutral wire. **(2 marks)**

   b) Some electrical appliances only have live and neutral wires in their plugs.
   Explain the reason for this. **(2 marks)**

Permanent and induced magnetism, magnetic forces and fields

Poles of a magnet

The poles of a magnet are the places where the magnetic forces are strongest. When two magnets are brought close together they exert a force on each other.

> Two like poles repel. Two unlike poles attract.

Attraction between opposite poles

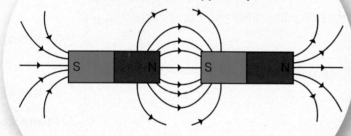

Repulsion between like poles

Neutral or null point

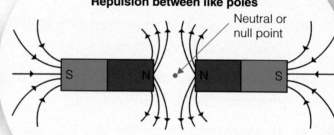

Magnetism is an example of a non-contact force.

Keywords

Permanent magnet ➤ Magnet which produces its own magnetic field

Magnetic field ➤ Region around a magnet where a force acts on another magnet or on a magnetic material

Permanent magnetism vs induced magnetism

A **permanent magnet** . . .
➤ produces its own **magnetic field**.

An induced magnet . . .
➤ becomes a magnet when placed in a magnetic field
➤ always experiences a force of attraction
➤ loses most or all of its magnetism quickly when removed from a magnetic field.

Magnetic field

The region around a magnet – where a force acts on another magnet or on a magnetic material (iron, steel, cobalt, magnadur and nickel) – is called the magnetic field.

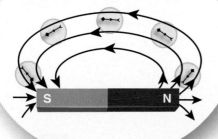

A compass can be used to plot a magnetic field

The **force** between a magnet and a magnetic material is always attraction.

The **strength** of the magnetic field depends on the distance from the magnet.

The **field** is strongest at the poles of the magnet.

The **direction** of a magnetic field line is from the north pole of the magnet to the south pole of the magnet.

Compasses

A magnetic compass contains a bar magnet that points towards magnetic north. This provides evidence that the Earth's core is magnetic and produces a magnetic field.

85

Make your own compass using a bowl of water, a small dish, a magnet and a nail. To make a magnet for your compass, take the nail and magnet and stroke one end of the magnet along the length of the nail, always going in the same direction. Once your nail is magnetised, you need to float it in the water. Start by putting a dish into the water, then place the nail into the centre of the dish. Let it settle a bit, to move around a little until it has found north.

1. What happens if the two north poles of a bar magnet are brought together?
2. When will a magnetic material become an induced magnet?
3. Where is the magnetic field of a magnet strongest?
4. Why does a magnetic compass point north?

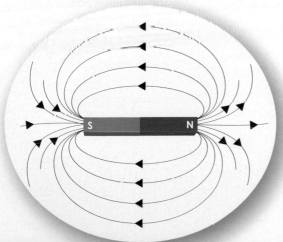

Electromagnets and the motor effect

Electromagnets

When a current flows through a conducting wire a magnetic field is produced around the wire.

The shape of the magnetic field can be seen as a series of concentric circles in a plane, perpendicular to the wire.

The direction of these field lines depends on the direction of the current.

The strength of the magnetic field depends on the current through the wire and the distance from the wire.

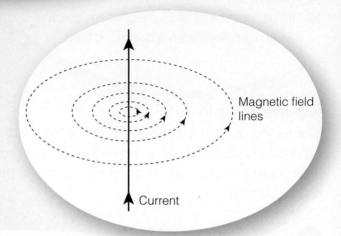

Magnetic field lines

Current

Coiling the wire into a **solenoid** (a helix) increases the strength of the magnetic field created by a current through the wire.

Features of a solenoid

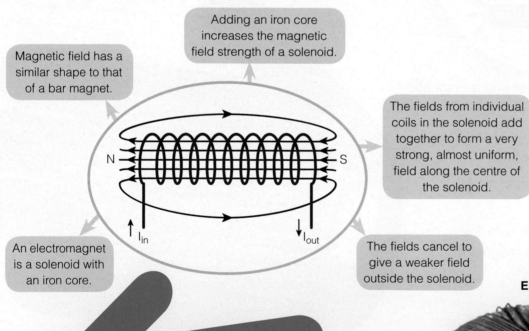

Magnetic field has a similar shape to that of a bar magnet.

Adding an iron core increases the magnetic field strength of a solenoid.

The fields from individual coils in the solenoid add together to form a very strong, almost uniform, field along the centre of the solenoid.

An electromagnet is a solenoid with an iron core.

The fields cancel to give a weaker field outside the solenoid.

I_{in} I_{out} N   S

🎧 86

Go around the house and make a list of all the devices that contain an electric motor. For each one, explain why the motor is important to the device's function. (Hint: Any device that is electrically powered and has moving parts will have a motor.)

Electromagnetic coil

Fleming's left-hand rule and the motor effect

HT

When a conductor carrying a current is placed in a magnetic field, the magnet producing the field and the conductor exert an equal and opposite force on each other. This is the motor effect and is due to interactions between magnetic fields.

The direction of the force on the conductor can be identified using Fleming's left-hand rule.

If the direction of the current or the direction of the magnetic field is reversed, the direction of the force on the conductor is reversed.

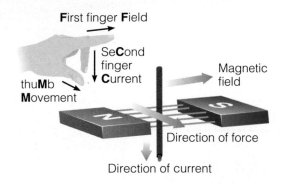

First finger **Field**

SeCond finger Current

thuMb Movement

Magnetic field

Direction of force

Direction of current

The size of the force on the conductor depends on:

➤ the magnetic flux density
➤ the current in the conductor
➤ the length of conductor in the magnetic field.

For a conductor at right angles to a magnetic field and carrying a current, the force can be calculated using the following equation:

> force = magnetic flux density × current × length
>
> $$F = BIl$$
>
> ➤ force, F, in newtons, N
> ➤ magnetic flux density, B, in tesla, T
> ➤ current, I, in amperes, A (or amp)
> ➤ length, l, in metres, m

Example:

What is the force produced by a 0.5 m long conductor, with a magnetic flux of 1.2 T and a current of 16 A flowing through it?

$$F = BIl$$
$$F = 1.2 \times 16 \times 0.5 = 9.6 \text{ N}$$

Electric motors

A coil of wire carrying a current in a magnetic field experiences a force, causing it to rotate. This is the basis of an **electric motor**.

The commutator and graphite brush allow the current to be reversed every half turn to keep the coil spinning.

Simple electric motor

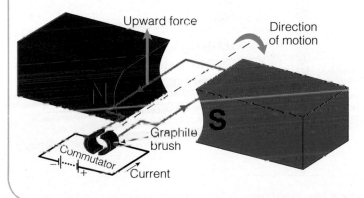

Upward force

Direction of motion

N

S

Graphite brush

Commutator

Current

Keyword

Solenoid ➤ Coil wound into a helix shape

1. What two things does the strength of a magnetic field around a wire depend on?
2. What shape is the magnetic field around a solenoid?
HT 3. What three variables are related by Fleming's left-hand rule?

Mind map

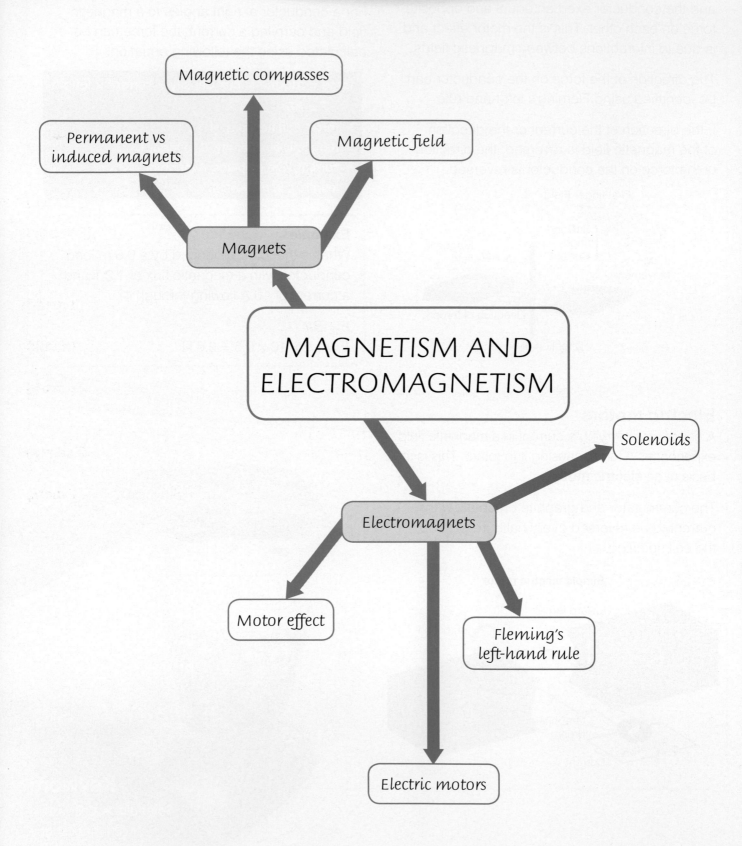

Magnetic compasses

Permanent vs induced magnets

Magnetic field

Magnets

MAGNETISM AND ELECTROMAGNETISM

Solenoids

Electromagnets

Motor effect

Fleming's left-hand rule

Electric motors

Practice questions

1. The diagram below shows a bar magnet.

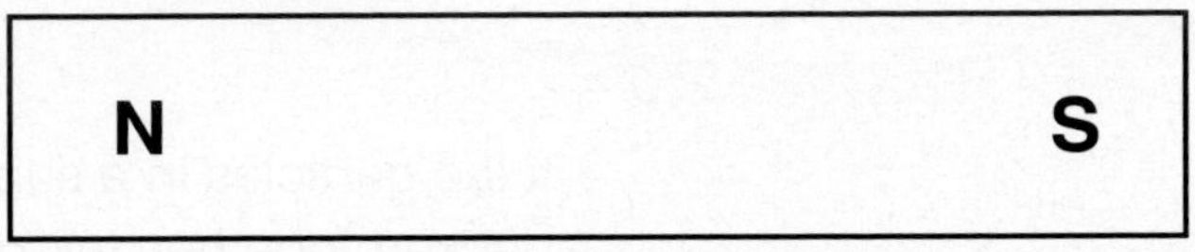

   | N   S |

   a) Draw the shape of the magnetic field around this magnet. **(2 marks)**

   b) What would happen if the south pole of a bar magnet was brought into contact with the north pole of another magnet? **(1 mark)**

   c) Give two differences between a bar magnet and an induced magnet. **(2 marks)**

2. A wire is used in an investigation into magnetism.

   a) i) How can a magnetic field be produced around a wire? **(1 mark)**

      ii) What effect would coiling the wire into a solenoid have? **(1 mark)**

      iii) How could this wire be turned into an electromagnet? **(1 mark)**

   HT b) i) What force does the wire experience if it is 0.3 m long, has a magnetic flux density of 3.5 T, and has a current of 8 A flowing through it? **(2 marks)**

      ii) If the current through the wire is reversed, what happens to the force on the wire? **(1 mark)**

The particle model and pressure

The particle model

Matter can exist as a solid, liquid or as a gas.

Solid – particles are very close together and vibrating. They are in fixed positions.

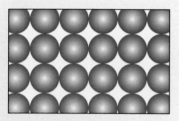

Liquid – particles are very close together but are free to move relative to each other. This allows liquids to flow.

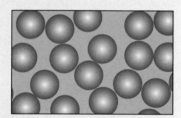

Gas – particles in a gas are not close together. The particles move rapidly in all directions.

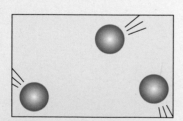

If the particles in a substance are more closely packed together, the density of the substance is higher. This means that liquids have a higher density than gases. Most solids have a higher density than liquids.

Density also increases when the particles are forced into a smaller volume.

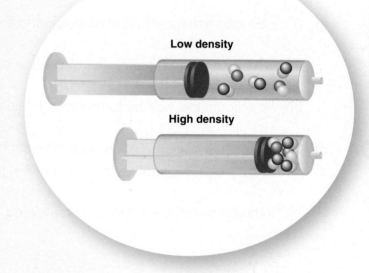

Low density

High density

The density of a material is defined by the following equation:

$$\text{density} = \frac{\text{mass}}{\text{volume}}$$

$$\rho = \frac{m}{V}$$

➤ density, ρ, in kilograms per metre cubed, kg/m³
➤ mass, m, in kilograms, kg
➤ volume, V, in metres cubed, m³

Example:

What is the density of an object that has a mass of 56 kg and a volume of 0.5 m³?

$$\rho = \frac{m}{V}$$

$$= \frac{56}{0.5} = 112 \text{ kg/m}^3$$

When substances change state (melt, freeze, boil, evaporate, condense or sublimate), mass is conserved (it stays the same).

Changes of state are physical changes: the change does not produce a new substance, so if the change is reversed the substance recovers its original properties.

Ice

Water

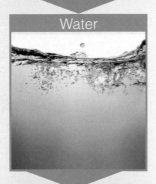

Steam

Keyword

Gas pressure ➤ Total force exerted by all of the gas molecules inside the container on a unit area of the wall

Gas under pressure

The molecules of a gas are in constant random motion.

When the molecules collide with the wall of their container they exert a force on the wall. The total force exerted by all of the molecules inside the container on a unit area of the wall is the **gas pressure**.

Increasing the temperature of a gas, held at constant volume, **increases** the pressure exerted by the gas.

Decreasing the temperature of a gas, held at constant volume, **decreases** the pressure exerted by the gas.

The temperature of the gas is related to the average kinetic energy of the molecules. The higher the temperature, the greater the average kinetic energy, and so the faster the average speed of the molecules. At higher temperatures, the particles collide with the walls of the container at a higher speed.

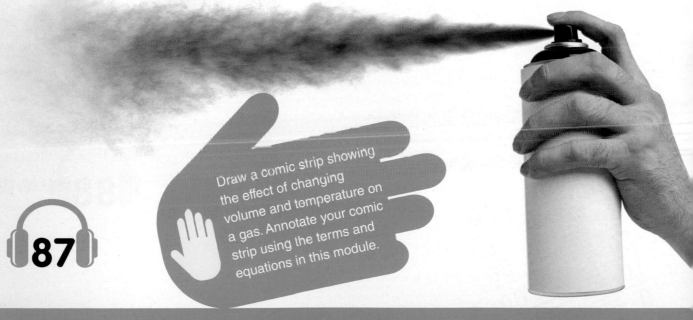

Draw a comic strip showing the effect of changing volume and temperature on a gas. Annotate your comic strip using the terms and equations in this module.

87

1. Explain how gases exert pressure.
2. What is the density of a 2 kg object with a volume of 0.002 m³?
3. What happens to the mass of a liquid when it freezes?

Internal energy and change of state

Internal energy

Energy is stored inside a system by the particles (atoms and molecules) that make up the system. This is called **internal energy**.

Internal energy of a system is equal to the total kinetic energy and potential energy of all the atoms and molecules that make up the system.

Heating changes the energy stored within the system by increasing the energy of the particles that make up the system. This either raises the temperature of the system or produces a change of state.

Heat and temperature are related but are not a measure of the same thing.
- Heat is the amount of thermal energy and is measured in Joules (J).
- Temperature is how hot or cold something is and is measured in degrees Celsius (°C).

Changes of heat and specific latent heat

When a change of state occurs, the stored internal energy changes, but the temperature remains constant. The graph below shows the change in temperature of water as it is heated; the temperature is constant when the water is changing state.

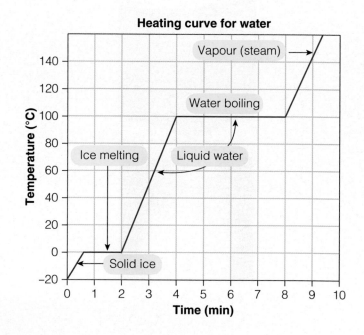

The **specific latent heat** of a substance is equal to the energy required to change the state of one kilogram of the substance with no change in temperature.

The energy required to cause a change of state can be calculated by the following equation:

energy for a change of state	= mass × specific latent heat

$$E = mL$$

➤ energy, E, in joules , J
➤ mass, m, in kilograms, kg
➤ specific latent heat, L, in joules per kilogram, J/kg

Keyword
Specific latent heat ➤ The energy required to change the state of one kilogram of the substance with no change in temperature

> **Example:**
> What is the energy needed for 600 g of water to melt? (The specific latent heat of water melting is 334 kJ/kg.)
>
> $$E = mL$$
> $$0.6 \times 334 = 200.4 \text{ kJ}$$

The specific latent heat of fusion is the energy required for a change of state from solid to liquid.

The specific latent heat of vapourisation is the energy required for a change of state from liquid to vapour

Temperature can be measured in degrees Celsius (°C) or Kelvin (K). To convert from Celsius to Kelvin, add 273.

For example:
➤ 10°C + 273 = 283 K

0 Kelvin (−273°C) is **absolute zero**. At this point, the particles have no kinetic energy so are not moving.

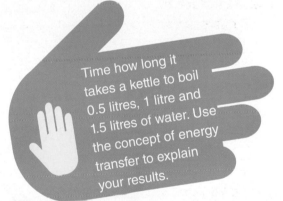

Time how long it takes a kettle to boil 0.5 litres, 1 litre and 1.5 litres of water. Use the concept of energy transfer to explain your results.

1. What energy is needed for 200 kg of cast iron to turn from a solid to a liquid? (The specific latent heat of iron melting is 126 kJ/kg.)
2. Explain the difference between the specific latent heat of fusion and the specific latent heat of vapourisation.
3. If a substance is heated but its temperature remains constant, what is happening to the substance?
4. What is 32 °C in Kelvin?

Mind map

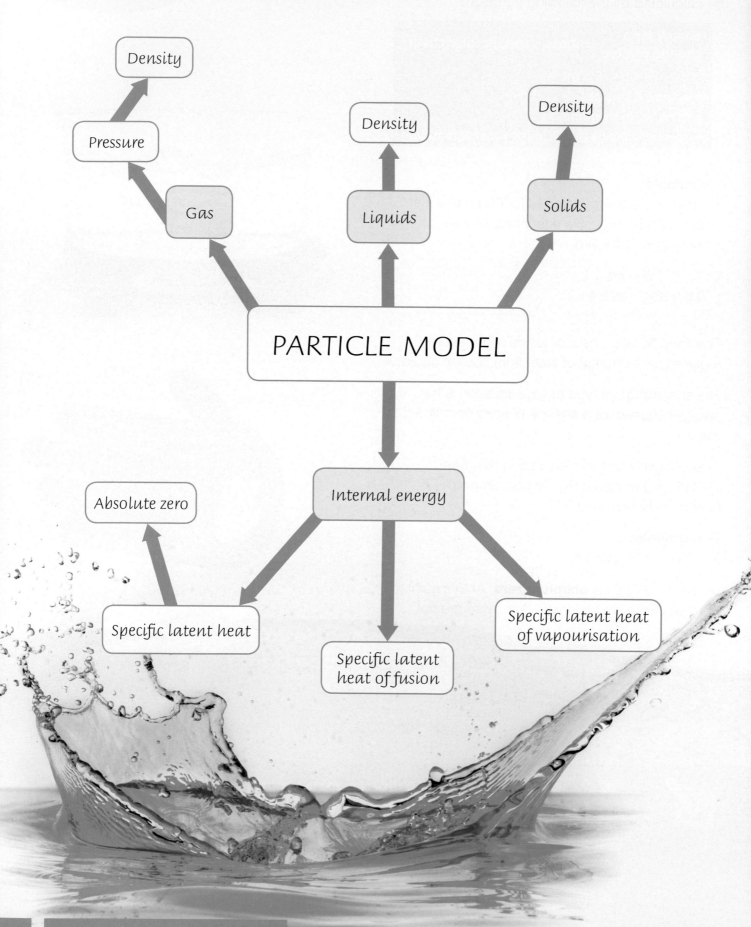

Density

Pressure

Gas

Density

Liquids

Density

Solids

PARTICLE MODEL

Internal energy

Absolute zero

Specific latent heat

Specific latent heat of fusion

Specific latent heat of vapourisation

Practice questions

1. A solid has a mass of 150 g and a volume of 0.0001 m³.

   a) What is the density of the solid? **(2 marks)**

   b) What happens to the mass and density of the solid when it sublimes? **(2 marks)**

   c) Explain what would happen to the stored internal energy and the temperature of the solid as it sublimed. **(2 marks)**

   d) The specific latent heat of the solid is 574 kJ/kg.

      What is the energy required for the solid to sublime? **(2 marks)**

2. Explain, using the particle model, why:

   a) a gas at a constant volume has a higher pressure when the temperature increases. **(2 marks)**

   b) a gas at a constant temperature has a lower pressure when the volume increases. **(2 marks)**

3. A solid has a temperature of 300 Kelvin.

   a) What is this temperature in °C? **(1 mark)**

   b) If the temperature fell to 250 Kelvin, how would the average kinetic energy and average speed of the particles in the solid change? **(1 mark)**

4. What term is given to the energy required for 1 kg of a liquid to become a gas? **(1 mark)**

Atoms and isotopes

Structure of atoms

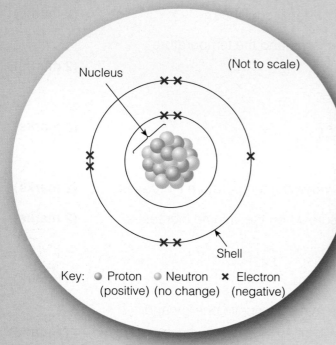

Nucleus

(Not to scale)

Shell

Key: ● Proton ● Neutron ✕ Electron
(positive) (no change) (negative)

Atoms have a radius of around 1×10^{-10} metres.

The radius of a nucleus is less than $\dfrac{1}{10\,000}$ of the radius of an atom.

Most of the mass of an atom is concentrated in the nucleus. Protons and neutrons have a relative mass of 1 while electrons have a relative mass of 0.0005. The electrons are arranged at different distances from the nucleus (are at different energy levels).

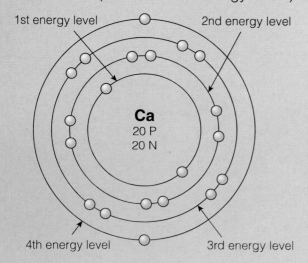

1st energy level

2nd energy level

Ca
20 P
20 N

4th energy level

3rd energy level

Absorption of electromagnetic radiation causes the electrons to become excited and move to a higher energy level and further from the nucleus.

Emission of electromagnetic radiation causes the electrons to move to a lower energy level and move closer to the nucleus.

If an atom loses or gains an electron, it is ionised.

The number of electrons is equal to the number of protons in the nucleus of an atom.

Atoms have no overall electrical charge.

All atoms of a particular element have the same number of protons. The number of protons in an atom of an element is called the **atomic number**.

The total number of protons and neutrons in an atom is called the **mass number**.

Mass number $\longrightarrow$
Atomic number $\longrightarrow$ $_{2}^{4}\text{He}$ $\longleftarrow$ Element symbol

Atoms of the same element can have different numbers of neutrons; these atoms are called isotopes of that element. For example, below are some isotopes of nitrogen. They each have 7 protons in the nucleus but different numbers of neutrons, giving the different isotopes.

$$^{14}\text{N} \quad ^{15}\text{N} \quad ^{13}\text{N}$$

Atoms turn into **positive ions** if they lose one or more outer electrons and into **negative ions** if they gain one or more outer electrons.

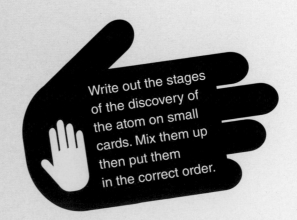

Write out the stages of the discovery of the atom on small cards. Mix them up then put them in the correct order.

The development of the atomic model

Before the discovery of the electron, atoms were thought to be tiny spheres that could not be divided.

The discovery of the electron led to further developments of the model. The plum pudding model suggested that the atom is a ball of positive charge with negative electrons embedded in it.

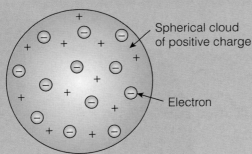

Spherical cloud of positive charge

Electron

Rutherford, Geiger and Marsden's alpha scattering experiment led to the conclusion that the mass of an atom was concentrated at the centre (nucleus) and that the nucleus was charged.

The nucleus

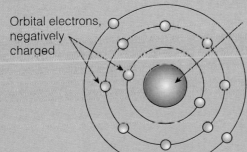

Orbits

Electrons

This evidence led to the nuclear model replacing the plum pudding model.

Niels Bohr suggested that the electrons orbit the nucleus at specific distances. The theoretical calculations of Bohr agreed with experimental observation.

Orbital electrons, negatively charged

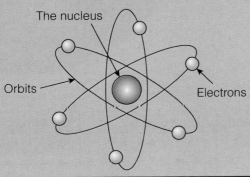

Nucleus, containing positively charged protons

Later experiments led to the idea of the nucleus containing smaller particles with the same amount of positive charge (**protons**).

In 1932, the experimental work of James Chadwick provided evidence of the existence within the nucleus of the **neutron**.

Keywords

Atomic number ➤ Number of protons in an atom

Mass number ➤ Total number of protons and neutrons in an atom

1. What is the effect on the electrons when an atom absorbs electromagnetic radiation?
2. What name is given to atoms of the same element that have different numbers of neutrons?
3. What is the difference between the plum pudding model and the nuclear model?

Radioactive decay, nuclear radiation and nuclear equations

Radioactive decay

Some atomic nuclei are unstable. The nucleus gives out radiation as it changes to become more stable. This is a random process called **radioactive decay**. Changes in atoms and nuclei can also generate and absorb radiation over the whole frequency range.

Activity is the rate at which a source of unstable nuclei decays, measured in **becquerel** (Bq).

➤ 1 becquerel = 1 decay per second

Count rate is the number of decays recorded each second by a detector, such as a Geiger-Müller tube).

➤ 1 becquerel = 1 count per second

Radioactive decay can release a neutron, alpha particles, beta particles or gamma rays. If radiation is ionising, it can damage materials and living cells.

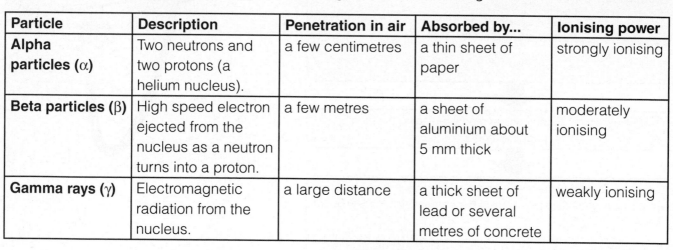

Particle	Description	Penetration in air	Absorbed by...	Ionising power
Alpha particles (α)	Two neutrons and two protons (a helium nucleus).	a few centimetres	a thin sheet of paper	strongly ionising
Beta particles (β)	High speed electron ejected from the nucleus as a neutron turns into a proton.	a few metres	a sheet of aluminium about 5 mm thick	moderately ionising
Gamma rays (γ)	Electromagnetic radiation from the nucleus.	a large distance	a thick sheet of lead or several metres of concrete	weakly ionising

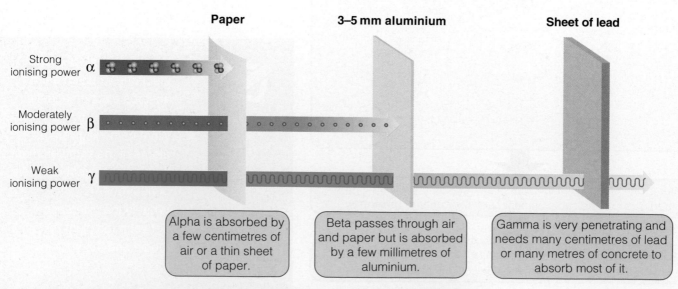

Alpha is absorbed by a few centimetres of air or a thin sheet of paper.

Beta passes through air and paper but is absorbed by a few millimetres of aluminium.

Gamma is very penetrating and needs many centimetres of lead or many metres of concrete to absorb most of it.

Nuclear equations

Nuclear equations are used to represent radioactive decay.

Nuclear equations can use the following symbols:

$^{4}_{2}\textbf{He}$ alpha particle

$^{0}_{-1}\textbf{e}$ beta particle

Alpha decay causes both the mass and charge of the nucleus to decrease, as two protons and two neutrons are released.

$$^{219}_{86}\textbf{radon} \rightarrow {}^{215}_{84}\textbf{polonium} + {}^{4}_{2}\textbf{He}$$

Beta decay does not cause the mass of the nucleus to change but does cause the charge of the nucleus to increase, as a proton becomes a neutron.

$$^{14}_{6}\textbf{carbon} \rightarrow {}^{14}_{7}\textbf{nitrogen} + {}^{0}_{-1}\textbf{e}$$

The above example is β– decay as a neutron has becomes a proton and an electron has been ejected. In β+ decay a proton becomes a neutron plus a positron.

The emission of a gamma ray does not cause the mass or the charge of the nucleus to change.

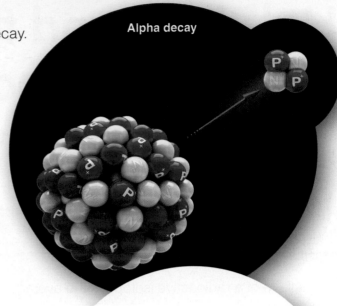

Alpha decay

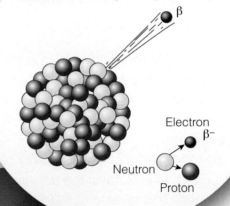

Beta-minus decay with gamma ray

β

Electron
β⁻

Neutron

Proton

Make a large version of the radioactive decay table on p. 222. Cut out each individual box to form separate cards. Mix the cards up and then group them to show the features of alpha, beta and gamma particles.

Keywords

Radioactive decay ➤ Random release of radiation from an unstable nucleus as it becomes more stable

Becquerel ➤ Unit of rate of radioactive decay

1. How far does alpha radiation penetrate in air?
2. What material is required to absorb gamma rays?
3. What effect does beta decay have on the mass and charge of the nucleus of an atom?

Half-lives and the random nature of radioactive decay

Uranium

Half-life

Radioactive decay occurs randomly. It is not possible to predict which nuclei will decay.

The half-life of a radioactive isotope is the average time it takes for:

➤ the number of nuclei in a sample of the isotope to halve

or

➤ the count rate (or activity) from a sample containing the isotope to fall to half of its initial level.

For example:

A radioactive sample has an activity of 560 counts per second. After 8 days, the activity is 280 counts per second. This gives a half-life of 8 days.

The decay can be plotted on a graph and the half-life determined from the graph.

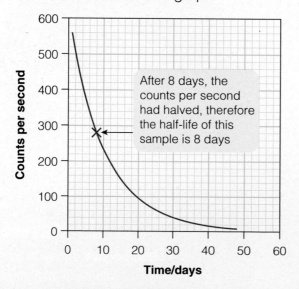

After 8 days, the counts per second had halved, therefore the half-life of this sample is 8 days

HT After another 8 days, the activity would now be 140 counts per second. As a ratio the total net decline is 140 : 560 or 1 : 4.

Radioactive contamination

Radioactive contamination is the unwanted presence of materials containing radioactive atoms or other materials.

This is a hazard due to the decay of the contaminating atoms. The level of the hazard depends on the type of radiation emitted.

Irradiation is the process of exposing an object to nuclear radiation. This is different from radioactive contamination as the irradiated object does not become radioactive.

Suitable precautions must be taken to protect against any hazard from the radioactive source used in the process of irradiation. In medical testing using radioactive sources, the doses patients receive are limited and medical staff wear protective equipment.

Keyword

Irradiation ➤ Exposing an object to nuclear radiation without the object becoming radioactive itself

It is important for the findings of studies into the effects of radiation on humans to be published and shared with other scientists. This allows the findings of the studies to be checked by other scientists by the peer review process.

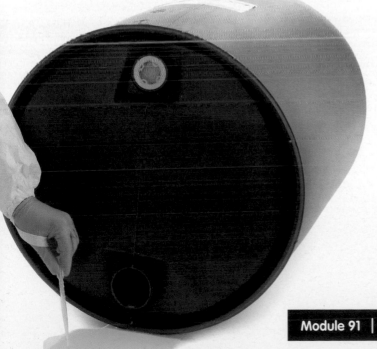

Shake ten or more coins in your hand and then drop them. Remove all the coins that are heads and record the number you've removed. Repeat the experiment until you have one or no coins left. Now plot a graph of how the number of coins in your hand decreased over time. Then, research graphs showing radioactive decay and compare them to the graph from your experiment.

1. Give the two definitions of half-life.
2. What is the half-life of a sample that goes from a count per second of 960 to 240 in 10 months?
3. Why is radioactive contamination a hazard?

Mind map

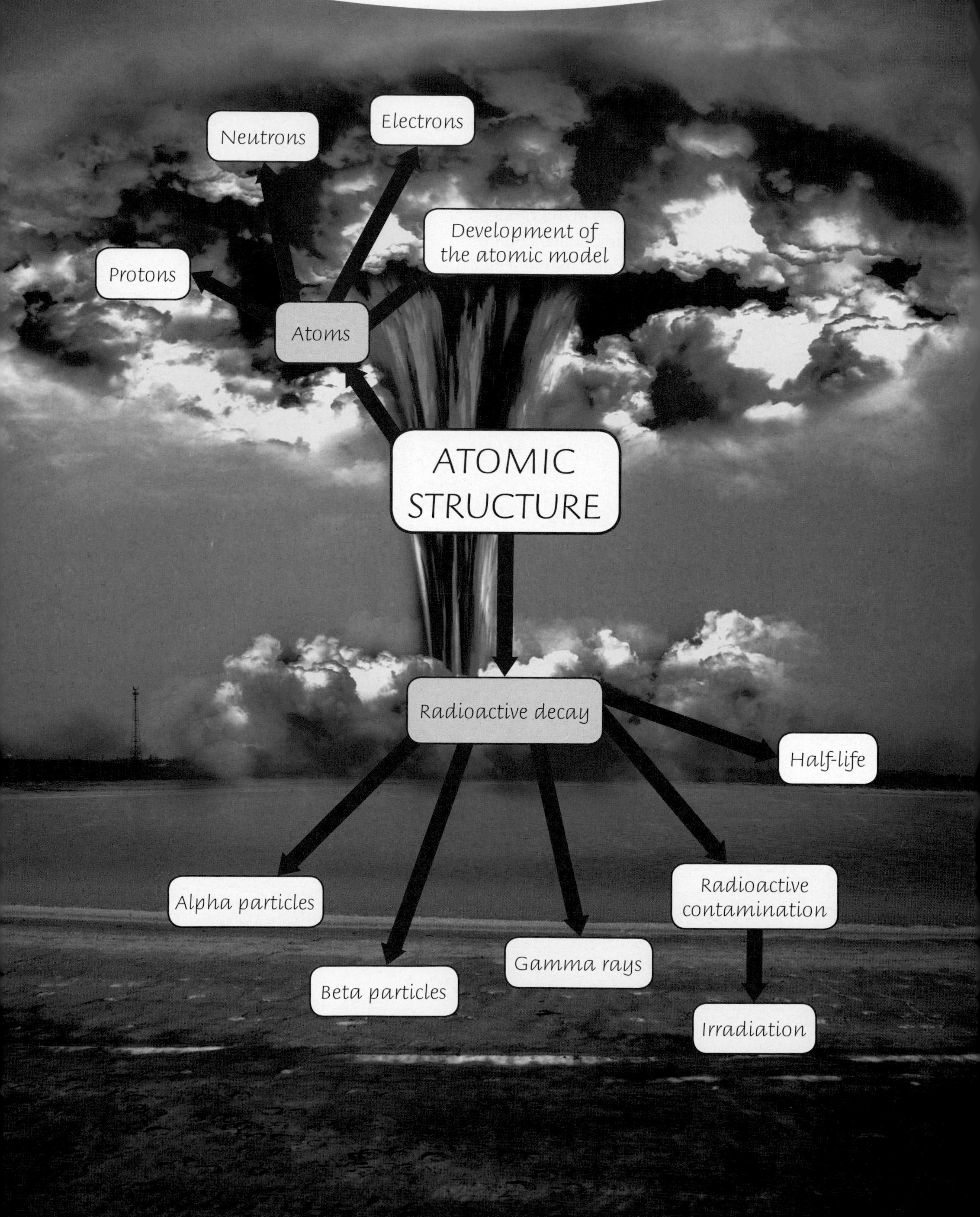

Neutrons

Electrons

Development of
the atomic model

Protons

Atoms

ATOMIC
STRUCTURE

Radioactive decay

Half-life

Alpha particles

Radioactive
contamination

Beta particles

Gamma rays

Irradiation

Practice questions

1. The symbol below shows an element.

$$^{48}_{22}\text{Ti}$$

   a) What is its . . .

   i) number of protons? **(1 mark)**

   ii) number of electrons? **(1 mark)**

   iii) number of neutrons? **(1 mark)**

   b) For parts i)–iii) above, explain how you arrived at your answers. **(6 marks)**

2. Experiments by Rutherford, Geiger and Marsden led to the plum pudding model being replaced by the nuclear model.

   a) Explain the differences between the plum pudding model and the nuclear model. **(2 marks)**

   b) How did the further work of Bohr and the further work of Chadwick refine the nuclear model? **(2 marks)**

3. The graph below shows the activity of a radioactive sample over time.

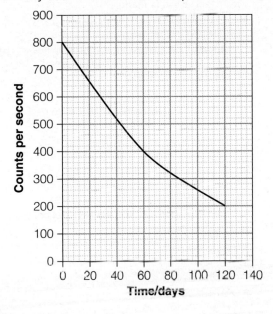

   a) What is the half-life of this sample?
      Explain how you arrived at your answer. **(2 marks)**

   b) Would this sample be useful as a radioactive tracer in medicine?
      Explain your answer. **(2 marks)**

   c) Balance the equation below to show the alpha decay of uranium.

$$^{238}_{92}\text{U} \rightarrow \,^{234}_{90}\text{Th} + \,^{4}_{2}\text{H}$$

   (2 marks)

Answers

Biology

Page 7

1. **Prokaryotes:** any three bacteria or archaebacteria, e.g. cholera, *E. coli* and salmonella. **Eukaryotes:** any three from the plant, animal, protist or fungal kingdoms, e.g. geranium (plant), tiger (animal), amoeba (protist) and mushroom (fungus).
2. A prokaryote has a DNA loop and plasmids. A eukaryote's DNA is found in the nucleus.
3. True – all cells do have a cell membrane.
4. Mitochondrion.
5. Chloroplasts contain chlorophyll to absorb sunlight for photosynthesis.

Page 9

1. An organ.
2. It is able to contract (shorten).
3. Phloem.
4. **Any one benefit**, e.g. can be used to treat serious conditions, cancer research, organ transplants. Any one objection, e.g. the embryo has the potential to be a living human and shouldn't be experimented with, risk of viral transmission.

Page 11

1. **Any two from:** electron microscopes use electrons to form images, light microscopes use light waves; electron microscopes produce 2D and 3D images, light microscopes use 2D images only; electron microscopes have a magnification up to ×500 000 (2D), light microscopes have a magnification of up to ×1500; electron microscopes are able to observe small organelles, light microscopes are only able to observe cells and larger organelles; electron microscopes enable you to see things at high resolution, light microscopes allow you to see things at low resolution.
2. The resolving power of a light microscope can only be used for objects that are greater than 200 nm across.

Page 13

1. For growth, repair and reproduction.
2. Chromosomes.
3. **Mitosis:** asexual reproduction, repair and growth; **meiosis:** sexual reproduction.
4. DNA/chromosomes and all other organelles.

Page 15

1. **Building** – any one from: converting glucose to starch in plants/glucose to glycogen in animals; synthesis of lipid molecules, formation of amino acids in plants (which are built up into proteins). **Breaking down** – any one from: breaking down excess proteins to form urea, respiration.
2. Aerobic.

Page 17 (col 2)

3. **Any two from:** transmitting nerve impulses, active transport, muscle contraction/ movement, maintaining a constant body temperature, synthesis of molecules.
4. **Humans:** lactic acid; **yeast:** ethanol and carbon dioxide.
5. To pay back the oxygen debt, i.e. take in oxygen to remove the lactic acid in muscles.

Page 17

1. pH and temperature.
2. A substrate molecule fits exactly into a specific enzyme's active site.
3. It emulsifies fat and helps neutralise acid from the stomach.
4. Amino acids.

Page 19

1. **A:** cell membrane, **B:** DNA, **C:** cell wall, **D:** plasmid. (**1 mark for each correct**)
2. a) Lactic acid increase in muscles causes muscle fatigue/tiredness (**1 mark**); lactic acid is toxic (**1 mark**).
   b) Anaerobic respiration releases lower amounts of energy than aerobic respiration; not enough energy available for extended periods of intense activity. (**1 mark**)
   c) Glucose is completely broken down (to carbon dioxide and water). (**1 mark**)
3. a) Denaturing/denaturation. (**1 mark**)
   b) Change in shape of active site (**1 mark**); substrate no longer fits active site (**1 mark**).
4. A specialised system is needed to transport oxygen over long distances (**1 mark**); paramecium can rely on simple diffusion due to its larger surface area / volume ratio (**1 mark**).

Page 21

1. A shrew – the proportion of its area to its volume is greater, despite the fact that its **total** body area is less than that of an elephant.
2. The plant cells have a higher water potential/lower solute concentration. The water moves **down** an osmotic gradient from inside the cells into the salt solution.

Page 23

1. Root hair cells.
2. To allow space for gases to be exchanged more freely.
3. So that cells can freely carry water up the plant.

Page 25

1. It would increase the (evapo)transpiration rate.
2. When temperatures are high (during the day) and loss of water through open stomata would cause the plant to dehydrate and wilt.
3. Osmosis.
4. Water enters the xylem at root level due to a 'suction' force caused by evaporation from the leaves, called (evapo) transpiration. The water is drawn up as a column within the stem's xylem.

Page 27

1. Valves prevent backflow of blood and ensure it reaches the heart (especially from parts of the body vertically below the heart).
2. Excess fat (particularly saturated fat) in the diet causes cholesterol to build up and block the coronary artery. This restricts the supply of blood to the heart muscle, which then does not receive enough oxygen and glucose. The heart muscle therefore dies.

Page 29

1. **Red blood cells** do not have a nucleus, are biconcave in shape, contain haemoglobin and carry oxygen. **Lymphocytes** have a nucleus, are irregular in shape and are involved in the immune response.
2. Oxygen is breathed into alveoli, diffuses across alveolar wall and combines with haemoglobin in a red blood cell. Blood enters the heart, from which it is pumped to the respiring muscle tissue. The oxygen diffuses from the red blood cell into a muscle cell, where it reacts with glucose during aerobic respiration.

Page 31

1. Photosynthesis takes **in** carbon dioxide and water, and requires an energy input. It produces glucose and oxygen. Respiration **produces** carbon dioxide and water, and releases energy. It absorbs glucose and oxygen.
2. Balancing investment costs with increased profit from increased yield.

Page 33

1. a, d and e (**1 mark** for each correct answer)
2. a) Healthy man (**1 mark**)
   b) **Any two from:** less oxygen absorbed into blood; longer diffusion distance across alveolar wall; insufficient oxygen delivered to muscles to release energy for exercise (**2 marks**)
3. a) **A:** artery (**1 mark**); **B:** vein (**1 mark**).
   b) **Any one from:** an artery has to withstand/recoil with higher pressure; elasticity allows smoother blood flow/ second boost to blood when recoils. (**1 mark**)
   c) **Any one from:** to prevent backflow of blood; compensate for low blood pressure. (**1 mark**)

Page 35

1. **Any three from:** smoking tobacco, drinking excess alcohol, carcinogens, ionising radiation.
2. The body is more prone to infections.

Page 37

1. Cholera bacteria are found in human faeces, which contaminate water supplies.
2. **Any two reasonable answers, e.g.:** measles, athlete's foot.

Page 39

1. Phagocyte engulfs a pathogen where it is digested by the cell's enzymes.
2. Lymphocytes detect antigen; this triggers production of antibodies; once pathogens are destroyed, memory cells are produced; further infection with same pathogen dealt with swiftly, as antibodies produced rapidly in large numbers. The process can also be triggered via vaccination.

Page 41

1. An antibiotic is a drug that kills bacteria; an antibody is a protein produced by the immune system that kills bacteria.
2. An antiviral alleviates symptoms of an infection; analgesics are painkillers.
3. Do not prescribe antibiotics for viral/non-serious infections; ensure that the full course of antibiotics is completed.

Page 43

1. Human volunteers; computer simulations/modelling; cells grown in tissue culture.
2. **Any two from:** to see if they work; to make sure they are safe; to make sure that they are given at the correct dose.

Page 45

1. **Any two from:** apply a fungicide; remove affected leaves; don't plant roses too close together; avoid wetting leaves
2. Photosynthesis and growth is affected.

Page 47

1. Bacterium – cholera; fungus – athlete's foot; virus – HIV; protist – malaria.
   (**3 marks** for all answers correct;
   2 marks for 2 or 3 answers correct;
   1 mark for 1 answer correct)
2. a) i) Phagocytes engulf the pathogen, then digest it **(1 mark)**
      ii) Antibodies lock onto antigen/pathogen/clump pathogens together. **(1 mark)**
   b) Vaccine contains dead/heat-treated pathogen/microbe. **(1 mark)**
      Antigen recognised as foreign **(1 mark)**; lymphocytes produce antibodies against it **(1 mark)**; memory cells remain in system ready to produce antibodies if re-infection occurs **(1 mark)**.
   c) Antibiotics don't work against viruses **(1 mark)**, over-prescription may lead to antibiotic resistance **(1 mark)**.
   d) **Any one from:** antiviral drug/analgesic **(1 mark)**
3. a) Yes (no marks). Any two for **2 marks**: DDD results in a greater weight loss; 5.8 compared with 3.2; significantly higher than the placebo.
      No (no marks). Any two for **2 marks**: Number of volunteers for the DDD trial is very small compared with the other two trials; more trials need to be carried out; data is unreliable.

b) In a double blind trial, neither the volunteers nor the doctors know which drug has been given **(1 mark)**; this eliminates all bias from the test/scientists cannot influence the volunteers' response in any way **(1 mark)**.

Page 49

1. **Any two from:** osmoregulation/water balance; balancing blood sugar levels; maintaining a constant body temperature; controlling metabolic rate.
2. The pituitary.

Page 51

1. Axons/dendrites.
2. They ensure a rapid response to a threatening/harmful stimulus, e.g. picking up a hot plate. As a result, they reduce harm to the human body.
3. Flow diagram with the following labels: (stretch) receptor at knee joint stimulated; sensory neurone sends impulse to spine; intermediate/relay neurone relays impulse to motor neurone; motor neurone sends impulse to (thigh) muscle; (thigh) muscle contracts.

Page 53

1. It releases a range of hormones that control other processes in the body.
2. In the ovaries and the pituitary (female); in the testes (male).
3. Reduced ability of cells to absorb insulin and therefore high levels of blood glucose. This leads to tiredness, frequent urination, poor circulation, eye problems, etc.

Page 55

1. **Any three from:** glucose, amino acids, fatty acids, glycerol, some water.
2. Makes urine more concentrated.
3. It diffuses down a concentration gradient from the patient's blood into the dialysis fluid.

Page 57

1. FSH acts on the ovaries, causing an egg to mature; oestrogen inhibits further production of FSH, stimulates the release of LH and promotes repair of the uterus wall; LH stimulates release of an egg; progesterone maintains the lining of the uterus after ovulation has occurred and inhibits FSH and LH.
2. Just after menstruation has stopped/from day 7.
3. **Any one from:** production of sperm in testes; development of muscles and penis; deepening of the voice, growth of pubic, facial and body hair.

Page 59

1. Oral contraceptive, hormone injection or implant.
2. They provide a barrier/prevent transferral of the virus during sexual intercourse.
3. Microscopes enable scientists to observe in vitro fertilisation and retrieval of zygote/fertilised egg for implantation in the woman.

Page 61

1. a) Stimulus. **(1 mark)**
   b) The response is automatic/unconscious **(1 mark)**; response is rapid **(1 mark)**.
   c) Stimulus at receptor triggers sensory neurone to send impulse **(1 mark)**; impulse received in brain and/or spinal cord and signal sent to intermediate/relay neurone **(1 mark)**; impulse then sent to motor neurone **(1 mark)**; motor neurone sends impulse to effector/muscles in hand **(1 mark)**.
2. a) The person's blood sugar level **(1 mark)** fluctuates dramatically **(1 mark)**.
   b) The person has eaten their breakfast at A and their lunch at B. **(1 mark)**
   c) There would be a slight rise in blood sugar level, followed by a swift drop back to normal level. **(1 mark)**
   d) Their blood sugar level had dropped too low/below normal. **(1 mark)**
3. a) They release (more) sweat **(1 mark)**; sweat evaporates, taking heat from the skin **(1 mark)**.
   b) Excretion. **(1 mark)**
   c) Amino acids. **(1 mark)**
   d) **Top box:** Urea enters/is carried in blood **(1 mark)**; **box below it:** Urine stored in bladder **(1 mark)**.

Page 63

1. It allows variation, which gives an evolutionary advantage when the environment changes.
2. **Any one from:** produces clones of the parent – if these are successfully adapted individuals, then rapid colonisation and survival can be achieved; only one parent required; fewer resources required than sexual reproduction; faster than sexual reproduction.

Page 65

1. It has allowed the production of linkage maps that can be used for tracking inherited traits from generation to generation. This has led to targeted treatments for these conditions.
2. Proteins.

Page 67

1. A dominant allele controls the development of a characteristic even if it is present on only one chromosome in a pair. A recessive allele controls the development of a characteristic only if a dominant allele is not present.
2. Wrong base sequences may lead to incorrect or no protein being produced. This may have consequences for health/wrong base sequence may not affect function of protein produced.

Page 69

1. Zero/0%.
2. XX.
3. Causes production of thick mucus in respiratory pathways and interferes with enzyme production.

Page 71

1. **Any two from:** the fossil record; comparative anatomy (pentadactyl limb); looking at changes in species during modern times; studying embryos and their similarities; comparing genomes of different organisms.
2. The conditions for their formation are rare, e.g. rapid burial and a lower chance of being discovered before they are eroded.

Page 73

1. **Evolution:** the long-term changes seen in species over a long period of time. **Natural selection:** the mechanism by which evolution occurs.
2. **Any two examples,** e.g. Kettlewell's moths; antibiotic resistance in bacteria.
3. They must be passed on by the well-adapted individual that contains them, through reproduction, to the next generation.

Page 75

1. Genetic engineering is more precise and it takes less time to see results.
2. **Reason for:** food production improved through increased yields and better nutritional content. **Reason against:** GM plants may spread their genetic material into the wider ecosystem, resulting in, for example, herbicide-resistant weeds/ possible harmful effect of GM foods on consumers.

Page 77

1. Genus and species.
2. Invertebrates, vertebrates, protists, higher plants.
3. Common ancestor.

Page 79

1. **Any four from:**
   - adapted to environment/had different characteristics
   - named examples of different characteristics, e.g. some horse-like mammals had more flipper-like limbs (as whales have flippers); idea of competition for limited resources
   - examples of different types of competition; idea of survival of the fittest
   - adaptations being advantageous to living in water/idea that adaptations helped them survive
   - named examples of different adaptations, e.g. some horse-like mammals had more flipper-like limbs that allowed them to swim well in water; idea of inheritance of successful characteristics
   - (named) characteristics/adaptations passed on (through breeding). **(4 marks)**
2. a) Ff
   b) ff
3. a) **Step 3:** section of human DNA inserted into plasmid by ligase enzyme **(1 mark)**. **Step 5:** bacterium replicates/cultivated in fermenter. **(1 mark)**
   b) Restriction enzyme. **(1 mark)**

4. a) Nitrogenous base. **(1 mark)**
   b) Double helix. **(1 mark)**

Page 81

1. A **habitat** is the part of the physical environment in which an animal lives. An **ecosystem** includes the habitat, its communities of animals and plants, together with the physical factors that influence them.
2. **A mixed-leaf woodland:** the biodiversity is greater and so the links between different organisms are more extensive.
3. A **population** is the number of individuals of a species in a defined area. A **community** contains many different populations of species.
4. **Any two examples,** e.g. chemotrophs (live in deep ocean trenches and volcanic vents) and icefish (exist in waters less than 0°C in temperature).
5. So that they survive to reproductive age and pass on their genes to the next generation.

Page 83

1. Where you have a transition from one habitat to the next. It would tell you how numbers of different species vary along the line of the transect.

Page 85

1. The level that an organism feeds at, e.g. producer, primary consumer level. It refers to layers in a pyramid of biomass.
2. As the rabbit population decreases, there is less food available for foxes; so the fox population decreases. Fewer rabbits are therefore eaten, so the rabbit population then increases.

Page 87

1. **One from:** sulfur dioxide; nitrogen dioxide.
2. Numbers increase at a rapidly increasing rate.
3. With more species, there are more relationships between different organisms and therefore more resistance to disruption from outside influences.
4. Plant a variety of trees, especially deciduous; protect rare species; make it a Site of Special Scientific Interest (SSSI); protect against invasive species, e.g. red squirrel.

Page 88

1. Condensation and evaporation.
2. As coal.
3. **Any two from:** combustion, animal respiration, plant respiration, microbial respiration (including decay).

Page 89

1. As bacteria feed on the dead organisms they use up oxygen. This causes larger organisms and plants to die because they are unable to respire.
2. Setting quotas and increasing mesh size of nets.

Page 91

1. a) Respiration. **(1 mark)**
   b) **Any two from:** Fossil fuels represent a carbon 'sink'/they absorbed great quantities of carbon many millions of years ago from the atmosphere; combustion in power stations returns this carbon dioxide; less burning of fossil fuels cuts down on carbon emissions; alternative sources of energy may not return as much carbon dioxide to the atmosphere. **(2 marks)**
2. a) 120–125 **(1 mark)**
   b) When kingfishers increase, fish decrease/when kingfishers decrease, fish increase. **(1 mark)**
   c) This is a model answer that would score the full **6 marks**: Three rivers is too small a sample so not all birds would be observed, and ringing birds might affect their survival. Some fish may evade capture by anglers and not all anglers will cooperate with the scientist. Not all species will be caught and kingfishers do not feed on every species of fish. Improvements could be made by sampling many more rivers, using more observers, sampling fish directly, e.g. mark/ recapture technique, observing which species of fish the kingfishers take, or by using more efficient capture methods for fish, e.g. netting.
3. features; characteristics (either way around); suited; environment; evolutionary; survival. (**6 words correct = 3 marks, four or five words correct = 2 marks, two or three words correct = 1 mark, one or 0 words correct = 0 marks.**)

Chemistry

Page 93
1. A compound.
2. Simple distillation.

Page 95
1. The plum pudding model suggests that the electrons are embedded within the positive charge in an atom. The nuclear model suggested that the positive charge was confined in a small volume (the nucleus) of an atom.
2. Because most of the positive charge passed straight through the atom. As only a few alpha particles were deflected, this suggested that the positive part of the atom was very small.
3. 6 protons, 6 electrons and 7 neutrons.
4. Isotopes.

Page 97
1. 2, 8, 1
2. He predicted that there were more elements to be discovered. He predicted their properties and left appropriate places in the periodic table based on his predictions.
3. A metal.

Page 99
1. Because they have full outer shells of electrons.
2. Lithium hydroxide and hydrogen.
3. The reactivity decreases.
4. Potassium bromide and iodine.

Page 101
1. a) protons = 17 (**1 mark**), electrons = 17 (**1 mark**), neutrons = 18 (**1 mark**).
   b) 2, 8, 7 (**1 mark**).
   c) Similarity: same number of protons in each atom, same number of electrons in each atom, same chemical properties (**1 mark**). Difference: different number of neutrons in each atom (**1 mark**).
   d) **One from**: does not conduct heat/electricity; gas at room temperature (**1 mark**).
   e) $Cl_2 + 2NaI \rightarrow 2NaCl + I_2$ (**1 mark for correct formula, 1 mark for correct balancing**).
   f) Chlorine is less reactive than fluorine (**1 mark**), so it is unable to displace fluorine from a compound (**1 mark**).
2. a) Filtration (**1 mark**).
   b) Flask connected to condenser with bung/thermometer in place (**1 mark**).
   Water flowing in at the bottom and leaving at the top (**1 mark**).
   Salt water and pure water labelled (**1 mark**).

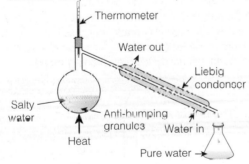
Thermometer
Water out
Liebig condenser
Salty water
Anti-bumping granules
Water in
Heat
Pure water

   c) The water is lost/evaporates during crystallisation (**1 mark**).
3. $\frac{(10 \times 20) + (11 \times 80)}{100}$ (**1 mark**)
   = 10.8 (**1 mark**)
   Answer to 3 significant figures. (**1 mark**)

Page 103
1. Ionic.
2. Two.
3. A lattice (regular arrangement) of cations surrounded by a sea of (delocalised) electrons.

Page 105
1. Electrostatic forces/strong forces between cations and anions
2. Simple molecular, polymers, giant covalent
3.

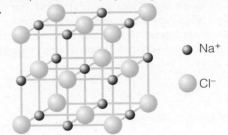
● Na⁺
○ Cl⁻

Page 107
1. The strength of the forces acting between the particles present.
2. The electrostatic forces of attraction between the ions are strong.
3. The intermolecular forces/forces between the molecules.
4. Polymers have larger molecules therefore there are more forces between the molecules.
5. There are lots of strong covalent bonds that need lots of energy to break them all.

Page 109
1. Because there are strong forces of attraction between the metal cations and delocalised electrons.
2. In alloys, the layers of metal ions are not able to slide over each other.
3. Each carbon atom has a spare electron that allows it to conduct electricity.
4. **Two from**: high tensile strength; high electrical conductivity; high thermal conductivity.
5. **Two from**: drug delivery into the body; lubricants; reinforcing materials.

Page 111
1. a) Ionic (**1 mark**)
   b)

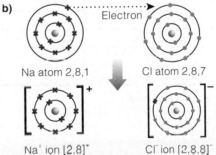
Electron
Na atom 2,8,1
Cl atom 2,8,7
Na⁺ ion [2,8]⁺
Cl⁻ ion [2,8,8]⁻

   (**Correct electronic structure of atoms, 1 mark; correct electronic structure of ions, 1 mark; correct charges on ions, 1 mark**)
   c) There are strong electrostatic forces of attraction (**1 mark**) between the ions (**1 mark**).
   d) High (**1 mark**). Lots of energy is needed to overcome the forces holding the ions together (**1 mark**).
   e)

Negatively charged chloride ions

Positively charged sodium ions (**1 mark**)

2. a) Covalent **(1 mark)**.
  b) i) Two **(1 mark)**.
    ii) Simple molecular **(1 mark)**.
  c) i) Giant covalent (macromolecular) **(1 mark)**.
    ii) Simple molecular structures consist of many individual molecules held together by weak intermolecular forces **(1 mark)**. Giant covalent structures are lots of atoms all held together by covalent bonds **(1 mark)**.
  d) Silicon dioxide will have a higher boiling point **(1 mark)**. The covalent bonds in silicon dioxide that need to be broken in order to boil it are much stronger than the intermolecular forces that need to be broken in order to boil carbon dioxide **(1 mark)**.

Page 113
1. The same.
2. **a)** 80
   b) 58
3. Lower.

Page 115
1. 100 g
2. 124 g
3. Li_2O
4. P_4O_{10}

Page 117
1. 2.3 g
2. $Si + 2Cl_2 \rightarrow SiCl_4$

Page 119
1. **a)** Lower **(1 mark)**, because the $CaCO_3$/calcium carbonate will have thermally decomposed meaning that some of the $CaCO_3$ will have decomposed into carbon dioxide, which will have gone into the air **(1 mark)**.
   b) 100 **(1 mark)**.
   c) 100 g of $CaCO_3$ forms 44 g of CO_2; therefore 10 g of $CaCO_3$ will have formed 4.4 g of CO_2 **(1 mark for working, 1 mark for the correct answer based on working; correct answer on its own scores 2 marks. The final answer must include the units)**.
   d) moles of Mg: $0.15 \div 24 = 0.00625$ **(1 mark)**; number of atoms: $0.00625 \times 6 \times 10^{23} = 3.75 \times 10^{21}$ **(1 mark)**.
2. **a)** $100 - (40 + 6.67) = 53.33$ **(1 mark)**
   b)

Element	Mass	Moles = mass ÷ Ar	÷ smallest
C	40	$40 \div 12 = 3.33$	$3.33 \div 3.33 = 1$
H	6.67	$6.67 \div 1 = 6.67$	$6.67 \div 3.33 = 2$
O	53.33	$53.33 \div 16 = 3.333125$	$3.333125 \div 3.33 = 1$
		(1 mark)	**(1 mark)**

   Empirical formula = CH_2O **(1 mark)**
   c) Relative formula mass of empirical formula
   $= 12 + (1 \times 2) + 16 = 30$
   $$\frac{\text{Actual } M_r}{\text{relative formula mass of empirical formula}} = \frac{60}{30} = 2 \text{ (1 mark)}$$
   Molecular formula = $C_2H_4O_2$ **(1 mark)**

Page 121
1. magnesium + oxygen → magnesium oxide
2. Sodium (because it is more reactive).
3. **Two from**: zinc, iron, copper.
4. Magnesium is being oxidised (because it loses electrons) and Zn^{2+} is being reduced (because it gains electrons).

Page 123
1. zinc + sulfuric acid → zinc sulfate + hydrogen.
2. Fe
3. A metal, metal oxide or metal carbonate.
4. Lithium nitrate.
5. Add solid until no more reacts, filter off the excess solid, crystallise the remaining solution.
6. Barium sulfate.

Page 125
1. An acid.
2. OH^-
3. $H^+_{(aq)} + OH^-_{(aq)} \rightarrow H_2O_{(l)}$
4. A strong acid fully ionises/dissociates in solution. A weak acid only partially ionises/dissociates in solution.
5. So that the ions are able to move.

Page 127
1. Potassium will be formed at the cathode; iodine will be formed at the anode.
2. Hydrogen will be formed at the cathode; iodine will be formed at the anode.
3. $4OH^- \rightarrow O_2 + 2H_2O + 4e^-$ (or $4OH^- - 4e^- \rightarrow O_2 + 2H_2O$).

Page 129
1. It cools down.
2.

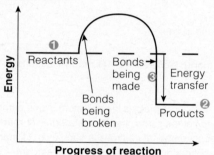

3. -1299 kJ (allow 1299 kJ).
4. Exothermic – more energy is released when bonds are made than is used up in breaking the bonds in the reactants/ΔH is negative.

Page 131
1. **a)** $2 Zn_{(s)} + O_{2(g)} \rightarrow 2 ZnO_{(s)}$ (state symbols are not required.
   1 mark awarded for the correct symbols/formulae and for the equation being correctly balanced).
   b) ZnO/zinc oxide **(1 mark)**, because it loses oxygen **(1 mark)**.
   c) Less reactive **(1 mark)**; magnesium is able to displace zinc from zinc oxide, meaning that magnesium is more reactive than zinc **(1 mark)**.
   d) By reduction with carbon **(1 mark)**, because it is below carbon in the reactivity series **(1 mark)**.
   e) Zinc **(1 mark)**, because it loses electrons **(1 mark)**.
2. **a)**

(1 mark for each label numbered on the graph.)

b) Bonds broken:

4 C–H: $4 \times 413 = 1652$ kJ

2 O=O: $2 \times 498 = 996$ kJ

Total = 2648 kJ **(1 mark)**

Bonds formed:

2 C=O: $2 \times 803 = 1606$ kJ

4 O–H: $4 \times 464 = 1856$ kJ

Total = 3462 kJ **(1 mark)**

ΔH = Bonds broken – bonds formed = 2648 – 3462

= – 814 kJ/mol **(1 mark for correct calculation, including correct sign)**.

c) It increases **(1 mark)**

Page 133

1. 0.75 g/s
2. **Two from**: the concentrations of the reactants in solution; the pressure of reacting gases; the surface area of any solid reactants; temperature; presence of a catalyst.
3. By attaching a gas syringe and recording the volume of gas collected in a certain amount of time, e.g. volume collected every 10 seconds.
4. The rate increases.

Page 135

1. The idea that, for a chemical reaction to occur, the reacting particles must collide with sufficient energy.
2. The minimum amount of energy that the particles must have when they collide in order to react.
3. There are more particles in the same volume of liquid and so there are more chances of reactant particles colliding.
4. A species that speeds up a chemical reaction but is not used up during the reaction.
5. They provide an alternative pathway of lower activation energy.

Page 137

1. $\rightleftharpoons$
2. Endothermic.
3. **a)** The amount of nitrogen will decrease.
   b) The amount of nitrogen will decrease.

Page 139

1. **a)** 50 seconds **(1 mark)**, as after this time no more gas was collected/the volume of gas did not change **(1 mark)**.
   b) $40 \div 50 = 0.8$ cm³/s (working **1 mark**: allow $40 \div$ answer to part a; answer with units, **1 mark**).
   c) The gradient was steeper after 10 seconds than after 40 seconds. **(1 mark)**
   d)

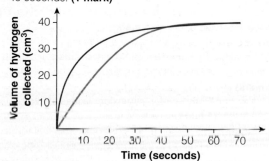

   (**Curve is steeper than in original graph, 1 mark; final volume is 40 cm³, 1 mark.**)
   e) At a higher concentration there will be more particles of acid in the same volume of solution **(1 mark)**, and so there will be more/an increased probability/more likelihood of/collisions **(1 mark)**.
2. **a)** The water in the equation appears as a gas **(1 mark)**.
   b) That the reaction is reversible **(1 mark)**.

c) High pressure favours the reaction that produces the smaller number of molecules of gas; i.e. the reverse reaction will be favoured, which uses up hydrogen **(1 mark)**.

d) The yield of hydrogen will increase **(1 mark)**; increasing temperature favours the endothermic (in this case forward) reaction **(1 mark)**.

Page 141

1. Dead biomass.
2. Molecules that contain carbon and hydrogen atoms only.
3. C_3H_8
4. Fractional distillation.

Page 143

1. $C_2H_6 + 3.5 O_2 \rightarrow 2CO_2 + 3H_2O$ or $2C_2H_6 + 7 O_2 \rightarrow 4CO_2 + 6H_2O$
2. C_4H_{10}
3. By heating with steam
4. Add bromine water. Alkenes decolourise bromine water / turn it from orange to colourless.
5. To make plastics / polymerisation

Page 145

1. **a)** Dead biomass sinks to ocean bottom **(1 mark)**; decaying biomass is covered in mud, which turns to rock **(1 mark)**; biomass decays, slowly forming crude oil under the rock **(1 mark)**.
   b) Fractional distillation **(1 mark)**; the molecules in crude oil are separated according to their boiling points **(1 mark)**.
   c) Saturated **(1 mark)**; hydrocarbons/molecules with the general formula C_nH_{2n+2} **(1 mark)**.
   d) Cracking turns relatively useless long-chain molecules **(1 mark)** into more useful products **(1 mark)**.
   e) By passing the hydrocarbon vapour over a hot catalyst/mixing the hydrocarbon with steam at high temperatures **(1 mark)**.
   f) C_4H_{10} **(1 mark)**.
2. **a)** Kerosene – aircraft fuel / fuel for stoves **(1 mark)**; Bitumen – tar for roads / roofing **(1 mark)**
   b) bitumen **(1 mark)**
   c) kerosene **(1 mark)**
   d) bitumen **(1 mark)** because the molecules in bitumen are larger / stronger intermolecular forces **(1 mark)**
3. **a)** Molecules that contain carbon and hydrogen **(1 mark)** only **(1 mark)**.
   b) **Any two from:** differ by CH_2 in their molecular formula from neighbouring compounds; show a gradual trend in physical properties; have similar chemical properties. **(2 marks)**
   c) 17 **(1 mark)**
   d)

   H–C–C–C–H structure with H atoms **(1 mark)**

   e) $C_4H_{10\,(g)} + 6\frac{1}{2} O_{2\,(g)} \rightarrow 4CO_{2\,(g)} + 5H_2O_{\,(l)}$ **(Ignore state symbols)** (**Allow any correct multiple, e.g.:**
   $2C_4H_{10\,(g)} + 13O_{2\,(g)} \rightarrow 8CO_{2\,(g)} + 10H_2O_{\,(l)}$)
   (1 mark for correct formula of reactants and products; 1 mark for correct balancing)
   f) Add bromine water / bubble the gases through bromine water **(1 mark)**.
   The alkene will decolourise the bromine water / turn it from brown / orange to colourless. **(1 mark)**
   The bromine water remains orange in the alkane **(1 mark)**

Page 147
1. A single element or compound.
2. A mixture that has been designed as a useful product.
3. **Two from**: fuels; cleaning materials; paints; medicines; foods; fertilisers.
4. 0.55

Page 149
1. Oxygen.
2. Add a lit splint and there will be a squeaky pop.
3. Calcium hydroxide solution.
4. It turns milky.
5. It turns it red before bleaching it.

Page 151
1. a) Z **(1 mark)**. There are three 'spots' on the chromatogram of Z **(1 mark)**.
   b) W and Z **(1 mark)**
   c) Red and yellow **(1 mark)**
   d) X **(1 mark)**. None of the spots in X are at the same height of the spots in the red, yellow or blue ink **(1 mark)**.
   e) $\frac{22.5}{29}$ **(1 mark)** = 0.78 (allow between 0.76 and 0.79) **(1 mark)**
   f) W **(1 mark)**. It contains a single compound **(1 mark)**.
   g) **Any one from:** a mixture that has been designed as a useful product; a mixture made by mixing the individual components in carefully measured quantities. **(1 mark)**

2.
Gas	Test	Observation
Hydrogen	**Add a lit splint**	A 'squeaky pop' is heard
Oxygen	**Add a glowing splint**	**Splint relights**
Chlorine	Add moist blue litmus paper	**Litmus paper turns red and is then bleached / turns white**
Carbon dioxide	Add limewater	**The limewater turns milky / cloudy**

(1 mark for each correctly filled in box up to a maximum of 8 marks)

Page 153
1. **Two from**: carbon dioxide; water vapour; methane; ammonia; nitrogen.
2. As a product of photosynthesis.
3. Approximately $\frac{4}{5}$ or 80%.
4. Because it was used in photosynthesis and to form sedimentary rocks.

Page 155
1. **Two from**: water vapour; carbon dioxide; methane.
2. Increased animal farming/rubbish in landfill sites.
3. **Two from**: rising sea levels leading to flooding/coastal erosion; more frequent/severe storms; changes to the amount, timing and distribution of rainfall; temperature and water stress for humans and wildlife; changes in the food producing capacity of some regions; changes to the distribution of wildlife species.
4. **One from**: disagreement over the causes and consequences of climate change; lack of public information and education; lifestyle changes, e.g. greater use of cars and aeroplanes; economic considerations, i.e. the financial costs of reducing the carbon footprint; incomplete international cooperation.

Page 157
1. **Two from**: carbon dioxide; carbon monoxide; water vapour; sulfur dioxide; nitrogen oxides.
2. From the incomplete combustion of fossil fuels.
3. They cause respiratory problems and can form acid rain.

Page 159
1. Living such that the needs of the current generation are met without compromising the ability of future generations to meet their own needs.
2. Pure water has no chemicals added to it. Potable water may have other substances in it but it is safe to drink.
3. Filtered and then sterilised.
4. Distillation or reverse osmosis.

Page 161
1. **One from**: electrical wiring; water pipes.
2. We are running out of metal ores.
3. Bioleaching.
4. **One from**: displacement using scrap iron; electrolysis.

Page 163
1. The environmental impact of a product over the whole of its life.
2. **Two from**: how much energy is needed; how much water is used; what resources are required; how much waste is produced; how much pollution is produced.
3. Some of the values are difficult to quantify, meaning that value judgements have to be made which could be biased/based on opinion.
4. **One from**: using fewer items that come from the earth; reusing items; recycling more of what we use.

Page 165
1. a) Volcanoes **(1 mark)**.
   b) Nitrogen **(1 mark)**.
   c) Oxygen is formed by photosynthesis **(1 mark)**; oxygen has not always been present in the atmosphere because green plants/algae have not always existed **(1 mark)**.
   d) Carbon dioxide is absorbed into the oceans/forms carbonate rocks **(1 mark)**, and is used in photosynthesis **(1 mark)**.
   e) There has been increased consumption of fossil fuels **(1 mark)**, e.g. since the Industrial Revolution/greater use of transport such as cars which produce carbon dioxide when they burn fuel **(1 mark)**.
2. a) **Any two from:** increased animal farming; deforestation; rubbish in landfill sites. **(2 mark)**
   b) A measure of the total amount of carbon dioxide (and other greenhouse gases) **(1 mark)** emitted over the life cycle of a product, service or event **(1 mark)**
   c) **Any two from:** use of alternative energy supplies; energy conservation; CCS (carbon capture and storage); carbon taxes or licences; carbon offsetting measures; carbon neutrality. **(2 mark)**
   d) i) **Any one from:** carbon monoxide; oxides of nitrogen; sulfur dioxide. **(1 mark)**
      ii) **Either from:** carbon monoxide – toxic gas that reduces the ability of blood to carry oxygen; sulfur dioxide/oxides of nitrogen – cause respiratory problems in humans and animals / can form acid rain. **(1 mark)**

Physics

1. A scalar quantity only has a magnitude, a vector quantity has both a magnitude and a direction.
2. **Two from**: friction; air resistance; tension; normal contact force
3. $0.067 \times 10 = 0.67$ N
4. 78 J

Page 169
1. $0.1 \times 2 = 0.2$ N
2. Any point where the limit of proportionality hasn't been exceeded
3. Elastic potential energy

Page 171
1. Speed has a magnitude but not a direction.
2. $\frac{10}{2.5} = 4$ km/h
3. Speed is a scalar quantity as it only has a magnitude. Velocity is speed in a given direction. Velocity has a magnitude and a direction so it is a vector quantity.

Page 173
1. Speed
2. A negative acceleration
3. The distance the object travels

Page 175
1. 67 N
2. $89 \times 10 = 890$ N
3. It continues to move at the same speed.

Page 177
1. Thinking distance and braking distance
2. **Two from**: rain; ice; snow
3. It may lead to brakes overheating and/or loss of control.
4. $6 \times 4 = 24$ kg m/s
5. conservation of momentum

Page 179
1. a) weight = mass × gravitational field strength
   $3.7 \times 187 = 691.9$ N **(2 marks)**
   b) Yes. The rover would weigh more (1870 N) **(1 mark)** as the gravitational field strength on Earth is greater than that on Mars **(1 mark)**
2. a) i) Gradient of graph from 0–3 s $= \frac{25}{3} = 8.33$
      Acceleration = 8.33 m/s² **(2 marks)**
   ii) Area under graph 0–3 s $= 0.5 \times (3 \times 25) = 37.5$
      Distance travelled = 37.5 m **(2 marks)**
   b) Yes **(1 mark)** as the line on the graph is steeper from 0–3 than 3–6 / A steeper line indicates a faster acceleration **(1 mark)**
3. a) The upward force from the ground is 890 N **(1 mark)** as it is equal and opposite to the force the cyclist is exerting on the ground **(1 mark)**.
   b) As the forces on the rider are balanced **(1 mark)** there is no resultant force and the rider would continue to move at a constant speed. This is Newton's first law **(1 mark)**.
   c) The resultant force would be smaller **(1 mark)** so the rider would slow down **(1 mark)**.
4. a) resultant force = mass × acceleration
      $= 1200 \times 2.5 = 3000$ N or 3 kN **(2 marks)**
   b) momentum = mass × velocity
      $= 1200 \times 16 = 19\,200$ N kg m/s **(3 marks)**

Page 181
1. $0.5 \times 0.065 \times 6^2 = 11.7$ J
2. $17 \times 987 \times 10 = 167.79$ kJ
3. It is the amount of energy required to raise the temperature of one kilogram of a substance by one degree Celsius.

Page 183
1. To ensure more energy is usefully transferred and less is wasted
2. $\frac{400}{652} = 0.61 = 61\%$
3. It reduces the thermal conductivity.

Page 185
1. Renewable. **Three from**: bio-fuel; wind; hydro-electricity; geothermal; tidal power; solar power; water waves
   Non-renewable. **Three from**: coal; oil; gas; nuclear fuel
2. The wind doesn't always blow and it's not always sunny, so electricity isn't always generated.
3. They produce carbon dioxide, which is a greenhouse gas. Increased greenhouse gas emissions are leading to climate change. Particulates and other pollutants are also released, which cause respiratory problems.

Page 187
1. a) Renewable resources can be replenished as they are used **(1 mark)** whilst non-renewable energy resources will eventually run out **(1 mark)**
   b) Accidents at nuclear power stations could have devastating health and environmental effects **(1 mark)**. Nuclear waste is very hazardous **(1 mark)**.
   c) **Two from**: building tidal power stations involves the destruction of habitats; wind energy doesn't produce electricity all the time; some people think wind turbines are ugly and spoil the landscape **(2 marks)**
2. a) kinetic energy = 0.5 × mass × (speed)²
      $= 0.5 \times 1600 \times 32^2$
      $= 819\,200$ N or 819.2 kN **(2 marks)**
   b) efficiency $= \frac{\text{useful output energy transfer}}{\text{useful input energy transfer}}$
      $= \frac{819.2}{1500} = 0.55$ or 55% **(2 marks)**
   c) Sound **(1 mark)** and heat **(1 mark)**
   d) **One from**: lubrication; oil **(1 mark)**
3. a) g.p.e. = mass × gravitational field strength × height
      $= 77 \times 150 \times 10$
      $= 115.5$ kN **(2 marks)**
   b) kinetic energy = 0.5 × mass × (speed)²
      $= 0.5 \times 77 \times 20^2$
      $= 15.4$ kN **(2 marks)**
   c) Gravitational potential energy to kinetic energy **(1 mark)** to elastic potential energy **(1 mark)**

Page 189
1. Longitudinal: Sound wave
   Transverse: **One from**: water wave; electromagnetic wave
2. The distance from a point on one wave to the equivalent point on an adjacent wave
3. 1792 m/s

Page 191
1. Infrared radiation
2. Visible light
3. Towards the normal

Page 193
1. By oscillations in electrical circuits
2. Mutation of genes and cancer
3. **One from**: energy efficient lamps; sun tanning

Page 195
1. a) Compression is a region in a longitudinal wave where the particles are closer together **(1 mark)**. Rarefaction is a region in a longitudinal wave where the particles are further apart **(1 mark)**

b) frequency = $\dfrac{\text{wave speed}}{\text{wavelength}}$

$= \dfrac{200}{3.2}$

$= 62.5$ Hz **(2 marks)**

2. a) Ultraviolet radiation **(1 mark)**
   b) It can increase the chance of developing skin cancer. **(1 mark)**
   c) Human eyes can only perceive a limited range of electromagnetic radiation (visible light) **(1 mark)**

3. a) Refraction **(1 mark)**
   b) Waves travel slower in a denser medium and faster in a less dense medium **(1 mark)**. When the edge of a wave hits a boundary between media, the edge of the wave either slows down or speeds up **(1 mark)**. The rest of the wave continues at the same speed, causing the light to bend. **(1 mark)**
   c) **Any two from:** when the light moves from water to air / it bends away from the normal / meaning when the light hits the eye the fish appears to be in a different position to what it actually is. **(2 marks)**

4. Sound travels as a **longitudinal** wave. When a sound wave travels in air the oscillations of the air particles are **parallel** to the direction of energy transfer. The sound wave **doesn't transfer matter, only energy. (3 marks)**

Page 197
1. The symbol for a variable resistor has an arrow through it.
2. 4.2 C
3. 90 A

Page 199
1. Because resistance depends on light intensity
2. An ammeter and a voltmeter
3. 8 V
4. 2 Ω

Page 201
1. 5 A
2. Add the resistances of both resistors together
3. Lower

Page 203
1. An earth connection is not required as it is impossible for the case to become live.
2. Circuit breakers can be reset and operate faster than a fuse.
3. Touching a live wire would produce a large potential difference across the body.

Page 205
1. $5^2 \times 2 = 50$ W
2. $60 \times 12 = 720$ J
3. They lower the potential difference of the transmission cables to a safe level for domestic use.

Page 207
1. a) current = $\dfrac{\text{potential difference}}{\text{resistance}}$

$= \dfrac{15}{3}$

$= 5$ A **(3 marks)**
   b) 5 A **(1 mark)**. The current is the same at all points in a series circuit **(1 mark)**.
   c)

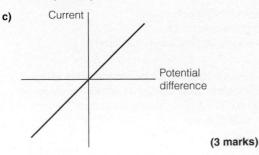

(3 marks)

   d) **One from:** filament lamp; LDR; diode; thermistor **(1 mark)**

2. a) i) Brown **(1 mark)**
       ii) **Any two points from:** The live wire carries the alternating potential difference from the supply / whilst the neutral wire completes the circuit and is at earth potential. / Mixing the two up could lead to damage to the appliance or injury. **(2 marks)**
   b) The appliances are double insulated **(1 mark)** so it is impossible for the case to become live, so there is no need for an earth wire. **(1 mark)**

Page 209
1. They would repel
2. When it's placed in a magnetic field
3. At the poles of the magnet
4. The Earth's core is magnetic and produces a magnetic field.

Page 211
1. The current through the wire and the distance from the wire
2. The same shape as the magnetic field around a bar magnet
3. Magnetic field, force and current

Page 213
1. a)

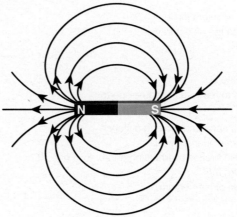

(2 marks)

   b) The magnets would attract **(1 mark)**.
   c) An induced magnet is only magnetic when placed in a magnetic field whilst a bar magnet is always magnetic **or** An induced magnet always experiences a force of attraction while a bar magnet can experience a force of attraction or repulsion. **(2 marks)**

2. a) i) If an electrical current passes through the wire. **(1 mark)**
       ii) It would increase the strength of the magnetic field produced by the wire. **(1 mark)**
       iii) If the wire was wrapped around an iron core. **(1 mark)**
   b) i) $F = BI\ell$
       $F = 3.5 \times 8 \times 0.3 = 8.4$ N **(1 mark for correct working, 1 mark for answer)**
       ii) The direction of the force would be reversed. **(1 mark)**

Page 215
1. When the molecules collide with the wall of their container they exert a force on the wall, causing pressure.
2. $\dfrac{2}{0.002} = 1000$ kg/m³
3. The mass stays the same

Page 217
1. $200 \times 126 = 25\ 200$ kJ or 25.2 ms
2. Specific latent heat of fusion is the energy required for a change of state from solid to liquid. Specific latent heat of vapourisation is the energy required for a change of state from liquid to vapour.
3. It is changing state.
4. 305 Kelvin

Page 219

1. a) density $= \dfrac{\text{mass}}{\text{volume}}$

   $= \dfrac{0.15}{0.0001}$

   $= 1500 \text{ kg/m}^3$ **(2 marks)**

   b) The mass remains constant **(1 mark)** and the density decreases **(1 mark)**.

   c) The temperature would remain constant as it was changing state **(1 mark)** and the solid's internal energy would increase **(1 mark)**.

   d) energy for a change of state = mass × specific latent heat

   $= 0.15 \times 574\,000$

   $= 86.1 \text{ kJ or } 86100 \text{ J}$ **(2 marks)**

2. a) The particles gain kinetic energy as the temperature increases **(1 mark)**. This increases the speed at which the particles collide with the sides of the container they are in **(1 mark)**.

   b) The same number of particles occupy a greater volume **(1 mark)**, reducing the rate of collisions with the sides of the container **(1 mark)**.

3. a) 300 − 273 = 27 °C **(1 mark)**

   b) The average kinetic energy and average speed of the particles in the solid would both decrease **(1 mark)**.

4. Specific latent heat of vaporisation **(1 mark)**

Page 221

1. The electrons become excited and move to a higher energy level, further from the nucleus.

2. Isotopes

3. The plum pudding model suggested the atom was a ball of positive charge with negative electrons embedded in it. The nuclear model has a nucleus with electrons orbiting.

Page 223

1. A few centimetres

2. **Accept any dense material**, e.g.: concrete or lead.

3. The mass of the nucleus doesn't change but the charge of the nucleus does change.

Page 225

1. When the time taken for the number of nuclei in a sample of the isotope halves, or when the count rate (or activity) from a sample containing the isotope falls to half of its initial level.

2. 5 months

3. The radioactive atoms decay and release radiation.

Page 227

1. a) i) 22 **(1 mark)**

   ii) 22 **(1 mark)**

   iii) 26 **(1 mark)**

   b) i) Number of protons is the atomic number **(1 mark)**, which is the bottom number on the symbol **(1 mark)**.

   ii) The number of electrons equals the number of protons **(1 mark)**. The number of protons is 28 **(1 mark)**.

   iii) The number of neutrons is the mass number **(1 mark)**. The number of protons is 48 − 22 = 26 **(1 mark)**.

2. a) The plum pudding model suggested that the atom is a ball of positive charge with negative electrons embedded in it **(1 mark)**. Rutherford, Geiger and Marsden said the mass of an atom was concentrated in the nucleus with electrons orbiting the nucleus **(1 mark)**.

   b) Niels Bohr suggested that the electrons orbit the nucleus at specific distances **(1 mark)**. Chadwick provided the evidence for the existence of the neutron within the nucleus **(1 mark)**.

3. a) 60 days **(1 mark)**. This is the point where the counts per second have halved (Also accept $\dfrac{800}{2} = 400$) **(1 mark)**

   b) No **(1 mark)** because its half-life is too long so it would persist in the body for too long **(1 mark)**.

   c) $^{238}\text{U} \rightarrow \,^{234}\text{Th} + \,^{4}\text{He}$ **(2 marks)**

Index

Index

The Periodic Table

Key

Metals
Non-metals

Relative atomic mass	→	1
Atomic symbol	→	**H**
Name	→	hydrogen
Atomic number	→	1

Group 1	Group 2											Group 3	Group 4	Group 5	Group 6	Group 7	0 or 8
																	4 **He** helium 2
7 **Li** lithium 3	9 **Be** beryllium 4											11 **B** boron 5	12 **C** carbon 6	14 **N** nitrogen 7	16 **O** oxygen 8	19 **F** fluorine 9	20 **Ne** neon 10
23 **Na** sodium 11	24 **Mg** magnesium 12											27 **Al** aluminium 13	28 **Si** silicon 14	31 **P** phosphorus 15	32 **S** sulfur 16	35.5 **Cl** chlorine 17	40 **Ar** argon 18
39 **K** potassium 19	40 **Ca** calcium 20	45 **Sc** scandium 21	48 **Ti** titanium 22	51 **V** vanadium 23	52 **Cr** chromium 24	55 **Mn** manganese 25	56 **Fe** iron 26	59 **Co** cobalt 27	59 **Ni** nickel 28	63.5 **Cu** copper 29	65 **Zn** zinc 30	70 **Ga** gallium 31	73 **Ge** germanium 32	75 **As** arsenic 33	79 **Se** selenium 34	80 **Br** bromine 35	84 **Kr** krypton 36
85 **Rb** rubidium 37	88 **Sr** strontium 38	89 **Y** yttrium 39	91 **Zr** zirconium 40	93 **Nb** niobium 41	96 **Mo** molybdenum 42	[98] **Tc** technetium 43	101 **Ru** ruthenium 44	103 **Rh** rhodium 45	106 **Pd** palladium 46	108 **Ag** silver 47	112 **Cd** cadmium 48	115 **In** indium 49	119 **Sn** tin 50	122 **Sb** antimony 51	128 **Te** tellurium 52	127 **I** iodine 53	131 **Xe** xenon 54
133 **Cs** caesium 55	137 **Ba** barium 56	139 **La*** lanthanum 57	178 **Hf** hafnium 72	181 **Ta** tantalum 73	184 **W** tungsten 74	186 **Re** rhenium 75	190 **Os** osmium 76	192 **Ir** iridium 77	195 **Pt** platinum 78	197 **Au** gold 79	201 **Hg** mercury 80	204 **Tl** thallium 81	207 **Pb** lead 82	209 **Bi** bismuth 83	[209] **Po** polonium 84	[210] **At** astatine 85	[222] **Rn** radon 86
[223] **Fr** francium 87	[226] **Ra** radium 88	[227] **Ac*** actinium 89	[261] **Rf** rutherfordium 104	[262] **Db** dubnium 105	[266] **Sg** seaborgium 106	[264] **Bh** bohrium 107	[277] **Hs** hassium 108	[268] **Mt** meitnerium 109	[271] **Ds** darmstadtium 110	[272] **Rg** roentgenium 111							

Elements with atomic numbers 112–116 have been reported but not fully authenticated

*The lanthanoids (atomic numbers 58–71) and the actinoids (atomic numbers 90–103) have been omitted.

The relative atomic masses of copper and chlorine have not been rounded to the nearest whole number.

GCSE
Success

Combined Science

Higher Tier

Exam Practice Workbook

Tom Adams
Dan Evans
Dan Foulder

Biology

Contents

Chemistry

Physics

Contents

Electricity

Magnetism and Electromagnetism

Particle Model of Matter

Atomic Structure

Practice Exam Papers

Answers

The Periodic Table

1 This image shows some human liver cells, as seen through a very powerful light microscope.

(a) Which organelle is labelled X? .... (1)

(b) Unlike skin cells, these cells contain many mitochondria, but they cannot be seen in the image. Suggest why not.

(1)

....

(c) Why do the cells have many mitochondria?

(2)

....

....

(d) Liver cells have different features.
Arrange the features in order of size, starting with the largest.

(2)

| gene | nucleus | cell | chromosome | cytoplasm |

....

2 **(a)** A student is observing bacterial cells under the high power lens of a light microscope. She cannot see a nucleus in the cells and concludes that the cells do not contain DNA. Explain why this conclusion is wrong.

(1)

....

....

(b) Which of the following words best describes a bacterial cell? Tick (✓) **one** box.

(1)

Prokaryotic ☐

Eukaryotic ☐

Multicellular ☐

Undifferentiated ☐

For more help on this topic, see Letts GCSE Combined Science Higher Revision Guide pages 6–7

1 The diagram shows a fertilised egg cell (a zygote).

(a) The zygote is described as a **stem cell**. What does this term mean? (1)

....

(b) The zygote has a very different appearance to the root hair cell (pictured right). However, all cells have some structures in common. Write down **two** of these structures. (2)

1. ....

2. ....

2 (a) A student attends a school trip to a medical research laboratory, where he is given a talk from a scientist on the techniques and benefits of stem cell research.

Describe **two** applications of stem cell research that the scientist is likely to mention. (2)

1. ....

2. ....

(b) After the visit, one of the student's friends says she is opposed to stem cell research. Describe **one** objection that people have to stem cell research. (1)

....

....

3 A live sperm cell is observed under the microscope beating its tail. It moves across the field of view at a rate of 200 μm every 30 seconds.

Assuming the sperm travels at the same rate and in the same direction, how far will it have travelled in one hour? Give your answer in mm. (3)

....

For more help on this topic, see Letts GCSE Combined Science Higher Revision Guide pages 8–9

Organisation and differentiation

Module 2

1 (a) Daljit is looking at some cheek cells using a light microscope under low power. He decides that he wants a more magnified view. How should he adjust the microscope?

Draw a line from X to show which part of the microscope he should adjust.

X

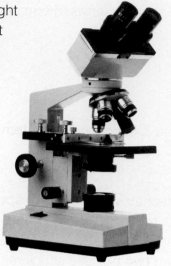

(1)

(b) Under higher power, Daljit clearly sees the nucleus, cytoplasm and cell membrane of the cheek cells. He would also like to see mitochondria and ribosomes. Give **two** reasons why he cannot see these structures.

(2)

....

....

(c) Using a specially fitted camera, Daljit takes a picture of the cells he sees. He measures the diameter of one cell on his photograph by drawing a line and using a ruler. The line is shown on the picture. It measures 3 cm.

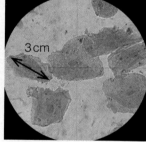

3 cm

If the microscope magnifies the image 400 times, calculate the actual size of the cell in μm.

You can use the following formula:

$$\text{magnification} = \frac{\text{size of image}}{\text{size of real object}}$$

Answer: .... μm   (3)

2 (a) Look at the photograph on the right. What type of microscope was used to take this picture?

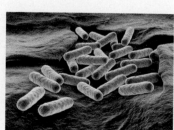

(1)

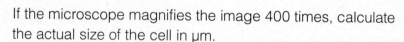

(b) There are 27 bacterial cells in this picture. If the bacteria have reproduced from 1 cell every 20 minutes, how long have the bacteria been growing?

(2)

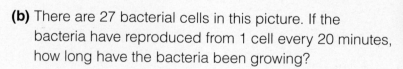

.... minutes

For more help on this topic, see Letts GCSE Combined Science Higher Revision Guide pages 10–11

1 The illustrations show a single-celled organism, called an amoeba, and a multicellular organism (a horse).

Not to scale

Explain why the horse has specialised organs in its breathing and digestive system, and the amoeba has none. (2)

....

....

....

....

2 Complete the following table, which compares the processes of mitosis and meiosis. (3)

Mitosis	Meiosis
Involved in asexual reproduction	....
....	Produces variation
Produces cells with 46 chromosomes	....

3 Jenny is studying chicken cells and is looking at some examples down the microscope. She draws these cells.

(a) Which type of cell division is shown here? .... (1)

(b) Give a reason for your answer to **(a)**. (1)

....

4 (a) Explain the difference between a **benign** and a **malignant** tumour. (2)

....

....

....

(b) Write down **two** lifestyle choices a person could make to reduce their chances of developing cancer. (2)

....

For more help on this topic, see Letts GCSE Combined Science Higher Revision Guide pages 12–13

Cell division

Module 4

HT **1** Isaac is running a marathon. Write a balanced symbol equation for the main type of respiration that will be occurring in his muscles. (2)

....

2 Isaac's metabolic rate is monitored as part of his training schedule. He is rigged up to a metabolic rate meter. This measures the volumes of gas that he breathes in and out. The difference in these volumes represents oxygen consumption. This can be used in a calculation to show metabolic rate.

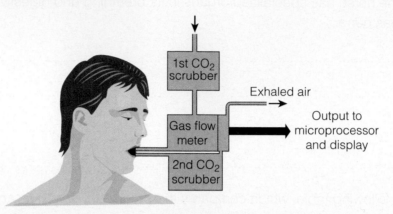

The table below shows some measurements taken from the meter over a period of one hour.

	Five minutes of jogging	Five minutes of rest	Five minutes of sprinting	Five minutes sprinting on an incline
Mean metabolic rate per ml oxygen used per kg per min	35	20	45	60

(a) The units of metabolic rate are expressed in the table as 'per kg'. Why is this adjustment made? (2)

....

....

(b) Using the table, explain the difference in readings for jogging and sprinting. (2)

....

(c) Isaac does quite a lot of exercise. His friend Boris does not. How might Boris' readings compare with Isaac's? Give a reason for your answer. (2)

....

....

For more help on this topic, see Letts GCSE Combined Science Higher Revision Guide pages 14–15

1 In an experiment to investigate the enzyme catalase, potato extract was added to a solution of hydrogen peroxide. The catalase in the potato catalysed the decomposition of the hydrogen peroxide and produced oxygen bubbles. The experiment was carried out at different temperatures and the results recorded in the table below.

Temperature / °C	0	10	20	30	40	50	60	70	80
Number of bubbles produced in one minute	0	10	24	40	48	38	8	0	0

(a) Plot a graph of these results on the graph paper. (3)

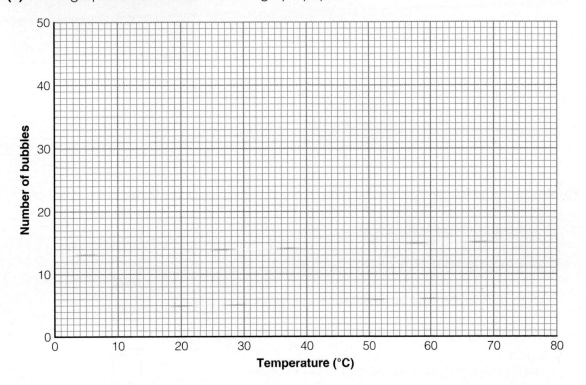

(b) Describe how the number of bubbles produced varies with the temperature of the reacting mixture. (2)

....

....

(c) Using the graph, estimate the optimum temperature for catalase to work at. (1)

....

(d) Factors other than temperature affect the activity of enzymes. Explain why the enzyme amylase, found in saliva, stops working when it gets to the stomach. (2)

....

....

For more help on this topic, see Letts GCSE Combined Science Higher Revision Guide pages 16–17

1 Cells rely on diffusion as a way of transporting materials inwards and outwards.

(a) Name **two** substances that move by diffusion **into** animal cells.   (2)

.... and ....

(b) Name **one** substance that might diffuse **out** of an animal cell. .... (1)

2 Osmosis is a special case of diffusion involving water. Plants rely on osmosis for movement of materials around their various structures.

On the right is a diagram of three plant cells in the root of a plant. Cell **A** has a higher concentration of water than cell **C**.

(a) Explain how water can keep moving from cell **A** to cell **C**. .... (3)

....

....

(b) Which of the following are examples of osmosis? Tick (✓) the **three** correct options.   (3)

Water evaporating from leaves   ☐

Water moving from plant cell to plant cell   ☐

Mixing pure water and sugar solution   ☐

A pear losing water in a concentrated solution of sugar   ☐

Water moving from blood plasma to body cells   ☐

Sugar being absorbed from the intestine into the blood   ☐

3 Rabia is investigating how plant cells respond to being surrounded by different concentrations of sugar solution. She places some rhubarb tissue into pure water and then observes the cells under the microscope.

(a) Describe and explain the appearance of the rhubarb cells.   (2)

....

....

(b) Rabia then puts some rhubarb tissue into a strong salt solution. Describe how the cells would change in appearance if she observed them under the microscope.   (2)

....

....

For more help on this topic, see Letts GCSE Combined Science Higher Revision Guide pages 20–21

1 This diagram shows a magnified view of the inside of a leaf. Complete the missing labels. (3)

Waxy cuticle

Palisade cells

Stoma

(a) _____

(b) _____

(c) _____

2 Plants all share a basic structure consisting of four main organs.

Describe the function that each organ performs in the plant. (4)

Roots: ....

Stem: ....

Leaf: ....

Flower: ....

3 Describe **three** adaptations of xylem vessels that make them suited to the job they do. (3)

....

....

4 The diagram shows xylem and phloem tissue.

(a) State **one** structural difference between the two tissues. (1)

....

....

Xylem Phloem

Xylem   Phloem

(b) Small, herbivorous insects called aphids are found on plant stems. They have piercing mouthparts that can penetrate down to the phloem.

Explain the reasons for this behaviour. (2)

....

....

For more help on this topic, see Letts GCSE Combined Science Higher Revision Guide pages 22–23

Plant tissues, organs and systems

Module 8

1 In an experiment, a plant biologist carried out an investigation to measure the rate of transpiration in a privet shoot. She set up three tubes like the one in the diagram, measured their mass and exposed them each to different conditions.

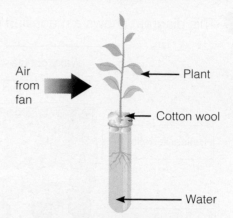

Air from fan

Plant

Cotton wool

Water

- **A** – Left to stand in a rack

- **B** – Cold moving air from a fan was blown over it

- **C** – A radiant heater was placed next to it

The tubes were left for six hours and then their masses were re-measured. The biologist recorded the masses in this table.

Tube	A	B	C
Mass at start (g)	41	43	45
Mass after six hours (g)	39	35	37
Mass loss (g)	2	8	5
% mass loss	4.9		11.9

(a) Calculate the percentage mass loss in tube B. Show your working. (2)

....

....

(b) Which factor increased the rate of transpiration the most? .... (1)

(c) Evaporation from the leaves has increased in tubes B and C. Describe how this would affect water in the xylem vessels of the plant. (1)

....

2 Guard cells respond to light intensity by opening and closing stomata. Explain how this occurs. In your answer, use ideas about osmosis and turgidity. (6)

....

....

....

....

....

....

Continue your answer for this question on a separate piece of paper.

For more help on this topic, see Letts GCSE Combined Science Higher Revision Guide pages 24–25

1 The graph shows the number of people who die from coronary heart disease per 100 000 people in different parts of the UK.

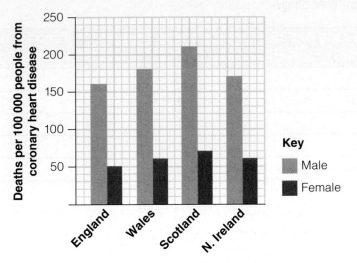

(a) (i) Which country has the highest number of deaths per 100 000? (1)

....

(ii) Calculate the difference between this country's death rate for males and the country with the smallest death rate for males. (1)

....

(b) Describe the pattern between death rates from coronary heart disease in men and women. (1)

....

2 The diagram shows the human circulatory system.

Match the numbers on the diagram with the words listed below. Write the appropriate numbers in the boxes. (4)

Artery ☐

Capillaries in the body ☐

Vein ☐

Capillaries in the lungs ☐

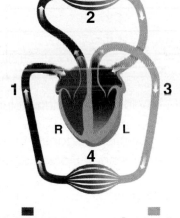

■ Deoxygenated blood   ■ Oxygenated blood

For more help on this topic, see Letts GCSE Combined Science Higher Revision Guide pages 26–27

Transport in humans 1

Module 10

1 The table shows some data from an experiment measuring the effect of different doses of warfarin in two samples of rat blood. Warfarin prevents blood from clotting, killing the rat as a result of internal bleeding.

Warfarin dose / mg per kg body weight	Time for clot to form in sample 1	Time for clot to form in sample 2
0.2	52	61
0.4	101	99
0.6	193	197
0.8	300	311
1	978	984

(a) Calculate the average change in clotting rate between 0.2 and 1.0 mg of warfarin per kilogram of body weight. Show your working. (2)

....

....

(b) Explain why the warfarin dose was measured in mg per kg of body weight. (1)

....

(c) Describe the pattern of results shown in the data. (1)

....

2 Scientists are studying the performance of pearl divers living on a Japanese island. They have timed how long they can stay underwater. The scientists have also measured recovery time for the divers' breathing rates after a dive. The data is shown in the table below.

Vital capacity / litres	Max. time under water / mins
3.5	2.5
4.0	2.7
4.3	2.8
4.5	2.9
4.6	3.0

Vital capacity is the maximum volume of air that the lungs can hold at any one time.

One of the scientists suggests that having a larger vital capacity allows a diver to stay underwater for longer. Do you agree with her? Give a reason for your answer. (2)

Agree / disagree: ....

Reason: ....

....

For more help on this topic, see Letts GCSE Combined Science Higher Revision Guide pages 28–29

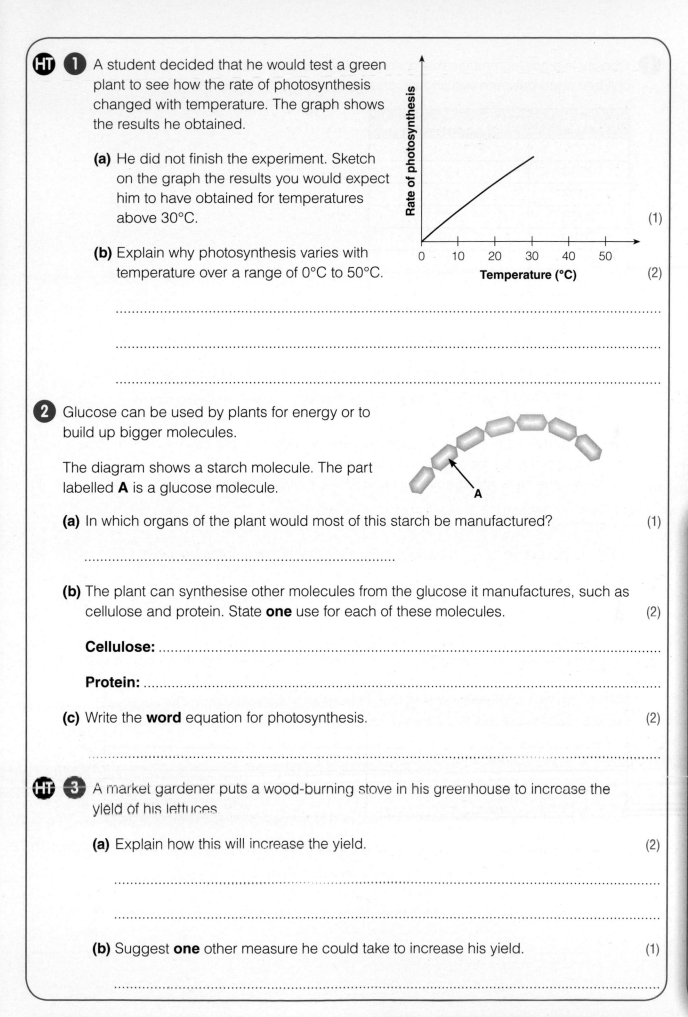

HT 1 A student decided that he would test a green plant to see how the rate of photosynthesis changed with temperature. The graph shows the results he obtained.

(a) He did not finish the experiment. Sketch on the graph the results you would expect him to have obtained for temperatures above 30°C.

(1)

(b) Explain why photosynthesis varies with temperature over a range of 0°C to 50°C.

(2)

....

....

....

2 Glucose can be used by plants for energy or to build up bigger molecules.

The diagram shows a starch molecule. The part labelled **A** is a glucose molecule.

(a) In which organs of the plant would most of this starch be manufactured? (1)

....

(b) The plant can synthesise other molecules from the glucose it manufactures, such as cellulose and protein. State **one** use for each of these molecules. (2)

Cellulose: ....

Protein: ....

(c) Write the **word** equation for photosynthesis. (2)

....

HT 3 A market gardener puts a wood-burning stove in his greenhouse to increase the yield of his lettuces

(a) Explain how this will increase the yield. (2)

....

....

(b) Suggest **one** other measure he could take to increase his yield. (1)

....

For more help on this topic, see Letts GCSE Combined Science Higher Revision Guide pages 30–31

1 Obesity is a non-communicable condition. The table shows how obesity in a population of children aged between two and ten changed between 2005–2013.

Year	% of obese children
2005	9.9
2006	10.2
2007	10.8
2008	11.3
2009	11.8
2010	12.3
2011	12.8
2012	13.3
2013	13.7

(a) Predict the percentage of obese children in the UK for 2014 based on this trend. (1)

...............................%

(b) If the body's daily energy requirements are exceeded, sugar can be converted to storage products; for example, fat under the skin.
Name **one** other storage product and where it would be found. (2)

....

(c) Write down **two** other conditions / diseases that are non-communicable. (2)

....

....

2 The table shows how smoking can affect a person's chances of getting lung cancer.

Number of cigarettes smoked per day	Increased chance of lung cancer compared to non-smokers
5	×4
10	×8
15	×12
20	×16

(a) Estimate the increased chance of lung cancer if someone smoked 25 cigarettes a day. (1)

....

(b) Write down **one** harmful effect that smoking can have on unborn babies. (1)

....

....

For more help on this topic, see Letts GCSE Combined Science Higher Revision Guide pages 34–35

1 Microorganisms consist of bacteria, viruses, fungi and protists. Many cause harm to the human body.

(a) Write down the term that describes these disease-causing organisms. (1)

....

(b) Harmful microorganisms produce symptoms when they reproduce in large numbers. Write down **two** ways in which microorganisms cause these symptoms. (2)

1. ....

2. ....

2 The picture below shows the bacterium that causes cholera.

(a) Write down **two** symptoms of cholera. (2)

1. ....

2. ....

(b) Explain why cholera spreads rapidly in natural disaster zones. (2)

1. ....

2. ....

3 Malaria kills many thousands of people every year. The disease is common in areas that have warm temperatures and stagnant water.

(a) Explain why this is. (2)

....

....

(b) A protist called *Plasmodium* lives in the salivary glands of the female *Anopheles* mosquito.

From the box below, choose a word that describes each organism. (2)

parasite	disease	symptom	vector	consumer	host

Mosquito: .... **Plasmodium:** ....

(c) Samit, an African villager, believes that having mosquito nets around the beds of family members and taking antiviral remedies will reduce their risk of catching malaria.

Explain why he is only partially correct. (2)

....

....

For more help on this topic, see Letts GCSE Combined Science Higher Revision Guide pages 36–37

Communicable diseases

Module 14

1 The diagram shows a white blood cell producing small proteins as part of the body's immune system.

(a) What is the name of these proteins?

.... (1)

(b) These proteins will eventually lock on to specific invading pathogens. Describe what happens next to disable the pathogens. (1)

....

....

(c) Below are the names of some defence mechanisms that the body uses. Match each defence mechanism with the correct function. The first one has been done for you. (3)

Epithelial cells in respiratory passages		engulf pathogens.
Phagocytes		contain enzymes called lysozymes that break down pathogen cells.
Tears		contains acid to break down pathogen cells.
Stomach		trap pathogens in mucus.

2 The graph shows the antibody levels in Dominic after he contracted the flu. The flu pathogen first entered his body two days before point X. There was then a second invasion at point Y.

(a) Name **one** transmission method by which Dominic could have caught the flu virus. (1)

....

(b) After how many days did the antibodies reach their maximum level? (1)

.... days

(c) What is the difference in antibody level between point Y and this maximum? Show your working. (2)

.... arbitrary units

(d) Explain, using your knowledge of memory cells, the difference between these two levels. (2)

....

....

For more help on this topic, see Letts GCSE Combined Science Higher Revision Guide pages 38–39

1 The photograph shows the structure of the human immunodeficiency virus (HIV). For decades it has spread throughout the world, especially in developing countries.

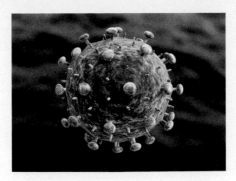

A vaccine is now being developed that shows promising results. It works by mimicing the shapes and structures of HIV proteins. Scientists hope the immune system may be 'educated' to attack the real virus. A specially designed adenovirus shell can protect the vaccine genes until they are in a cell that can produce the vaccine protein.

Using your knowledge of the immune response and immunological memory, describe and explain how antibodies can be produced against the HIV virus. (6)

....

....

....

....

....

....

....

....

....

2 Explain why antibiotics are becoming increasingly less effective against 'superbugs' such as MRSA. (3)

....

....

....

....

Fighting disease

Module 16

For more help on this topic, see Letts GCSE Combined Science Higher Revision Guide pages 40–41

1 A pharmaceutical company is carrying out a clinical trial on a new drug called alketronol. They are testing it to see whether it produces significant adverse (harmful) events in a sample of 226 patients.

(a) Apart from checking for adverse events, write down **two** other reasons that a company carries out clinical trials. (2)

1. ....

2. ....

(b) The kind of trial carried out is a double blind trial. What does this term mean? (2)

....

....

....

(c) Data from the trial is shown in the table below.

Adverse event	Alketronol	Placebo
	Number of patients	**Number of patients**
Pain	4	3
Cardiovascular	21	20
Dyspepsia	7	6
Rash	10	1

(i) Calculate the percentage of patients **in the trial** who suffered a cardiovascular event while taking alketronol. Show your working. (2)

.... %

(ii) A scientist is worried that alketronol may trigger heart attacks. Is there evidence in the data to support this view? Explain your answer. (2)

....

....

....

(iii) Which other adverse event might cause concern? Give a reason for your decision. (2)

....

....

For more help on this topic, see Letts GCSE Combined Science Higher Revision Guide pages 42–43

1 Ash dieback, or *Chalara*, is caused by a fungus called *Hymenoscyphus fraxineus*. *Chalara* results in loss of leaves, crown dieback and bark damage in ash trees. Once a tree is infected, the disease is usually fatal because the tree is weakened and becomes prone to pests or pathogens.

The map gives an indication of where cases of *Chalara* were reported in 2012 in the UK.

Scientists have also discovered that:

- *Chalara* spores are unlikely to survive for more than a few days
- spores can be dispersed by winds blowing from mainland Europe
- trees need a high dose of spores to become infected
- there is a low probability of dispersal on clothing or animals and birds.

Key:
■ = infection confirmed

(a) Damage to leaves can be caused by lack of certain minerals that plants need.

Write down **one** mineral deficiency and how it can affect leaves.

Mineral deficiency: .... **Leaf appearance:** .... (2)

(b) Which **one** of the following conclusions is supported by evidence from the map?
Tick (✓) **one** box. (1)

Chalara is limited to the East of England. ☐

Spores of *Chalara* arrived in England by being carried on winds from Europe. ☐

There is a high concentration of *Chalara* cases in the East of England. ☐

Ash trees in north-west Scotland are resistant to *Chalara*. ☐

(c) One scientist suggests that culling down and burning infected trees could eradicate the disease.

(i) Explain how this method could be effective. (2)

....

....

(ii) Give **one** reason why this control method may not stop the spread of *Chalara*. (1)

....

For more help on this topic, see Letts GCSE Combined Science Higher Revision Guide pages 44–45

1 From the box below, choose three words to complete the information about how conditions are kept stable in the human body. (3)

effectors	spine	receptors	homeostasis	hormones	glands

Certain factors have to be kept constant in the body. This is achieved by a process called .... In order for this to happen, the central nervous system (CNS) needs to receive information from the environment. This is accomplished through .... such as light-sensitive cells on the retina. Once the information has been relayed, the CNS brings about appropriate changes through ....

HT 2 This diagram shows how production of the hormone adrenaline is controlled.

Hypothalamus → **CRH** Corticotropin-releasing hormone → Pituitary → **ACTH** Adrenocorticotropic hormone → Adrenal glands → **Adrenaline**

(a) What name is given to this process, where a system resists a change from a norm (set point) level? .... (1)

(b) Another hormone, cortisol, is produced by the adrenal glands. Its production is also governed by CRH and ACTH production, in the same way as adrenaline. Cortisol increases nutrient distribution, reduces inflammation, and also takes part in water control. In Addison's disease, the adrenal glands fail to produce enough cortisol.

(i) What is the effect of Addison's disease on the production of ACTH? (1)

....

(ii) Using the information above, give **one** symptom of Addison's disease. (1)

....

(iii) Here is some data taken from adult blood samples.

Patient	A	B	C	D	E
Cortisol in blood / µg per litre	31.0	19.2	20.5	1.2	16.0

Which patient is most likely to have Addison's disease? .... (1)

(iv) A doctor injects some cortisol into this patient's blood, then takes another sample. The reading is now 7 µg per litre. If we assume that the patient has 5 litres of blood in their body, calculate the amount of cortisol in this person's blood. Show your working. (2)

....

For more help on this topic, see Letts GCSE Combined Science Higher Revision Guide pages 48–49

1 Complete the missing labels in this diagram of a motor neurone. (2)

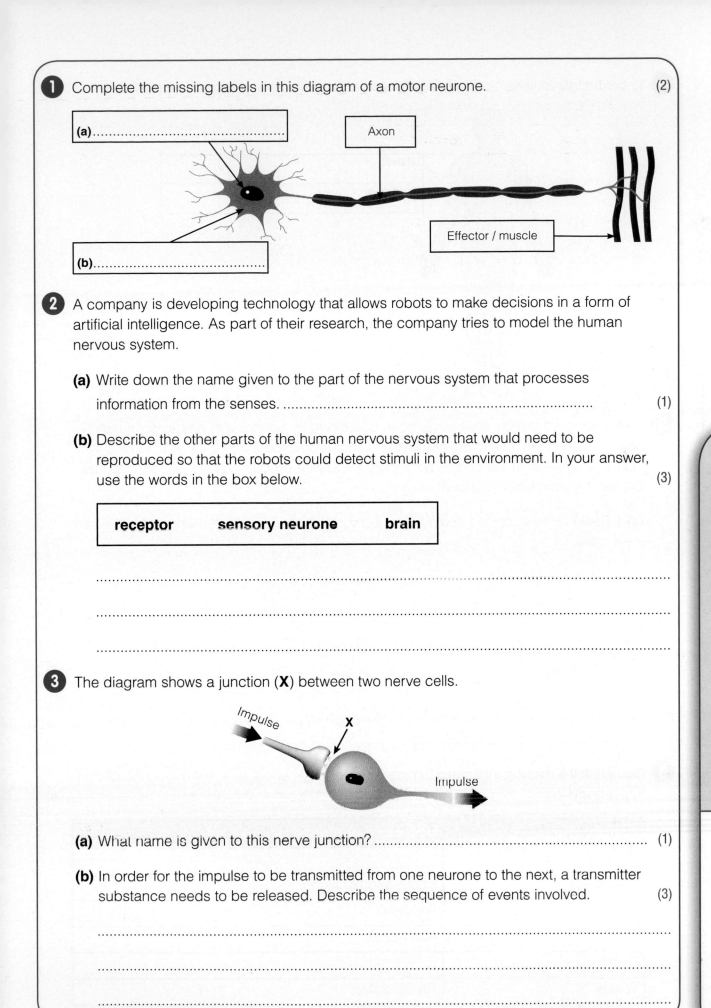

(a)...

Axon

Effector / muscle

(b)...

2 A company is developing technology that allows robots to make decisions in a form of artificial intelligence. As part of their research, the company tries to model the human nervous system.

(a) Write down the name given to the part of the nervous system that processes information from the senses. .... (1)

(b) Describe the other parts of the human nervous system that would need to be reproduced so that the robots could detect stimuli in the environment. In your answer, use the words in the box below. (3)

| receptor | sensory neurone | brain |

....

....

....

3 The diagram shows a junction (**X**) between two nerve cells.

Impulse

X

Impulse

(a) What name is given to this nerve junction? .... (1)

(b) In order for the impulse to be transmitted from one neurone to the next, a transmitter substance needs to be released. Describe the sequence of events involved. (3)

....

....

....

For more help on this topic, see Letts GCSE Combined Science Higher Revision Guide pages 50–51

1 Label the gland shown on the diagram and add the name of a hormone it produces. (2)

Gland:	
Hormone:	

2 A new nanotechnology device has been developed for people with diabetes – it can detect levels of glucose in the blood and communicate this information to a hormone implant elsewhere in the body. The implant releases a precise quantity of hormone into the bloodstream when required.

(a) Explain how this device could help a person with type 1 diabetes who has just eaten a meal. (2)

....

....

(b) Explain why a person with type 2 diabetes might not have as much use for this technology. (2)

....

....

3 Complete the missing information in the table, which is about different endocrine glands in the body. (4)

Gland	Hormones produced
Pituitary gland	.... and ....
Pancreas	Insulin and glucagon
....	Thyroxine
....	Adrenaline
Ovary	.... and ....
Testes	Testosterone

For more help on this topic, see Letts GCSE Combined Science Higher Revision Guide pages 52–53

1 A marathon runner is resting the day before she competes in a race. The table shows the water that she gains and loses during the day.

Gained	Water gained (ml)	Lost	Water lost (ml)
In food	1000	In urine	
From respiration	300	In sweat	800
Drinking	1200	In faeces	100
Total gained		**Total lost**	2500

(a) How much water does the runner lose in urine during the day? .... (1)

(b) What can you say about the total water gained and the total water lost in the day? Why is this important? (2)

....

....

(c) The runner runs a marathon the next day. Suggest and explain how the figures shown in the table may alter during the day of the race. (4)

....

....

....

2 The diagram shows a nephron.

Your responses to the following questions should be **A**, **B** or **C**.

(a) Where does selective reabsorption occur?   (1)

....

(b) Where does salt regulation occur? .... (1)

(c) In which region does filtration occur? .... (1)

(d) Explain how the brain and kidneys work together to restore water levels in the blood when the body is dehydrated. (4)

....

....

....

For more help on this topic, see Letts GCSE Combined Science Higher Revision Guide pages 54–55

Water and nitrogen balance

Module 22

1 The graph shows the thickness of the uterus during the menstrual cycle. Use the graph and your scientific knowledge to explain what happens in the woman's ovaries and uterus between days 5 and 28. (3)

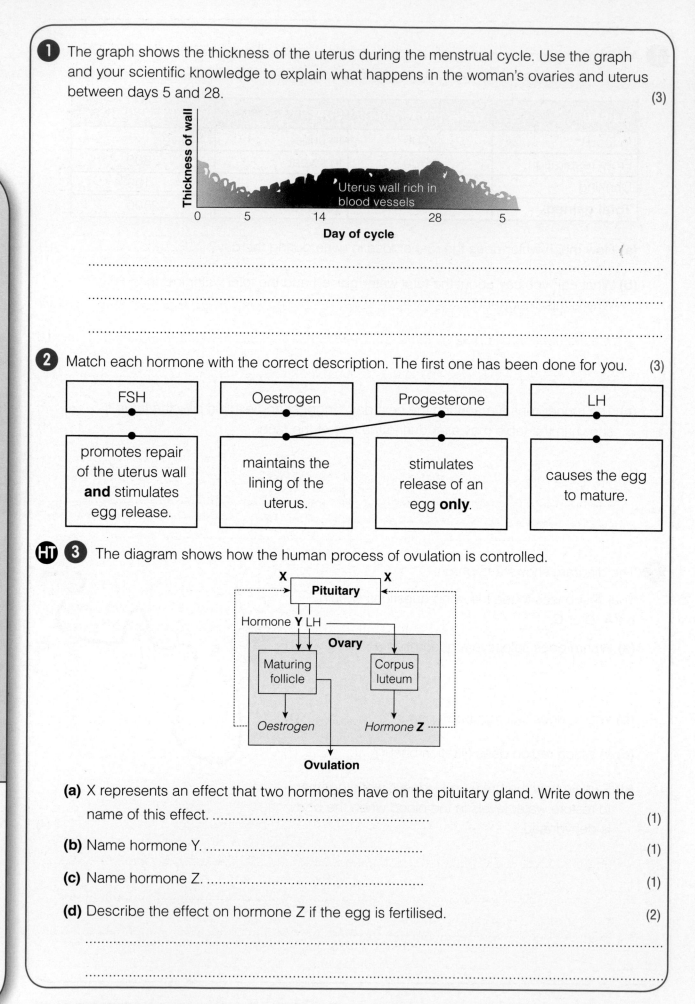

....

....

....

2 Match each hormone with the correct description. The first one has been done for you. (3)

| FSH | Oestrogen | Progesterone | LH |

| promotes repair of the uterus wall **and** stimulates egg release. | maintains the lining of the uterus. | stimulates release of an egg **only**. | causes the egg to mature. |

HT 3 The diagram shows how the human process of ovulation is controlled.

(a) X represents an effect that two hormones have on the pituitary gland. Write down the name of this effect. .... (1)

(b) Name hormone Y. .... (1)

(c) Name hormone Z. .... (1)

(d) Describe the effect on hormone Z if the egg is fertilised. (2)

....

....

For more help on this topic, see Letts GCSE Combined Science Higher Revision Guide pages 56–57

1 Tim and Margaret are finding it hard to conceive a child. They visit a fertility clinic and meet some other couples. The table shows some information about the problem that each couple has.

Couple	Problem causing infertility	Percentage of infertile couples with this problem	Percentage success rate of treatment
Tim and Margaret	Blocked fallopian tubes	13	20
Rohit and Saleema	Irregular ovulation	16	75
Leroy and Jane	No ovulation	7	95
Gary and Charlotte	Low sperm production	15	10
Ian and Kaye	No sperm production	21	10
Stuart and Mai	Unknown cause	28	–

(a) Which couple has the best chance of being successfully treated? (1)

....

(b) In how many of the six couples is the problem known to be with the female? (1)

....

(c) The treatment of irregular ovulation and no ovulation have the highest success rates. Explain why treating irregular ovulation would produce more pregnancies in the whole population. (2)

....

(d) Leroy and Jane are considering two methods to help them have children. The first is to have an egg donated by another woman. The second is to arrange for another woman to conceive the child using sperm from Leroy, then give birth to it (surrogacy). What are the advantages and disadvantages of each method? (4)

....

....

....

....

....

2 Explain how the contraceptive pill works. In your answer, name any hormones involved. (2)

....

....

....

For more help on this topic, see Letts GCSE Combined Science Higher Revision Guide pages 58–59

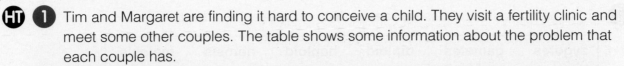
Contraception and infertility

Module 24

1 From the box below, choose **three** words to complete these sentences. (3)

| zygotes | gametes | diploid | haploid | mitosis | meiosis |

Eggs and sperm are .... They are .... because they contain one set of chromosomes. Eggs and sperm are produced in the ovaries and testes by ....

2 Tick (✓) the **two** statements about causes of variation that are true. (2)

Meiosis shuffles genes, which makes each gamete unique. ☐

Gametes fuse randomly. ☐

Zygotes fuse randomly. ☐

Mitosis shuffles genes, which makes each gamete the same. ☐

3

Sexual reproduction is the best strategy for organisms because it allows variation and therefore greater adaptation.

Asexual reproduction is better because when an organism is well adapted, it can produce exact copies of itself.

(a) John and Ayesha disagree about which type of reproduction is most beneficial to organisms. State which explanation, if any, is correct. Give the reasons for your choice. (3)

....

....

....

....

(b) Apart from variation, write down **one** other difference between sexual and asexual reproduction. (1)

....

....

(c) Describe how yeast carries out asexual reproduction. (2)

....

....

For more help on this topic, see Letts GCSE Combined Science Higher Revision Guide pages 62–63

1 Tick (✓) the statements about the Human Genome Project (HGP) that are true. (3)

The genome of an organism is the entire genetic material present in its adult body cells. ☐

The data produced from the HGP produced a listing of amino acid sequences. ☐

The HGP involved collaboration between US and UK geneticists. ☐

The project allowed genetic abnormalities to be tracked between generations. ☐

The project was controversial as it relied on embryonic stem cells. ☐

2 Studies of genomes can help scientists work out the evolutionary history of organisms by comparing the similarity of particular DNA sequences that code for a specific protein.

The table shows the percentage DNA coding similarity for protein A in different organisms.

Species	% DNA coding similarity between species and humans for protein A
Human	100
Chimpanzee	100
Horse	88.5
Fish	78.6
Yeast	67.3
Protist	56.6

(a) What evidence is there in the table that closely related organisms developed from a recent common ancestor? (1)

....

(b) Using only the information from the table, which invertebrate is the most closely related to humans? .... (1)

3 The Human Genome Project has enabled specific genes to be identified that increase the risk of developing cancer in later life. Two of these genes are the *BRCA1* and *BRCA2* mutations that increase the risk of developing breast cancer.

(a) If women are prepared to take a genetic test, how could this information help doctors advise women about breast cancer? (2)

....

....

(b) If a woman possesses these mutations, it does not mean that she will definitely develop breast cancer. Why is this? (2)

....

....

DNA

Module 26

For more help on this topic, see Letts GCSE Combined Science Higher Revision Guide pages 64–65

1 The molecule DNA is a double helix made of two complementary strands.

(a) Write down the bases that pair with **T** and **C**. (1)

T pairs with ....

C pairs with ....

(b) How many bases code for **one** amino acid when a protein molecule is made? (1)

....

HT **2** Mutations occur when genes on DNA cause them to code for different proteins (or sequences of amino acids).

(a) State **two** causes of mutation. (2)

1. ....

2. ....

(b) A change occurs in a section of DNA that leads to a new protein being formed.

Explain how this is possible and why the protein is not able to perform its function. (3)

....

....

....

HT **3** DNA is constructed from individual building blocks called **nucleotides**.

Describe the structure of a nucleotide and how the sequence of these building blocks codes for amino acids. (4)

....

....

....

....

....

For more help on this topic, see Letts GCSE Combined Science Higher Revision Guide pages 66–67

1 Raj is the owner of two dogs, both of which are about two years old. Both dogs are black in colour and came from the same litter of puppies.

(a) A dog's adult body cell contains 78 chromosomes. How many chromosomes would be in a male dog's sperm cells? (1)

....

(b) The dogs' mother had white fur and the father had black fur. Using what you know about dominant genes, suggest why there were no white puppies in the litter. (2)

....

....

HT **(c)** One year later, one of the black puppies mated with a white-haired dog. She had four puppies. Two had black fur and two had white fur. The letters **B** and **b** represent the alleles for fur colour: **B** for black fur and **b** for white fur.

Draw a fully labelled genetic diagram to explain this. Show which offspring would be black and which would be white. (3)

2 Complete these two different crosses between a brown-eyed parent and a blue-eyed parent. (4)

(a) Brown eyes × Blue eyes

Parents (BB) × (bb)

Gametes ◯ ◯ ◯ ◯

Offspring ◯ ◯ ◯ ◯

Phenotype ▢ ▢ ▢ ▢

(b) Brown eyes × Blue eyes

Parents (Bb) × (bb)

Gametes ◯ ◯ ◯ ◯

Offspring ◯ ◯ ◯ ◯

Phenotype ▢ ▢ ▢ ▢

Inheritance and genetic disorders

Module 28

For more help on this topic, see Letts GCSE Combined Science Higher Revision Guide pages 68–69

1 This is an evolutionary tree for some of our present-day vertebrates. Where possible, use the diagram to answer these questions.

Million years ago		Geological time period
50	Turtle Terrapin Tortoise Snake Lizard Birds Crocodile	Tertiary
100	Tuarta (giant lizard)	Cretaceous
150	Crocodilia Dinosaurs	Jurassic
		Triassic
200	Testudina Archosaurs	Permian
250		
		Carboniferous
300	Sauropods	

(a) How many millions of years ago did the testudina appear? (1)

....

(b) (i) In what geological time period did the dinosaurs become extinct? (1)

....

(ii) How do scientists know that dinosaurs once lived on Earth? (1)

....

(c) What group of animals alive today is most closely related to the snake? (1)

....

(d) Which ancestor is shared by dinosaurs, crocodiles and the giant lizard, but is not an ancestor of tortoises? (1)

....

For more help on this topic, see Letts GCSE Combined Science Higher Revision Guide pages 70–71

1 Peppered moths are usually pale and speckled. They are often found amongst the lichens on silver birch tree bark. The data below estimates the average number of peppered moths spotted in a city centre before and after the Industrial Revolution.

Month	Before Industrial Revolution		After Industrial Revolution	
	Pale	**Dark**	**Pale**	**Dark**
June	1261	102	87	1035
July	1247	126	108	1336
August	1272	93	72	1019

(a) Complete the table by calculating the mean number of each colour of moth during the summer months. (2)

Before Industrial Revolution		After Industrial Revolution	
Pale	**Dark**	**Pale**	**Dark**
....	....	....	....

(b) Draw a bar graph to represent your results. (2)

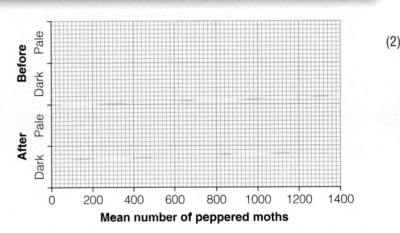

Mean number of peppered moths

(c) Why do you think there were more pale-coloured moths than dark-coloured moths before the Industrial Revolution? (1)

....

(d) Explain why the number of dark-coloured peppered moths increased significantly during the Industrial Revolution. (2)

....

....

....

2 Lucy is an early hominid fossil that is 3.2 million years old. Why was this a significant find? (1)

....

For more help on this topic, see Letts GCSE Combined Science Higher Revision Guide pages 72–73

1 **(a)** A sheep farmer wants to breed sheep that grow high quality wool. What four stages of selective breeding can he use to produce his desired variety? (3)

The first stage has been done for you.

1. Choose males and females that produce good quality wool.

2. ....

3. ....

4. ....

(b) Apart from high quality wool, name another characteristic that a farmer might want to selectively breed into his flock. (1)

....

2 Describe how genetic engineering is different from selective breeding. (2)

....

....

....

3 Explain the benefit of each of these examples of genetic engineering.

(a) Resistance to herbicide in soya plants (1)

....

....

(b) Inserting beta-carotene genes into rice plants (1)

....

....

4 Some people think that genetically engineering resistance to herbicides in plants could have unforeseen consequences. Give **one** example of a harmful effect. (1)

....

....

....

For more help on this topic, see Letts GCSE Combined Science Higher Revision Guide pages 74–75

1 Lions, tigers and leopards are all carnivorous big cats. They have five toes on their front paws and four toes on their back paws. Their claws can be drawn back to avoid damage. They all roar. Tigers and leopards tend to be solitary animals but lions live in prides of females with one dominant male.

(a) Underline **one** piece of evidence from the information above that suggests that lions, tigers and leopards are all descended from a common ancestor. (1)

(b) This table shows how some scientists have named four species of large cat.

	Genus	Species
Lion	Panthera	leo
Tiger	Panthera	tigris
Leopard	Panthera	pardus
Snow leopard	Uncia	uncia

Are leopards more closely related to tigers or snow leopards? Explain your answer. (2)

....

....

....

2 Archaeopteryx is an ancient fossilised species of bird. When first discovered, scientists found it hard to classify.

Using features shown in the picture, explain why Archaeopteryx is difficult to classify. (2)

....

....

....

For more help on this topic, see Letts GCSE Combined Science Higher Revision Guide pages 76–77

Classification Module 32

1 Complete the following passage about adaptations using words from the box below. (3)

environment	population	features	community	characteristics
survival	evolutionary	predatory	suited	

Adaptations are special .... or .... that make a living

organism particularly well .... to its .... Adaptations

are part of an .... process that increases a living organism's chance of

....

2 A new species of insectivorous mammal has been discovered in Borneo. It has been observed in rainforest undergrowth and more open savannah-like areas. Scientists have called the creature a *long-nosed batink*. They have studied its diet and obtained this data.

Food	Ants	Termites	Aphids	Beetles	Maggots	Bugs	Grubs
Mass eaten per day / g	275	380	320	75	150	20	110

(a) Plot the data for termites, beetles, bugs and grubs as a bar chart. (3)

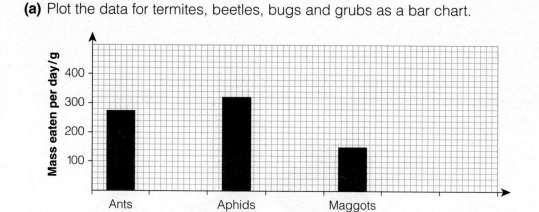

(b) Calculate the percentage of the batink's diet that is made up from termites. Show your working. (2)

.... %

(c) From what you know about the batink, suggest **two** behavioural adaptations it might have that makes it successful. (2)

....

....

For more help on this topic, see Letts GCSE Combined Science Higher Revision Guide pages 80–81

1 A meadow supports a wide variety of animals and plants. George is carrying out a survey of the meadow to assess the populations of organisms found there.

(a) State the term that describes the meadow as a place for organisms to live. (1)

....

(b) Which word describes the different populations in the meadow and their interaction with the physical factors found there? (1)

....

(c) George has laid pitfall traps in the meadow to capture and count soil invertebrates. He notices that there are many flying insects that are too difficult to count and identify.

Suggest an item of apparatus he could use to survey the flying insects. (1)

....

(d) George uses a 0.25 m² quadrat to survey the plant populations. He lays ten quadrats in one corner of the field and finds a mean count of 16 meadow buttercups per quadrat. He estimates the area of the meadow to be 5000 m².

Calculate the expected number of buttercups in the whole meadow.
Show your working. (2)

....

....

(e) George finds these two invertebrates in his pitfall traps.

Beetle   Snail

(i) The beetle feeds off other insects. Explain how a decrease in the number of beetles will eventually result in their numbers rising. (2)

....

....

(ii) Thrushes eat snails and worms. Describe what would happen to the number of snails if large numbers of thrushes arrived in their habitat. (1)

....

For more help on this topic, see Letts GCSE Combined Science Higher Revision Guide pages 82–83

Studying ecosystems

Module 34

1 Apple trees are grown in orchards in temperate climates. They are part of a wider food web.

wasp   ladybird   hoverfly

caterpillar   apple sawfly   aphids

apple tree

(a) The apple tree is a **producer**. What is meant by this term? (1)

....

(b) What is the source of energy for this food web? .... (1)

(c) Name a secondary consumer in the food web. .... (1)

2 Bird populations are a good indicator of environmental sustainability and allow scientists to track environmental changes in particular habitats.

Scientists measured the numbers of farmland birds and woodland birds in the UK between 1972 and 2002. The results are show below.

(a) Explain clearly how the numbers of farmland birds have changed between 1972 and 2002. (4)

....

....

....

....

(b) Suggest a reason for the overall change in numbers of farmland birds. (1)

....

(c) The government wants to reverse these changes by 2020. Suggest **one** thing it could do that would help to achieve this. (1)

....

For more help on this topic, see Letts GCSE Combined Science Higher Revision Guide pages 84–85

1 Circle the renewable resources. (1)

water   minerals   oil   wind   coal   wood

2 Explain how rising average global temperatures may have an effect on the Earth.
Use the headings below to structure your answer. (3)

Climate zones around the world:

....

....

Sea levels:

....

....

Ice caps and glaciers:

....

....

3 At the moment, the human population is increasing exponentially.

(a) Sketch a graph that shows this increase. (2)

(b) On the *y*-axis, add a suitable unit for the population. (1)

(c) Suggest **two** reasons for this 'population explosion'. (2)

....

....

For more help on this topic, see Letts GCSE Combined Science Revision Guide page 86

1. In Ireland, four species of bumble bee are now endangered. Scientists are worried that numbers may become so low that they are inadequate to provide pollination to certain plants.

State **two** reasons why some organisms become endangered. (2)

....

....

2. **(a)** What is deforestation? Tick (✓) the correct definition. (1)

Planting new trees ☐

Forest fires caused by hot weather ☐

Cutting down large areas of forest ☐

Polluting national parks with litter ☐

(b) Which of the following is a consequence of deforestation? Tick (✓) the correct answer. (1)

Decrease in soil erosion in tropical regions ☐

Increase in atmospheric carbon dioxide ☐

Increase in average rainfall ☐

Increase in habitat area ☐

3. Other than using wood for timber, give **two** other reasons for large-scale deforestation. (2)

....

....

4. Circle the correct options in the sentences below. (6)

When deforestation occurs in **tropical / arctic / desert** regions, it has a devastating impact on the environment.

The loss of **trees / animals / insects** means less photosynthesis takes place, so less **oxygen / nitrogen / carbon dioxide** is removed from the atmosphere.

It also leads to a reduction in **variation / biodiversity / mutation**, because some species may become **protected / damaged / extinct** and **habitats / land / farms** are destroyed.

5. Sometimes when land has been cleared of forests to grow crops, farmers stop producing good yields after a few years. Explain why. (1)

....

....

For more help on this topic, see Letts GCSE Combined Science Revision Guide page 87

1 Choose the correct words from the list to complete this paragraph on the water cycle: (3)

| boiled | precipitation | rivers | organisms | evaporated | condensation |

The water cycle provides fresh water for .... on land before draining into the seas. Water is .... from seawater to form vapour in the atmosphere. This vapour then forms clouds and falls as ....

2 A group of students wanted to investigate factors affecting decay. They mixed soil with small discs cut from leaves. They divided the leaf disc / soil mixture equally into four test tubes, as shown below.

Leaf disc cut from leaf

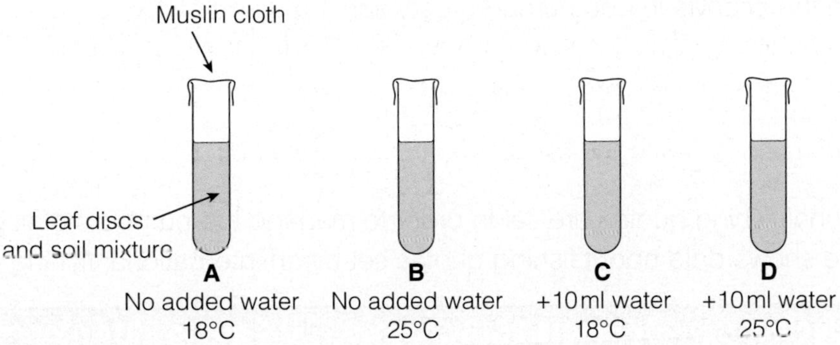

Muslin cloth

Leaf discs and soil mixture

A	**B**	**C**	**D**
No added water	No added water	+10ml water	+10ml water
18°C	25°C	18°C	25°C

(a) In which tube would you expect the leaf discs to decay fastest? Give a reason for your answer. .... (2)

....

(b) The students did not add any microorganisms to the test tubes. Where will the microorganisms that cause decay come from? (1)

....

(c) Why did the students seal the tubes with muslin cloth instead of a rubber bung? (1)

....

(d) Suggest **one** way in which the students could use the leaf discs to measure the rate of decay. (1)

....

For more help on this topic, see Letts GCSE Combined Science Revision Guide page 88

Recycling

Module 37

1 Some scientists studied the numbers of cod caught in cool to temperate waters in the northern hemisphere. They obtained the following data, which is expressed in a graph.

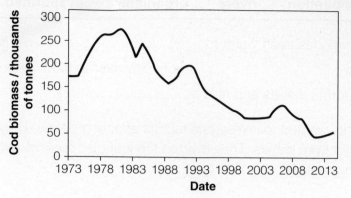

(a) What was the estimated cod biomass in 1988? (1)

.... thousand tonnes

(b) Describe the change in cod numbers between 1988 and 2013. (2)

....

....

(c) International fishing quotas are set in order to manage the numbers of fish in our seas. The table shows data about fishing quotas set by an international fishing commission.

Fish species	UK quota 2013 / tonnes	UK quota 2014 / tonnes
Cod	11 216	13 123
Haddock	27 507	23 381
Whiting	8426	3287

(i) By how much did the cod quota change between 2013 and 2014? (1)

.... tonnes

(ii) Suggest possible reasons for the decreased quota for haddock. (2)

....

....

(d) Suggest **one** other measure that fisheries councils could take to prevent over-fishing. (1)

....

For more help on this topic, see Letts GCSE Combined Science Revision Guide page 89

1 The chemical sodium chloride is more commonly known as 'salt' (i.e. the food flavouring).

Sodium chloride can be made in the laboratory by reacting sodium with chlorine gas. Salt is very soluble in water.

(a) Give the chemical symbols for the two elements present in sodium chloride. Use the periodic table on page 200 to help you. (2)

....

(b) Write a word equation to show the reaction between sodium and chlorine to produce sodium chloride. (2)

....

....

(c) Is sodium chloride a mixture or a compound? Explain your answer. (2)

....

....

(d) When salt dissolves in water, does it form a mixture or a compound? Explain your answer. (2)

....

....

(e) A student wants to separate salt and water from salty water. Which two methods of separation listed below would be appropriate for the student to use? Tick the relevant box or boxes. (2)

Filtration ☐   Simple distillation ☐

Crystallisation ☐   Chromatography ☐

For more help on this topic, see Letts GCSE Combined Science Higher Revision Guide pages 92–93

1 One of the early representations of the atom, the 'plum pudding' model, was further developed in light of Rutherford, Geiger and Marsden's scattering experiment. This led to the conclusion that the positive charge of an atom is contained within a small volume known as the nucleus. Niels Bohr improved this model and it is this model that forms the basis of the way in which we represent the structure of atoms today.

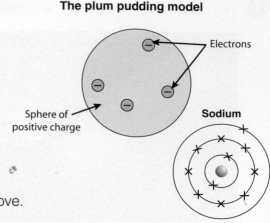

The plum pudding model

Electrons

Sphere of positive charge

Sodium

The plum pudding version of an atom is shown above.

Today, an atom such as sodium is represented by a diagram like the one above.

(a) Give **two** differences between the 'plum pudding' model of an atom and today's model. (2)

energy levels ~outer shell electrons electrons didn't move in orbits

(b) What observation in Rutherford, Geiger and Marsden's scattering experiment led them to conclude that the positive charge of an atom was contained in a small volume? (1)

....

(c) What improvements did Niels Bohr make to the nuclear model and what evidence did he have to support these changes? (2)

....

....

(d) James Chadwick developed the idea that the nucleus of an atom contains protons and neutrons.

Complete the table below showing the properties of the sub-atomic particles. (4)

Particle	Relative charge	Relative mass
Proton	+ 1	
Neutron		1
Electron		

(e) An atom of sodium contains 11 protons, 12 neutrons and 11 electrons.

(i) What is the atomic number of sodium? ....11............... mass no = mass — atomic no (1)

(ii) What is the mass number of sodium? ....23.............. (1)

mass no = proton + neutron

For more help on this topic, see Letts GCSE Combined Science Higher Revision Guide pages 94–95

1 The diagrams below represent an atom of magnesium and an atom of fluorine:

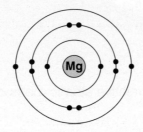 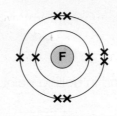

The electronic structure of magnesium can also be written as 2,8,2

(a) How many shells of electrons does a magnesium atom have? (1)

....

(b) What is the electronic structure of fluorine? (1)

....

(c) In which group of the periodic table would you expect to find fluorine?
Explain your answer. (2)

....

....

2 Dmitri Mendeleev is often referred to as the father of the periodic table, as he was instrumental in its construction.

Mendeleev placed the metals lithium and sodium in the same group of the periodic table.

(a) How are the elements arranged in the periodic table? (1)

....

(b) Explain why Mendeleev placed sodium and lithium in the same group of the periodic table. (1)

....

(c) Give **two** characteristic properties of metals. (2)

....

....

For more help on this topic, see Letts GCSE Combined Science Higher Revision Guide pages 96–97

1 (a) Explain why the noble gases are chemically inert. (2)

....

....

(b) What is the trend in boiling point as the relative atomic mass of the noble gases

increases? .... (1)

2 The element sodium reacts vigorously with water. When universal indicator solution is
added to the resulting solution a colour change is observed.

(a) Write a balanced symbol equation for the reaction between sodium and water. (2)

....

(b) What colour would universal indicator solution turn when it is added to the resulting
solution? Explain your answer. (2)

....

....

(c) The element potassium reacts more vigorously with water than sodium. Explain why. (2)

....

....

3 Sodium reacts with bromine gas as shown by the equation below:

........$Na_{(s)}$ + ...$Cl_{2(g)}$ $\longrightarrow$ ....$NaCl_{(s)}$

(a) Balance the above equation. (2)

(b) What type of bonding is present in sodium chloride (NaCl)? (1)

....

(c) When chlorine gas is bubbled through sodium bromide solution a chemical reaction
occurs. Write a word equation for this reaction. (2)

....

(d) What name is given to the type of reaction that occurs when chlorine gas reacts with
sodium bromide solution? Explain why the reaction occurs. (2)

....

....

For more help on this topic, see Letts GCSE Combined Science Higher Revision Guide pages 98–99

1 Consider the structures of sodium (Na), chlorine (Cl_2) and sodium chloride (NaCl).

Draw arrows from each substance to its correct structure. One structure will not have an arrow drawn to it. (3)

Sodium

Chlorine

Sodium chloride

• Ionic

• Simple molecular

• Giant molecular

• Metallic

2 Calcium reacts with oxygen to form calcium oxide. The bonding in calcium oxide is ionic.

(a) Complete the diagrams below to show the electronic configurations and charges of the calcium and oxygen ions. (2)

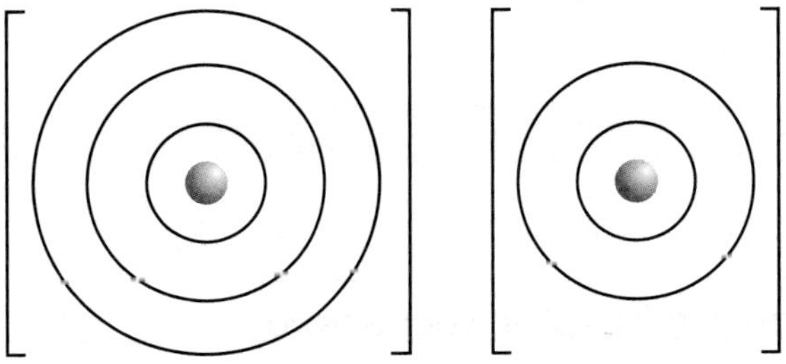

(b) State the charges on each ion. (2)

....

....

3 (a) Draw a dot-and-cross diagram to show the structure of HCl. (1)

(b) The dot-and-cross diagram for a molecule of oxygen is shown below.

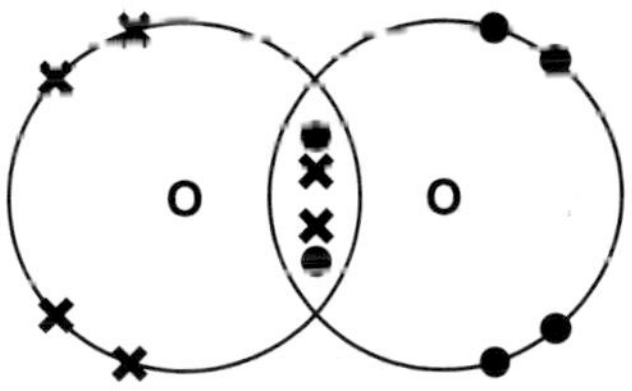

How many covalent bonds are there between the two oxygen atoms? (1)

....

For more help on this topic, see Letts GCSE Combined Science Higher Revision Guide pages 102–103

1 Calcium reacts with oxygen present in the air to form calcium oxide.

(a) Write a word equation for this reaction. (2)

....

(b) Explain why this is an oxidation reaction. (2)

....

....

(c) Name a metal that could be used to displace calcium from calcium oxide. Explain your choice of metal. (2)

....

....

(d) Write a word equation for this reaction. (2)

....

(e) In your equation from part **d**, give the name of the substance that has been reduced. (1)

....

2 Many metals are found in the Earth's crust as ores. For example, haematite is an ore containing iron(III) oxide (Fe_2O_3); bauxite is an ore containing aluminium oxide (Al_2O_3). Both metals can be extracted from their ores by reduction.

(a) What process is used to extract metals above carbon in the reactivity series from

their ores? .... (1)

(b) When iron(III) oxide is reduced by carbon, iron and carbon dioxide are formed. Write a balanced symbol equation for this reaction. (2)

....

(HT) **(c)** In the extraction of aluminium the following equation occurs: $Al^{3+} + 3e^- \longrightarrow Al$

Is this an oxidation or reduction reaction? Explain your answer. (3)

....

....

(HT) **(d)** Aluminium can also be formed by reacting a reactive metal such as potassium. An ionic equation for this reaction would be: $3K + Al^{3+} \longrightarrow Al + 3K^+$ Which substance is oxidised in this reaction? Explain your answer. (2)

....

....

For more help on this topic, see Letts GCSE Combined Science Higher Revision Guide pages 120–121

1 Zinc, zinc oxide and zinc carbonate all react with acids.

(a) Name the salt formed when zinc, zinc oxide and zinc carbonate react with sulfuric acid.

(1)

....

(b) Write a word equation for the reaction between zinc oxide and hydrochloric acid. (2)

....

(c) Name and give the formula of the gas formed when zinc carbonate reacts with nitric acid. (2)

....

HT **(d)** The ionic equation for the reaction between calcium and acid is:

$$Ca_{(s)} + 2H^+_{(aq)} \longrightarrow Ca^{2+}_{(aq)} + H_{2(g)}$$

    (i) Which substance is oxidised in the above reaction? (1)

    ....

    (ii) Which substance is reduced? (1)

    ....

HT **(e)** In terms of electrons, what is meant by an oxidation reaction? (2)

....

2 Copper(II) oxide (CuO) reacts with sulfuric acid to make the soluble salt copper(II) sulfate according to the equation below.

$$CuO_{(s)} + H_2SO_{4(aq)} \longrightarrow CuSO_{4(aq)} + H_2O_{(l)}$$

(a) Describe the steps you would take to prepare a sample of solid copper(II) sulfate, starting from copper(II) oxide and sulfuric acid solution. (3)

....

....

....

(b) The salt sodium nitrate can be formed by the reaction of sodium carbonate with an acid. Name this acid. (1)

....

(c) Is sodium nitrate a soluble or insoluble salt? .... (1)

For more help on this topic, see Letts GCSE Combined Science Higher Revision Guide pages 122–123

1 Hydrogen chloride (HCl) and ethanoic acid (CH$_3$COOH) both dissolve in water to form acidic solutions.

(a) What is the pH range of acids? (1)

....

(b) Give the name and formula for the ion present in solutions of hydrogen chloride and ethanoic acid. (2)

....

(c) What is the common name for hydrogen chloride solution? (1)

....

(d) Acids can be neutralised by reaction with an alkali such as sodium hydroxide.

Write an ionic equation for the reaction that occurs when an acid is neutralised by an alkali. Include state symbols in your equation. (2)

....

HT 2 Ethanoic acid is a key ingredient in vinegar. It is a weak acid. Nitric acid is a strong acid.

(a) What is the difference between a weak acid and a strong acid? (2)

....

....

(b) Write a balanced symbol equation for the dissociation of ethanoic acid in water. (2)

....

(c) Will a solution of nitric acid of the same concentration as a solution of ethanoic acid have a higher or lower pH?

Explain your answer. (2)

....

....

(d) What happens to the pH value of an acid when it is diluted by a factor of 10? (2)

....

....

For more help on this topic, see Letts GCSE Combined Science Higher Revision Guide pages 124–125

1 The diagram shows how a molten salt such as lead(II) bromide ($PbBr_2$) can be electrolysed. Lead(II) bromide consists of Pb^{2+} and Br^- ions.

Molten lead(II) bromide

(a) What general name is given to positive ions? (1)

....

(b) What general name is given to negative ions?

.... (1)

(c) Explain why the lead(II) bromide needs to be molten. (2)

....

....

HT (d) At the anode, the following reaction occurs: $2Br^- \longrightarrow Br_2 + 2e^-$

Is this an oxidation or a reduction reaction? Explain your answer. (2)

....

....

2 (a) The table below shows the products at each electrode when the following solutions are electrolysed. Some answers have already been filled in. Complete the table. (6)

Solution	Product at anode	Product at cathode
NaCl	H_2	
KNO_3		
$CuSO_4$		
Water diluted with sulfuric acid		O_2

(b) Explain why sodium is not formed at the cathode when aqueous sodium chloride is electrolysed. (2)

....

....

HT (c) Write a half-equation for the formation of oxygen at the anode in the electrolysis of water diluted with sulfuric acid. (2)

....

For more help on this topic, see Letts GCSE Combined Science Higher Revision Guide pages 126–127

Applications of electrolysis

Module 53

1 When methane burns in air an exothermic reaction takes place. The equation for the reaction is shown here:

$$CH_{4(g)} + 2O_{2(g)} \longrightarrow CO_{2(g)} + 2H_2O_{(l)}$$

(a) On the axes, draw and label a reaction profile for an exothermic reaction. Label the reactants, products, activation energy and ΔH. (5)

(b) In terms of bond energies, explain why this reaction is exothermic. (2)

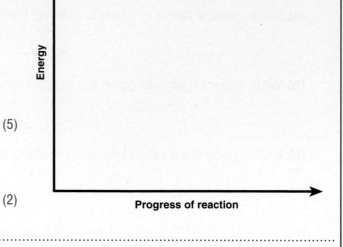

Energy

Progress of reaction

....

....

(c) Give an example of an endothermic chemical reaction. (1)

....

HT **2** Hydrogen peroxide (H_2O_2) decomposes in air to form water and oxygen. The diagram below shows this reaction by displaying all of the bonds present in the reactants and products.

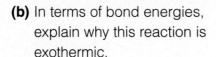

The table states the bond energy values of the bonds present in hydrogen peroxide, water and oxygen.

Bond	Bond energy kJ/mol
H–O	463
O–O	146
O=O	496

For the decomposition of hydrogen peroxide:

(a) Calculate ΔH for the reaction. (3)

....

....

(b) Is this reaction exothermic or endothermic? Explain your answer. (2)

....

....

For more help on this topic, see Letts GCSE Combined Science Higher Revision Guide pages 128–129

1 A pupil was investigating the effect of temperature on the rate of reaction between aqueous sodium thiosulfate with dilute hydrochloric acid. When the acid is added to the sodium thiosulfate solution, a precipitate of sulfur gradually forms. The pupil recorded the time taken for a cross written on a piece of paper to disappear from view.

The experiment was repeated at different temperatures. The results are shown in the table below.

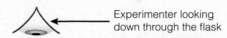 Experimenter looking down through the flask

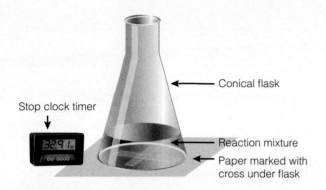
Conical flask

Stop clock timer

Reaction mixture
Paper marked with cross under flask

Temperature (°C)	Time taken for cross to disappear from view (s)
15	70
25	44
40	30
55	22
70	14

(a) At which temperature was the reaction the fastest? .... (1)

(b) Suggest how the rate of this reaction at 30°C will change when the concentration of hydrochloric acid is increased. Explain your answer. (2)

....

....

2 A student investigating the rate of reaction between magnesium and hydrochloric acid carried out two experiments: one using magnesium ribbon and the other using magnesium powder.

The equation for the reaction is shown here: $Mg_{(s)} + 2HCl_{(aq)} \longrightarrow MgCl_{2(aq)} + H_{2(g)}$

In the first experiment, 69 cm³ of hydrogen gas was collected in 46 seconds. In the second experiment, 18 cm³ of hydrogen gas was collected in 10 seconds.

(a) Calculate the rate of reaction in both experiments. (3)

....

....

(b) Which experiment was carried out using magnesium powder? Explain your answer. (2)

....

For more help on this topic, see Letts GCSE Combined Science Higher Revision Guide pages 132–133

Rates of reaction

Module 55

1 One aspect of collision theory states that, for a chemical reaction to occur, the reacting particles must first collide with each other.

(a) What else must occur in order for the collision to be successful? (1)

....

(b) Explain how:

(i) Increasing the pressure of a gas increases the rate of a reaction. (2)

....

....

(ii) Increasing the temperature of a solution increases the rate of a reaction. (3)

....

....

....

(c) Adding a catalyst to a reaction increases the rate of reaction. Draw, on the diagram below, the reaction profile for the reaction when a catalyst is added. (1)

(d) Explain how a catalyst is able to increase the rate of a reaction. (2)

....

....

For more help on this topic, see Letts GCSE Combined Science Higher Revision Guide pages 134–135

1 In an experiment, a student heated some blue crystals of hydrated copper(II) sulfate in an evaporating dish.

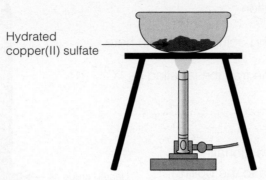

Hydrated copper(II) sulfate

(a) State what colour change will be observed during the reaction. (1)

....

(b) Write a word equation for the change that occurs to the hydrated copper(II) sulfate during this experiment. (2)

....

(c) Describe what will be observed when water is added to the solid remaining at the end of the experiment. (1)

....

(d) Is the addition of water an exothermic or endothermic reaction? (1)

....

2 Consider the reaction given here: $2SO_{2(g)} + O_{2(g)} \rightleftharpoons 2SO_{3(g)}$

(a) What does the $\rightleftharpoons$ symbol represent? .... (1)

HT **(b)** What would be the effect on the yield of SO_3 if the above reaction was carried out at a higher pressure? Explain your answer. (3)

....

....

....

HT **(c)** The forward reaction is exothermic. What would be the effect on the yield of SO_3 if the above reaction was carried out at a higher temperature? Explain your answer. (3)

....

....

....

For more help on this topic, see Letts GCSE Combined Science Higher Revision Guide pages 136–137

Reversible reactions and equilibrium

Module 57

1 Crude oil is separated into its constituent components by fractional distillation. A fractionating column is used to carry out fractional distillation.

A diagram of a fractionating column is shown here.

→ Refinery gases

→ Gasoline (petrol)

→ X

→ Diesel oil

→ Fuel oil

Heated crude oil →

→ Bitumen

(a) What is the name of the fraction labelled as 'X'?   (1)

....

(b) As you go down the fractionating column, what happens to the boiling point of the fractions?   (1)

....

(c) Explain how crude oil is separated in a fractionating column.   (3)

....

....

....

2 Most of the hydrocarbons found in crude oil are members of the homologous series of hydrocarbons called the alkanes.

(a) What is the general formula of alkanes?   (1)

....

(b) In the space below, draw the displayed formula for propane.   (1)

(c) What is the molecular formula of the member of the homologous series after propane?   (1)

....

(d) Other than the same general formula, give one other feature of a homologous series.   (1)

....

For more help on this topic, see Letts GCSE Combined Science Higher Revision Guide pages 140–141

1 Propane (C_3H_8) is an alkane frequently bottled and used as a fuel.

(a) Name the products produced when propane undergoes complete combustion. (2)

....

....

(b) Write a balanced symbol equation for the complete combustion of propane. (2)

....

....

(c) In the complete combustion of propane which substance has been oxidised? (1)

....

2 Cracking is a method of converting long-chain hydrocarbons into shorter, more useful hydrocarbons.

(a) Name a catalyst used to crack hydrocarbons. (1)

....

(b) Other than use of a catalyst, state an alternative method for cracking hydrocarbons. (2)

....

....

(c) The equation for a reaction that occurs during this process is:

$$C_{12}H_{26} \longrightarrow C_2H_4 + C_6H_{12} + X$$

In the balanced equation, what is the molecular formula of X? (1)

....

(d) Describe how the gas collected during cracking can be shown to contain a double bond. (2)

....

....

For more help on this topic, see Letts GCSE Combined Science Higher Revision Guide pages 142–143

1 Paint and household cleaning chemicals are typical examples of everyday chemical formulations.

(a) What is a formulation? (1)

....

(b) Are formulations chemically pure? Explain your answer. (2)

....

....

(c) Give **one** other example of a type of formulation. (1)

....

2 Pen ink is typically a mixture of dyes. The individual dyes in pen ink can be separated by paper chromatography. The chromatogram below is for an unknown ink 'X' and the standard colours blue, red and green.

(a) What is the mobile phase in paper chromatography? (1)

....

(b) Which colours are present in ink X? Explain your answer. (2)

....

....

(c) Calculate the R_f for the blue ink. (2)

....

....

(d) The sample of ink could also have been separated using gas chromatography. State **one** advantage that gas chromatography has over paper chromatography. (1)

....

For more help on this topic, see Letts GCSE Combined Science Higher Revision Guide pages 146–147

1 When carbon dioxide gas is bubbled through limewater the following reaction occurs:

$$Ca(OH)_{2(aq)} + CO_{2(g)} \longrightarrow CaCO_{3(s)} + H_2O_{(l)}$$

(a) What is the chemical name for limewater? (1)

....

(b) With reference to the above equation, explain why limewater turns cloudy when carbon dioxide is bubbled through it. (2)

....

....

2 (a) Describe what would be observed when moist blue litmus paper is added to a gas jar containing chlorine gas. (2)

....

....

(b) Is chlorine an acidic or alkaline gas?

What evidence is there to support your answer? (2)

....

....

3 Hydrogen and oxygen gases are both colourless, odourless gases.

(a) What is the chemical test and observation for hydrogen gas? (2)

....

....

(b) What is the chemical test and observation for oxygen gas? (2)

....

....

(c) When hydrogen gas burns in air it reacts with oxygen to form water. Write a balanced symbol equation for the reaction taking place. (2)

....

....

Identification of gases

Module 61

For more help on this topic, see Letts GCSE Combined Science Higher Revision Guide pages 148–149

1 Many scientists think that the Earth's early atmosphere may have been similar in composition to the gases typically released by volcanoes today.

The pie charts below show the composition of the atmosphere today and the composition of gases released by a volcano.

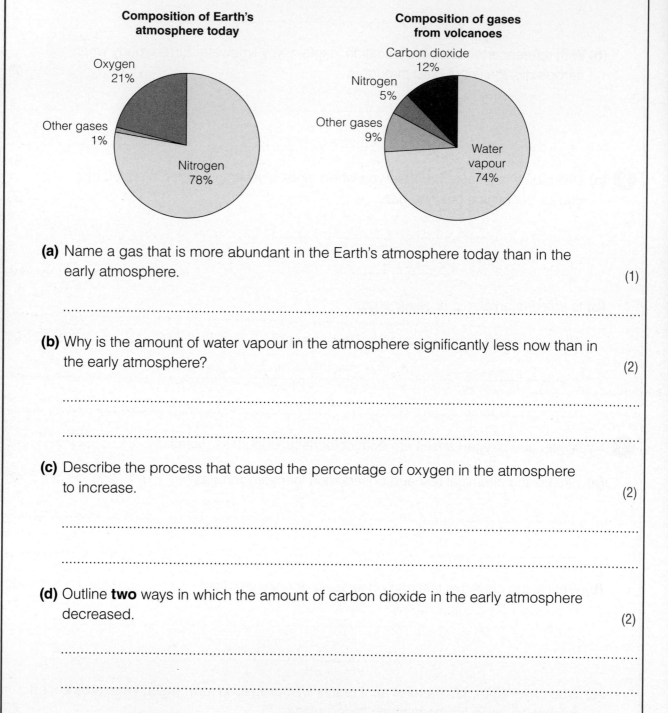

Composition of Earth's atmosphere today

Oxygen 21%

Other gases 1%

Nitrogen 78%

Composition of gases from volcanoes

Carbon dioxide 12%

Nitrogen 5%

Other gases 9%

Water vapour 74%

(a) Name a gas that is more abundant in the Earth's atmosphere today than in the early atmosphere. (1)

....

(b) Why is the amount of water vapour in the atmosphere significantly less now than in the early atmosphere? (2)

....

....

(c) Describe the process that caused the percentage of oxygen in the atmosphere to increase. (2)

....

....

(d) Outline **two** ways in which the amount of carbon dioxide in the early atmosphere decreased. (2)

....

....

For more help on this topic, see Letts GCSE Combined Science Higher Revision Guide pages 152–153

1 When fossil fuels are burnt, carbon dioxide gas is produced and released into the atmosphere. Some people believe carbon dioxide to be a greenhouse gas.

(a) Explain how greenhouse gases maintain the temperature on Earth. (2)

....

....

(b) Name **one** other greenhouse gas. (1)

....

(c) Outline **two** ways in which human activity increases the amounts of greenhouse gases in the atmosphere. (2)

....

....

(d) Why is it not easy to predict the impact of changes on global climate change? (2)

....

....

(e) Describe **two** potential effects of increasing average global temperature. (2)

....

....

(f) Describe **two** forms of global action that can be taken to reduce the carbon footprint. (2)

....

....

(g) Outline **two** potential problems that governments might face when trying to reduce the carbon footprint. (2)

....

....

For more help on this topic, see Letts GCSE Combined Science Higher Revision Guide pages 154–155

1 The combustion of fossil fuels, e.g. from cars, is a major source of atmospheric pollution.

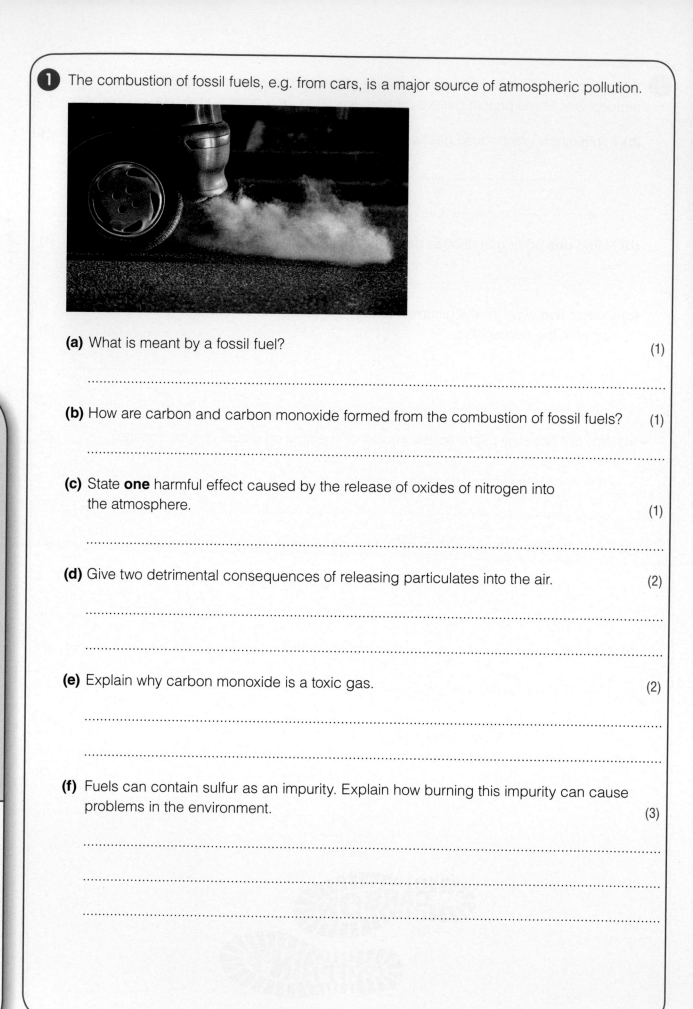

(a) What is meant by a fossil fuel? (1)

....

(b) How are carbon and carbon monoxide formed from the combustion of fossil fuels? (1)

....

(c) State **one** harmful effect caused by the release of oxides of nitrogen into
the atmosphere.

(1)

....

(d) Give two detrimental consequences of releasing particulates into the air. (2)

....

....

(e) Explain why carbon monoxide is a toxic gas. (2)

....

....

(f) Fuels can contain sulfur as an impurity. Explain how burning this impurity can cause
problems in the environment.

(3)

....

....

....

For more help on this topic, see Letts GCSE Combined Science Higher Revision Guide pages 156–157

1 We use the Earth's resources to provide us with warmth, shelter, food and transport. As the Earth is a finite source of resources, we need to ensure that we use them sustainably.

(a) What is sustainable development? (1)

....

(b) What is meant by the term 'potable water'? (1)

....

(c) After identification of an appropriate source of fresh water, what two stages then need to occur to turn this into potable water? (2)

....

....

(d) Outline the processes that are used to treat sewage. (3)

....

....

....

2 Salty water, e.g. seawater, can be desalinated (i.e. treated to reduce its salt content). One such method is distillation.

(a) In the space below, draw a labelled diagram to show how seawater can be distilled. Describe how distillation produces desalinated water. (5)

....

....

(b) What method of desalination involves the use of membranes? (1)

....

For more help on this topic, see Letts GCSE Combined Science Higher Revision Guide pages 158–159

Module 65

HT **1** As we mine more and more of the Earth's natural resources, we need to develop alternative methods of extracting metals such as copper. One such recently developed method is phytomining.

(a) What is an ore?

(2)

....

....

(b) Aside from environmental reasons, why are methods of extracting metals such as phytomining being developed?

(2)

....

....

(c) State two uses of copper and describe the properties that make it suitable for each purpose.

(4)

....

....

(d) Describe the process of phytomining.

(3)

....

....

....

(e) How can bacteria be used to extract metals such as copper?

(1)

....

(f) Scrap metals, such as iron, can be used to obtain copper from solutions. Write a word equation for the reaction that occurs when iron reacts with copper sulfate solution.

(2)

....

(g) Why would platinum not be a suitable metal for extracting copper from copper sulfate solution?

(1)

....

(h) What is the name of the process involving electricity that can be used to extract a metal from a solution of its ions?

(1)

....

For more help on this topic, see Letts GCSE Combined Science Higher Revision Guide pages 160–161

1 Life-cycle assessments (LCAs) are carried out to evaluate the environmental impact of products at different stages of the life of a product.

(a) Other than transport and distribution, state **two** other stages of a product life cycle that will be considered when carrying out an LCA. (2)

....

....

(b) State **two** quantities that are considered when conducting an LCA. (2)

....

....

(c) Explain why the pollution value in a life-cycle value may result in the LCA not being totally objective. (2)

....

....

(d) Why might selective or abbreviated LCAs be misused? (1)

....

2 The table below shows an example of an LCA for the use of plastic (polythene) and paper shopping bags.

	Amounts per 1000 bags over the whole LCA	
	Paper	Plastic (polythene)
Energy use (mJ)	2590	713
Fossil fuel use (kg)	28	12.8
Solid waste (kg)	34	6
Greenhouse gas emissions (kg CO_2)	72	36
Fresh water use (litres)	3387	198

Based on the above figures, why might some people think that plastic (polythene) bags should be used instead of paper bags? Use information from the table in your answer. (3)

....

....

....

For more help on this topic, see Letts GCSE Combined Science Higher Revision Guide pages 162–163

1 Neil, an astronaut, has a mass of 78 kg.

(a) Calculate Neil's weight.

(gravitational field strength = 10 N/kg)   (1)

....

(b) The Moon has a gravitational field strength of 1.6 N/kg.

What would Neil's mass and weight be on the Moon?   (2)

....

....

(c) Neil also has a gravitational field that causes attraction.

Explain why this has no measurable effect on either the Moon or the Earth.   (2)

....

....

2 The diagram shows Louise, a runner.

(a) Calculate the resultant force acting on Louise.

30 N   120 N   (2)

....

....

(b) The forces on Louise changed as shown by the diagram below.

(i) What is the resultant force on Louise now?

90 N   90 N   (1)

....

(ii) What statement can be made about her speed now? Explain your answer.   (2)

....

....

(c) Louise uses 90 N of force and the work done is 25 kJ. What distance does she cover? (2)

....

....

For more help on this topic, see Letts GCSE Combined Science Higher Revision Guide pages 166–167

1 The graph below shows the results of an extension of a spring in response to different forces.

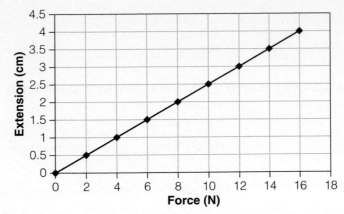

(a) What term is given to the relationship shown in this graph? (1)

....

(b) Calculate the spring constant for this spring. (3)

....

....

....

(c) The results were repeated, but with a larger range of masses providing the force. The results are shown in the graph below.

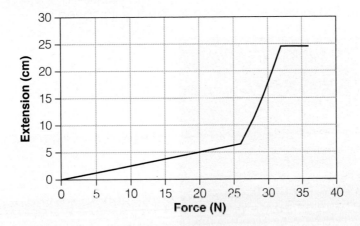

(i) What term is given to the relationship shown in this graph? (1)

....

(ii) Explain the difference in the shapes of the two graphs. (3)

....

....

....

For more help on this topic, see Letts GCSE Combined Science Higher Revision Guide pages 168–169

1 (a) Explain why speed is a scalar quantity while velocity is a vector quantity. (2)

....

....

HT (b) Why does a car travelling around a bend at a constant speed have a constantly changing velocity? (2)

....

....

(c) Draw lines to match the following average speeds to the methods of travel. (4)

Average speed	Travel method
1.5 m/s	Car
6 m/s	Plane
20 m/s	Bicycle
250 m/s	Walking

2 (a) A jet ski travels 180 metres in 13 seconds. What is its speed? (2)

....

....

(b) How long would it take for the same jet ski travelling at the same speed to travel 500 m? (2)

....

....

For more help on this topic, see Letts GCSE Combined Science Higher Revision Guide pages 170–171

1 The graph shows the distance a boat travels over time.

    (a) What is the average speed of the boat over the first 350 seconds? (2)

....

....

....

....

    (b) What is the velocity of the boat at 265 seconds? (2)

....

....

2 The graph shows the velocity of a car.

    (a) (i) During what time period is the greatest acceleration of the car? (1)

....

....

    (ii) What is the acceleration during this time period? (2)

....

....

HT **(b)** How far did the car travel in 0 50 seconds? (3)

....

....

3 Explain why a skydiver in free fall accelerates for a time before maintaining a

constant speed. .... (4)

....

....

....

For more help on this topic, see Letts GCSE Combined Science Higher Revision Guide pages 172–173

1 **(a)** What will happen if a resultant force greater than zero is applied to:

    (i) a stationary object? (1)

    ....

    (ii) a moving object? (1)

    ....

  (b) Which of Newton's laws deals with the effect of resultant force? (1)

  ....

HT **(c)** What term is given to the tendency of objects to continue in their state of rest? (1)

  ....

2 **(a)** The acceleration of an object is inversely proportional to the mass of an object. How does the acceleration relate to the resultant force? (1)

  ....

  (b) (i) Adele, a cyclist, who has a total mass of 110 kg, accelerates at 5 m/s^2. What is the resultant force on Adele? (2)

  ....

  ....

  (ii) Explain how the resultant force on Adele will change as she slows down and comes to a stop. (3)

  ....

  ....

  ....

3 State Newton's third law. (1)

....

4 Use Newton's laws to explain the events that the sign below is warning about. (3)

....

....

....

....

Weak bridge
^{1}4 mile
ahead

17T

For more help on this topic, see Letts GCSE Combined Science Higher Revision Guide pages 174–175

1 (a) Increasing speed increases the thinking distance and the braking distance of a car. Explain why. (2)

(i) Thinking distance: ....

....

(ii) Braking distance: ....

....

(b) Give **two** other factors that could increase the thinking distance. (2)

....

....

(c) The table shows the temperatures of brakes when a car decelerates to zero in a set amount of time. The test was repeated at four different initial speeds.

Test	Brake temperature (°C)
A	150
B	800
C	320
D	560

(i) Put the tests in order of initial speed, from highest speed to lowest speed. (1)

....

(ii) Explain the difference in the results of A and B. Use the concepts of work done and kinetic energy in your answer. (3)

....

....

....

HT **2 (a)** What is the momentum of a 50 kg cheetah running at 20 m/s? (2)

....

....

(b) What will happen to the cheetah's momentum as it decelerates? (1)

....

For more help on this topic, see Letts GCSE Combined Science Higher Revision Guide pages 176–177

Forces, braking and momentum

Module 73

1. Jessica, a sky diver, is in a plane at a height of 3900 m. She has a mass of 60 kg.

   (a) What is Jessica's gravitational potential energy?

   (Assume gravitational field strength is 10 N/kg.)   (2)

   ....

   ....

   (b) Jessica jumps from the plane and accelerates to a terminal velocity of 55 m/s.
   What is Jessica's kinetic energy at this point?   (2)

   ....

   ....

   (c) Jessica deploys her parachute and slows to a speed of 5 m/s.
   What is her new kinetic energy?   (2)

   ....

   ....

   (d) When Jessica lands on the ground, she is stationary. What is her kinetic energy now? (1)

   ....

2. The table below shows the specific heat capacity of different substances.

Substance	Specific heat capacity J/kg/°C
Water	4180
Copper	390
Ethanol	2440
Titanium	520

   (a) Which substance would require the least energy to raise 1 kg by 1°C?
   Explain how you arrived at your answer.   (2)

   ....

   ....

   (b) Calculate the mass of copper that requires 76 kJ of energy to increase in temperature
   from 16°C to 35°C.   (3)

   ....

   ....

   ....

For more help on this topic, see Letts GCSE Combined Science Higher Revision Guide pages 180–181

1 Which of the below is an incorrect ending to the following sentence?
Tick the correct options. (2)

Energy cannot be...

created. ☐

transferred. ☐

destroyed. ☐

dissipated. ☐

2 The table below shows the average cost of heating three different houses.
Each home is the same size.

House	Heating cost per hour / p
A	105
B	88
C	150

(a) Which house is likely to have the best insulation in its walls?
Explain how you arrived at your answer. (3)

....

....

....

(b) Can you be certain about your conclusion?
Explain your answer. (3)

....

....

....

(c) The boiler in another house is 65% efficient. If the energy input is 5400 kJ,
what is the useful energy output? (2)

....

....

For more help on this topic, see Letts GCSE Combined Science Higher Revision Guide pages 182–183

1 Complete the table below to give **three** examples of renewable energy and **three** examples of non-renewable energy. (3)

Renewable energy	Non-renewable energy

2 The graph below shows the percentage of the total electricity in the UK generated by wind turbines.

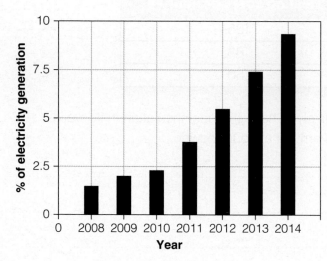

(a) Describe the trend shown by the graph. (1)

....

(b) Describe the main advantage of wind power over burning fossil fuels. (2)

....

....

(c) Will wind turbines ever make up 100% of electricity generation? Explain your answer. (3)

....

....

....

(d) Why might some people not want wind turbines to be placed on the tops of hills? (1)

....

For more help on this topic, see Letts GCSE Combined Science Higher Revision Guide pages 184–185

1 The speed of sound in water is 1482 m/s.

(a) What type of wave is a sound wave when travelling in air? (1)

....

(b) Calculate the wavelength of a sound wave in water that has a frequency of 120 Hz. (2)

....

....

(c) The speed of sound in air is 330 m/s.
Suggest a reason for the difference between this speed and the speed of sound
in water. (2)

....

....

(d) How do the oscillations in a water wave differ to the oscillations in a sound wave
travelling in air? (2)

....

....

2 Draw lines to match the following terms to their correct definitions. (3)

| Amplitude |
| Wavelength |
| Frequency |

| The distance from a point on one wave to the equivalent point on the adjacent wave. |
| The number of waves passing a point each second. |
| The maximum displacement of a point on a wave away from its undisturbed position. |

For more help on this topic, see **Letts GCSE Combined Science Higher Revision Guide pages 188–189**

1 The image below shows the electromagnetic spectrum.

Wavelength (metres)	**A**	Microwave	**B**	Visible	Ultraviolet	X-ray	**C**
	10^3	10^{-2}	10^{-5}	10^{-6}	10^{-8}	10^{-10}	10^{-12}

What are the names of the different types of electromagnetic radiation **A**–**C**? (3)

A: ....

B: ....

C: ....

HT **2** The diagram shows the effect of light entering water from the air.

Air

A

B

Water

(a) Give the names of angles **A** and **B**. (2)

A: ....

B: ....

(b) Explain why the light changes direction as it moves from air to water. (3)

....

....

....

(c) How would refraction differ if the light was entering air from water? (1)

....

For more help on this topic, see Letts GCSE Combined Science Higher Revision Guide pages 190–191

HT **1** Draw lines to match up the following types of radiation to their uses and why they are suitable for that use. (3)

Radiation type	Use	Why suitable for use?
Radio waves	Heating a room	Don't require a direct line of sight between transmitter and receiver.
Ultraviolet	Television	Require less energy than conventional lights.
Infrared	Energy efficient lamps	Thermal radiation heats up objects.

2 **(a)** From where do gamma rays originate? (1)

....

(b) Give **one** potential use of gamma rays. (1)

....

(c) Why are gamma rays potentially harmful? (2)

....

....

3 What variable could be measured to determine the possible harm caused by radiation? (1)

....

HT **4** This photograph shows a medical image.

(a) What type of electromagnetic radiation is used to produce this image? (1)

....

(b) Explain why this type of radiation is used in medical imaging. (3)

....

....

....

For more help on this topic, see Letts GCSE Combined Science Higher Revision Guide pages 192–193

Electromagnetic waves and properties 2 | Module 79

1 Identify the following circuit symbols:

(a)  (1)

....

(b) 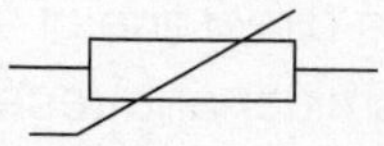 (1)

....

(c)  (1)

....

2 The diagram shows a circuit.

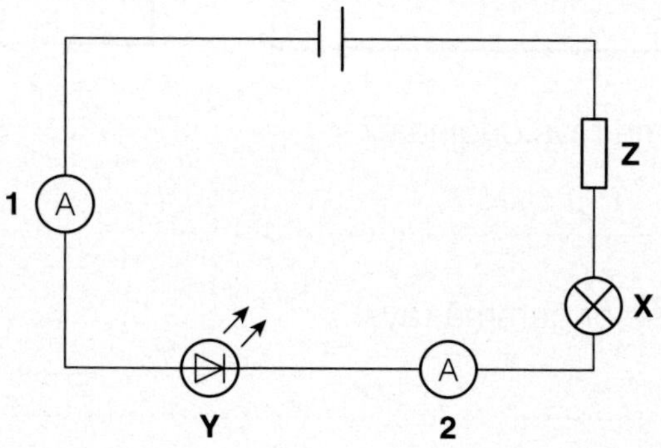

(a) Identify components **X**, **Y** and **Z**. (3)

X: ....

Y: ....

Z: ....

(b) Ammeter **1** gave a reading of 5 amps.
What is the reading of ammeter **2**? (1)

....

(c) What is 'electric current'? (1)

....

(d) If the charge flow through the circuit was 780 C, for how long was the current
flowing through the circuit? (2)

....

....

For more help on this topic, see Letts GCSE Combined Science Higher Revision Guide pages 196–197

1 The graph shows the relationship between the current and potential difference of a component.

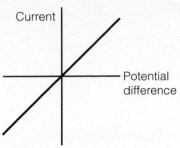

(a) What general name could be given to this type of conductor? (1)

....

(b) What environmental factor could change and lead to a change in the shape of the graph above? (1)

....

(c) On the axis, sketch a graph to show the relationship between current and potential difference through a diode. (2)

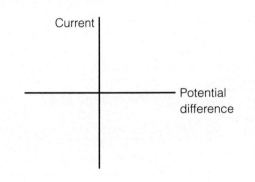

2 Calculate the current flowing through a 4 Ω resistor when there is a potential difference of 15 V across it. (2)

....

....

3 Look at the circuit below.

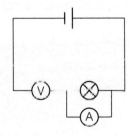

Explain why this circuit could not be used to determine the resistance of the bulb. (3)

....

....

....

For more help on this topic, see Letts GCSE Combined Science Higher Revision Guide pages 198–199

1 The diagram shows a circuit.

(a) What type of circuit is shown? (1)

....

....

(b) What is the total resistance of the three resistors
in the circuit? Show how you arrived at your answer. (2)

....

....

2 The diagram shows a circuit.

(a) What is the current at **1**? (1)

....

....

(b) What is the voltage at **2**? (1)

....

....

(c) What is the resistance at **3**? (1)

....

....

(d) The circuit was rewired so that the bulb and resistor were wired in series. How would this
change the total resistance of the two components?

Explain your answer. (3)

....

....

....

For more help on this topic, see Letts GCSE Combined Science Higher Revision Guide pages 200–201

1 (a) Draw lines to match the names of the wires in a plug to its colour and function. (3)

Wire	Colour	Function
Live wire	Blue	Completes the circuit.
Neutral wire	Brown	Only carries a current if there is a fault.
Earth wire	Green and yellow stripes	Carries the alternating potential difference from the supply.

(b) Why does a double insulated appliance not require an earth connection? (2)

....

....

2 An electric sander is being used during a house renovation. The sander is plugged into a socket in the wall.

(a) Is the sander powered by direct current or alternating current?
Explain your answer. (2)

....

....

(b) When using the sander, a wire in a wall is damaged and trips the house circuit breakers.

What are the advantages, in this case, of the house mains supply having a circuit breaker rather than a fuse? (2)

....

....

For more help on this topic, see Letts GCSE Combined Science Higher Revision Guide pages 202–203

Domestic uses and safety

Module 83

1 **(a)** A tumble dryer has a current flowing through it of 3 A and a resistance of 76.7 Ω.

Calculate its power. (2)

....

....

(b) What useful energy transfers are occurring in the tumble dryer? (2)

....

....

(c) If the tumble dryer transfers 180 kJ of energy in a cycle, how long is the cycle
in seconds? (2)

....

....

(d) The mains electricity used by the tumble dryer has a potential difference of 230 V.
Some of the overhead cables that carry the electricity in the National Grid have a
potential difference of 138 kV.

Explain the reasons for this difference in potential difference. (3)

....

....

....

For more help on this topic, see Letts GCSE Combined Science Higher Revision Guide pages 204–205

1 Complete the diagram below to show the poles of the three bar magnets interacting. (3)

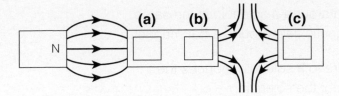

2 The diagram below shows an experiment into magnets and magnetic objects.

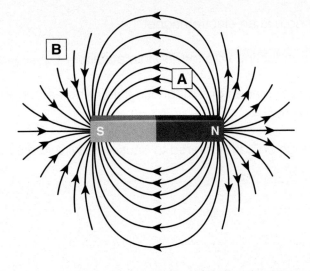

(a) What name is given to the region around the magnet where magnetic objects or magnets experience a force? (1)

....

(b) What type of force would a magnetic object placed at **A** experience? (1)

....

(c) Would the force at **A** be stronger than the force experienced by a magnetic object at **B**? Explain your answer. (2)

....

....

3 The bar magnet in a compass points towards magnetic north. What can be concluded about the Earth's core from this fact? (3)

....

....

....

For more help on this topic, see Letts GCSE Combined Science Higher Revision Guide pages 208–209

1 Tick each of the following statements that correctly describe the features of a solenoid.   (2)

The magnetic field around a solenoid is the same
shape as the magnetic field around a bar magnet. ☐

Adding an iron core to a solenoid reduces the
magnetic strength of the solenoid. ☐

A solenoid with an iron core is an electromagnet. ☐

A solenoid with a tin core is an electromagnet ☐

A solenoid is a non-conducting wire formed into a helix. ☐

HT **2** A conducting wire is placed in a magnetic field. When a current is passed through the wire it begins to move.

(a) What **two** things could be altered to cause the wire to move in the opposite direction?   (2)

....

....

(b) What name is given to this effect?   (1)

....

(c) The wire is at a right angle to the magnetic field. The wire is 30 cm long and has a current of 15 A flowing through. This produces 25 N of force.

What is the magnetic flux density?   (2)

....

....

HT **3** In an electric fan, electrical energy is transferred to kinetic energy. Explain how this is made possible by the motor effect.   (3)

....

....

....

For more help on this topic, see Letts GCSE Combined Science Higher Revision Guide pages 210–211

1 **(a)** A full fire extinguisher has a mass of 5 kg and a volume of 0.002 m³. What is the density of a fire extinguisher? (2)

....

....

(b) What would happen to the density of the fire extinguisher after it had been used to put out a fire? Explain your answer. (3)

....

....

....

2 In an investigation into the link between pressure and molar concentration of a gas, the temperature and volume are kept constant.

Explain the importance of controlling the following variables:

(a) Constant temperature (1)

....

(b) Constant volume (1)

....

3 **(a)** What mass of water is produced by heating 3 kg of ice until it has completely melted? Explain how you arrived at your answer. (2)

....

....

(b) The temperature of the water is then lowered past its freezing point and ice reforms. How does this prove that the original melting was a physical change as opposed to a chemical change? (2)

....

....

....

For more help on this topic, see Letts GCSE Combined Science Higher Revision Guide pages 214–215

1 The graph below shows the results of an investigation into the heating of a substance.

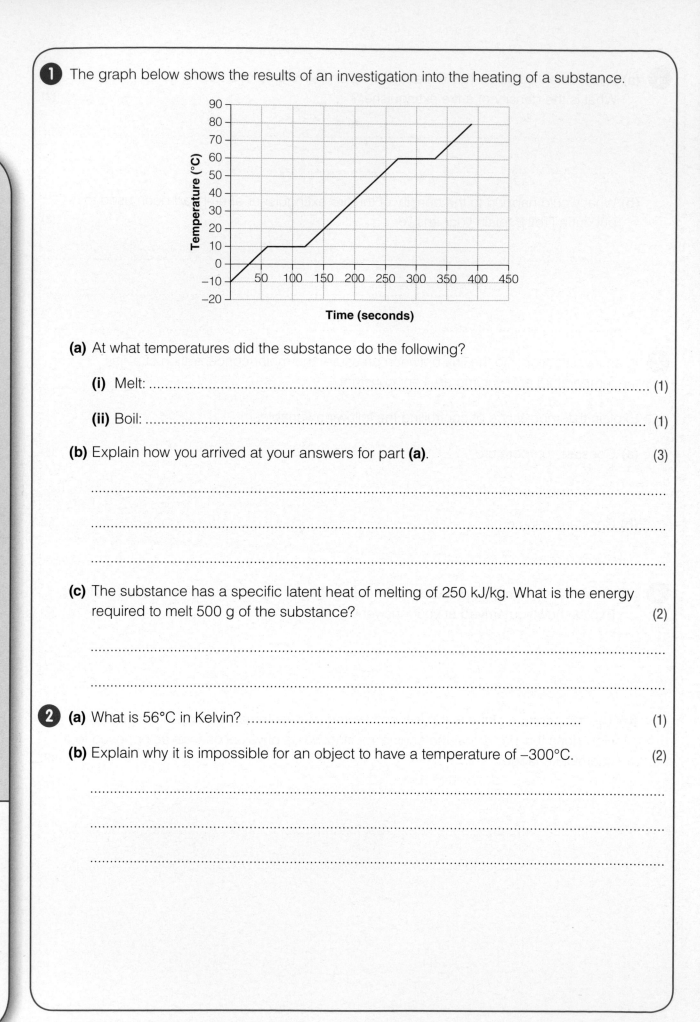

(a) At what temperatures did the substance do the following?

(i) Melt: .... (1)

(ii) Boil: .... (1)

(b) Explain how you arrived at your answers for part **(a)**. (3)

....

....

....

(c) The substance has a specific latent heat of melting of 250 kJ/kg. What is the energy required to melt 500 g of the substance? (2)

....

....

2 **(a)** What is 56°C in Kelvin? .... (1)

(b) Explain why it is impossible for an object to have a temperature of −300°C. (2)

....

....

....

For more help on this topic, see Letts GCSE Combined Science Higher Revision Guide pages 216–217

1 An element symbol is shown below.

(a) State the numbers of the following subatomic particles that an atom of the element contains.

    (i) Protons: .... (1)

    (ii) Neutrons: .... (1)

    (iii)Electrons: .... (1)

(b) The element is also found in the following forms:

^{12}C ^{13}C ^{14}C

    (i) What name is given to these forms? (1)

....

    (ii) How do they differ from each another? (1)

....

2 (a) Give **two** differences between the plum pudding model of atomic structure and Rutherford, Geiger and Marsden's nuclear model. (2)

....

....

(b) Why was James Chadwick's experimental work in 1932 important in further developing the model of atomic structure? (1)

....

For more help on this topic, see Letts GCSE Combined Science Higher Revision Guide pages 220–221

1 An investigation was carried out into the penetration of radiation emitted from different radioactive sources.

Type of radiation	Radiation released	Penetration distance in air
A	Two neutrons and two protons (a helium nucleus).	A few centimetres.
B	Electromagnetic radiation from the nucleus.	A large distance.
C	High speed electron ejected from the nucleus as a neutron turns into a proton.	A few metres.

(a) (i) Identify the types of radiation **A–C**. (3)

A: ....

B: ....

C: ....

(ii) Rank the radiations in **(i)** from most ionising to least ionising. (2)

....

Most ionising   **Least ionising**

2 The equation below shows the decay of a radioactive element.

$$^{238}_{\text{A}} U \longrightarrow ^{\text{B}}_{90} Th + ^{\text{C}}_{\text{D}} \alpha$$

(a) What type of decay is shown by the equation? (1)

....

(b) Complete the missing parts (**A–D**) of the equation. (3)

A: ....

B: ....

C: ....

D: ....

(c) What effect does gamma emission have on the nucleus of a radioactive element? (1)

....

....

For more help on this topic, see Letts GCSE Combined Science Higher Revision Guide pages 222–223

1 Complete the following paragraph using some of the words below. (3)

decay	irradiation	Sievert	contamination
radioactive	half-life	emit	radiation

Radioactive .... is the unwanted presence of materials containing

radioactive atoms on other materials. This is a hazard due to the .... of

the contaminating atoms. The atoms will .... radiation so may be a hazard.

.... is the process of exposing an object to nuclear ....

without the object itself becoming ....

2 The graph below shows the decay of a radioactive element.

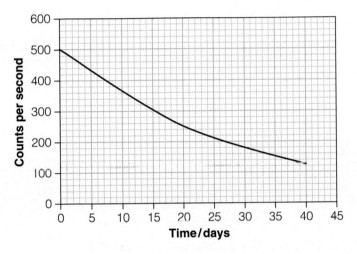

(a) (i) Estimate the half-life of this element. (1)

....

(ii) Explain how you arrived at your answer. (1)

....

(iii) Estimate the counts per second of the sample after 60 days. (2)

....

....

For more help on this topic, see Letts GCSE Combined Science Higher Revision Guide pages 224–225

GCSE
Combined Science
Paper 1: Biology 1

Higher
Time: 1 hour 15 minutes

You may use:
- a calculator
- a ruler.

Instructions

- Use black ink or black ball-point pen. Draw diagrams in pencil.
- Read each question carefully before you start to write your answer.
- Answer **all** questions in the spaces provided.
- Show your working in any calculator question and include units in your answer where appropriate.
- In questions marked with an asterisk (*), marks will be awarded for your ability to structure your answer logically, showing how the points that you make are related or follow on from each other where appropriate.

Information

- The marks for each question are shown in brackets.
  Use this as a guide to how much time to spend on each question.
- The maximum mark for this paper is 70.
- Diagrams are not accurately drawn unless otherwise stated.

Name: ....

1 **(a)** Which substance is a product of anaerobic respiration in humans? Tick (✓) **one** box. **[1]**

Carbon dioxide ☐

Ethanol ☐

Glucose ☐

Lactic acid ☐

(b) Which substance is a product of aerobic respiration in plants? Tick (✓) **one** box. **[1]**

Carbon dioxide ☐

Ethanol ☐

Glucose ☐

Lactic acid ☐

2

Figure 1

(a) Niamh in **Figure 1** is training for a marathon. Every few days she runs a long distance. This builds up the number of mitochondria in her muscle cells.

What is the advantage for Niamh of having extra mitochondria in her muscle cells?
Tick (✓) **one** box. **[1]**

Her muscles become stronger. ☐

Her muscles can contract faster. ☐

Her muscles can release more energy. ☐

Her muscles can repair faster after injury. ☐

*(b) Bob in **Figure 2** has been running hard and has an oxygen debt. Describe what causes an oxygen debt after a session of vigorous exercise and how Bob can recover from its effects. [3]

Figure 2

....

....

....

....

*(c) Tariq is competing in a 10-mile running race. His heart rate and breathing rate increase. Describe how this helps his muscles during the race. [3]

....

....

....

3 Which of the following structures are in the correct size order, starting with the smallest? Tick (✓) **one** box. [1]

cell, tissue, organ, system ☐

tissue, organ, system, cell ☐

cell, organ, system, tissue ☐

tissue, system, cell, organ ☐

4 Which part of the blood helps protect the body from pathogens? Tick (✓) **one** box. [1]

Plasma ☐

Platelets ☐

Red blood cells ☐

White blood cells ☐

5 (a) From which section of the human heart is blood pumped to the lungs?
Tick (✓) **one** box. [1]

Left atrium ☐

Right atrium ☐

Left ventricle ☐

Right ventricle ☐

(b) Explain why the left side of the heart is more muscular than the right side. [1]

....

....

(c) The heart contains a number of valves.

Describe how the valves help the heart pump blood more effectively. [1]

....

....

(d) There are around 105 650 deaths in the UK from smoking-related causes each year. The number of deaths due to cardiovascular disease that is linked to smoking is estimated to be 22 100.

What percentage of deaths from smoking each year is due to cardiovascular disease? Show your working. Give your answer to two significant figures. [2]

....

(e) The chance of heart disease can be reduced by lowering alcohol intake and by not smoking. Write about **two** other choices that can be made to reduce the chance of heart disease. [2]

....

....

6 (a) Explain how skin defends the human body against disease. [2]

....

....

(b) Disease can be caused by bacteria. Bacteria multiply very quickly – the numbers of cholera bacteria can double every 20 minutes.

Ten cholera bacteria were kept in ideal conditions for growth. How many cholera bacteria were there after two hours? Show your working. **[2]**

....

....

(c) Explain why measles cannot be treated with antibiotics. **[2]**

....

....

(d) **Figure 3** shows a photomicrograph of the bacterium *E. coli*, which is a common cause of stomach upsets. The magnification of the photo is × 5000.

Figure 3

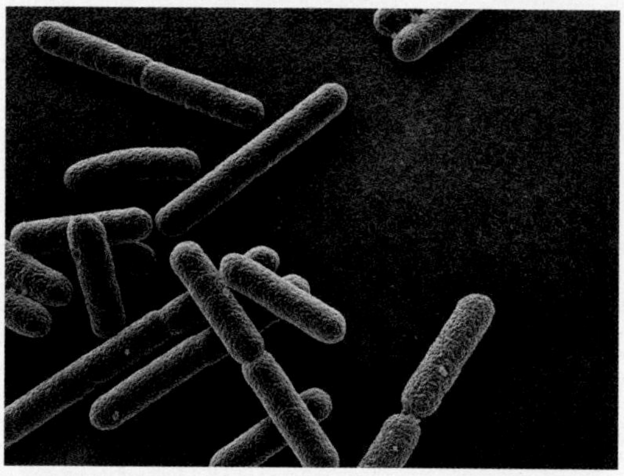

The average magnified length of the bacteria shown in **Figure 3** is 10 mm. Calculate the actual length of an *E. coli* bacterium in µm (1 µm = 1×10^{-3} mm). Show your working. **[2]**

....

....

(e) The spread of cholera is often a problem in temporary refugee camps. One way cholera is spread is through contaminated water.

What simple measures can be taken to reduce the spread of cholera in the camps? **[2]**

....

....

(f) If a disease is infectious, an epidemic can be prevented by vaccination.

Explain why a very high percentage of the population need to be vaccinated for the prevention to be successful. **[2]**

....

....

7 Which of the following is found in a plant cell but not in an animal cell?
Tick (✓) **one** box. **[1]**

Cell membrane ☐

Cytoplasm ☐

Nucleus ☐

Cell wall ☐

*__8__ Describe the aseptic method used to grow a colony of bacteria cells from pond water using a sterilised petri dish containing nutrient agar jelly. **[4]**

....

....

....

....

9 Human stem cell research could lead to new treatments for conditions such as diabetes.

(a) Outline **two** reasons why some people think that human stem cell research should not be allowed. **[2]**

....

....

(b) Look at **Figure 4**. What is the name of the process by which a stem cell becomes a new cell type? **[1]**

Figure 4

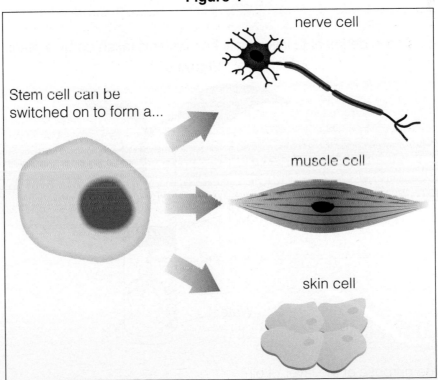

....

10 (a) Stomata are found on the underside of a plant leaf. During the day the stomata open to allow carbon dioxide into the leaf. Outline how the stomata open. **[2]**

....

....

(b) Carbon dioxide moves into a leaf by diffusion. Describe the process of diffusion. **[2]**

....

....

11 (a) Figure 5 shows a celery plant. The stalk of a celery plant contains xylem vessels.

Figure 5

Describe the structure of xylem vessels. **[2]**

....

....

(b) Describe how root cells are adapted to allow the efficient absorption of water. **[2]**

....

....

12 Figure 6 shows an experiment to investigate how water is taken up by a plant.

Figure 6

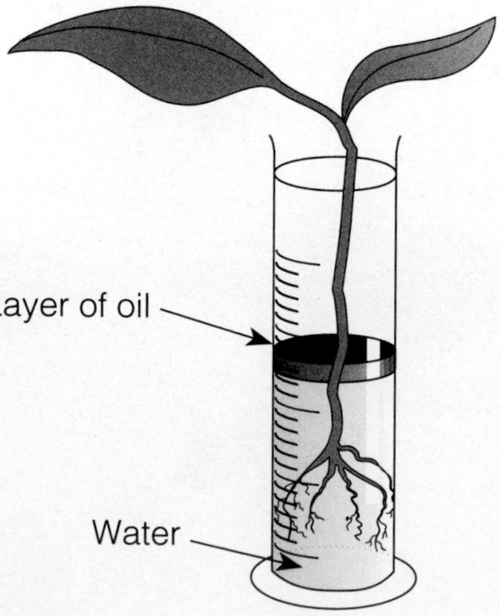

Layer of oil

Water

(a) What is the purpose of the layer of oil? **[1]**

....

(b) Table 1 shows the results of the experiment.

Table 1

Time (days)	0	1	2	3	4
Volume of water in cylinder (cm³)	50	47	43	42	40

Calculate the average water loss per day from the measuring cylinder in **Figure 6**.
Show your working. **[2]**

....

....

Average water loss: .... cm³ per day

13 Plants and animals use glucose for respiration. Plants also convert glucose into different substances.
Name **three** of these substances and give a reason why each one is important. **[3]**

....

....

....

14 **Figure 7** shows an experiment to demonstrate osmosis.

Figure 7

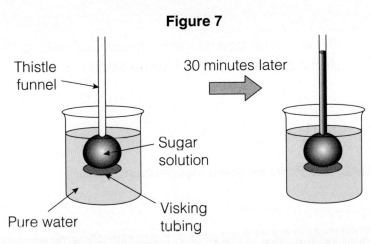

Explain why the volume of solution inside the thistle funnel has increased. **[3]**

....

....

....

*15 Black spot is a fungal disease that affects rose leaves (see **Figure 8**). Fatima has noticed that roses growing in areas with high air pollution are less affected by the disease. She thinks that regular exposure to acid rain is stopping the disease from developing.

Figure 8

Describe a simple experiment that Fatima could carry out to test her theory.   [3]

....

....

....

....

16 (a) Thomas burns paraffin in a small stove inside his greenhouse during March and April.
         How does this benefit the growth of his greenhouse plants?   [2]

....

....

(b) Complete the balanced symbol equation for photosynthesis.   [2]

$6\,CO_2$ + ... $\longrightarrow$ $C_6H_{12}O_6$ + ...

*(c) Anoushka investigates the effect of light on photosynthesis at 25°C.
     She uses the apparatus shown in **Figure 9**.

Figure 9

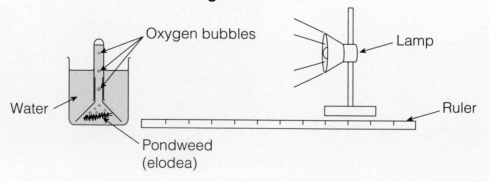

She moves the lamp and counts the bubbles at different distances from the pondweed. **Table 2** shows her results.

Table 2

Distance from lamp to pondweed (cm)	Number of bubbles counted in five minutes
10	241
20	124
30	60
40	36
50	24

Describe the pattern in the results in **Table 2** and predict how the pattern would change if the experiment was repeated at 35 °C and at 55 °C. Explain your answers. **[6]**

....

....

....

....

....

....

....

....

....

17 Outline why it is difficult to develop drugs that disable or destroy viruses. **[2]**

....

....

TOTAL FOR PAPER = 70 MARKS

GCSE
Combined Science

Paper 2: Biology 2

Higher

Time: 1 hour 15 minutes

You may use:

- a calculator
- a ruler.

Instructions

- Use black ink or black ball-point pen. Draw diagrams in pencil.
- Read each question carefully before you start to write your answer.
- Answer **all** questions in the spaces provided.
- Show your working in any calculator question and include units in your answer where appropriate.
- In questions marked with an asterisk (*), marks will be awarded for your ability to structure your answer logically, showing how the points that you make are related or follow on from each other where appropriate.

Information

- The marks for each question are shown in brackets.
  Use this as a guide to how much time to spend on each question.
- The maximum mark for this paper is 70.
- Diagrams are not accurately drawn unless otherwise stated.

Name: ....

1 **Figure 1** shows a simple food chain. The arrows represent the transfer of energy in the food chain.

Figure 1

Sun   A   Grass   B   Rabbit   C   Stoat   D   Fox

Which arrow shows the greatest transfer of energy?
Tick (✓) **one** box. [1]

A ☐

B ☐

C ☐

D ☐

2 **Figure 2** shows a flock of seagulls. The number of seagulls in a flock is affected by both abiotic and biotic factors.

Figure 2

Which of the following is a biotic factor?
Tick (✓) **one** box. [1]

Temperature ☐

Rainfall ☐

Disease ☐

Ocean tides ☐

6 The following text is one of the instructions on a packet of antibiotic tablets (see **Figure 5**):
Complete the prescribed course of treatment as directed by your doctor.

Figure 5

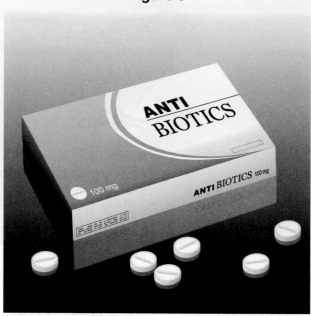

Explain why this instruction is important to stop bacteria becoming resistant to this antibiotic. **[3]**

....

....

....

7 Genetically engineered bacteria can be used to make human insulin to treat diabetes. The human genes to make insulin are inserted into the bacteria DNA.

Outline **three** reasons why bacteria are chosen for this process. **[3]**

....

....

....

8 In a recent newspaper article, the following statement appeared:

You can only get cancer if you have the wrong genes.

This is not true.

Write down **two** other factors that could be involved in the formation of cancer cells. **[2]**

....

....

....

9 Outline **two** reasons why Darwin's theory of evolution took many years to gain acceptance by the scientific community. **[2]**

....

....

10 **Figure 6** shows some of the endocrine system.

Figure 6

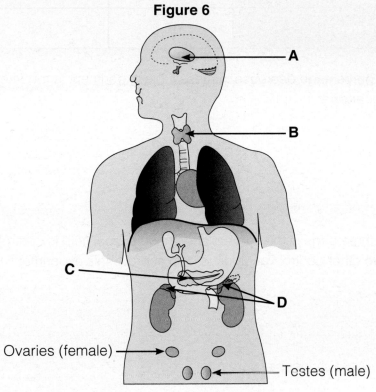

Ovaries (female)

Testes (male)

Which label shows the adrenal gland?
Tick (✓) **one** box. **[1]**

A ☐

B ☐

C ☐

D ☐

11 Two students carried out an experiment to investigate the decay of grass cuttings.

- They put the cuttings in three different-coloured plastic bags – each bag had a few very small holes for ventilation.

- The bags were placed together at the edge of the school field.

- The bags were weighed at the start of the experiment and again three months later.

Table 1 shows the results.

Table 1

	Black bag (A)	Yellow bag (B)	White bag (C)
Mass of bag and grass cuttings at the start (g)	320.4	350.6	325.7
Mass of bag and grass cuttings after three months (g)	271.7	305.7	290.9
% decrease in mass	15.2	12.8	10.7

(a) Predict the percentage decrease in mass if the experiment is repeated with a dark brown bag. Explain your answer. [3]

....

....

....

(b) Putting the three bags in the same place on the school field is controlling a variable. Suggest **two** other control variables to help improve this experiment. [2]

1. ....

2. ....

12 The reaction times of six people were measured.

They put on headphones and were asked to push a button when they heard a sound. The button was connected to a timer.

Table 2 shows the results.

Table 2

Person	Gender	Reaction time in seconds				
		1	2	3	4	5
A	Male	0.26	0.25	0.27	0.25	0.27
B	Female	0.25	0.25	0.26	0.22	0.24
C	Male	0.31	1.43	0.32	0.29	0.32
D	Female	0.22	0.23	0.25	0.22	0.23
E	Male	0.27	0.31	0.30	0.28	0.26
F	Female	0.23	0.19	0.21	0.21	0.22

(a) Describe a pattern in these results. [1]

....

(b) Calculate the mean reaction time for person C, ignoring any outliers. Show your working. **[2]**

....

....

(c) When person D was concentrating on the test, someone touched her arm and she jumped. Her response was a reflex action. What are the **two** main features of a reflex action? **[2]**

....

....

*(d) A reflex action involves a 'message' travelling along a sensory neurone as an electrical impulse. The electrical impulse reaches a junction called a synapse.

Describe what happens at the synapse for the 'message' to continue its journey. **[4]**

....

....

....

....

13 **Figure 7** shows hormone levels in a woman's bloodstream during her menstrual cycle.

Figure 7

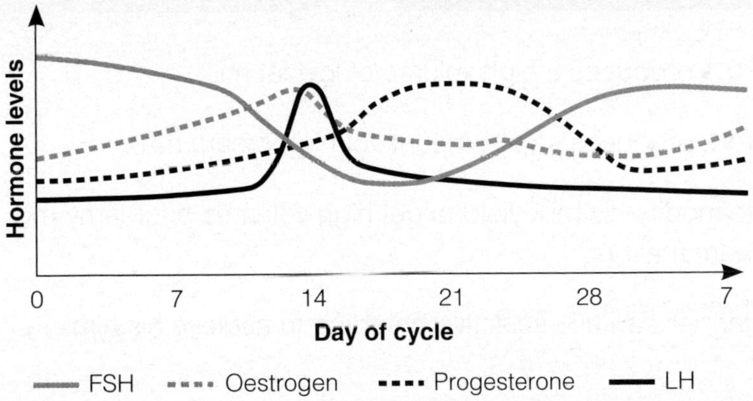

(a) The woman believes that her best chance of becoming pregnant is after day 21 of the cycle. Is she correct? Use the levels of hormones in **Figure 7** to explain your answer. **[2]**

....

....

(b) What is the role of progesterone in the menstrual cycle? **[2]**

....

....

(c) Explain how the hormones used in oral contraceptives prevent conception. **[2]**

....

....

(d) Fertility drugs have helped many couples have children, where previously they could not. However, the process is not without its problems.

Outline **two** problems with this type of treatment. **[2]**

....

....

***14** A farmer keeps two different herds of cows. The two types of cow are shown in **Figure 8**.

Figure 8

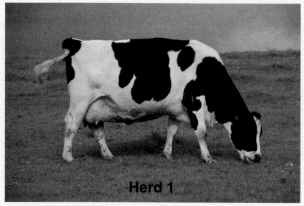

- Each cow in herd 1 produces a high volume of low fat milk.

- Each cow in herd 2 produces small amounts of high cream milk.

The farmer wants to modify his milk yield to get high volumes of creamy milk. He can sell the creamy milk to local ice-cream makers.

Describe how the farmer can use selective breeding to achieve his aim. **[4]**

....

....

....

....

15 **Figure 9** shows a sheepdog puppy. There are 39 pairs of chromosomes in the skin cell of a sheepdog puppy. Two of the chromosomes determine the sex of the puppy.

Figure 9

(a) How many chromosomes are there in the sperm cell of a sheepdog? Tick (✓) **one** box. **[1]**

39 ☐

76 ☐

78 ☐

80 ☐

(b) The number of skin cells increases as the puppy grows.

A skin cell grows and then divides into two skin cells. What is the name of this process? Explain why each skin cell has the same number of chromosomes. **[4]**

....

....

....

....

Cystic fibrosis is a genetic disorder. Adam has the disorder but his mother and father did not show signs of the condition.

(a) Complete the Punnett diagram to show how this could occur. Use f as the allele for cystic fibrosis. **[2]**

(b) Before Adam was conceived, what was the probability that his parents would have a child with cystic fibrosis? **[1]**

....

(c) Which phrase describes the genotype of Adam's parents? **[1]**

....

*17 **(a)** Diabetes is a condition where the body cannot control the level of glucose in the blood.

Describe how the human body normally controls the level of glucose in the blood and how people with type 1 and type 2 diabetes maintain the correct levels of glucose in the blood. **[6]**

....

....

....

....

....

....

....

....

....

....

(b) Diabetes can adversely affect the kidneys.

Kidneys remove urea from the bloodstream. Outline what other jobs the kidneys do. **[2]**

....

....

(c) A person with kidney disease must control their diet to reduce the kidneys' workload.

Explain in detail why the amount of protein in the diet must be limited. **[4]**

....

....

....

....

....

18 Large areas of Amazon rainforest are cleared to provide land for farming every year.
Explain how deforestation is linked to global warming. **[2]**

....

....

....

19 Write down **two** reasons why biodiversity is important. **[2]**

....

....

TOTAL FOR PAPER = 70 MARKS

GCSE
Combined Science
Paper 3: Chemistry 1

Higher

Time: 1 hour 15 minutes

You may use:

- a calculator
- a ruler.

Instructions

- Use black ink or black ball-point pen. Draw diagrams in pencil.
- Read each question carefully before you start to write your answer.
- Answer **all** questions in the spaces provided.
- Show your working in any calculator question and include units in your answer where appropriate.
- In questions marked with an asterisk (*), marks will be awarded for your ability to structure your answer logically, showing how the points that you make are related or follow on from each other where appropriate.

Information

- The marks for each question are shown in brackets.
  Use this as a guide to how much time to spend on each question.
- The maximum mark for this paper is 70.
- Diagrams are not accurately drawn unless otherwise stated.

Name: _____

1 The periodic table lists all known elements.

(a) Which statement about the periodic table is correct?
Tick (✓) **one** box. [1]

Each row begins with elements with one outer electron. ☐

The columns are called periods. ☐

The elements are arranged in mass number order. ☐

The metallic elements are on the right. ☐

(b) Which of these statements about the elements in Group 0 is correct?
Tick (✓) **one** box. [1]

They are all liquids at room temperature. ☐

Their boiling points increase as you go down the group. ☐

They have very high melting points. ☐

Their molecules are made from pairs of atoms. ☐

(c) Element X is a solid with a low melting point. When it reacts it forms covalent bonds with other elements or it forms negative ions.

Put an X where you would expect to find element X on the periodic table. [1]

2 (a) Which statement explains why group 1 elements are known as the alkali metals?
Tick (✓) **one** box. [1]

They are tested with an alkali to show they are reactive. ☐

They are in the first column in the periodic table. ☐

They all react strongly with alkalis. ☐

They make an alkali when reacted with water. ☐

(b) Sodium is below lithium in group 1 of the periodic table.

Explain why sodium reacts more vigorously with water than lithium. **[2]**

....

....

(c) Figure 1 shows the arrangement of particles in a metal.

Figure 1

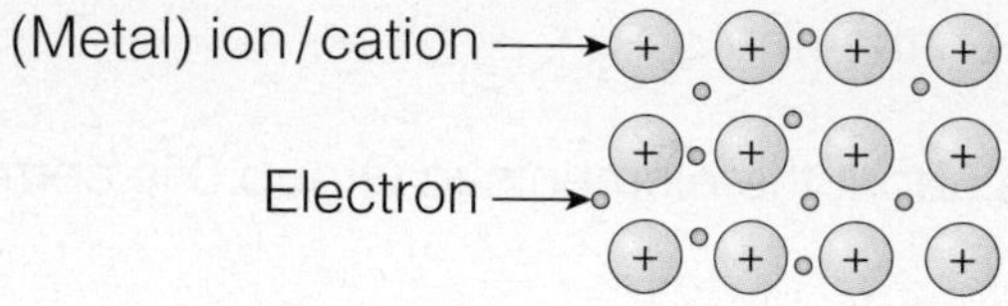

(Metal) ion/cation ⟶

Electron ⟶

Explain how metals conduct electricity. **[2]**

....

....

3 **(a)** Graphite is commonly used as a lubricant in machines that operate at high temperatures.

Which properties of graphite explain why it is suitable for this use?
Tick (✓) **one** box. **[1]**

Electrical conductor and high melting point ☐

Good heat and electrical conductor ☐

Good heat conductor and slippery ☐

High melting point and slippery ☐

(b) Graphene is a form of carbon. It is formed of a sheet of carbon atoms, one atom thick.

A graphene sheet has a thickness of 3.4×10^{-8} cm. Calculate the area covered by 1 cm³ of graphene.
Tick (✓) **one** box. **[1]**

3.4×10^8 cm² ☐

2.9×10^7 cm² ☐

2.9×10^{-7} cm² ☐

3.4×10^{-8} cm² ☐

(c) Carbon nanotubes are cylindrical fullerenes.

Outline two important physical properties of nanotubes. **[2]**

....

....

(d) Diamond has a tetrahedral structure, as shown in **Figure 2**.

Figure 2

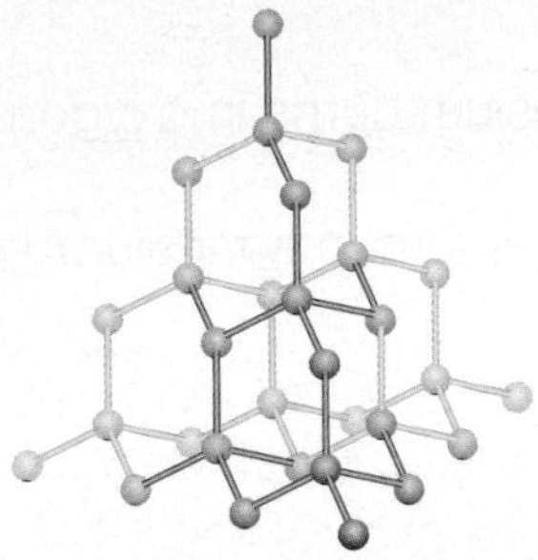

Explain why diamond has a very high melting point and why, unlike graphite, it does not conduct electricity. **[3]**

....

....

....

4 **(a)** Carbon dioxide is made by the thermal decomposition of copper(II) carbonate (see **Figure 3**). Copper(II) oxide is also made.

Figure 3

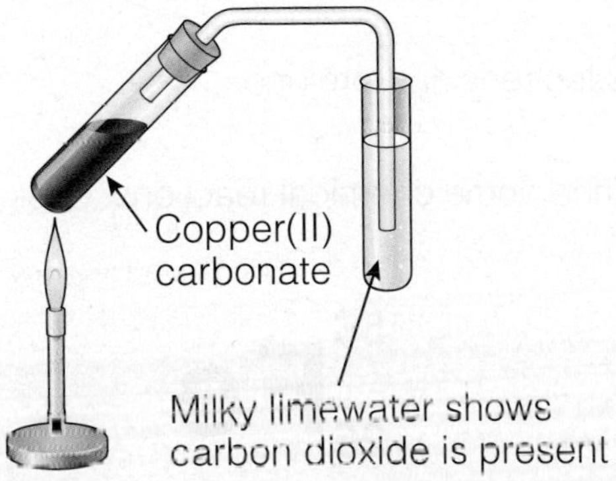

Copper(II) carbonate

Milky limewater shows carbon dioxide is present

Write the word equation for the decomposition reaction. **[1]**

....

(b) Calculate the mass of carbon dioxide made when 12.35 g of copper(II) carbonate is heated to make 7.95 g of copper(II) oxide. Show your working. **[2]**

....

....

5 **Figure 4** shows the electronic structure of an oxygen atom and a magnesium atom.

Figure 4

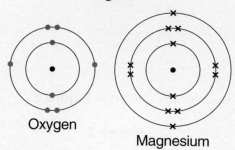

Oxygen

Magnesium

Electrons are transferred when magnesium burns in oxygen to produce magnesium oxide.

(a) Describe how the magnesium atoms form magnesium ions and the oxygen atoms form oxide ions. [2]

....

....

(b) Give the charge of each ion. [2]

....

6 **(a)** Which of these statements about a neutral atom is always correct?
Tick (✓) **one** box. [1]

It has the same number of electrons and neutrons. ☐

It has the same number of protons and neutrons. ☐

It has the same number of protons, neutrons and electrons. ☐

It has the same number of electrons and protons. ☐

(b) (i) Fe^{2+} ions are formed during some chemical reactions. Look at the information given below and then complete **Table 1**. [1]

$$^{56}_{26}Fe$$

Table 1

Number of protons in the ion	
Number of neutrons in the ion	
Number of electrons in the ion	

*(ii) Explain how you worked out each of the three numbers. **[3]**

Number of protons:

....

....

Number of neutrons:

....

....

Number of electrons:

....

....

7 Gold metal can be rolled into very thin sheets called gold leaf.

The radius of a gold atom is 1.5×10^{-10} m.

Gold leaf has a typical thickness of 1.2×10^{-6} m.

Calculate how many gold atoms are packed on top of each other to achieve this thickness. **[2]**

....

....

....

8 (a) Acids react with bases to form salts and water. Which pair of reactants can be used to prepare copper sulfate?
Tick (✓) **one** box. **[1]**

Copper and sulfuric acid ☐

Copper hydroxide and nitric acid ☐

Copper oxide and sulfuric acid ☐

Copper oxide and hydrochloric acid ☐

(b) Josh put a sample of potassium hydroxide solution into a beaker. He measured the pH. Then he slowly added dilute nitric acid until no further reaction took place.

How would the pH of the solution in the beaker change?
Tick (✓) **one** box. [1]

The pH would start high and decrease to below 7. ☐

The solution would change to a pH of 7. ☐

The pH would stay the same. ☐

The pH would start low and increase to above 7. ☐

(c) Which of the following 0.1 mol/dm³ acid solutions has the lowest pH?
Tick (✓) **one** box. [1]

Carbonic acid ☐

Citric acid ☐

Ethanoic acid ☐

Nitric acid ☐

(d) An acid–base reaction was completed between hydrochloric acid (HCl) and calcium oxide (CaO) to make calcium chloride ($CaCl_2$).

This is the equation for the reaction: $2HCl + CaO \rightarrow CaCl_2 + H_2O$

An excess of solid calcium oxide was added to the acid.

Calculate the minimum mass of calcium oxide needed to make 5.55 g of calcium chloride.
Show your working. [4]

....

....

....

....

9 Iron(III) oxide is roasted with carbon (coke) in a blast furnace to produce iron. In one of the reactions in the furnace, carbon reacts with oxygen in the air to make carbon monoxide.

Carbon monoxide (CO) then reacts with the iron(III) oxide (Fe_2O_3) to make iron (Fe). The other product is carbon dioxide.

(a) Write a balanced symbol equation for the reaction of carbon monoxide with iron(III) oxide. [2]

....

(b) Heating a metal oxide with carbon is a common method used to extract the metal.

Explain why copper can be extracted from copper oxide but aluminium cannot be extracted from its oxide by this method. **[2]**

....

....

(c) Aluminium is extracted by the electrolysis of molten aluminium oxide (Al_2O_3).

Write the ionic half equation for the reaction at each electrode. **[2]**

Cathode: ....

Anode: ....

10 Iris measured 15 cm³ of water into a test tube, as shown in **Figure 5**.

Figure 5

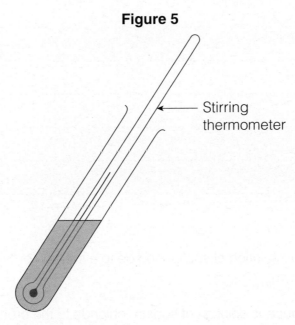

Stirring thermometer

She measured the temperature of the water and added 2 g of a solid. She stirred until there was no further temperature change. She repeated the experiment with other solids.

(a) Complete the results table (**Table 2**). **[2]**

Table 2

Solid	Start temperature (°C)	End temperature (°C)	Temperature change (°C)
Ammonium chloride	15	9	–6
Potassium hydroxide	16	29	+13
Ammonium nitrate	18	4	....
Sodium hydroxide	17	35	....

*(b) Which of the solids had the largest endothermic energy change? Explain your answer. **[3]**

....

....

....

*11 Our understanding of the model of the atom has developed from the work of a number of scientists, starting from Dalton's theory that an atom was a solid sphere.

Outline how our understanding of the atom has changed. Link the key scientists with the improvements they made to our understanding. **[6]**

....

....

....

....

....

....

....

....

....

....

*12 (a) Finlay added an aqueous solution of sodium iodide to a solution of bromine. The colour changed from orange to deep brown.

Finlay then added an aqueous solution of sodium chloride to the bromine solution. The orange colour did not change.

Explain these observations. **[4]**

....

....

....

....

(b) Chlorine is composed of diatomic molecules, Cl_2.

Draw a dot-and-cross diagram to show the bonding in a chlorine molecule. You should only show the outer shell electrons in your diagram. **[2]**

(c) Chlorine and iodine are both in group 7 of the periodic table.

Explain why chlorine is a gas and iodine is a solid at room temperature. **[2]**

....

....

(d) Explain why solid iodine does not conduct electricity. **[1]**

....

13 **(a)** When 1 mole of carbon burns completely, 393 kJ of energy is released.

$$C_{(s)} + O_{2(g)} \rightarrow CO_{2(g)}$$

The relative atomic mass (A_r) of carbon = 12.

Calculate the energy released when 14.4 g of carbon is burned. Show your working. **[2]**

....

....

....

***(b)** Energy is released when carbon burns. Use ideas about bond making and bond breaking to explain why. **[3]**

....

....

....

....

(c) Amy measured the energy released by reacting hydrochloric acid with sodium hydroxide solution. Both solutions had the same concentration.

This was the method used.

1 Measure 25 cm³ sodium hydroxide solution using a 100 cm³ measuring cylinder.

2 Pour the sodium hydroxide solution into a 250 cm³ beaker.

3 Use the 100 cm³ measuring cylinder to measure 25 cm³ hydrochloric acid.

4 Pour the acid into the sodium hydroxide in the beaker.

5 Measure the start temperature with a thermometer.

6 After one minute, measure the final temperature.

This method gave a poor result. Suggest three improvements to the method. **[3]**

1: ....

....

2: ....

....

3: ....

....

TOTAL FOR PAPER = 70 MARKS

GCSE

Combined Science

Paper 4: Chemistry 2

Higher

Time: 1 hour 15 minutes

You may use:

- a calculator
- a ruler.

Instructions

- Use black ink or black ball-point pen. Draw diagrams in pencil.
- Read each question carefully before you start to write your answer.
- Answer **all** questions in the spaces provided.
- Show your working in any calculator question and include units in your answer where appropriate.
- In questions marked with an asterisk (*), marks will be awarded for your ability to structure your answer logically, showing how the points that you make are related or follow on from each other where appropriate.

Information

- The marks for each question are shown in brackets.
  Use this as a guide to how much time to spend on each question.
- The maximum mark for this paper is 70.
- Diagrams are not accurately drawn unless otherwise stated.

Name: ....

1 **(a)** Which one of the following gases will bleach damp litmus paper?
Tick (✓) **one** box. [1]

Carbon dioxide ☐

Chlorine ☐

Hydrogen ☐

Methane ☐

(b) Which one of the following gases is made when ethanoic acid reacts with calcium carbonate?
Tick (✓) **one** box. [1]

Carbon dioxide ☐

Chlorine ☐

Hydrogen ☐

Methane ☐

2 The apparatus used in the laboratory for cracking long-chain hydrocarbons is shown in **Figure 1**.

Figure 1

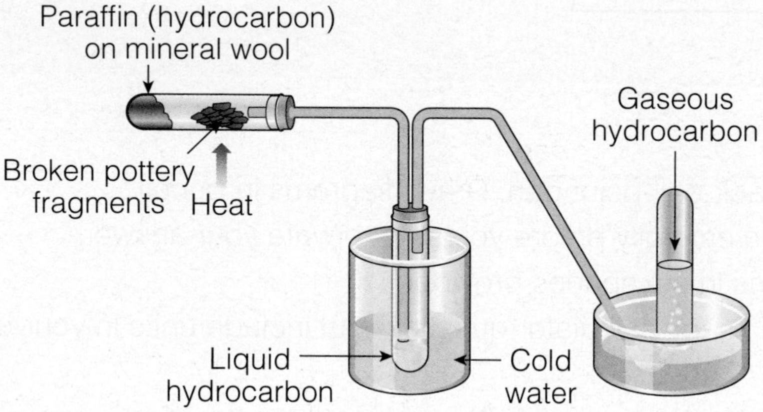

(a) Explain what is meant by **cracking** long-chain hydrocarbons. [2]

....

....

(b) What is the purpose of the broken pottery fragments? [1]

....

(c) The paraffin on the mineral wool has the formula $C_{16}H_{34}$. The gaseous product is ethene (C_2H_4) and the liquid hydrocarbon is decane ($C_{10}H_{22}$).

Construct a balanced symbol equation for the reaction. [2]

....

*3 Explain how the difference in strength of intermolecular forces between hydrocarbons allows them to be separated by fractional distillation. [3]

....

....

....

4 Which of the following hydrocarbons is the most flammable?
   Tick (✓) **one** box. [1]

C_8H_{18} ☐

$C_{11}H_{24}$ ☐

C_5H_{12} ☐

$C_{14}H_{30}$ ☐

5 Five students each have a test tube containing $10\,cm^3$ of hydrochloric acid of the same concentration. They each have a different-sized strip of magnesium ribbon.

They drop the magnesium into the acid and time how long it takes for the fizzing to stop.

Table 1 shows the results of the experiment.

Table 1

Student	Iram	Alex	Dylan	Georgie	Noah
Time (s)	246	258	204	300	272

(a) Which student had the fastest reaction? [1]

....

(b) Georgie noticed that there was some magnesium left in the test tube when the fizzing stopped. In all the other test tubes, there was no magnesium left. Explain these two observations. [2]

....

....

....

(c) (i) Georgie repeated her experiment.

This time she measured the volume of gas made with a gas syringe. She measured 94.5 cm³ of gas made in 225 seconds.

Calculate the mean rate of reaction. Show your working and include the unit in your answer. **[3]**

....

....

....

(ii) Georgie repeated her experiment again. This time she used double the volume of acid and double the amount of magnesium.

Predict what happened to the amount of gas made in the reaction. Explain your answer. **[2]**

....

....

....

6 **Figure 2** shows the result of a chromatography experiment on an unknown black ink.

Figure 2

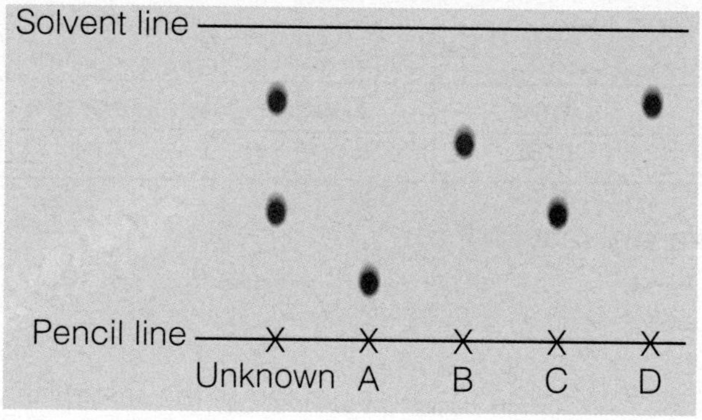

(a) Which inks does the unknown ink in **Figure 2** contain?
Tick (✓) **one** box. **[1]**

A and B ☐

A and C ☐

B and D ☐

C and D ☐

(b) The R_f value of ink B is 0.86. The solvent line moved 7.91 cm from the pencil line.

Calculate how far ink B moved up the paper. Show your working. Give your answer to an appropriate number of significant figures. **[2]**

....

....

7 **(a)** Which of the following molecules has the formula C_4H_{10}? Tick (✓) **one** box. **[1]**

☐ ☐ ☐ ☐

(b) Write the balanced symbol equation for the complete combustion of C_4H_{10}. **[2]**

....

8 A nine carat wedding ring weighs 4.5 g. What is the weight of pure gold in the ring?
Pure gold is 24 carats.
Tick (✓) **one** box. **[1]**

0.50 g ☐

0.90 g ☐

1.69 g ☐

4.05 g ☐

9 **(a)** These statements describe the process by which the Earth's atmosphere has changed.

   A Oceans formed as the temperature at the surface fell below 100°C.

   B Photosynthesis released oxygen into the atmosphere and used up carbon dioxide.

   C Nitrifying bacteria used up ammonia and released nitrogen.

   D Hot volcanic earth released carbon dioxide and ammonia into the atmosphere.

Put each letter in the correct box to show the order that scientists now believe the atmosphere developed. **[2]**

☐ → ☐ → ☐ → ☐

(b) How the Earth's atmosphere evolved is a theory. What is a theory? **[2]**

....

....

(c) Explain why the way that the Earth's atmosphere evolved can only be a theory. **[1]**

....

....

(d) Which pie chart shows the composition of the Earth's atmosphere today? Tick (✓) **one** box.　　　**[1]**

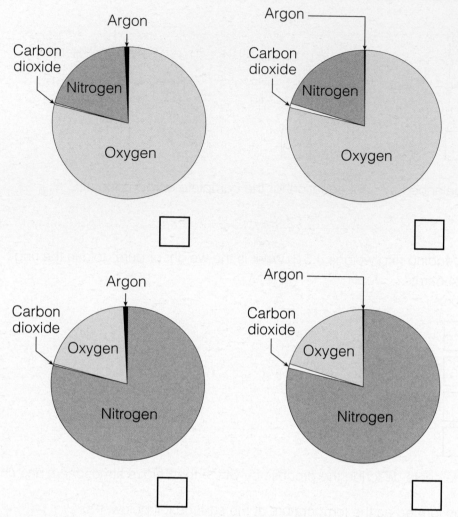

10 Meg carried out a rate of reaction experiment by reacting hydrochloric acid with sodium thiosulfate solution. A yellow precipitate of sulfur formed.

As shown in **Figure 3**, the reaction was followed by timing how long it took a cross drawn under a flask to disappear.

Figure 3

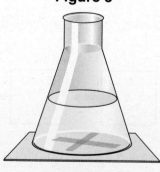

All reactions were carried out at 25°C. **Table 2** shows the results.

Table 2

Concentration of acid (mol/dm³)	Time taken for cross to disappear (s)
0.1	60
0.2	40
0.4	24
0.6	13
0.8	8
1.0	4

(a) Plot the results on the graph paper in **Figure 4**. [3]

Figure 4

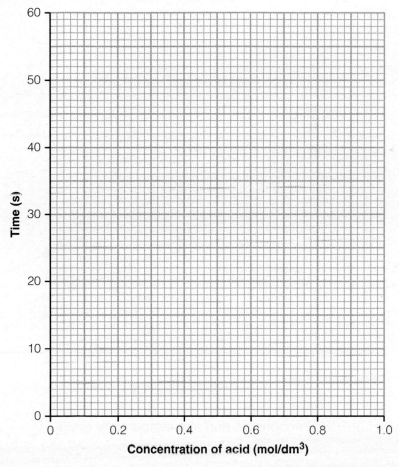

*(b) Describe and explain how the rate of reaction changes as the concentration of acid changes. [3]

....

....

....

(c) The experiment was repeated at 35°C. Predict how the reaction times would change. [1]

....

11 Explain the purpose of desalination and chlorination in making safe drinking water. **[2]**

Desalination:

....

....

Chlorination:

....

....

12 **Figure 5** shows how the yield of the Haber process changes with different conditions.

Figure 5

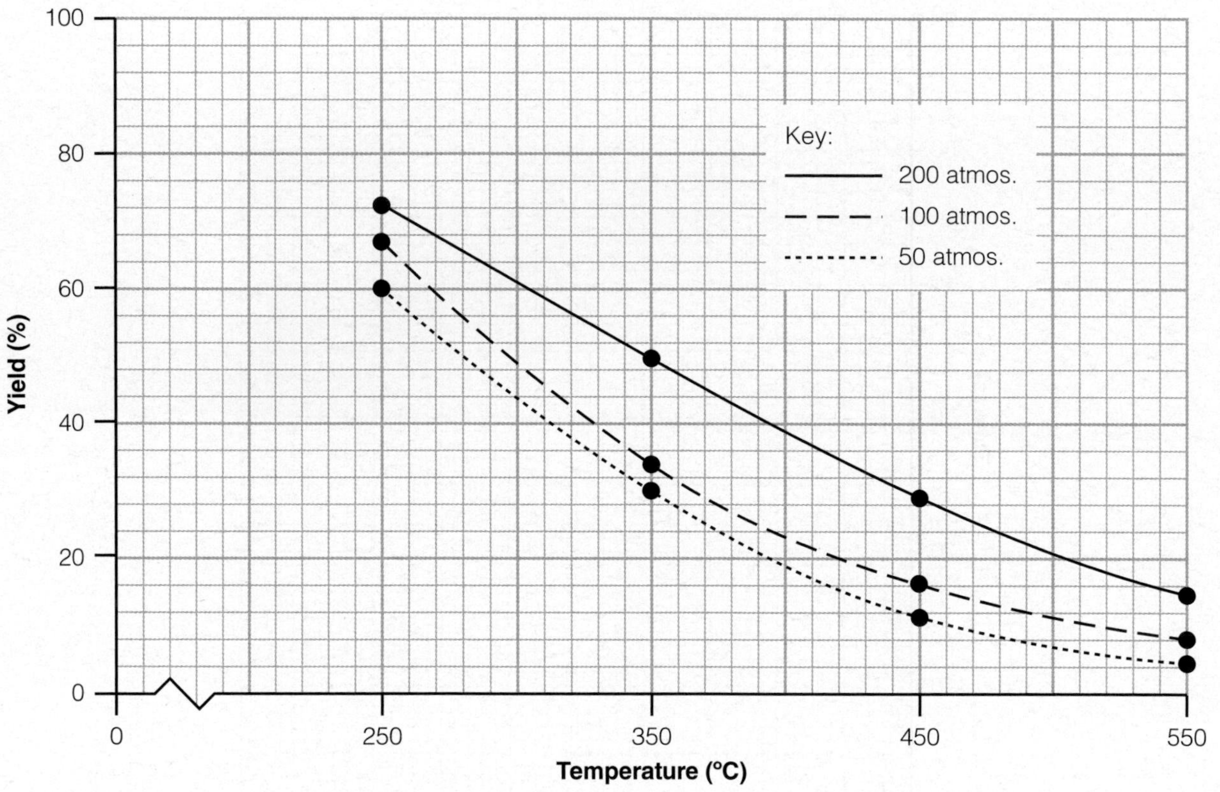

(a) Write down the yield at 200 atmospheres and at a temperature of 350°C. **[1]**

....

(b) Describe what happens to the yield as the temperature is increased. **[1]**

....

(c) This is the equation for the reaction: $N_{2(g)} + 3H_{2(g)} \rightleftharpoons 2NH_{3(g)}$

Use the equation to explain why the yield increases with increased pressure. **[2]**

....

....

(d) Very high yields of ammonia can be achieved at a pressure of 500 atmospheres.

Explain why the normal operating pressure for the Haber process is much lower. **[2]**

....

....

....

13 **Figure 6** shows the results of an investigation into the reaction of zinc metal with hydrochloric acid.

Experiments A and B used 2 g of zinc: one experiment used zinc powder and the other used zinc granules.

Figure 6

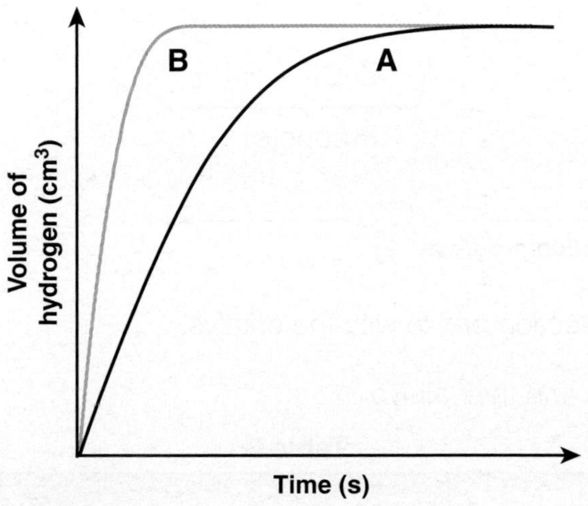

*(a) Which line on the graph represents the reaction with powdered zinc?
Explain your answer using the idea of reacting particles. **[4]**

....

....

....

....

(b) Copper ions (Cu^{2+}) act as a catalyst for the reaction.

Figure 7 shows the reaction profile without a catalyst.

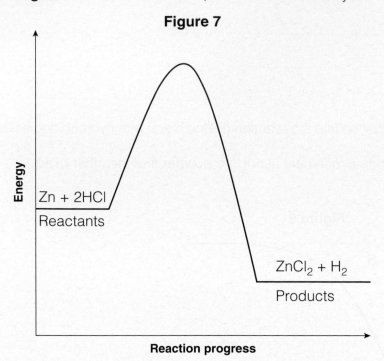

Figure 7

Draw on the graph the reaction profile with the catalyst.   [1]

*14 **Table 3** shows some metals and their alloys.

Table 3

	Order of hardness	Density (g/cm³)	Melting point (°C)	Order of strength
Copper	5	8.9	1083	5
Brass (alloy of copper)	3	8.6	920	3
Iron	2	7.9	1538	2
Steel (alloy of iron)	1	7.8	1420	1
Lead	6	11.3	327	6
Solder (alloy of lead)	5	9.6	170	4

Use the data in the table to outline what alloying does to the properties of pure metals.   [4]

....

....

....

....

15 Look at the displayed formula of propene in **Figure 8**.

Figure 8

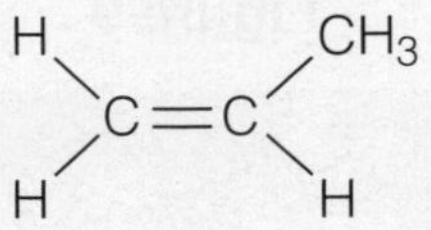

Propene molecules can join together to form the addition polymer, poly(propene).

Draw a diagram to show the structure of the polymer. **[3]**

16 Sulfuric acid is manufactured in the contact process.

In one of the reactions in the process, sulfur dioxide is converted to sulfur trioxide:

$$2SO_{2(g)} + O_{2(g)} \rightleftharpoons 2SO_{3(g)}$$

This is a reversible reaction and it will reach a position of equilibrium.

(a) Describe how the reaction reaches equilibrium from the start. Use ideas about rate of reaction. **[2]**

....

....

(b) Predict and explain the effect of reducing the pressure on the position of equilibrium for this reaction. **[2]**

....

....

(c) What is the effect of using a catalyst on the position of equilibrium in this reaction? **[1]**

....

(d) Outline the extra information you need to determine the effect on the equilibrium position of increasing the temperature of the reaction mixture. **[1]**

....

17 Catalytic converters are fitted to modern cars to reduce carbon monoxide and nitrogen dioxide emissions formed during the combustion of fuel (see **Figure 9**).

Figure 9

*(a) Describe how nitrogen dioxide gas is formed by the car. **[3]**

....

....

....

(b) Sulfur dioxide can also be formed from burning fuels such as petrol or diesel. Catalytic converters cannot reduce sulfur dioxide emissions.

(i) Give one reason why sulfur dioxide is an atmospheric pollutant. **[1]**

....

(ii) Suggest how emissions of sulfur dioxide can be reduced from cars that use diesel and petrol. **[1]**

....

TOTAL FOR PAPER = 70 MARKS

GCSE

Combined Science

Paper 5: Physics 1

Higher

Time: 1 hour 15 minutes

Instructions

- Use black ink or black ball-point pen. Draw diagrams in pencil.
- Read each question carefully before you start to write your answer.
- Answer **all** questions in the spaces provided.
- Show your working in any calculator question and include units in your answer where appropriate.
- In questions marked with an asterisk (*), marks will be awarded for your ability to structure your answer logically, showing how the points that you make are related or follow on from each other where appropriate.

Information

- The marks for each question are shown in brackets.
  Use this as a guide to how much time to spend on each question.
- The maximum mark for this paper is 70.
- Diagrams are not accurately drawn unless otherwise stated.

Name: ....

1 **(a)** Which of the following circuit diagram symbols represents a thermistor?
Tick (✓) **one** box. [1]

(b) The diagrams below show four circuits. Each circuit has two **identical** bulbs connected in parallel.

In which circuit will the ammeters have the same reading?
Tick (✓) **one** box. [1]

(c) A torch bulb has a resistance of 1200 Ω. The bulb operates when the current through it is 0.005 A.
How many 1.5 V batteries will the torch need to operate? [3]

....

....

....

*(d) Alex and Louise want to find out the identity of the mystery electrical component contained in Box Z. They connect it in the circuit shown in **Figure 1**.

Figure 1

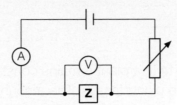

They change the potential difference, measure the current and plot the results (see **Figure 2**).

Figure 2

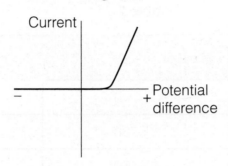

Write down the name of the mystery component in Box Z.
Explain your answer using ideas about resistance.   [3]

....

....

....

2 (a) Complete **Table 1** to show the atomic structures of the three isotopes of carbon.   [3]

Table 1

Isotope	Number of protons	Number of neutrons	Number of electrons
Carbon-12	6	6	6
Carbon-13			
Carbon-14			

(b) Carbon-14 is an unstable isotope. It undergoes beta decay to form nitrogen-14.

Describe what happens in the nucleus of an atom to form a beta particle.   [2]

....

....

(c) The half-life for the decay of carbon-14 is 5730 years.

Explain what is meant by the term half-life. **[1]**

....

....

(d) The very small amount of carbon-14 in a plant remains constant until the plant dies. The amount of carbon-14 then falls steadily as the plant decays. The amount of carbon-12 stays the same.

The plant material can be dated by measuring the ratio of carbon-14 to carbon-12.

Complete **Table 2**. **[1]**

Table 2

Number of half-lives	Time after death of organism in years	$^{14}C : ^{12}C$ ratio/10^{-12}
0	0	1.000
1	5730	0.500
2	11 460	0.250
3	....	0.125

(e) Use the data from **Table 2** to plot a decay curve for carbon-14 (see **Figure 3**). **[2]**

Figure 3

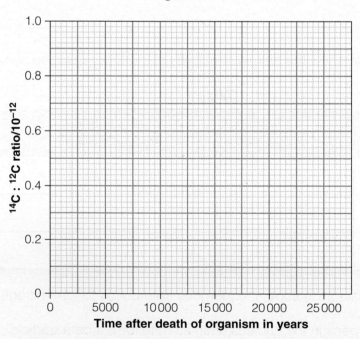

(f) A sample of wood taken from an old shipwreck had a carbon-14 : carbon-12 ratio/10^{-12} of 0.3.

Use **Figure 3** to estimate the age of the wood. **[1]**

....

3 **(a)** Look at **Figure 4**. Which set of conditions would you find on the label of a microwave oven that operates with the mains electricity supply in the UK?
Tick (✓) **one** box. [1]

Figure 4

50 Hz, 230 V, ac ☐

50 Hz, 230 V, dc ☐

60 Hz, 230 V, dc ☐

60 Hz, 230 V, ac ☐

(b) Figure 5 shows a symbol found on hairdryers.

Figure 5

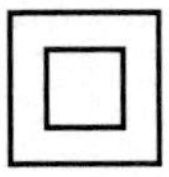

☐

The symbol shows that the hairdryer is double insulated. What does this mean?
Tick (✓) **one** box. [1]

It has a moulded plastic plug. ☐

It does not need an earth wire. ☐

The case has metal parts on the outside. ☐

The dryer has double plastic coating on the wires. ☐

4 Look at the diagram of a three-pin plug in **Figure 6**.

Figure 6

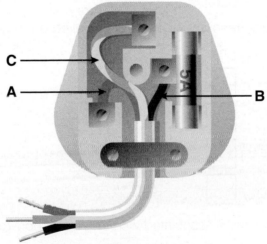

(a) Complete **Table 3**. [2]

Wire	Name	Colour
A	....	Blue
B	Live	....
C	....	Green and yellow stripes

(b) Give **two** reasons why wire C is connected to some domestic appliances. [2]

....

....

....

*(c) The plug is connected to an electric drill and contains a 5 A fuse.

The electric drill has a power rating of 960W.

Calculate the value of the current passing through the fuse when the drill is operating normally at 230 V. Show all your working. Give your answer to two significant figures. [3]

....

....

....

Answer: .... A

5 **(a)** Which of the following energy resources is non-renewable?
Tick (✓) **one** box. [1]

Bio-fuel ☐

Coal ☐

Hydro-electricity ☐

Wind ☐

(b) Which of the following energy resources can be most relied on to give a constant supply of energy?
Tick (✓) **one** box. [1]

Geothermal ☐

Tidal ☐

Wave ☐

Wind ☐

(c) (i) State **one** environmental issue associated with the use of non-renewable fuels. [1]

....

(ii) Give **two** reasons why we still use non-renewable fuels. [2]

....

....

6 Look at the picture of the roller coaster in **Figure 7**.

Figure 7

(a) At what position have the roller coaster cars got maximum kinetic energy?
Tick (✓) **one** box.   **[1]**

Position 1 ☐

Position 2 ☐

Position 3 ☐

Position 4 ☐

(b) Describe the energy changes that take place as the roller coaster cars travel from position 1 to position 4.   **[2]**

....

....

....

*(c) Explain why the next 'hill' on the roller coaster after position 4 has to be lower than position 1.   **[3]**

....

....

....

7 **Figure 8** shows an electric screwdriver. This question is about motors used in electric screwdrivers.

Figure 8

Table 4

Electric motor	Input electrical power (W)	Useful output power (W)	Wasted power (W)
A	209	220	11
B	172	160	12
C	235	223	12
D	205	193	12
E	242	....	20

(a) (i) Complete **Table 4**. [1]

(ii) Name the motor with the largest useful power output. .... [1]

(b) Describe how the electrical power is used and suggest how some power is wasted. [2]

....

....

....

(c) Calculate the efficiency of electric motor B. [2]

....

....

....

8 **(a)** Which of the following vehicles has the greatest kinetic energy?
Tick (✓) **one** box. [1]

A van with a mass of 1500 kg travelling at 11 m/s ☐

A car with a mass of 1400 kg travelling at 12 m/s ☐

A van with a mass of 1200 kg travelling at 12 m/s ☐

A car with a mass of 1100 kg travelling at 13 m/s ☐

(b) Figure 9 shows an electric motor lifting a load.

Figure 9

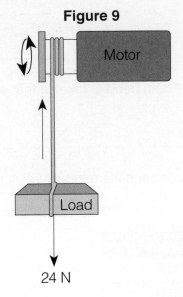

24 N

How much work (in joules) is done when the load is lifted through a height of 2.5 m?
Show all your working. **[2]**

....

....

(c) It takes four seconds to lift the load through 2.5 m. Calculate the power of the motor
Show all your working. **[2]**

....

....

9 **Figure 10** shows some meteorites that Mahri is investigating.

Figure 10

(a) Draw a labelled diagram to describe how she can measure the volume of each meteorite. **[2]**

(b) Mahri measures the volume of each meteorite three times. How does this improve her results? **[2]**

....

....

(c) What other measurement does Mahri need to take so that she can calculate the density of the meteorites? **[1]**

....

(d) **Table 5** shows the densities of common elements found in meteorites.

Table 5

Element	Density kg/m³
Aluminium	2712
Iron	7850
Magnesium	1738
Nickel	8908
Silicon	2328

The mean density of the three meteorites was 7965 kg/m³. Analysis indicated that two elements were present. Iron formed 90% of the composition. What was the element making up the remaining 10%? Tick (✓) **one** box. **[1]**

Aluminium ☐

Magnesium ☐

Nickel ☐

Silicon ☐

10 Look at **Table 6**, which shows the specific heat capacity of four metals.

Table 6

Metal	Aluminium	Copper	Iron	Lead
Specific heat capacity J/kg °C	900	490	390	130

(a) If you were given a 2 kg block of each metal, which metal would take the least amount of energy to raise its temperature from 20°C to 25°C?

Tick (✓) **one** box. [1]

Aluminium ☐

Copper ☐

Iron ☐

Lead ☐

(b) As shown in **Figure 11**, a 500 g block of copper was heated with a 100 W electric immersion heater for 85 seconds.

Figure 11

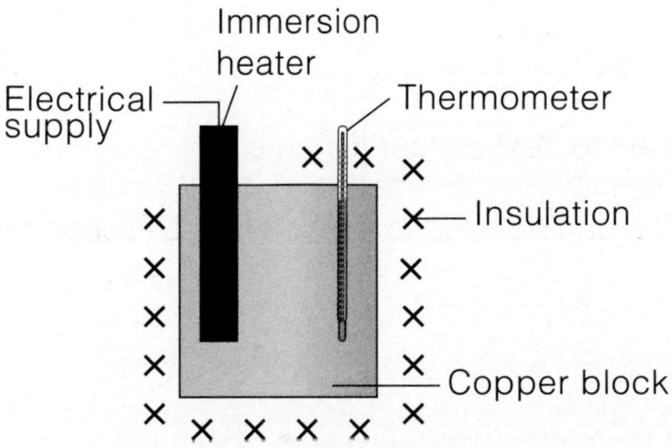

Calculate the amount of energy in joules supplied to the copper block. Show all your working. [2]

....

....

....

(c) In a repeat experiment, the copper block started at a temperature of 22°C and was supplied with 9065 J of energy. What was its final temperature? Show all your working. [3]

change in thermal energy = mass × specific heat capacity × temperature change

....

....

....

*11 A well-insulated beaker contains 200 g of water at 20°C. This will release 16800 J of energy to cool down to 0°C.

60 g of ice at 0°C is added to the water.

If no heat energy is lost or gained by the beaker, will all of the ice melt? Explain your answer. [3]

> energy for a change of state = mass × specific latent heat
>
> specific latent heat of fusion of water = 334 000 J/kg

....

....

....

*12 Gamma radiation can be used to treat cancer tumours.

Explain why gamma radiation can be used to treat cancer. Describe the risks and how the risks are controlled. [6]

....

....

....

....

....

....

....

....

....

....

TOTAL FOR PAPER = 70 MARKS

GCSE
Combined Science

Paper 6: Physics 2

Higher

Time: 1 hour 15 minutes

> **You may use:**
> - a calculator
> - a ruler.

Instructions

- Use black ink or black ball-point pen. Draw diagrams in pencil.
- Read each question carefully before you start to write your answer.
- Answer **all** questions in the spaces provided.
- Show your working in any calculator question and include units in your answer where appropriate.
- In questions marked with an asterisk (*), marks will be awarded for your ability to structure your answer logically, showing how the points that you make are related or follow on from each other where appropriate.

Information

- The marks for each question are shown in brackets.
  Use this as a guide to how much time to spend on each question.
- The maximum mark for this paper is 70.
- Diagrams are not accurately drawn unless otherwise stated.

Name: _____

1 (a) Which of the following is a vector quantity?
Tick (✓) **one** box. [1]

Distance ☐

Mass ☐

Speed ☐

Velocity ☐

(b) A small solid steel cube is taken from the Earth's surface to the International Space Station.

Which of the following properties will change?
Tick (✓) **one** box. [1]

Mass ☐

Surface area ☐

Volume ☐

Weight ☐

2 Look at **Figure 1**, which shows a velocity–time graph of a car travelling on a road.

Figure 1

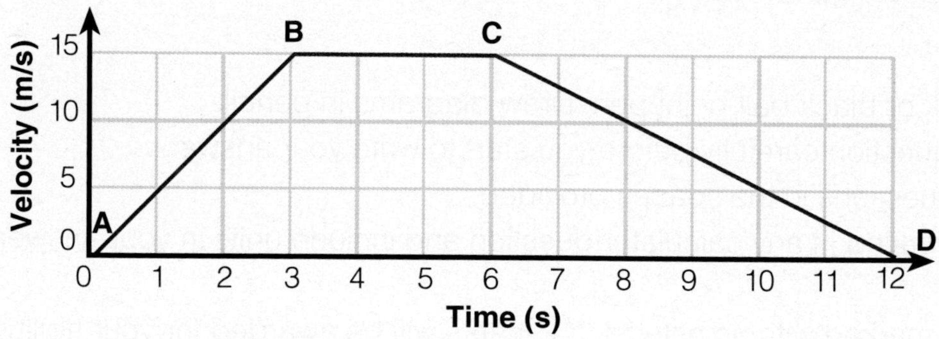

(a) What is the velocity of the car after two seconds? [1]

....

(b) Calculate the acceleration of the car between points **A** and **B**.
Show all your working and include the unit in your answer. [3]

....

....

....

....

(c) Calculate the distance travelled between 0 and 6 seconds. Show all your working. **[3]**

....

....

....

(d) Describe the motion of the car between points **C** and **D**. **[2]**

....

....

3 **(a)** Look at **Figure 2**, which shows a wave.

Figure 2

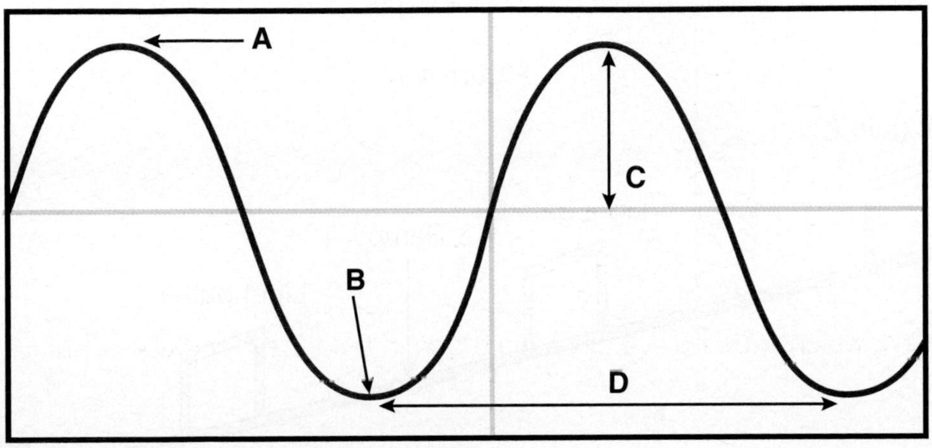

Which letter represents the amplitude of the wave?
Tick (✓) **one** box. **[1]**

A ☐

B ☐

C ☐

D ☐

(b) Microwaves can be used to cook food in a microwave oven, shown in **Figure 3**.
Microwaves are part of the electromagnetic spectrum.

Figure 3

Which other part of the electromagnetic spectrum is commonly used to cook food? **[1]**

....

(c) The microwaves used in ovens have a wavelength of 0.12 m.

The speed of electromagnetic waves is 3×10^8 m/s.

Calculate the frequency of the microwaves used in ovens. Show all your working and include the unit. **[3]**

....

....

....

4 David and Gemma are investigating the motion of a toy car. David says that the car will go down the ramp at constant velocity. Gemma disagrees. She thinks the car will gradually go faster.

They design the experiment shown in **Figure 4** to settle the argument. Light gates are attached to a data logger that records the time the car passes through.

Figure 4

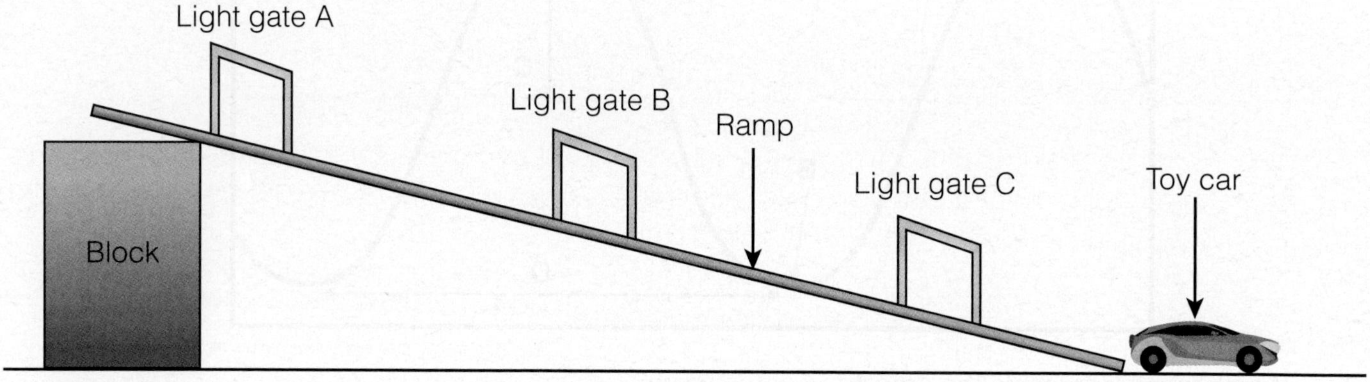

(a) Explain why David and Gemma must use three light gates to time the car. **[1]**

....

....

(b) Describe how they can use the times to decide who is correct. **[2]**

....

....

....

(c) Table 1 shows their results.

Table 1

	Run 1	Run 2	Run 3	Run 4
Time at A (s)	0	0	0	0
Time at B (s)	0.141	0.229	0.152	0.139
Time at C (s)	0.249	0.342	0.270	0.251

Identify the anomalous result.
Tick (✓) **one** box. **[1]**

Run 1 ☐

Run 2 ☐

Run 3 ☐

Run 4 ☐

(d) The distance between light gate A and light gate C is 1.50 m.

Ignoring the anomalous result, calculate the overall mean speed of the car from the other runs, in m/s. Show all your working and give your answer to the appropriate number of significant figures. **[3]**

....

....

....

....

.... m/s

5 **Figure 5** shows an astronaut doing a spacewalk. He can move about using small jets of air blown in directions A, B, C and D. He is stationary.

Figure 5

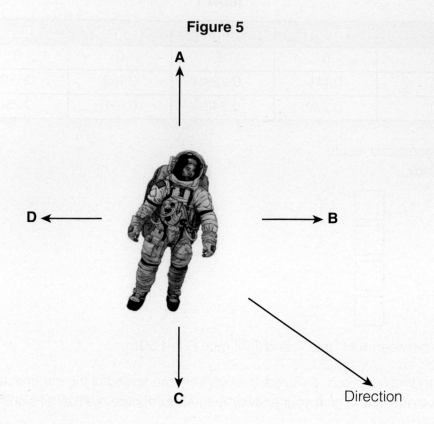

Which two jets should the astronaut use to move in the direction of the arrow shown?
Tick (✓) **one** box.   [1]

A and B ☐

A and D ☐

B and C ☐

C and D ☐

6 **Figure 6** shows a skydiver.

Figure 6

(a) X and Y are forces acting on the skydiver as she falls. Describe what happens to the size of force X as she accelerates. **[1]**

....

(b) The skydiver has a weight of 550 N.

What will be the value of force X when she stops accelerating and falls at terminal velocity? Explain your answer. **[2]**

....

....

(c) **Figure 7** shows the velocity of the skydiver as she descends through the air.

Figure 7

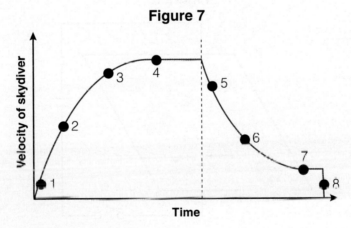

Between which two points does the skydiver open her parachute?
Tick (✓) **one** box. **[1]**

4 and 5 ☐

5 and 6 ☐

6 and 7 ☐

7 and 8 ☐

*(d) Explain why the skydiver has a lower terminal velocity when the parachute is open. **[4]**

....

....

....

....

7 **(a)** **Figure 8** illustrates an experiment to show a magnetic field around a bar magnet using plotting compasses.

Figure 8

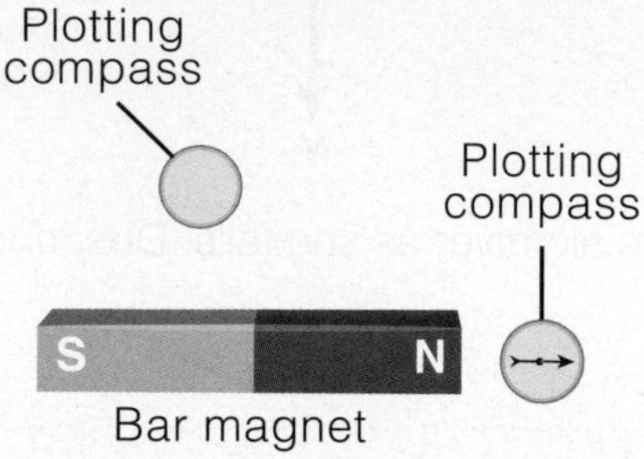

Plotting compass

Plotting compass

S   N

Bar magnet

Which direction will the arrow point in the top plotting compass?
Tick (✓) **one** box. **[1]**

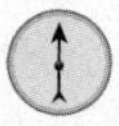

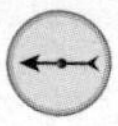

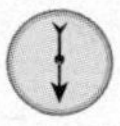

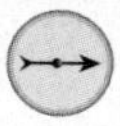

(b) Look at **Figure 9**.

Figure 9

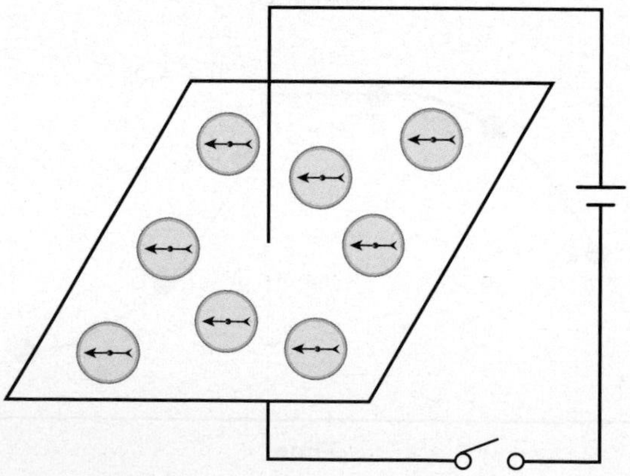

Describe what happens to the plotting compass arrows when the current is switched on. **[2]**

....

....

8 **(a)** Raj is trying to make an electromagnet that will pick up as many paperclips as possible. As shown in **Figure 10**, he adds a soft iron core to the coil.

Figure 10

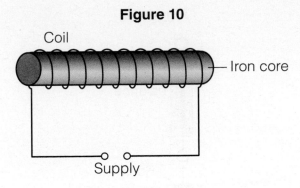

Coil

Iron core

Supply

What **two** other changes could he make to increase the strength of the electromagnet? **[2]**

....

....

(b) As shown in **Figure 11**, a wire is placed in a magnetic field and the current is switched on.

Figure 11

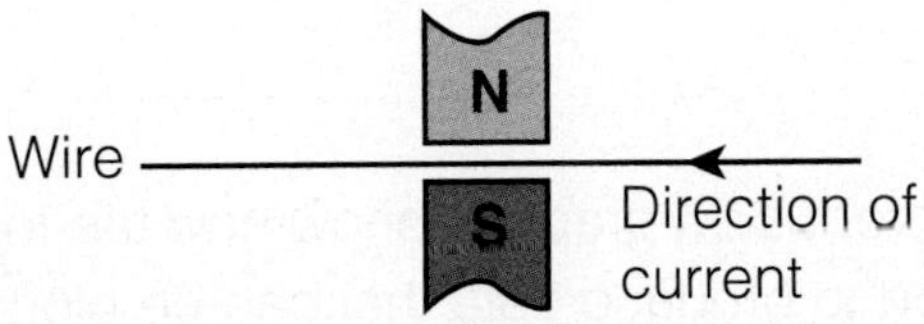

N

Wire

S
Direction of
current

In what direction will the wire move?
Tick (✓) **one** box. **[1]**

Down into the page, away from you ☐

Towards the north pole of the magnet ☐

Towards the south pole of the magnet ☐

Up from the page, towards you ☐

(c) Explain why the wire only moves once the current is on. **[2]**

....

....

....

9 Navjot and Shaleen are investigating the forces involved in floating and sinking. **Figure 12** shows their experiment.

Figure 12

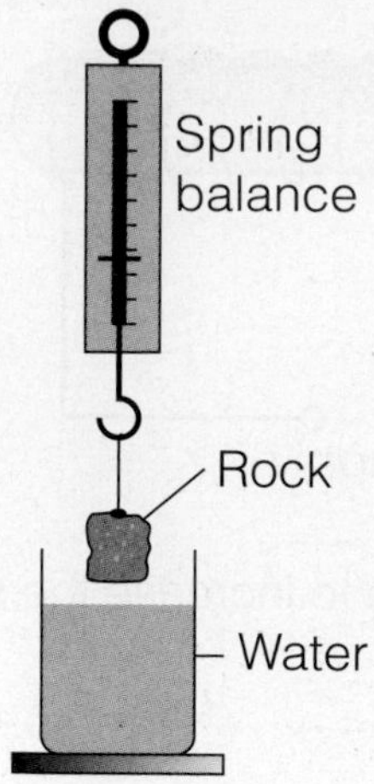

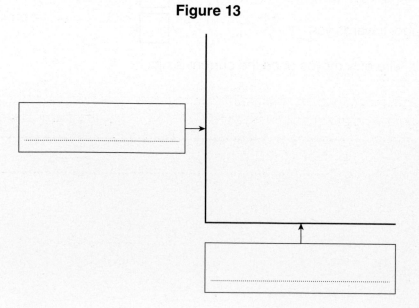

Spring balance

Rock

Water

(a) Describe what happens to the reading on the spring balance as Navjot and Shaleen slowly lower the rock into the water until it is fully submerged. **[2]**

....

....

(b) Navjot and Shaleen want to produce a graph to show how the force changes. Describe how they can improve their method to produce data that can be plotted on a line graph. **[2]**

....

....

....

(c) Label the axes on **Figure 13** to show how Navjot and Shaleen could plot their results. **[1]**

Figure 13

....

....

*10 (a) Explain why, theoretically, a ship would rise as it travelled from fresh water into seawater. [3]

....

....

....

....

(b) A diver uses echo sounding from his boat to measure the depth of water, as shown in **Figure 14**.

Figure 14

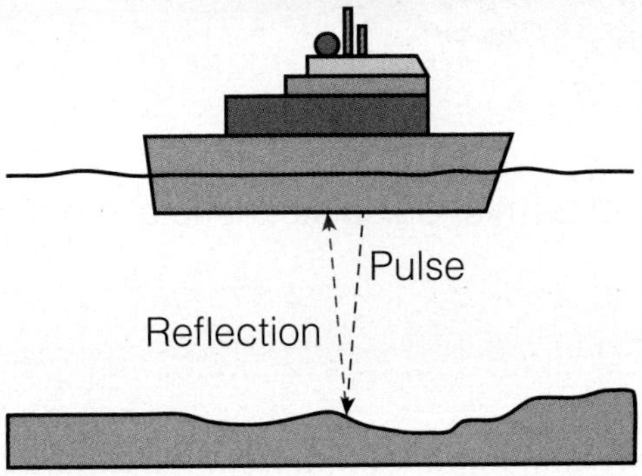

The pulse of sound takes 0.0270 s to be reflected back to be detected on the boat. If sound travels at a speed of 1500 m/s in water, what is the depth of the water in metres under the boat?
Show all your working. [3]

....

....

....

....

(c) Josh wears a pressure gauge on his wrist. He notices that when he dives 10 m under the water, the pressure around him doubles. When he climbs 10 m to the top of the boat the pressure hardly changes at all.

Explain these observations. [2]

pressure = height of column × density of fluid × gravitational field strength

....

....

....

11 **Figure 15** shows a car in a crash test. The car has a mass of 1200 kg.

Figure 15

(a) The car travels at a velocity of 20 m/s. Calculate the total momentum of the car. Show all your working. **[2]**

....

....

....

(b) When the car is crashed into a wall its momentum becomes zero in 0.50 seconds. What is the size of the force that the car exerts on the wall? **[2]**

$$\text{force} = \frac{\text{change in momentum}}{\text{time}}$$

....

....

....

*12 A car driver's awareness of stopping distances is an important part of driving safely.

(a) The thinking distance and the braking distance can be affected by different factors. Explain how speed, alcohol and road conditions can affect driving safety. [6]

....

....

....

....

....

....

....

....

....

(b) Stopping distance is also affected by tiredness. Why is tiredness not a very good variable for a scientific experiment? [1]

....

13 **Figure 16** demonstrates the motor effect.

Figure 16

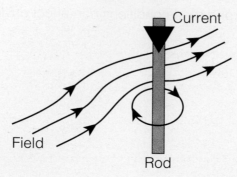

*(a) Use Fleming's left hand rule to explain in which direction the rod will move. **[4]**

....

....

....

....

(b) How could you increase the movement of the wire? **[2]**

....

....

TOTAL FOR PAPER = 70 MARKS

Answers

Biology

CELL BIOLOGY

Page 6

1. (a) Nucleus **(1)**
   (b) Mitochondria are too small to see with a light microscope / require an electron microscope / resolution of microscope not high enough. **(1)**
   (c) Liver cells require the release of a lot of energy **(1)**; mitochondria release energy for muscle contraction **(1)**.
   (d) Cell, cytoplasm, nucleus, chromosome, gene **(2 marks for everything in the correct order, 1 mark if cell, cytoplasm and nucleus are in the correct order, reading left to right)**

2. (a) Bacteria have a chromosomal loop; have plasmids; no nuclear membrane / nucleus. **(1)**
   (b) Prokaryotic ✓ **(1)**

Page 7

1. (a) An undifferentiated cell that can develop into one of many different types. **(1)**
   (b) **Any two from:** nucleus, cytoplasm, cell / plasma membrane, mitochondria, ribosomes. **(2)**

2. (a) **Any two from:** therapeutic cloning, treating paralysis, repairing nerve damage, cancer research, grow new organs for transplantation. **(2)**
   (b) **Any one from:** stem cells are sometimes obtained from human embryos and people believe it is wrong to use embryos for this purpose, risk of viral infections. **(1)**

3. $\frac{3600}{30} \times 200$ **(1)** $= 24\,000$ µm **(1)** $= 24$ mm **(1)**

Page 8

1. (a) Line should point to one of the objective lenses / rotating nose cone. **(1)**
   (b) The organelles are too small to see **(1)** / microscope doesn't have a high enough resolving power. **(1)**
   (c) Size of real object $= \frac{3}{400}$ **(1)** $= 0.0075$ cm **(1)** $= 75$ µm **(1)**

2. (a) Scanning electron microscope **(1)**
   (b) **For 2 marks, accept any answer between 80–100 minutes**; if answer is incorrect, award 1 mark for the idea that there have been 4 divisions.

Page 9

1. **Any two from:** specialised organs carry out a specific job; multicellular organisms are complex and require specialised organs so they can grow larger; single-celled organisms are small enough not to require specialised cells and transport systems. **(2)**

2.

Mitosis	Meiosis
Involved in asexual reproduction	**Involved in sexual reproduction (1)**
Produces clones / no variation (1)	Produces variation
Produces cells with 46 chromosomes	**Produces cells with 23 chromosomes (1)**

3. (a) Meiosis **(1)**
   (b) Four cells produced (in second meiotic division) **(1)**

4. (a) Benign tumours don't spread from the original site of cancer in the body **(1)**; Malignant tumour cells invade neighbouring tissues / spread to other parts of the body / form secondary tumours. **(1)**

   (b) **Any two from:** not smoking tobacco products; not drinking too much alcohol; avoiding exposure to UV rays; eating a healthy diet; taking moderate exercise / reduce obesity. **(2)**

Page 10

1. $C_6H_{12}O_6 + 6O_2 \longrightarrow 6CO_2 + 6H_2O$ **(1 mark for correct formulae, 1 mark for correct balancing)**

2. (a) **Any two from:** larger athletes will use more oxygen due to their higher muscle mass; the adjustment allows rates to be fairly / accurately compared; different athletes may have different masses. **(2)**
   (b) Sprinting has a greater energy demand **(1)**, so more oxygen is needed **(1)**.
   (c) Boris' consumption rate would be lower **(1)** because his lungs, heart and muscles are less efficient at transporting / using oxygen **(1)**.

Page 11

1. (a)

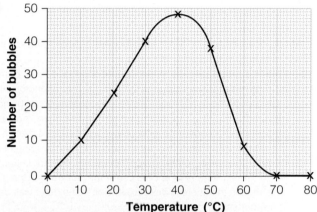

   (2 marks for correct plotting; 1 mark for smooth curve; subtract 1 mark for every incorrect plot)
   (b) The rate of bubbles produced increases until it reaches an optimum / maximum **(1)**; then it decreases rapidly, producing no bubbles at 70°C **(1)**.
   (c) 40°C **(1)**
   (d) **Any two from:** enzyme / active site has changed shape / become denatured; substrate / hydrogen peroxide no longer fits active site, so substrate cannot be broken down; low pH of the stomach **or** amylase works best at alkaline pH and stomach is acid. **(2)**

TRANSPORT SYSTEMS AND PHOTOSYNTHESIS

Page 12

1. (a) **Any two named small nutrient molecules**, e.g. glucose, vitamins, minerals, ions, amino acids, oxygen **(2)**.
   (b) **Any one from:** carbon dioxide or urea. **(1)**

2. (a) Water moves down concentration gradient from high water concentration to low water concentration **(1)**, across a partially / differentially permeable membrane / plasma membrane **(1)**; gradient maintained by input and output of water at each end of cell line **(1)**.
   (b) Water moving from plant cell to plant cell ✓ **(1)**; A pear losing water in a concentrated solution of sugar ✓ **(1)**; Water moving from blood plasma to body cells ✓ **(1)**.

3. (a) Rhubarb cells turgid **(1)**; because water moves into cells due to osmosis **(1)**.
   (b) **Any two from:** plasmolysed; plant cell vacuole extremely small; membrane pulled away from wall. **(2)**

Page 13

1. **(a)** (upper) epidermis **(1)**; **(b)** spongy layer / mesophyll **(1)**;
   (c) air space **(1)**.

2. **Roots:** anchor plant in soil / absorb water and minerals **(1)**
   Stem: supports leaves and flowers, transports substances up and down the plant **(1)**
   Leaf: organs of photosynthesis **(1)**
   Flower: reproductive organs, formation of seeds **(1)**

3. **Any three from:** dead cells without cytoplasm; no end walls; hollow lumen; continuous tubes – all adaptations allow efficient movement of water in columns. **(3)**

4. **(a) Any one from:** phloem have perforated end walls / xylem has no end wall; xylem have hard cell walls (contain lignin) / phloem have soft cell walls. **(1)**
   (b) Aphids extract / eat sugar **(1)**; sugar solution transported in phloem **(1)**.

Page 14

1. **(a)** $\frac{8}{43} \times 100 = 18.6\%$ **(1 mark for calculation, 1 mark for correct answer)**
   (b) B (cold moving air) **(1)**
   (c) Water column in xylem would move upwards / towards the leaves more quickly. **(1)**

2. **This is a model answer, which would score the full 6 marks:** As light intensity increases during the day, the rate of photosynthesis increases in the guard cells. This results in more sugar being manufactured, which raises the solute concentration. Increased potassium ions contribute to increased solute concentration too. The guard cells therefore draw in water from surrounding cells by osmosis, becoming more turgid. This causes the stoma to become wider. The arrangement of cellulose in the cell walls of the guard cells means that there is more expansion in the outer wall, resulting in a wider stoma.

Page 15

1. **(a) (i)** Scotland **(1)**
   (ii) 50 deaths per 100 000 (210 – 160) **(1)**
   (b) Men have higher death rates than women. **(1)**

2. Artery – 3 **(1)**; Capillaries in the body – 4 **(1)**; Vein – 1 **(1)**; Capillaries in the lungs – 2 **(1)**

Page 16

1. **(a)** 924.5 **(2)**; **if the answer is incorrect then showing the working (926 + 923 = 1849, then $\frac{1849}{2}$) will gain 1 mark**
   (b) Rats have different body masses / to standardise results. **(1)**
   (c) As the warfarin dose increases, the time to clot also increases. **(1)**

2. Agree **(1)** because as vital capacity increases the time underwater also increases **(1)**.
   Or disagree **(1)** due to **any one from:** only five subjects / not enough data; need to find divers with higher / lower vital capacities **(1)**.

Page 17

1. **(a)**

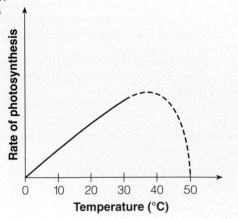

(1)

(b) As the temperature increases, the rate of photosynthesis increases due to more rapid molecular movement and therefore more frequent successful collisions between molecules **(1)**. By 40 °C, the rate peaks and beyond this point enzymes controlling photosynthesis become denatured and the reaction stops **(1)**.

2. **(a)** Leaves **(1)**
   (b) Cellulose: cell walls for support **(1)**; **Protein:** growth / cell membranes / enzyme production **(1)**.
   (c) carbon dioxide + water $\longrightarrow$ glucose + oxygen
   (1 mark for reactants, 1 mark for products)

3. **(a) Any two from:** the increased temperature from the stove will increase photosynthesis rate; increased carbon dioxide concentration will have the same effect; increased photosynthesis means increased starch production / yield. **(2)**
   (b) Any one from: increase light regime, e.g. artificial lighting switched on at night time; increased light intensity / brighter lights. **(1)**

HEALTH, DISEASE AND THE DEVELOPMENT OF MEDICINES
Page 18

1. **(a)** 13.8–14.8% **(1)**
   (b) Glycogen **(1)** found in liver / muscles **(1)**
   (c) Any two from: heart disease / CVD / stroke; cancer; diabetes; asthma / eczema / autoimmune diseases; poor nutrition – named example, e.g. rickets; genetic conditions, e.g. cystic fibrosis; eating disorders, e.g. anorexia; mental health conditions; alcoholism / addiction; named inherited disease. **(2)**

2. **(a)** ×20 **(1)**
   (b) Any one from: low birth weight; premature birth; higher risk of still birth. **(1)**

Page 19

1. **(a)** Pathogen **(1)**
   (b) Cause cell damage **(1)**; the toxins produced damage tissues. **(1)**

2. **(a) Any two from:** diarrhoea; vomiting; dehydration. **(2)**
   (b) Cholera spread by drinking contaminated water **(1)**; water easily contaminated because water supply / sewage systems damaged **or** overcrowding and poor hygiene in disaster zones **(1)**.

3. **(a) Any two from:** malaria is transmitted by the mosquito; warm temperatures are ideal for mosquitos to thrive; stagnant water is an ideal habitat for mosquito eggs to be laid / larvae to survive **(2)**.
   (b) Mosquito: vector **(1)**
   Plasmodium: parasite **(1)**
   (c) Nets will deter mosquitoes / prevent bites / prevent transferral of plasmodium **(1)**; antivirals are ineffective as plasmodium is a protist / not a virus **(1)**.

Page 20

1. **(a)** Antibodies **(1)**
   (b) Pathogens are clumped together to prevent their further reproduction, to make them easier for phagocytes to digest. **(1)**
   (c)

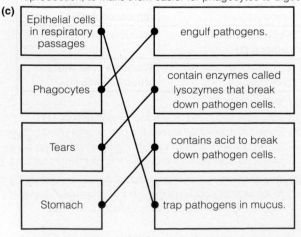

(1 mark for each correct line up to 3 marks, subtract 1 mark for any additional lines)

2. **(a) Any one from:** droplet infection / coughing / sneezing / water droplets in breath / aerosol. **(1)**
   (b) Answer in the range 16–17 days **(1)**
   (c) 9 arbitrary units **(1)** (9.5 – 0.5) **(1)**
   (d) Memory cells recognise future invasion of pathogen **(1)**; they can produce the necessary antibodies much quicker, and at higher levels, if the same pathogen is detected again **(1)**.

Page 21

1. **This is a model answer, which would score the full 6 marks:**
   HIV proteins can be triggered and manufactured in existing human cells. The genes that code for the viral proteins are injected into the bloodstream. An adenovirus shell prevents them from being destroyed by the body's general defences. Once inside a cell, the genes instruct it to produce viral proteins that are presented at the cell surface membrane. The body's lymphocytes then recognise these antigens and produce antibodies against them. Memory cells sensitive to the viral proteins are then stored in case the body is exposed to the antigens again.

2. **Accept any three from:** Bacteria are becoming resistant to many modern antibiotics; doctors have in the past over-prescribed antibiotics; mutations in bacteria have led to resistant strains developing; some people don't complete the course of antibiotics. **(3)**

Page 22

1. **(a) Any two from:** to ensure that the drug is actually effective / more effective than placebo; to work out the most effective dose / method of application; to comply with legislation. **(2)**
   (b) Double blind trials involve volunteers who are randomly allocated to groups – neither they nor the doctors / scientists know if they have been given the new drug or a placebo **(1)**; this eliminates all bias from the test **(1)**.
   (c) (i) Total patients = 226; $\frac{21}{226} \times 100$ **(1)** = 9.29% **(1)**
   (ii) Yes, there are more patients who took the drug and had a cardiovascular event than those who took the placebo. However, there is not a large difference between the groups. **(1)** No, the cardiovascular events could include other conditions apart from heart attacks. **(1)**
   (iii) Rash **(1)**; the difference in numbers of patients who got a rash between the alketronol and placebo groups is quite large **(1)**.

Page 23

1. **(a) Mineral deficiency:** lack of nitrates **(1) Leaf appearance:** yellow leaves and stunted growth **(1)** (Also accept **Mineral deficiency:** lack of magnesium / potassium / phosphate **(1)**; **Leaf appearance:** chlorosis / discolouration of the leaves **(1)**)
   (b) There is a high concentration of *Chalara* cases in the East of England ✓ **(1)**
   (c) (i) Any two from: burning trees destroys fungus / *Chalara*; prevents further spores being produced; reduces spread of spores. **(2)**
   (ii) Any one from: not all trees removed; trees may produce spores before being detected / destroyed; more spores could be introduced by wind from mainland Europe. **(1)**

COORDINATION AND CONTROL

Page 24

1. homeostasis **(1)**; receptors **(1)**; effectors **(1)**
2. **(a)** Negative feedback **(1)**
   (b) (i) It reduces production of ACTH. **(1)**
   (ii) Any one from: ineffective nutrient distribution; inability to reduce inflammation; inefficient water control. **(1)**
   (iii) Patient D **(1)**
   (iv) 5 × 7 = 35 µg per litre **(2 marks for correct answer; if answer is incorrect, 1 mark for showing working)**

Page 25

1. **(a)** Nucleus **(1)**; **(b)** Cell body / cytoplasm **(1)**
2. **(a)** Brain **(1)**
   (b) A means of detecting external stimuli, i.e. a **receptor (1)**; transferral of electrical impulses to the CNS, i.e. a **sensory neurone (1)**; a coordinator / control system, i.e. a **brain (1)**.
3. **(a)** Synapse **(1)**
   (b) Any three from: transmitter substance released at end of first neurone in response to impulse; travels across synapse by diffusion; transmitter binds with receptor molecules on next neurone; nervous impulse released in second neurone **(3)**.

Page 26

1. **Gland:** pancreas **(1)   Hormone:** insulin / glucagon **(1)**
2. **(a) Any two from:** after meal, a rise in glucose levels will be detected by device; which will cause hormone implant to release insulin; insulin released to bring blood glucose level down. **(2)**
   (b) People with type 2 diabetes can often control their sugar level by adjusting their diet **(1)**; body's cells often no longer respond to insulin **(1)**.

3.

Gland	Hormones produced
Pituitary gland	**TSH, ADH, LH** and **FSH** (accept any two)
Pancreas	Insulin and glucagon
Thyroid gland	Thyroxine
Adrenal gland	Adrenaline
Ovary	**Oestrogen** and **progesterone**
Testes	Testosterone

(1 mark for each correct line)

Page 27

1. **(a)** 1600 ml **(1)**
   (b) Amounts are equal **(1)**; important that water intake should balance water output to avoid dehydration **(1)**.
   (c) Intake of water greater **(1)**; output from sweating greater **(1)**; water gained from respiration greater **(1)**, as muscles contracting more / respiring more **(1)**.
2. **(a)** B **(1)**
   (b) C **(1)**
   (c) A **(1)**
   (d) Low water levels in blood detected by receptors / in blood vessels / in brain **(1)**; more ADH released by pituitary gland **(1)**, acts on collecting duct / kidney **(1)**; which is stimulated to absorb more water back into bloodstream **(1)**.

Page 28

1. Days 5–14: uterus wall is being repaired **(1)**; egg released at approximately 14 days from ovary **(1)**; days 14–28: uterus lining maintained **(1)**.

2.

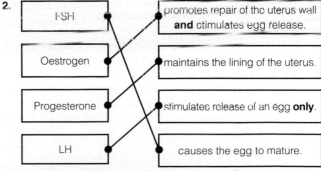

(1 mark for each correct line up to 3 marks)

3. **(a)** Negative feedback **(1)**
   (b) FSH **(1)**
   (c) Progesterone **(1)**
   (d) Continues to be produced **(1)** in large quantities / at high levels **(1)**.

Page 29

1. (a) Leroy and Jane **(1)**
   (b) **Three:** Tim and Margaret, Rohit and Saleema, and Leroy and Jane. **(1)**
   (c) Although irregular ovulation has a lower success rate **(1)**; it affects over twice as many couples (16 × 75 produces a larger total than 7 × 95). **(1)**
   (d) Both methods mean that Jane does not make any genetic contribution **(1)**; egg donation has a high rate of success but can be expensive **(1)**; surrogacy might be cheaper but there is a risk that the surrogate mother might develop an attachment to the baby / want to keep it **(1)**; egg donation requires invasive technique **(1)**.
2. **Any two from:** the contraceptive pill contains hormones that inhibit FSH production; e.g. oestrogen / progesterone; eggs therefore fail to mature; progesterone causes production of sticky cervical mucus that hinders movement of sperm **(2)**.

INHERITANCE, VARIATION AND EVOLUTION
Page 30

1. gametes **(1)**; haploid **(1)**; meiosis **(1)**
2. Meiosis shuffles genes, which makes each gamete unique ✓ **(1)**; Gametes fuse randomly ✓ **(1)**
3. (a) **Any three from:** sexual reproduction can be an advantage to a species if the environment changes; asexual reproduction is more advantageous when the environment is not changing; some organisms use both types of reproduction, therefore both have their advantages; sexual reproduction might yield disadvantageous adaptations in an individual when the environment changes. **(3)**
   (b) **Sexual:** male and female parents required; slower than asexual; requires meiosis; more resources (e.g. time, energy) required. **Asexual:** only one parent required; faster than sexual; requires mitosis only; less resources required. **(1)**
   (c) Cytoplasm and organelles duplicated **(1)**; as a 'bud' **(1)**

Page 31

1. The genome of an organism is the entire genetic material present in its adult body cells ✓ **(1)**; The HGP involved collaboration between US and UK geneticists ✓ **(1)**; The project allowed genetic abnormalities to be tracked between generations ✓ **(1)**.
2. (a) Organisms with very similar features / chimpanzee and human share equal DNA coding for protein A. **(1)**
   (b) Yeast **(1)**
3. (a) **Any two from:** warn women about the risk of cancer ahead of time; enable early and regular screening; enable early treatment; suggest treatment that is targeted. **(2)**
   (b) Other factors may contribute to onset of cancer **(1)**; risk is in terms of a probability (which is not 100%) **(1)**.

Page 32

1. (a) T pairs with A; C pairs with G **(both correct for 1 mark)**
   (b) 3 **(1)**
2. (a) **Any two from:** UV light; radioactive substances; X-rays; certain chemicals / mutagens. **(2)**
   (b) Base / triplet sequence changed **(1)**; leads to change in amino acid sequence **(1)**; protein no longer has correct shape to perform its job **(1)**.
3. Nucleotides are composed of a sugar-phosphate unit **(1)** and a nitrogenous base **(1)**. The bases are A, T, C and G **(1)**. The sequence of three bases / nucleotides / triplet / codes for a specific amino acid. **(1)**

Page 33

1. (a) 39 **(1)**
   (b) Black is the dominant gene / allele; white is recessive **(1)** (**no marks given for references to 'black chromosome' or 'white chromosome'**); the allele for black fur is passed on / inherited from the father **(1)**.
   (c) Correct genotype or gametes for both parents (Bb and bb) **(1)**; genotype of offspring correct (Bb and bb) **(1)**; correct phenotype of offspring **(1)**.

	b	**b**
B	Bb Black	Bb Black
b	bb White	bb White

Or

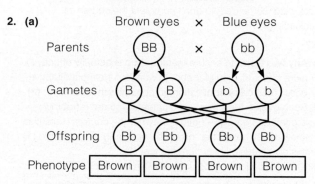

2. (a)

(1 mark will be awarded for the phenotype row and 1 mark for offspring row.)

(b)

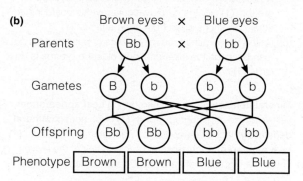

(1 mark will be awarded for the phenotype row and 1 mark for the offspring row.)

Page 34

1. **(a)** 205–215 million years ago **(1)**
   (b) (i) Cretaceous **(1)**
   (ii) They have discovered fossils. **(1)**
   (c) Lizard **(1)**
   (d) Archosaur **(1)**

Page 35

1. **(a)**

Before Industrial Revolution		After Industrial Revolution	
Pale	Dark	Pale	Dark
1260	107	89	1130

(1 mark for mean numbers before Industrial Revolution; 1 mark for mean numbers after Industrial Revolution)

   (b)

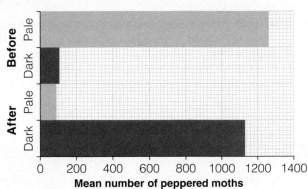

Mean number of peppered moths

(2 marks for correct plotting of bars; subtract 1 mark for every incorrect plot.)

   (c) The pale-coloured moths could camouflage themselves easily against the silver birch tree bark. **(1)**
   (d) Dark-coloured peppered moths were more camouflaged than pale moths after the Industrial Revolution due to the effects of air pollution **(1)**; dark moths had an increased chance of survival and consequently an increased chance of reproducing and passing on genes **(1)**.

2. Lucy was one of the earliest known hominids to have an upright stance. **(1)**

Page 36

1. **(a) Any three from:** Allow chosen males and females to mate / breed / reproduce together; select offspring from several matings that have high quality wool; allow these sheep to mate together; repeat the process over many generations **(stages must be in sequence). (3)**
   (b) Any one from: high quality meat / lamb; thick coat; hardiness / ability to withstand harsh winters; colouration / markings; disease resistance. **(1)**

2. **Any two from:** Involves genes, not whole organisms; genes transferred from one organism to another; much more precise in terms of passing on characteristics; rapid production; cheaper than selective breeding; (or reverse argument). **(2)**

3. **(a)** Crops containing soya can be sprayed with herbicide so weeds are killed rather than soya. **(1)**
   (b) Rice produces carotene, which provides poor populations with vitamin A. **(1)**

4. GM plants may cross-breed with wild plants, resulting in wild plants / weeds that are herbicide-resistant. **(1)**

Page 37

1. **(a) Underline any one of the following**; carnivorous big cats; five toes on their front paws and four toes on their back paws; claws can be drawn back. **(1)**
   (b) Leopards are more closely related to tigers **(1)**; both are the Panthera genus / snow leopards are a different genus **(1)**.

2. Possesses features that are found in reptiles and birds **(1)**; feathers place it with birds but it also has teeth / does not have a beak like reptiles – it is an intermediate form **(1)**.

ECOSYSTEMS

Page 38

1. features; characteristics **(either way round for features or characteristics)**; suited; environment; evolutionary; survival **(6 words correct = 3 marks, 4 or 5 words correct = 2 marks, 2 or 3 words correct = 1 mark, 1 or 0 words correct = 0 marks)**

2. **(a)**

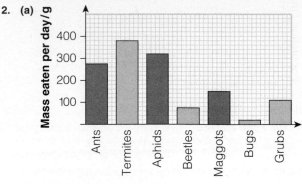

(2 marks for correctly plotting bars, 1 mark for correctly labelling x axis.)

   (b) $\frac{380}{1330} \times 100 = 28.6\%$
   (1 mark for correct answer, 1 mark for showing working)
   (c) It occupies more than one habitat / niche **(1)**; eats a wide variety of food / prey **(1)**.

Page 39

1. **(a)** Habitat **(1)**
   (b) Ecosystem **(1)**
   (c) Any one from: pooter; sweepnet; light trap. **(1)**
   (d) 16 × 4 × 5000 = 320 000 **(1 mark for correct answer, 1 mark for showing working)**
   (e) (i) Less competition for food between beetles **(1)**; numbers increase as a result **(1)**.
   (ii) Snail numbers would decline. **(1)**

Page 40

1. **(a)** A producer is an organism that produces its own food. **(1)**
   (b) Sunlight / the Sun **(1)**
   (c) Any one from: wasp; ladybird; hoverfly **(1)**

2. **(a)** There was a slight rise in 1974 **(1)**, but since then the numbers have decreased rapidly **(1)**, and then they have decreased slowly **(1)**. The numbers decreased rapidly between 1976 and 1986 and decreased slowly between 1986 and 2002 **(1)**.
   (b) Farmers have cut down hedgerows and/or trees, so the birds have had nowhere to nest and their food source has been reduced. **(1)**
   (c) Any one from: plant more trees; encourage farmers to plant hedgerows; encourage farmers to leave field edges wild as food for birds; use fewer pesticides. **(1)**

Page 41

1. water wind wood **(1)**

2. **Climate zones** shift, causing ecosystems and habitats to change; organisms are displaced and become extinct **(1) Sea levels** rise, causing flooding of coastal regions; islands are inundated and disappear beneath sea level. **(1) Ice caps and glaciers** melt and retreat, resulting in loss of habitat. **(1)**

3. (a) See graph **(2)**
(b) Millions (Also accept billions) **(1)**

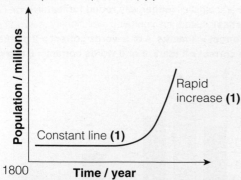

(c) Any two from: insufficient birth control; better life expectancy; better health care; better hygienic practice. **(2)**

Page 42

1. Any two from: climate change; new predators; habitat destruction; hunting; competition; pollution. **(2)**
2. (a) Cutting down large areas of forest ✓ **(1)**
(b) Increase in atmospheric carbon dioxide ✓ **(1)**
3. Any two from: provide land for agriculture; road building; mining; construction. **(2)**
4. tropical; trees; carbon dioxide; biodiversity; extinct; habitats **(6)**
5. Nutrients in the soil are absorbed by crops and are not replaced. **(1)**

Page 43

1. organisms **(1)**, evaporated **(1)**, precipitation **(1)**
2. (a) Tube D **(1)**; because it is warm and moist **(1)**.
(b) The soil / air / surface of the leaf **(1)**
(c) So that air / oxygen can get in **(1)**
(d) Accept one from: they could count the number of whole discs left at the end; they could record what fraction / percentage of leaf discs decayed and find an average; they could measure the percentage decrease in mass of discs by measuring mass before and after time in soil. **(1)**

Page 44

1. (a) 160 thousand tonnes (plus or minus 10 000 or in range 150–170) **(1)**
(b) Overall decrease in numbers **(1)**; temporary rises in 1988–1993 and 2003–2006 **(1)**.
(c) (i) 1907 tonnes **(1)**
(ii) Numbers of haddock still declining **(1)**; therefore less fish should be caught in order for fish stocks to recover **(1)**.
(d) Any one from: increasing mesh size to allow young cod to reach breeding age; increase quotas of other fish species. **(1)**

Chemistry

ATOMIC STRUCTURE AND THE PERIODIC TABLE

Page 45

1. **(a)** Na **(1)** Cl **(1)**
   (b) Sodium + chlorine ⟶ sodium chloride **(reactants 1, products 1)**
   (c) A compound **(1)** as the elements are chemically combined/joined **(1)**
   (d) A mixture **(1)** as the salt and water are together but not chemically combined **(1)**
   (e) Crystallisation **(1)**; simple distillation **(1)**

Page 46

1. **(a)** The plum pudding model proposed that an atom was a ball of positive charge/today's model has the positive charge contained in the nucleus/protons **(1)** The plum pudding model proposed that electrons were embedded/spread throughout the positive charge/today's model has the electrons in different energy levels/shells surrounding the positive charge **(1)**
   (b) Some of the positively charged particles/alpha particles (when fired at gold foil) were deflected **(1)**
   (c) Niels Bohr suggested that electrons orbit the nucleus at specific distances/are present in energy levels/shells **(1)** His calculations were backed up by experimental results **(1)**
   (d)

Particle	Relative charge	Relative mass
Proton	+1	1
Neutron	0	1
Electron	−1	Negligible/approx. 1/2000

   (4)

   (e) (i) 11 **(1)**
   (ii) 23 **(1)**

Page 47

1. **(a)** 3 **(1)**
   (b) 2,7 **(1)**
   (c) 7 **(1)** As an atom of fluorine has 7 electrons in its outer shell **(1)**
2. **(a)** By increasing atomic number **(1)**
   (b) Because they both have similar chemical properties **(1)**
   (c) Accept two from: have high melting/boiling points; conduct heat and electricity; react with oxygen to form alkalis; malleable/ductile **(2)**

Page 48

1. **(a)** The atoms have full outer shells/energy levels **(1)** so they do not bond **(1)**
   (b) It increases **(1)**
2. **(a)** $2Na_{(s)} + 2H_2O_{(l)} \longrightarrow 2NaOH_{(aq)} + H_{2(g)}$ **(1 for correct formula; 1 for correct balancing in equation. Ignore state symbols, even if wrong)**
   (b) Blue **(1)** as an alkali solution/the hydroxide ion is formed **(1)**
   (c) A potassium atom is larger (than a sodium atom), so the outer electron is further away from the nucleus **(1)** so there is less attraction/the electron is more easily lost **(1)**
3. **(a)** $2Na_{(s)} + Cl_{2(g)} \longrightarrow 2NaCl_{(s)}$ **(1 for each side; any correctly balanced equation scores both marks, e.g. 4Na + 2Br₂ ⟶ 4NaBr)**
   (b) Ionic **(1)**
   (c) chlorine + sodium bromide ⟶ sodium chloride **(1)** + bromine **(1)**
   (d) Displacement **(1)** A more reactive element (chlorine) takes the place of a less reactive element (bromine) in a compound **(1)**

STRUCTURE, BONDING AND THE PROPERTIES OF MATTER

Page 49

1. sodium – metallic **(1)**; chlorine – simple molecular **(1)**; sodium chloride – ionic **(1)**
2. **(a)**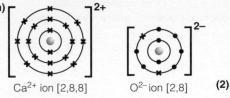
   Ca^{2+} ion [2,8,8] O^{2-} ion [2,8]   **(2)**
   (b) Calcium: 2+, oxygen: 2− **(2)**
3. **(a)**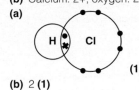
   (1)
   (b) 2 **(1)**

Page 50

1. **(a)** Electrostatic forces **(1)** between the anions and cations
   (b) CaO **(1)** There are an equal number of calcium ions and oxygen ions and so the ratio of each is 1:1 **(1)**
2. **(a)** A polymer **(1)**
   (b) CH_2 **(1)** There are twice as many hydrogen atoms as carbon atoms, so ratio of carbon to hydrogen is 1:2 **(1)**
3. Giant covalent/macromolecular **(1)** it is a large molecule consisting of atoms that are covalently bonded together with a theoretically infinite structure **(1)**

Page 51

1. **(a)** **(1 for regular arrangement of particles, 1 for no gaps between the particles)**
   (b) Intermolecular forces/forces between particles **(1)**
2. **(a)** It conducts electricity when liquid but not as a solid **(1)**
   (b) The ions **(1)** are not free to move **(1)**
   (c) Giant covalent/macromolecular **(1)** It has a high melting point **and** does not conduct electricity **(1)**
   (d) There are no free **(1)** charged particles/electrons/ions **(1)**

Page 52

1. **(a)** The layers **(1)** (of ions) are able to slide over each other **(1)**
   (b) There is a strong attraction **(1)** between the metal cations and the delocalised electrons **(1)**
   (c) The electrons **(1)** are free to move/flow through the structure **(1)**
2. **(a)** A mixture of metals/a metal mixed with another element **(1)**
   (b) The layers are not able to slide over each other **(1)** because the other atoms are larger and prevent movement **(1)**
3. **(a) Accept two from:** for drug delivery into the body/as lubricants/reinforcing materials, e.g. in tennis rackets **(2)**
   (b) Accept two from: tensile strength; electrical conductivity; thermal conductivity **(2)**
   (c) A carbon nanotube is a cylindrical fullerene **(1)**

QUANTITATIVE CHEMISTRY

Page 53

1. **(a)** Total mass of reactants = total mass of the products, i.e. there is no net mass loss or gain during a chemical reaction **(1)**
   (b)

Substance	A_r / M_r
Al	27
Fe_2O_3	160
Al_2O_3	102
Fe	56

   (4)

2. **(a)** Oxygen **(1)** is added **(1)** to the magnesium
    (b) $2Mg_{(s)} + O_{2(g)} \longrightarrow 2MgO_{(s)}$ **(1 for reactants and products, 1 for correct balancing)**
    (c) The magnesium carbonate loses/gives off **(1)** carbon dioxide **(1)**
    (d) $MgCO_{3(s)} \longrightarrow MgO_{(s)} + CO_{2(g)}$ **(1 for correct formulae products; 1 for balanced equation; ignore state symbols, even if wrong)**

Page 54

1. **(a)** 2.408×10^{24} $(4 \times 6.02 \times 10^{23})$ **(1)**
    (b) 92 g $(4 \times 23$ g) **(1)**
    (c) 0.5 $(11.5 \div 23)$ **(1)**
    (d) 4 moles of Na form 2 moles of Na_2O (2:1 ratio), therefore 0.5 mole of Na forms 0.25 mole of Na_2O mass = 0.5×62 **(1 for correct M_r of Na_2O)** = 31 g **(1)**
2. **(a)** $6 \div 12 = 0.5$, $1 \div 1 = 1$ **(1)**
    $0.5 \div 0.5 = 1$, $1 \div 0.5 = 2$ **(1)**
    Empirical formula = CH_2 **(1)**
    (b) (relative formula mass of empirical formula = 14), $98 \div 14 = 7$ **(1)**
    Molecular formula = C_7H_{14} **(1)**

Page 55

1. **(a)** $(5 \div 200) \times 1000 = 25$ g/dm³ **(1)**
    (b) $5 \div 200 \times 14 = 0.35$ g/dm³ **(1)**
    (Also accept $25 \times \left(\dfrac{14}{1000}\right) = 0.35$ g/dm³

2.

Chemical	Pb	O_2	PbO
Mass from question/g	41.4	3.2	44.6
A_r or M_r	207	**32**	223
Moles = $\dfrac{mass}{M_r}$	$\dfrac{41.4}{207}$ = 0.2	$\dfrac{3.2}{32}$ = 0.1	$\dfrac{44.6}{223}$ = 0.2
÷ smallest	$\dfrac{0.2}{0.1}$ = 2	$\dfrac{0.1}{0.1}$ = 1	$\dfrac{0.2}{0.1}$ = 2

Balanced equation: $2Pb + O_2 \longrightarrow 2PbO$ **(1 for each row in table, 1 for correct balanced equation)**

CHEMICAL AND ENERGY CHANGES

Page 56

1. **(a)** calcium + oxygen $\longrightarrow$ calcium oxide **(1 for reactants, 1 for product)**
    (b) Calcium gains **(1)** oxygen **(1)** (**Also accept** Oxygen **(1)** is added **(1)** or Calcium loses **(1)** electrons **(1)**)
    (c) Potassium, sodium or lithium (or any other metal in group 1 or strontium, barium or radium) **(1)** the metal is more reactive than calcium/is above calcium in the reactivity series **(1)**
    (d) Metal + calcium oxide $\longrightarrow$ metal oxide + calcium, e.g. potassium + calcium oxide $\longrightarrow$ potassium oxide + calcium **(1 for reactants, 1 for products)**
    (e) Calcium oxide **(1)**
2. **(a)** Electrolysis **(1)**
    (b) $2Fe_2O_3 + 3C \longrightarrow 4Fe + 3CO_2$ **(1 for correct formulae, 1 for balanced equation; allow any correct balanced equation, e.g. $4Fe_2O_3 + 6C \longrightarrow 8Fe + 6CO_2$ ignore state symbols)**
    (c) Reduction **(1)** as electrons are gained **(1)** by the Al^{3+} **(1)**
    (d) K **(1)** as it loses electrons **(1)** $K \longrightarrow K^+ + e$

Page 57

1. **(a)** Zinc sulfate **(1)**
    (b) Zinc oxide + hydrochloric acid $\longrightarrow$ zinc chloride **(1)** + water **(1)**
    (c) Carbon dioxide **(1)** CO_2 **(1)**
    (d) **(i)** calcium (as it loses electrons) **(1)**
       (ii) H^+ **(1; allow $2H^+$ not hydrogen)**
    (e) When a substance loses **(1)** electrons **(1)**
2. **(a)** **Accept three from:** measure out some sulfuric acid (e.g. 25 cm³ in a measuring cylinder); transfer to a beaker and warm the acid; add copper oxide, stir and repeat until no more copper oxide dissolves; filter the mixture; leave the filtrate somewhere warm/heat the filtrate **(3)**

    (b) Nitric acid **(1)**
    (c) Soluble salt **(1)**

Page 58

1. **(a)** 1–6 **(1)**
    (b) Hydrogen ion **(1)** H^+ **(1)**
    (c) Hydrochloric acid **(1)**
    (d) $H^+_{(aq)} + OH^-_{(aq)} \longrightarrow H_2O_{(l)}$ **(1 for correct formulae, 1 for correct state symbols)**
2. **(a)** A strong acid completely ionises/fully dissociates in water **(1)** a weak acid partially ionises/dissociates in water **(1)**
    (b) $CH_3COOH_{(aq)} \rightleftharpoons CH_3COO^-_{(aq)} + H^+_{(aq)}$ **or** $CH_3COOH_{(aq)} + aq \rightleftharpoons CH_3COO^-_{(aq)} + H^+_{(aq)}/CH_3COOH_{(aq)} + H_2O_{(l)} \rightleftharpoons CH_3COO^-_{(aq)} + H_3O^+_{(aq)}$ **(1 for reactants, 1 for products; ignore state symbols)**
    (c) Lower **(1)** Nitric acid is a stronger acid and so there will be more H^+ ions than in a weak acid and therefore will be more acidic **(1)**
    (d) It increases **(1)** by 1 **(1)**

Page 59

1. **(a)** Cations **(1)**
    (b) Anions **(1)**
    (c) So that the ions **(1)** are free to move **(1)**
    (d) Oxidation **(1)** as electrons are lost **(1)**
2. **(a)**

Solution	Product at anode	Product at cathode
NaCl	H_2	Cl_2
KNO_3	H_2	O_2
$CuSO_4$	Cu	O_2
Water diluted with sulfuric acid	H_2	O_2

(6)

    (b) Hydrogen is produced because hydrogen ions are present in the solution **(1)** and hydrogen is less reactive than sodium **(1)**
    (c) $4OH^- \longrightarrow O_2 + 2H_2O + 4e^-$ (or $4OH^- - 4e^- \longrightarrow O_2 + 2H_2O$) **(1 for reactants and products, 1 for balanced equation; ignore state symbols)**

Page 60

1. **(a)**

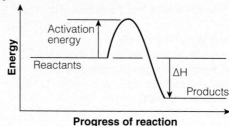

    (1 for products lower in energy than the reactants, each correct label scores 1)
    (b) More energy is released when the bonds in the product molecules are made **(1)** than is used to break the bonds in the reactant molecules **(1)**
    (c) **Accept one from**: any thermal decomposition reaction (e.g. metal carbonate $\longrightarrow$ metal oxide + carbon dioxide); The reaction between citric acid and sodium hydrogencarbonate **(1)**
2. **(a)** ΔH = Bonds broken – bonds formed = 2144 **(1)** – 2348 **(1)** = –204 kJ/mol **(1)**
    (b) Exothermic **(1)** the value of ΔH is negative/more energy is released when the bonds in the product molecules are made than is used to break the bonds in the reactant molecules **(1)**

THE RATE AND EXTENT OF CHEMICAL REACTIONS

Page 61

1. **(a)** 70°C **(1)**
    (b) Increased temperature increases the rate of reaction **(1)** the higher the temperature, the more kinetic energy the particles have and so the frequency of collisions/successful collisions increases **(1)**

2. (a) 1st experiment: $69 \div 46 = 1.5$ **(1)** cm³/s; 2nd experiment: $18 \div 10 = 1.8$ **(1)** cm³/s **(1 for correct units)**

    (b) The second experiment **(1)** as the rate is greater **(1)**

Page 62

1. (a) The particles must collide with enough energy/the activation energy **(1)**

    (b) (i) At a higher concentration, there are more particles per unit volume/in the same volume of solution **(1)** meaning that there will be more collisions **(1)**

        (ii) At a higher pressure there are more gas molecules per unit volume **(1)**, which means that there is an increased likelihood of a collision **(1)**

    (c)

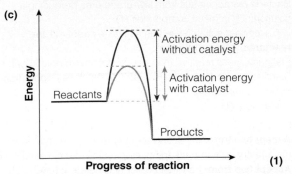

       (1)

    (d) Catalysts provide an alternative reaction pathway **(1)** of lower activation energy **(1)**

Page 63

1. (a) The blue crystals will turn white **(1)**

    (b) hydrated copper(II) sulfate $\rightleftharpoons$ anhydrous copper(II) sulfate + water **(allow arrow $\longrightarrow$ instead of $\rightleftharpoons$) (1 for formulae, 1 for balanced equation)**

    (c) The white powder will turn blue **(1)**

    (d) Exothermic reaction **(1)**

2. (a) A reversible reaction **(1)**

    (b) The yield of SO_3 would increase **(1)** higher pressure favours the reaction/shifts the equilibrium **(1)** to the side that produces fewer molecules of gas **(1)**

    (c) The yield of SO_3 would decrease **(1)** increasing temperature favours the endothermic reaction **(1)**, which in this case is the reverse reaction **(1)**

ORGANIC CHEMISTRY

Page 64

1. (a) Kerosene **(1)**

    (b) It increases **(1)**

    (c) 1. Crude oil is heated/boiled **(1)** 2. In the fractionating column there is a temperature gradient (hotter at bottom/cooler at top) **(1)** 3. The hydrocarbons travel up the fractionating column and condense at their boiling point **(1)**

2. (a) C_nH_{2n+2} **(1)**

    (b)

$$
\begin{array}{c}
\text{H} \quad \text{H} \quad \text{H} \\
| \quad\;\; | \quad\;\; | \\
\text{H}-\text{C}-\text{C}-\text{C}-\text{H} \\
| \quad\;\; | \quad\;\; | \\
\text{H} \quad \text{H} \quad \text{H}
\end{array}
$$
    (1)

    (c) C_4H_{10} **(1)**

    (d) Any one from: differ by CH_2 in their molecular formula from neighbouring compounds; show a gradual trend in physical properties; have similar chemical properties **(1)**

Page 65

1. (a) carbon dioxide **(1)** and water **(1)**

    (b) $C_3H_8 + 5O_2 \longrightarrow 3CO_2 + 4H_2O$ **(1 mark for correct formulae and 1 mark for correct balancing)**

    (c) propane **(1)**

2. (a) Accept one from: silica, alumina, porcelain **(1)**

    (b) by heating **(1)** with steam **(1)**

    (c) C_4H_{10} **(1)**

    (d) Bromine water **(1)** turns colourless / is decolourised / turns from orange to colourless when mixed with the gas **(1)**

CHEMICAL ANALYSIS

Page 66

1. (a) A mixture that has been designed as a useful product **(1)**

    (b) No **(1)** something that is chemically pure contains a single element or compound **(1)**

    (c) Accept one from: fuels; medicines; foods; fertilisers **(1)**

2. (a) The liquid solvent **(1 allow water)**

    (b) red and green **(1)** The spots of these colours are at the same height as spots in ink X **(1)**

    (c) $\dfrac{0.5}{4.65} = 0.11$ **(allow 0.10–0.12; 1 mark for working, 1 mark for correct answer)**

    (d) It is more accurate/relative amounts of different inks can be determined/smaller quantities can be used **(1)**

Page 67

1. (a) Calcium hydroxide **(1)**

    (b) A precipitate **(1)** of $CaCO_3$ **(1)** is formed

2. (a) The litmus paper turns red **(1)** before turning white/being bleached **(1)**

    (b) Acidic gas **(1)** as it turns litmus paper red **(1)**

3. (a) Hydrogen gives a squeaky pop **(1)** when exposed to a lit splint **(1)**

    (b) Oxygen relights **(1)** a glowing splint **(1)**

    (c) $2H_{2(g)} + O_{2(g)} \longrightarrow 2H_2O_{(l)}$ **(1 for formulae of reactants/ products, 1 for correctly balanced equation; ignore state symbols)**

THE EARTH'S ATMOSPHERE AND RESOURCES

Page 68

1. (a) Nitrogen or oxygen **(1)**

    (b) The water vapour originally in the atmosphere cooled **(1)** and condensed **(1)** forming the oceans

    (c) Green plants/algae **(1)** form oxygen as a waste product of photosynthesis **(1)**

    (d) Accept two from: green plants; algae use carbon dioxide for photosynthesis; carbon dioxide is used to form sedimentary rocks; carbon dioxide is captured in oil; coal **(2)**

Page 69

1. (a) Greenhouse gases allow short wavelength radiation from the Sun to pass through the atmosphere **(1)** but absorb long wavelength radiation reflected back from the earth trapping heat **(1)**

    (b) Accept one from: methane; water vapour **(1)**

    (c) Accept two from: combustion of fossil fuels; deforestation; increased animal farming; decomposing rubbish in landfill sites **(2)**

    (d) There are many different factors contributing to climate change **(1)** and it is not easy to predict the impact of each one **(1)**

    (e) Accept two from: rising sea levels, which may cause flooding and coastal erosion; more frequent and/or severe storms; changes to the amount, timing and distribution of rainfall, temperature and water stress for humans and wildlife; changes to the food-producing capacity of some regions/changes to the distribution of wildlife species **(2)**

    (f) Accept two from: use of alternative energy supplies; increased use of renewable energy; energy conservation; carbon capture and storage techniques; carbon taxes and licences; carbon offsetting/carbon neutrality **(2)**

    (g) Accept two from: disagreement over the causes and consequences of global climate change; lack of public information and education; lifestyle changes, e.g. greater use of cars and aeroplanes; economic considerations, i.e. the financial costs of reducing the carbon footprint; incomplete international co-operation **(2)**

Page 70

1. **(a)** Fuel formed in the ground over millions of years from the remains of dead plants and animals **(1)**
   (b) Due to incomplete combustion/burning of fuels in a poor supply of oxygen **(1)**
   (c) **Accept one from:** forms acid rain; can cause respiratory problems **(1)**
   (d) Global dimming **(1)** health problems due to lung damage **(1)**
   (e) It combines with haemoglobin/red blood cells **(1)** preventing the transport of oxygen **(1)**
   (f) When sulfur burns it react with oxygen to form sulfur dioxide **(1)** Sulfur dioxide dissolves in rain water **(1)** The rain water is now acidic/acid rain which can damage buildings and destroy wildlife **(1)**

Page 71

1. **(a)** The needs of the current generation are met without compromising the potential of future generations to meet their own needs **(1)** Improving agricultural practices/using chemical processes to make new materials **(1)**
   (b) Water that is safe to drink **(1)**
   (c) Filtration/passed through filter beds to remove solid impurities **(1)** sterilised to kill microbes **(1)**
   (d) **Accept three from:** screening and grit removal; sedimentation to produce sewage sludge and effluent; anaerobic digestion of sewage sludge; aerobic biological treatment of effluent **(3)**

2. **(a)**

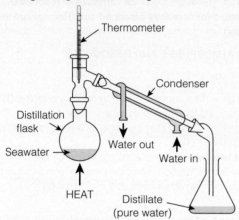

Thermometer
Condenser
Distillation flask
Water out
Seawater
Water in
HEAT
Distillate (pure water)

   (3 for labelled diagram: seawater in flask, condenser, pure water being collected)
   The water from the seawater boils/evaporates at 100°C and is condensed back into water in the condenser **(1)** the salt remains behind in the original flask **(1)**
   (b) Reverse osmosis **(1)**

Page 72

1. **(a)** A naturally occurring mineral **(1)** from which it is economically viable to extract a metal **(1)**
   (b) We still require the raw materials **(1)** but it is becoming increasingly difficult/uneconomic to mine them in traditional ways **(1)**
   (c) Electrical wiring **(1)** as it is a good conductor of electricity **(1)** water pipes **(1)** as it does not react with water/corrode **(1)**
   (d) Plants grow in a medium that enables them to absorb metal compounds **(1)** the plants are then harvested/burned leaving ash that is rich in the metal compounds **(1)** the ash is then further treated to extract the metal **(1)**
   (e) Bacteria extract metals from low-grade ores producing a solution rich in metal compounds **(1)**
   (f) iron + copper sulfate $\longrightarrow$ iron sulfate + copper **(1 for reactants, 1 for products)**
   (g) Platinum is less reactive than copper/too low in reactivity/in the reactivity series **(1)** and so is unable to displace copper from copper compounds
   (h) Electrolysis **(1)**

Page 73

1. **(a)** **Accept two from:** extracting and processing raw materials; manufacturing and packaging; disposal at end of useful life **(2)**
   (b) **Accept two from:** how much energy is needed; how much water is used; what resources are required; how much waste is produced; how much pollution is produced **(2)**
   (c) Allocating numerical values to pollutant effects is not always easy or straightforward **(1)** so value judgments have to be made which may not always be objective **(1)**
   (d) To support claims for advertising purposes **(1)**

2. Over the life of the product, plastic bags when compared with paper bags (**accept two from the following**): use less energy; use less fossil fuel; produce fewer CO$_2$ emissions; produce less waste; use less freshwater **(2)** meaning that plastic/polythene bags are less damaging to the environment/have less of an environmental impact **(1)** than paper bags (**Allow reverse argument**)

Physics

FORCES

Page 74

1. (a) weight = mass × gravitational field strength
   $78 × 10 = 780$ N **(1)**
   (b) Mass would be 78 kg (the same as on Earth) **(1)**.
   weight = mass × gravitational field strength
   $78 × 1.6 = 124.8$ N **(1)**
   (c) The gravitational attraction of Neil is very small **(1)**. The masses of the Moon and Earth are much larger than Neil so the gravitational attraction has no significant effect on them **(1)**.

2. (a) $120 − 30$ **(1)** $= 90$ N **(1)**
   (b) (i) 0 N **(1)**
   (ii) Louise is moving at a constant speed **(1)**. As the resultant force is zero she is neither accelerating nor decelerating **(1)**.
   (c) $\dfrac{\text{work done}}{\text{force}} = \dfrac{\text{distance moved along the}}{\text{line of action of the force}}$
   $= \dfrac{25\,000}{90}$ **(1)** $= 278$ m **(1)**

Page 75

1. (a) Linear **(1)**
   (b) force = spring constant × extension
   spring constant $= \dfrac{\text{force}}{\text{extension}}$ **(1)**
   $\dfrac{4}{0.01}$ – substitute numbers from graph **(1)**
   $= 400$ N/m **(1)**
   (c) (i) Non-linear
   (ii) The mass is too large **(1)** so the spring has exceeded the limit of proportionality **(1)**. The extension is no longer proportional to the force applied **(1)**.

Page 76

1. (a) Speed only has a magnitude **(1)**. Velocity has a magnitude and a direction **(1)**.
   (b) The direction of the car is changing **(1)**. A change in direction causes a change in velocity but not in speed **(1)**.
   (c) 1.5 m/s – Walking
   6 m/s – Bicycle
   20 m/s – Car
   250 m/s – Plane **(4 marks if fully correct; 1 mark per match)**

2. (a) speed $= \dfrac{\text{distance}}{\text{time}}$ **(1)** $= \dfrac{180}{13} = 14$ m/s (2 s.f.) **(1)**
   (b) speed $= \dfrac{\text{distance}}{\text{time}}$ **(1)**
   time $= \dfrac{\text{distance}}{\text{speed}}$
   $= \dfrac{500}{14}$ – 36 seconds (2 s.f.) **(1)**

Page 77

1. (a) speed $= \dfrac{\text{distance}}{\text{time}}$ **(1)** $= \dfrac{3500}{350} = 10$ m/s **(1)**
   (b) gradient $= \dfrac{1750}{50 \text{ seconds}}$ **(1)** $= 35$ m/s **(1)**

2. (a) (i) 250 – 300 seconds **(1)**
   (ii) gradient $= \dfrac{100}{50}$ **(1)** $= 2$ m/s² **(1)**
   (b) area under graph $= \dfrac{(36 × 50)}{2}$ **(2)**
   $= 900$ m **(1)**

3. A skydiver accelerates due to their weight **(1)** exceeding the air resistance **(1)**. As they reach terminal velocity **(1)** their weight balances the air resistance, or the resultant force is zero, so they stop accelerating and maintain a constant speed **(1)**.

Page 78

1. (a) (i) A stationary object will begin moving and accelerate **(1)**.
   (ii) A moving object will either accelerate or decelerate **(1)**.
   (b) Newton's first law **(1)**
   (c) Inertia **(1)**

2. (a) The acceleration of an object is proportional to the resultant force **(1)**.
   (b) (i) resultant force = mass × acceleration **(1)**
   $= 110 × 5$
   $= 550$ N **(1)**
   (ii) The resultant forces are unbalanced **(1)**. The force opposing the cyclist's movement is greater than the force of the cyclist's movement **(1)**. When she stops the resultant force on her is zero **(1)**.

3. Whenever two objects interact, the forces they exert on each other are equal and opposite **(1)**.

4. A vehicle with a mass over the limit would have a weight downwards greater **(1)** than the force upwards from the bridge **(1)**. There is a resultant force downwards and the bridge breaks **(1)**.

Page 79

1. (a) (i) Thinking distance: At higher speeds the car travels further in the time it takes to react or process the information and apply the brakes **(1)**.
   (ii) Braking distance: The car travels further in the time it takes the brakes to stop the car **(1)**.
   (b) **Two from**: tiredness; distraction; drugs; alcohol **(2)**
   (c) (i) B, D, C, A **(1)**
   (ii) Test B was done at a higher speed than A so the car had greater kinetic energy **(1)**. This meant the work done was also much greater in order to reduce this kinetic energy **(1)**. This meant there was much greater friction between the brakes and the wheel and so there was a much higher temperature in B than A **(1)**.

2. (a) momentum = mass × velocity **(1)**
   $= 50 × 20$
   $= 1000$ kg m/s **(1)**
   (b) The momentum will decrease. **(1)**

ENERGY

Page 80

1. (a) g.p.e. = mass × gravitational field strength × height **(1)**
   $= 60 × 10 × 3900$
   $= 2\,340\,000$ J or 2340 kJ **(1)**
   (b) kinetic energy = 0.5 × mass × (speed)² **(1)**
   $= 0.5 × 60 × 55^2$
   $= 90\,750$ J / 90.75 kJ **(1)**
   (c) kinetic energy = 0.5 × mass × (speed)² **(1)**
   $= 0.5 × 60 × 5^2$
   $= 750$ J **(1)**
   (d) 0 J **(1)**

2. (a) Copper **(1)** as it has the lowest specific heat capacity. **(1)**
   (b) Temperature change $= 35 − 16 = 19°C$ **(1)**
   $\dfrac{(\text{change in thermal energy} ÷ \text{temperature change})}{\text{specific heat capacity}} = \text{mass}$
   $= \dfrac{(76\,000 ÷ 19)}{390}$ **(1)**
   $= 10$ kg (2 s.f.) **(1)**

Page 81

1. transferred ✓ **(1)** dissipated ✓ **(1)**

2. (a) House B **(1)** has the lowest heating cost **(1)**. It is well insulated so loses less heat through the walls **(1)**.
   (b) No **(1)** not all heat is lost through walls **(1)**. Insulation in other areas could affect heating cost as could the efficiency of the boiler providing the heat **(1)**.
   (c) efficiency $= \dfrac{\text{useful output energy transfer}}{\text{useful input energy transfer}}$ **(1)**
   useful output energy transfer = efficiency × useful input energy transfer
   $= 0.65 × 5400 = 3510$ kJ **(1)**

Page 82

1. Renewable energy: **Three from**: solar; wind; wave; tidal; geothermal; hydroelectric
   Non-renewable energy: **Three from**: coal; oil; gas; nuclear
   (3 marks if fully correct; 2 marks if five correct; 1 mark if three correct)

2. **(a)** Over time the percentage of electricity generated by wind turbines has increased **(1)**.
   (b) Renewable energy so will not run out like fossil fuels **(1)**, doesn't release carbon dioxide or other pollutants **(1)**.
   (c) No **(1)**. Wind doesn't blow all the time **(1)** so we will always need another source of energy to provide 'back up' and supply electricity when wind turbines aren't turning **(1)**.
   (d) Some people think they are ugly and spoil views of landscapes **(1)**.

WAVES
Page 83

1. **(a)** A longitudinal wave **(1)**
   (b) wave speed = frequency × wavelength **(1)**
   wavelength = $\dfrac{\text{wave speed}}{\text{frequency}} = \dfrac{1482}{120} = 12.4$ metres **(1)**
   (c) Water is denser than air **(1)** so the sound wave is propagated faster **(1)**.
   (d) Water waves are transverse waves where the oscillations are perpendicular to the direction of energy transfer **(1)**. Sound waves are longitudinal waves where the oscillations are parallel to the direction of energy transfer **(1)**.

2. Amplitude – The maximum displacement of a point on a wave away from its undisturbed position. **(1)**
   Wavelength – The distance from a point on one wave to the equivalent point on the adjacent wave. **(1)**
   Frequency – The number of waves passing a point each second. **(1)**

Page 84

1. A: Radio **(1)** B: Infrared **(1)** C: Gamma **(1)**
2. **(a)** A: Angle of incidence **(1)**, B: Angle of refraction **(1)**
   (b) The light changes speed as it moves between media **(1)** as water is optically denser than air **(1)**. The wave travels slower in an optically denser medium so bends towards the normal **(1)**.
   (c) The light would bend away from the normal **(1)**.

Page 85

1. Radio waves – Television – Don't require a direct line of sight between transmitter and receiver.
   Ultraviolet – Energy efficient lamps – Require less energy than conventional lights.
   Infrared – Heating a room – Thermal radiation heats up objects.
   (3 marks if fully correct; 1 mark for each correct match of type, use and why suitable)

2. **(a)** Changes in the nucleus of a radioactive atom **(1)**.
   (b) Sterilisation of equipment or other suitable answer **(1)**.
   (c) They can cause gene mutations **(1)** and cancer **(1)**.
3. Radiation dose **(1)**
4. **(a)** X-rays **(1)**
   (b) X-rays are absorbed differently by different parts of the body **(1)**. More are absorbed by hard tissues, e.g. bone **(1)** and less are absorbed by soft tissues **(1)**.

ELECTRICITY
Page 86

1. **(a)** fuse **(1)**
   (b) thermistor **(1)**
   (c) switch (closed) **(1)**
2. **(a)** X: Filament lamp **(1)**, Y: LED **(1)**, Z: Resistor **(1)**
   (b) 5A **(1)**
   (c) The flow of electrical charge **(1)**
   (d) charge flow = current × time **(1)**
   time = $\dfrac{\text{charge flow}}{\text{current}} = \dfrac{780}{5}$
   = 156 seconds **(1)**

Page 87

1. **(a)** Ohmic conductor **(1)**
   (b) Temperature **(1)**
   (c)

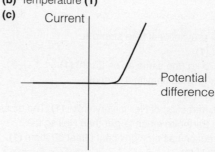

(2)

2. $\dfrac{\text{potential difference}}{\text{resistance}} = \text{current}$ **(1)** $= \dfrac{15}{4}$
   = 3.75 A **(1)**

3. The potential difference across a component and the current through it are required to calculate its resistance **(1)**. The ammeter is wired in parallel not in series so can't be used to measure the current **(1)**. The voltmeter is wired in series not in parallel so can't be used to measure the potential difference **(1)**.

Page 88

1. **(a)** A series circuit **(1)**
   (b) Total resistance = 4 + 5 + 2 **(1)**
   = 11 Ω **(1)**
2. **(a)** 2A **(1)**
   (b) 8V **(1)**
   (c) resistance = $\dfrac{\text{potential difference}}{\text{current}} = \dfrac{8}{2}$
   = 4 Ω **(1)**
   (d) The total resistance of all the components would be greater **(1)**. The total resistance of components wired in series is the sum of the individual resistors **(1)**. In parallel the total resistance is always lower than the resistance of an individual resistor **(1)**.

Page 89

1. **(a)** Live wire – Brown – Carries the alternating potential difference from the supply.
   Neutral wire – Blue – Completes the circuit.
   Earth wire – Green and yellow stripes – Only carries a current if there is a fault.
   (3 marks if fully correct; 1 mark for each correct match of wire, colour and function)
   (b) It is impossible for the case of the appliance to become live as it is plastic **(1)** and it is impossible for the live wire to come into contact with the case **(1)**.
2. **(a)** Alternating current **(1)**. The sander is plugged into the mains electricity which is a.c. **(1)**
   (b) The circuit breaker can be easily reset **(1)**. The circuit breaker operates much faster than a fuse **(1)**.

Page 90

1. **(a)** power = current^2 × resistance **(1)** = 3^2 × 76.7
   = 690.3 W **(1)**
   (b) Electrical **(1)** to kinetic and heat **(1)**.
   (c) energy transferred = power × time **(1)**
   time = $\dfrac{\text{energy transferred}}{\text{power}} = \dfrac{180\,000}{690.3} = 261$ seconds **(1)**
   (d) The potential difference is high in cables to reduce heat loss **(1)** and improve efficiency **(1)**. The potential difference is reduced in homes for safety **(1)**.

MAGNETISM AND ELECTROMAGNETISM
Page 91

1. **(a)** S **(1)**
   (b) N **(1)**
   (c) N **(1)**
2. **(a)** Magnetic field **(1)**
   (b) Attraction **(1)**
   (c) Force would be stronger at A than at B **(1)**. A is closer to the poles of the magnet / the magnetic field lines are closer together at A **(1)**.

3. The Earth's core is magnetic **(1)** and produces a magnetic field **(1)** so attracts the bar magnet **(1)**.

1. The magnetic field around a solenoid is the same shape as the magnetic field around a bar magnet. ✓ **(1)**
   A solenoid with an iron core is an electromagnet. ✓ **(1)**
2. **(a)** The direction of the current **(1)** and the direction of the magnetic field **(1)**.
   (b) The motor effect **(1)**
   (c) force = magnetic flux density × current × length **(1)**
   $$\text{magnetic flux density} = \frac{(\text{force} \div \text{current})}{\text{length}} = \frac{(25 \div 15)}{0.3}$$
   = 5.6 T **(1)**
3. In the fan there is a coil of wire carrying an electrical current **(1)** in a magnetic field **(1)**. The coil of wire experiences a force that causes the coil to rotate, so it now has kinetic energy **(1)**.

PARTICLE MODEL OF MATTER

1. **(a)** $\text{density} = \frac{\text{mass}}{\text{volume}}$ **(1)**
   $$\text{density} = \frac{5}{0.002}$$
   = 2500 kg/m³ **(1)**

   (b) The density would decrease **(1)** as gas was released **(1)**. The mass of the fire extinguisher would decrease but the volume would remain the same **(1)**.
2. **(a)** Differences in temperature would affect the pressure of the gas **(1)**.
   (b) Differences in volume would affect the pressure **(1)**.
3. **(a)** 3 kg of water **(1)**. Mass is conserved during changes of state **(1)**.
   (b) The change has been reversed and the ice has regained its original properties **(1)**. This occurs in physical changes but not in chemical changes **(1)**.

1. **(a)** **(i)** 10°C **(1)**   **(ii)** 60°C **(1)**
   (b) The temperature is staying the same **(1)** so it is changing state **(1)** and the stored internal energy is changing **(1)**.
   (c) energy for a change of state = mass × specific latent heat **(1)**
   = 0.5 × 250 000
   = 125 000 J **(1)** or 125 KJ
2. **(a)** 329K **(1)**
   (b) 0 Kelvin is –273°C, –300°C is below this **(1)**. 0 Kelvin is absolute zero and at this temperature the particles in the object have no kinetic energy so aren't moving, so it's impossible to have a temperature below this. **(1)**

ATOMIC STRUCTURE

1. **(a)** **(i)** 6 **(1)**
       (ii) 6 **(1)**
       (iii) 6 **(1)**
   (b) **(i)** Isotopes **(1)**
       (ii) They have different numbers of neutrons **(1)**.
2. **(a)** Nuclear model has a nucleus with electrons orbiting **(1)**. Plum pudding model suggested atom was a ball of positive charge with negative electrons embedded or scattered in it **(1)**.
   (b) It provided evidence of existence of neutrons **(1)**.

1. **(a)** **(i)** A: Alpha **(1)**, B: Gamma **(1)**, C: Beta **(1)**
       (ii) Most to least: Alpha, Beta, Gamma **(2 marks if fully correct; 1 mark for two correct)**
2. **(a)** Alpha **(1)**
   (b) A: 92, B: 234, C: 4, D: 2 **(3 marks if fully correct; 2 marks for three correct; 1 mark for two correct)**
   (c) There is no effect on the mass or the charge of the nucleus **(1)**.

1. contamination; decay; emit; Irradiation; radiation; radioactive **(3 marks if fully correct; 2 marks if one error; 1 mark if two errors)**
2. **(a)** **(i)** 20 days **(1)**
       (ii) This is the length of time it takes for the activity (counts per second) to halve **(1)**.
       (iii) Counts per second at 20 days = 250
       $$\text{Counts per second at 40 days} = \frac{250}{2} = 125 \textbf{ (1)}$$
       $$\text{Counts per second at 60 days} = \frac{125}{2} = 62.5 \textbf{ (1)}$$

Paper 1: Biology 1

Question number		Answer	Notes	Marks
1	(a)	Lactic acid		1
	(b)	Carbon dioxide		1
2	(a)	Her muscles can release more energy.		1
	(b)	**Cause:** build-up of lactic acid (in muscles)		1
		Recovery: heavy breathing / panting		1
		over a period of time		1
	(c)	**Any three from:**		
		More blood to the muscles.		
		More oxygen supplied to muscles.		
		Increased energy transfer in muscles.		
		More lactic acid to be removed from muscles.		3
3		cell, tissue, organ, system		1
4		White blood cells		1
5	(a)	Right ventricle		1
	(b)	Blood is pumped at a higher pressure. / Blood is pumped a greater distance.		1
	(c)	They stop the backflow of blood.	Allow: they stop blood flowing in the wrong direction.	1
	(d)	$\frac{22\,100}{105\,650} \times 100 = 20.91812\%$		1
		21% to two significant figures		1
	(e)	**Any two from:**		
		Low(er) fat intake		
		Low(er) salt intake		
		Regular exercise		
		Healthy body weight		
		Low stress levels		2
6	(a)	It's a physical barrier – prevents pathogens from entering.		1
		It produces antimicrobial secretions (peptides) to kill microorganisms.		1
	(b)	640		1
			Allow 1 mark for: number doubles six times in two hours.	1
	(c)	Measles is caused by a virus.		1
		Antibiotics only treat bacterial infections.		1
	(d)	$\frac{10}{5000} = 0.002 \times 1000$		1
		$= 2\ \mu m$		1
	(e)	**Any two from:**		
		Boil / sterilise all water.		
		Isolate infected individuals.		
		Any basic hygiene measure involving water.	Allow: wash hands / toilets away from water supply, etc.	2
	(f)	There is less chance of contracting the disease as it reduces possible contact with infected people.		1
		The disease cannot spread as people are immune.		1
7		Cell wall		1

For question 6 (b), the table referenced:

Time	Bacteria
0	10
20	20
40	40
60	80
80	160
100	320
120	640

Question number	Answer	Notes	Marks
8	**Any four from:** Sterilise wire / inoculating loop in flame. Transfer sample of pond water to agar. Seal lid with a cross of tape. Turn upside down (to stop condensation). Incubate at 25 °C.		4
9 (a)	Moral / religious / ethical reasons (e.g. use of embryos to obtain stem cells, it interferes with natural processes, 'plays God' or is against religious beliefs) Possibility of virus transfer		1 1
(b)	Differentiation		1
10 (a)	**Any two from:** Guard cells fill with water by osmosis. Guard cells change shape. Guard cells become turgid.		2
(b)	The net movement of particles from an area in which there is a high concentration to one of low concentration.	Allow molecules instead of particles. Allow 1 mark for either of the following: The (random / net) movement of particles. Particles spread out / particles mix up.	1 1
11 (a)	**Any two from:** Long Thin Tubes / hollow / no end walls		2
(b)	**Any two from:** Thin cell wall Large surface area Long, hair-like structure		2
12 (a)	To stop evaporation (of the water)		1
(b)	2.5 cm³ per day $\dfrac{50-40}{4}$	Allow 1 mark for: total volume lost = 10 cm³	1 1
13	**Any three from:** Starch – for storage Fat / oil – for storage Cellulose – to make cell walls Amino acids – to make protein	To score a mark, both the substance and reason must be noted.	3
14	Water has moved / diffused into sugar solution from a dilute to a more concentrated solution. Visking tubing is partially permeable.		1 1 1
15	Make up 'acid rain' solution (e.g. a dilute sulfuric acid or nitric acid solution, or a solution with a pH in the range 2–6). Minimum of two groups of infected roses – spray one group of roses with acid solution. Control variable, e.g. same place in garden.		1 1 1

Question number	Answer	Notes	Marks
16 (a)	Higher temperature leads to faster growth. More carbon dioxide leads to faster growth.		1 1
(b)	$6H_2O$ $6O_2$		1 1
(c)	**Level 3:** Correct patterns for linking both temperature and distance to *rate* of photosynthesis. Explanations linked to light intensity, energy and enzymes.		5–6
	Level 2: One correct pattern / prediction outlined for both distance and temperature. One correct explanation linked to one pattern / prediction.		3–4
	Level 1: One correct pattern / prediction outlined for either distance or temperature. One correct explanation linked to the pattern / prediction.		1–2
	No relevant content		0
	Indicative content **Patterns / predictions** • Fewer bubbles / less photosynthesis with increasing distance • More bubbles at 35 °C • Fewer / no bubbles at 55 °C • Rate of photosynthesis decreases with increasing distance • Rate of photosynthesis increases with temperature up to around 45 °C • Photosynthesis stops at higher temperature **Explanations** • Increase in distance reduces the amount of light • Less light, less photosynthesis • Higher temperature up to around 45 °C – more photosynthesis • More energy increases photosynthesis • Rate of photosynthesis decreases with decrease in light intensity • Correct mention of inverse square law • Rate of photosynthesis increases with increasing energy • Above 45 °C enzymes are denatured and so little or no photosynthesis		
17	**Any two from:** Viruses are found inside cells. Damaging a virus also damages cells. Viruses have a high mutation rate.		2

Paper 2: Biology 2

Question number	Answer	Notes	Marks
1	A		1
2	Disease		1
3	**Any two from:** Small ears (reduce heat loss) Thick fur (reduces heat loss) Thick fat / blubber (reduces heat loss) Sharp claws (for holding onto prey) Hair on pads of feet (to grip ice)		2
4	$\frac{15 \times 21}{4} = 78.75$ 79 (nearest whole number)		1 1
5 (a)	*Strigops*		1
(b)	Primary consumer		1
6	Less resistant bacteria are killed first / survival of the fittest. If course not completed, resistant bacteria survive. Resistant bacteria then reproduce.		1 1 1
7	Bacteria reproduce very quickly. They form clones / exact copies of the DNA. Bacteria DNA is easily altered / plasmids easily modified.		1 1 1
8	**Any two from:** Smoking Obesity Viruses UV exposure Excessive alcohol intake		2
9	**Any two from:** There was not enough evidence at the time. The mechanism through which variation was passed on was not known. It challenged religious beliefs.		2
10	D		1
11 (a)	Any figure in the range 12.9–15.1. Trend – darker colour to more mass loss. Darker colour – higher temperature / faster decay.		1 1 1
(b)	**Any two from:** Grass from same place Same mass of grass cuttings in each bag Same material for bag Same thickness of material for bag Same thickness / packing of material in the bag		2
12 (a)	Female reaction time better than male / females have faster reaction time than males.		1
(b)	$\frac{0.31 + 0.32 + 0.29 + 0.32}{4}$ Answer is 0.31		1 1
(c)	Rapid / fast Automatic / done without thinking		1 1
(d)	Impulse causes release of chemical / neurotransmitter from ends of sensory neurone. Chemical / neurotransmitter diffuses across gap. Chemical / neurotransmitter binds to receptor molecules on next / relay neurone. This triggers electrical impulse in next / relay neurone.		1 1 1 1

Question number	Answer	Notes	Marks
13 (a)	No The best chance is at or just after 14 days. That's when the egg is released / level of LH (luteinising hormone) is at its highest.	'No' on its own is not enough to obtain 1 mark.	0 1 1
(b)	Maintains lining of uterus Inhibits both FSH and LH		1 1
(c)	**Any two from:** They inhibit FSH. No eggs mature (and they cannot be fertilised). Progesterone causes production of sticky mucus, which hinders movement of sperm.		2
(d)	**Any two from:** Success rates are not high Can lead to multiple births Multiple births have a risk for mother / babies Very stressful		2
14	Select the cows and bulls that have the milk qualities required. Breed them. Select the offspring that have the best milk qualities. Repeat over a number of generations.		1 1 1 1
15 (a)	39		1
(b)	Mitosis **Any two from:** Chromosomes are copied. Two full sets of chromosomes are made. Each set moves to the opposite end of the cell. **Any one from:** Cell divides in two. Each new cell contains a complete set.		1 2 1
16 (a)	Both parents: Ff Four offspring: FF Ff Ff ff	Upper and lower case letters must be distinguishable.	1 1

Punnett square for 16 (a):

	F	f
F	FF	Ff
f	Ff	ff

Question number	Answer	Notes	Marks
(b)	25% or 1 in 4		1
(c)	Heterozygous		1
17 (a)	**Level 3:** Correct descriptions of all four control methods. **Level 2:** Correct description of control method 1 **and** one other control method (2, 3 or 4). **Level 1:** One correct description of any control method. No relevant content **Indicative content** **Control method 1** Pancreas monitors glucose level Pancreas produces insulin if glucose level high Glucose converted to glycogen Glycogen stored in liver / cells **Control method 2** Pancreas produces glucagon if glucose level low Glycogen converted to glucose by glucagon **Control method 3** Type 1: blood glucose levels tested regularly Insulin injections if glucose level high **Control method 4** Type 2: diet control Regular exercise	Allow 3 marks for a full description of methods 3 and 4 only.	5–6 3–4 1–2 0

Question number	Answer	Notes	Marks
(b)	**Any two from:** They: filter the blood remove water from the blood remove ions from the blood reabsorb glucose into the blood reabsorb water into the blood reabsorb ions into the blood.		2
(c)	Proteins broken down to amino acids.		1
	Excess amino acids form ammonia (in liver).		1
	(Toxic) ammonia converted to urea.		1
	Urea removed by kidneys / less protein – less urea.		1
18	Burning trees produces more carbon dioxide in the air. / Less photosynthesis means more carbon dioxide in the air.		1
	Carbon dioxide is a greenhouse gas / causes global warming.		1
19	**Any two from:** Stabilises ecosystems Preserves food chains Preserves possible future crops Preserves possible future medicines Preserves interdependence of species		2

Paper 3: Chemistry 1

Question number	Answer	Notes	Marks
1 (a)	Each row begins with elements with one outer electron.		1
(b)	Their boiling points increase as you go down the group.		1
(c)		Give 1 mark for an X anywhere in the grey area.	1
2 (a)	They make an alkali when reacted with water.		1
(b)	The outer electron in sodium is further from the nucleus.		1
	Less energy needed to remove the outer electron / the outer electron is less tightly held / less attractive force from nucleus to outer electron.		1
(c)	Electrons are delocalised / sea of electrons,		1
	which means they are free to move		1
3 (a)	High melting point and slippery		1
(b)	2.9×10^7 cm^2	This is how the answer is calculated: volume = area × height (thickness) $1 = \text{area} \times 3.4 \times 10^{-8}$ $\text{area} = \dfrac{1}{3.4 \times 10^{-8}}$ $= 2.9 \times 10^7$ cm^2	1
(c)	**Any two from:** high (tensile) strength high electrical conductivity high thermal conductivity.		2
(d)	High melting point because of: giant structure / lots of bonds / macromolecule		1
	strong bonds / lots of energy to break bonds.		1
	Does not conduct electricity because: there are no free / mobile electrons **or** all its electrons are used in bonding.		1
4 (a)	copper(II) carbonate $\rightarrow$ copper(II) oxide + carbon dioxide	Accept copper carbonate and copper oxide without (II).	1
(b)	12.35 – 7.95 =		1
	4.40 (g)	Accept 4.4 (g)	1
5 (a)	Magnesium loses electrons and oxygen gains electrons.		1
	Two electrons are transferred.		1
(b)	The magnesium ion has a charge of 2+.		1
	The oxide ion has a charge of 2–.		1
6 (a)	It has the same number of electrons and protons.		1
(b) (i)	Number of protons in the ion — 26; Number of neutrons in the ion — 30; Number of electrons in the ion — 24	Only award 1 mark if all three numbers are correct.	1
(ii)	**Protons:** the atomic number / number on the bottom left of symbol		1
	Neutrons: 56 – 26 = 30 / mass number – atomic number		1
	Electrons: 26 – 2 = 24 / atomic number but 2 electrons have been removed to make 2+		1
7	$\dfrac{1.2 \times 10^{-6}}{1.5 \times 10^{-10}} =$	Allow 1 mark for working, even if the answer is not correct.	1
	8000 or 8.0×10^3		1

Question number	Answer	Notes	Marks
8 (a)	Copper oxide and sulfuric acid		1
(b)	The pH would start high and decrease to below 7.		1
(c)	Nitric acid		1
(d)	M_r CaO = 56 **and** M_r $CaCl_2$ = 111		1
	5.55 g = $\frac{1}{20}$ mole or 0.05 mole $CaCl_2$		1
	Reaction ratio: 1:1		1
	$\frac{1}{20} \times 56$ or $0.05 \times 56 = 2.8$ g		1
9 (a)	$Fe_2O_3 + 3CO \rightarrow 2Fe + 3CO_2$	Allow 1 mark for: $Fe_2O_3 + CO \rightarrow Fe + CO_2$	2
(b)	Copper is less reactive than carbon / copper is lower in the reactivity series than carbon / or reverse argument (ora).		1
	Aluminium is more reactive than carbon / aluminium is higher in the reactivity series than carbon / ora.		1
(c)	**Cathode:** $Al^{3+} + 3e^- \rightarrow Al$		1
	Anode: $2O^{2-} \rightarrow O_2 + 4e^-$		1

10 (a)

Solid	Start temperature (°C)	End temperature (°C)	Temperature change (°C)
Ammonium chloride	15	9	−6
Potassium hydroxide	16	29	+13
Ammonium nitrate	18	4	**−14**
Sodium hydroxide	17	35	**+18**

Award 1 mark for two correct numbers and 1 mark for two correct signs. — 2 marks

Question number	Answer	Notes	Marks
(b)	Ammonium nitrate		1
	Endothermic reactions cause the temperature to decrease.		1
	Ammonium nitrate had the biggest drop in temperature.		1
11	**Level 3:** Correct descriptions of the development of at least three atomic models and the linking of two scientists.		5–6
	Level 2: Correct descriptions of the development of at least two atomic models and the linking of one scientist.		3–4
	Level 1: One correct description of the development of any atomic model.		1–2
	No relevant content		0

Indicative content

'Plum pudding' model of the atom / existence of electrons – J.J. Thomson

Nuclear model / 'solar system' atom – Marsden and Rutherford

Electron orbits – Niels Bohr

Existence of neutrons – James Chadwick

Question number	Answer	Notes	Marks
12 (a)	First test – the iodide converted (oxidised) to iodine		1
	Bromine is more reactive than iodine.		1
	No reaction in second test		1
	because bromine is less reactive than chlorine.		1
(b)			
		Give 1 mark for the shared pair of electrons.	1
		Give 1 mark if the rest of the diagram is correct.	1

Question number	Answer	Notes	Marks
(c)	Chlorine has weaker forces between molecules / weaker intermolecular forces than iodine. Less energy is needed to separate molecules in chlorine than iodine.	Allow 'stronger' forces for iodine. Allow 'more energy' for iodine.	1 1
(d)	It has no free electrons / the electrons cannot move / all outer electrons are involved in bonding.		1
13 (a)	$\dfrac{14.4}{12} = 1.2$ mole $1.2 \times 393 = 472$ kJ	Accept 471.6 kJ	1 1
(b)	Energy is taken in to break (oxygen) bonds. Energy is given out, making (C=O) bonds. More energy is given out than taken in.		1 1 1
(c)	**Any three from:** • Use a more accurate method of measuring the volumes, e.g. a 25 cm³ pipette or a 25 cm³ measuring cylinder. • Use an insulated beaker / polystyrene cup. • Use separate apparatus to measure the acid. • Measure the start temperature before adding the acid. • Wait until there is no further temperature change before measuring the final temperature. • Repeat the method at least two more times.		3

Paper 4: Chemistry 2

Question number	Answer	Notes	Marks
1 (a)	Chlorine		1
(b)	Carbon dioxide		1
2 (a)	Breaking up / decomposing (large molecules)		1
	into smaller / more useful substances / molecules.		1
(b)	**Any one from:** They act as a catalyst. They speed up the reaction. They provide a surface on which the reaction happens.		1
(c)	$C_{16}H_{34} \rightarrow C_{10}H_{22} + 3C_2H_4$	If balancing is not correct, allow 1 mark for: $C_{16}H_{34} \rightarrow C_{10}H_{22} + C_2H_4$	2
3	**Any three from:** Small molecules have weaker (intermolecular) forces / large molecules have stronger forces. Small molecules have lower boiling point / large molecules have higher boiling point. Stronger forces lead to a higher boiling point / weaker forces lead to a lower boiling point. Fractions are separated by different boiling points.		3
4	C_5H_{12}		1
5 (a)	Dylan		1
(b)	The acid was the limiting reagent in her experiment / all of the acid had been used up in her experiment.	Allow: magnesium in excess.	1
	Magnesium was the limiting reagent in the other experiments / all of the magnesium was used up in the other experiments.	Allow: acid in excess.	1
(c) (i)	mean rate = $\dfrac{\text{quantity of product formed}}{\text{time taken}} = \dfrac{94.5}{225} =$		1
	0.42		1
	Unit = cm^3/s		1
(ii)	The volume of gas will double		1
	because the volume of gas is dependent on the amount of magnesium.		1
6 (a)	C and D		1
(b)	$0.86 = \dfrac{\text{distance moved by B}}{7.91} = 0.86 \times 7.91$		1
	$= 6.80$	6.8 / 6.802 / 6.8026 is worth 1 mark.	1
7 (a)			1
(b)	$2C_4H_{10} + 13O_2 \rightarrow 8CO_2 + 10H_2O$	If balancing is not correct, allow 1 mark for: $C_4H_{10} + O_2 \rightarrow CO_2 + H_2O$ If all the numbers are correct, allow multiples for balancing.	2
8	1.69 g	Pure gold = 24 carats, 9 carats = $\dfrac{9}{24}$th gold $\dfrac{9}{24} \times 4.5 = 1.69$ (rounded up)	1

Question number	Answer	Notes	Marks
9 (a)	D, A, C, B	Allow 1 mark if D and A are in the correct order.	2
(b)	It is a simple or complex explanation put forward by scientists to try and explain observations/facts		1 1
(c)	It cannot be proved because it was so long ago / there is insufficient evidence to confirm the theory.		1
(d)	Argon Carbon dioxide Oxygen Nitrogen		1
10 (a)	**Time taken for cross to disappear (s)** Time (s) vs Concentration of acid (mol/dm³) All six points correctly plotted Smooth curve	Allow 1 mark for four or five points correctly plotted; 1 mark deducted if the graph is plotted dot to dot rather than as a smooth curve.	2 1
(b)	Rate increases as concentration increases. Increased concentration means more crowded particles / more particles in same space / volume. More chance of collision / more frequent collisions.		1 1 1
(c)	The reaction times would be smaller / shorter / less.		1
11	**Desalination:** removal of salt from the water / changing sea water into drinking water. **Chlorination:** adding chlorine to kill bacteria / germs / microorganisms.		1 1
12 (a)	50%		1
(b)	The yield decreases.		1
(c)	If pressure increases, the reaction goes in the direction that reduces the number of moles of gas / the volume of gases, i.e. the direction with the fewest number of moles of gas. The equilibrium moves to the right / forward direction / to the product side.		1 1
(d)	High pressures need energy / equipment that can tolerate high pressures, and this is expensive. The costs outweigh the benefits of a higher yield.		1 1

Question number	Answer	Notes	Marks
13 (a)	B Powder reacts faster / line steeper on graph because powder has a larger surface area. More chance of successful collisions / more frequent successful collisions.		1 1 1 1
(b)	 **Reaction progress** graph with Energy on y-axis. Zn + 2HCl / Reactants, ZnCl$_2$ + H$_2$ / Products.	The curve must start at reactants, be lower than the original curve and end at products.	1
14	Alloys are harder. Alloys have a lower density. Alloys have a lower melting point. Alloys are stronger.	Allow the reverse argument, e.g. pure metals are softer.	4
15	(structure diagram of polymer with H, CH$_3$, C—C, H, H and n) Accept curved or square brackets.	Award 1 mark for side links; 1 mark for n; 1 mark for the rest of the molecule (must have only one CH$_3$ group).	3
16 (a)	As the reaction progresses, the rate of the backward reaction increases until the rates of the forward and backward reactions are the same.		1 1
(b)	Favours the reverse reaction / equilibrium position moves to the left / moves to the reactant side. Reaction goes in the direction to increase the number of moles / reactants have a larger volume / reaction works to increase pressure on the side with higher moles of gas.		1 1
(c)	No effect on the equilibrium position.		1
(d)	Which reaction direction is exothermic / which reaction direction is endothermic.		1
17 (a)	Nitrogen **and** oxygen from the air react in the high temperatures in the engine.		1 1 1
(b) (i)	**One from:** causes acid rain / causes respiratory problems.		1
(ii)	Remove sulfur from the fuel before use.		1

Paper 5: Physics 1

Question number	Answer	Notes	Marks
1 (a)			1
(b)			1
(c)	$V = I \times R = 0.005 \times 1200$ $= 6\ V$ $\dfrac{6\ V}{1.5\ V} = 4$ batteries needed		1 1 1
(d)	Diode Because when it has a positive potential difference the resistance is low. Because when it has a negative potential difference the resistance is high.	Allow low resistance when potential difference is high enough Allow voltage for potential difference in both cases	1 1 1
2 (a)	<table><tr><td>Isotope</td><td>Number of protons</td><td>Number of neutrons</td><td>Number of electrons</td></tr><tr><td>Carbon-12</td><td>6</td><td>6</td><td>6</td></tr><tr><td>Carbon-13</td><td>6</td><td>7</td><td>6</td></tr><tr><td>Carbon-14</td><td>6</td><td>8</td><td>6</td></tr></table>	1 mark for each correct column	3
(b)	A neutron changes into a proton by emitting a (high speed) electron.		1 1
(c)	The time taken for the activity / count rate to halve **or** the time taken for the number of nuclei of the isotope to halve.		1
(d)	<table><tr><td>Number of half-lives</td><td>Time after death of organism in years</td><td>$^{14}C : {}^{12}C$ ratio / 10^{-12}</td></tr><tr><td>0</td><td>0</td><td>1.000</td></tr><tr><td>1</td><td>5730</td><td>0.500</td></tr><tr><td>2</td><td>11460</td><td>0.250</td></tr><tr><td>3</td><td>17190</td><td>0.125</td></tr></table>		1
(e)		Plotting points correctly Smooth curve	1 1
(f)	10 000 (years)	Accept answers in the range 9500–10 500	1
3 (a)	50 Hz, 230 V, ac		1
(b)	It does not need an earth wire.		1

Question number	Answer				Notes	Marks
4 (a)					2 marks for all three answers correct, 1 mark for two correct answers	2
	Wire	**Name**		**Colour**		
	A	**Neutral**		Blue		
	B	Live		**Brown**		
	C	**Earth**		Green and yellow stripes		
(b)	**Any two from:** • The earth wire stops the appliance becoming live. • It carries current if there is a fault. • It stops someone from being electrocuted if there is a fault.					2
(c)	power = potential difference × current P = V × I current = $\frac{960}{230}$ = 4.2(A)				Allow 2 marks for 4.17 or 4.173	1 1 1
5 (a)	Coal					1
(b)	Geothermal					1
(c) (i)	**Any one from:** • causes air pollution • emits greenhouse gases • mines spoil the countryside Accept any other reasonable answer.					1
(ii)	Economic/social reasons – it's cheaper to use fossil fuels. Political reasons – lots of jobs will be lost if we stop using fossil fuels.					1 1
6 (a)	Position 4					1
(b)	Maximum gravitational potential energy at position 1. Changes to kinetic energy in Positions 2–4 (as the cars go down the hill).					1 1
(c)	**Any three from:** The kinetic energy converts back to gravitational potential energy but some energy is lost due to friction / air resistance. Less energy means less height.					3
7 (a) (i)	Missing number is 222				242 – 20 = 222	1
(ii)	Motor C					1
(b)	Electrical power is used to turn around / spin the bit / screwdriver blade. Some power is wasted as heat / sound / vibration.					1 1
(c)	efficiency = $\frac{\text{useful output power}}{\text{total input power}} = \frac{160}{172}$ = 0.93 = 93%				Accept 0.93023 or 93.023%	1 1
8 (a)	A car with a mass of 1400 kg travelling at 12 m/s					1
(b)	work done = force × distance = 24 × 2.5 = 60 J					1 1
(c)	power = $\frac{\text{work done}}{\text{time}} = \frac{60}{4}$ = 15 W				Allow 2 marks for an incorrect answer to 8 (b) correctly divided by 4	1 1
9 (a)					1 mark for drawing appropriate apparatus 1 mark for showing that water is displaced The diagram must have labels to gain full marks	1 1

Question number	Answer	Notes	Marks
(b)	**Any two from:** reduces random experimental error can calculate a mean value can identify anomalous results.		2
(c)	Mass	Accept weight	1
(d)	Nickel		1
10 (a)	Lead		1
(b)	energy = power × time = 100 × 85 = 8500 J		1 1
(c)	temperature change = $\dfrac{\text{change in thermal energy}}{\text{mass} \times \text{specific heat capacity}}$ $= \dfrac{9065}{0.5 \times 490}$ = 37°C final temperature = 22 + 37 = 59°C		1 1 1
11	No Energy to melt ice = 0.06 × 334 000 = 20 040(J) 20 040 greater than 16 800 so there is not enough energy available from the water.	Also accept: Energy available in water would melt $\dfrac{16\,800}{334\,000}$ = 0.05 kg or 50 g of ice However, there is 60 g of ice present, so 10 g of ice would not melt.	1 1 1
12	**Level 3:** Correct explanation of why gamma radiation can be used to treat cancer, the risks involved and at least two control measures. **Level 2:** Correct explanation of why gamma radiation can be used and the risks involved, **or** explanation of why gamma radiation can be used and at least two control measures. **Level 1:** Correct explanation that gamma radiation kills cells and at least one risk or control measure. No relevant content **Indicative content** **Gamma radiation** Can penetrate to tumour Is ionising radiation Kills cancer cells Can be focused on particular area Dose can be controlled **Risks** Can kill healthy cells Radiation could cause normal cells to become cancerous and cause further problems **Risk control** Short exposure time Precise targeting of the radiation Calculating the correct dose Balancing risk with likelihood of successful treatment Using shielding on other parts of body		5–6 3–4 1–2 0

Paper 6: Physics 2

Question number		Answer	Notes	Marks
1	(a)	Velocity		1
	(b)	Weight		1
2	(a)	10 m/s		1
	(b)	acceleration = $\dfrac{\text{change of velocity}}{\text{time taken}}$		1
		$= \dfrac{15-0}{3}$		1
		$= 5$		1
		$= 5 \text{ m/s}^2$		1
	(c)	distance 0–3s = $0.5 \times 15 \times 3 = 22.5$ m	distance = area under line	1
		distance 3–6s = $15 \times 3 = 45$ m	distance = velocity × time	1
		total distance = 22.5 + 45 = 67.5 m		1
	(d)	Slowing down / decelerating / negative acceleration		1
		at a uniform / constant rate.		1
3	(a)	C		1
	(b)	Infrared		1
	(c)	frequency = $\dfrac{\text{wave speed}}{\text{wavelength}} = \dfrac{3 \times 10^8}{0.12}$	1 mark for showing working, 1 mark for the correct answer and 1 mark for the correct unit	1
		$= 2.5 \times 10^9$ Hz		2
4	(a)	To compare times / speeds in the two different sections.		1
	(b)	If the times are the same, David is correct.		1
		If the time for the car to travel down the second half of the ramp is less than the first, then Gemma is correct.		1
	(c)	Run 2		1
	(d)	Mean time = $\dfrac{(0.249 + 0.270 + 0.251)}{3}$		
		$= \dfrac{0.77}{3}$		
		$= 0.257$		1
		mean speed = $\dfrac{\text{distance}}{\text{time}} = \dfrac{1.50}{0.257}$		1
		$= 5.84$ m/s	Also accept 5.4, 5.836 or 5.8365.	1
5		A and D		1
6	(a)	Force X increases		1
	(b)	Force X = 550 N		1
		The forces balance each other / the forces reach an equilibrium / force X = force Y	Accept weight for force Y Accept air resistance for force X	1
	(c)	4 and 5		1
	(d)	Parachute has a larger surface area.		1
		Force X therefore increases.	Accept weight for force Y	1
		Force X greater than force Y.	Accept air resistance for force X	1
		Velocity reduces until the forces balance again.		1
7	(a)			1
	(b)	They will move		1
		to point in a circle.		1
8	(a)	Increase current		1
		Increase the number of coils		1
	(b)	Up from the page, towards you		1
	(c)	Wire has a magnetic field only when there is a current.		1
		The wire's magnetic field interacts with the magnet's field.		1

Question Number	Answer	Notes	Marks
9 (a)	The reading decreases as the rock is lowered in the water.		1
	No (further) change when the rock is fully submerged.		1
(b)	Use a ruler / measure distance lowered.		1
	Have suitable increments, e.g. measure force every 1 cm lowered		1
(c)			1
10 (a)	Seawater has a higher density than fresh water.		1
	Less seawater would be displaced		1
	to balance the weight of the ship.		1
(b)	distance = speed × time = 1500 × 0.0270		1
	= 40.5 m $\dfrac{40.5}{2}$	To find the distance travelled to the seabed and back, divide by 2	1
	= 20.25 m		1
(c)	Water is more dense than air. Pressure is proportional to density (if height and gravity are constant).		1
			1
11 (a)	momentum = mass × velocity = 1200 × 20 = 24 000 kg m/s		1
			1
(b)	force = $\dfrac{24\,000}{0.50}$ = 48 000 N		1
			1

Question number	Answer	Notes	Marks
12 (a)	**Level 3:** Use stopping distance equation to give a correct detailed explanation of how all three conditions affect the stopping distance, and one reference to adjusting driving to suit conditions.		5–6
	Level 2: Use stopping distance equation to give a correct detailed explanation of how two out of the three conditions affect the stopping distance.		3–4
	Level 1: Use stopping distance equation to give a correct detailed explanation of how one condition affects the stopping distance.		1–2
	No relevant content		0
	Indicative content Include the equation: stopping distance = thinking distance + braking distance **(Increased) speed** Increases thinking distance Same thinking time but greater distance travelled Increases braking distance More kinetic energy to be absorbed by the brakes Stopping distance increases **Road conditions** Anything on the road surface will increase braking distance. The surface will be slippery / less friction / less grip. No effect on thinking distance Stopping distance increases **Alcohol** Increases thinking distance Increases reaction time No effect on braking distance Stopping distance increases Idea that slower speeds reduce chance of accident or that adjusting speed to suit conditions reduces chance of accident.	Examples: water, snow, ice, leaves, mud Do not accept poor weather / poor visibility / fog	
(b)	It is difficult to measure / it is subjective.		1
13 (a)	Hold your left hand in a fist and then spread out the thumb, first finger and second finger so that they are at right angles to each other.		1
	Point the first finger in the direction of the magnetic field (N to S).		1
	Point the second finger in the direction of the current.		1
	The thumb now points in the direction of movement, i.e. out of the page towards you.		1
(b)	**Any two from:** • increase current flowing through the rod • increase the magnetic flux density • increase the length of the rod in the magnetic field.		2

The Periodic Table

Key

Metals

Non-metals

Relative atomic mass →		
Atomic symbol →	**1**	
	H	
Name →	hydrogen	
Atomic number →	1	

Group 1	Group 2											Group 3	Group 4	Group 5	Group 6	Group 7	0 or 8
																	4 **He** helium 2
7 **Li** lithium 3	9 **Be** beryllium 4											11 **B** boron 5	12 **C** carbon 6	14 **N** nitrogen 7	16 **O** oxygen 8	19 **F** fluorine 9	20 **Ne** neon 10
23 **Na** sodium 11	24 **Mg** magnesium 12											27 **Al** aluminium 13	28 **Si** silicon 14	31 **P** phosphorus 15	32 **S** sulfur 16	35.5 **Cl** chlorine 17	40 **Ar** argon 18
39 **K** potassium 19	40 **Ca** calcium 20	45 **Sc** scandium 21	48 **Ti** titanium 22	51 **V** vanadium 23	52 **Cr** chromium 24	55 **Mn** manganese 25	56 **Fe** iron 26	59 **Co** cobalt 27	59 **Ni** nickel 28	63.5 **Cu** copper 29	65 **Zn** zinc 30	70 **Ga** gallium 31	73 **Ge** germanium 32	75 **As** arsenic 33	79 **Se** selenium 34	80 **Br** bromine 35	84 **Kr** krypton 36
85 **Rb** rubidium 37	88 **Sr** strontium 38	89 **Y** yttrium 39	91 **Zr** zirconium 40	93 **Nb** niobium 41	96 **Mo** molybdenum 42	[98] **Tc** technetium 43	101 **Ru** ruthenium 44	103 **Rh** rhodium 45	106 **Pd** palladium 46	108 **Ag** silver 47	112 **Cd** cadmium 48	115 **In** indium 49	119 **Sn** tin 50	122 **Sb** antimony 51	128 **Te** tellurium 52	127 **I** iodine 53	131 **Xe** xenon 54
133 **Cs** caesium 55	137 **Ba** barium 56	139 **La*** lanthanum 57	178 **Hf** hafnium 72	181 **Ta** tantalum 73	184 **W** tungsten 74	186 **Re** rhenium 75	190 **Os** osmium 76	192 **Ir** iridium 77	195 **Pt** platinum 78	197 **Au** gold 79	201 **Hg** mercury 80	204 **Tl** thallium 81	207 **Pb** lead 82	209 **Bi** bismuth 83	[209] **Po** polonium 84	[210] **At** astatine 85	[222] **Rn** radon 86
[223] **Fr** francium 87	[226] **Ra** radium 88	[227] **Ac*** actinium 89	[261] **Rf** rutherfordium 104	[262] **Db** dubnium 105	[266] **Sg** seaborgium 106	[264] **Bh** bohrium 107	[277] **Hs** hassium 108	[268] **Mt** meitnerium 109	[271] **Ds** darmstadtium 110	[272] **Rg** roentgenium 111							

Elements with atomic numbers 112–116 have been reported but not fully authenticated.

*The lanthanoids (atomic numbers 58–71) and the actinoids (atomic numbers 90–103) have been omitted.

The relative atomic masses of copper and chlorine have not been rounded to the nearest whole number.

Periodic Table